FLYING THE KNIFE EDGE

Asoro mudmask

Highlands axe

Kundu drum

Sepik mask

Artwork by Matt McLaughlin.

A catalogue record for this book is available from the Books Registration Office of Hong Kong.

Published by A M McLaughlin in Hong Kong

ISBN 978-988-14036-0-5

Design: redinc. book design, Auckland, www.redinc.co.nz
Printed in China by Midas Printing International Ltd

FLYING THE KNIFE EDGE

MATT McLAUGHLIN

This book is dedicated to the memory of

Mack Lee

Ed Terry

Jim Millar

And all those pilots who died in Papua New Guinea

Come to the edge.
We might fall.
Come to the edge.
It's too high!
COME TO THE EDGE!
And they came,
and he pushed,
And they flew.

Christopher Logue[1]

ACKNOWLEDGEMENTS

This book would not have been possible without the generous assistance of the following people. Some helped a little, some helped a lot — all contributions were very much appreciated:

John Gilkes, MapArt; Godfrey Seeto; Paul and Kathy Chue; Rocky Roe; Georgie and Ron McKie; Ric Gillespie; Douglas Westfall; Juergen Ditz; Vicky Garrington, Simon Moody & Michelle Sim, researchers, Air Force Museum, Christchurch NZ; Matthew O'Sullivan, Air Force Museum; John Mowatt; Colin Cousten; Mike Feeney; Jim Sinclair; Michael Murphy; Sid Makary; Tim Johnston; Tony Froude; Dave Sarginson; Gerry Krynen, Charles Perry; Bryan Cox; Simon Wild and John Wild Senior; Sergeant Tim Jordan, Photographic Unit, RNZAF Base Ohakea; Martin Willing; Gail Thomas; Soc Kienzle; Michael Claringbould, Flightpath Magazine; Phil Vabre, CAHS; Will Rutledge; Ray Urlich; Paul Walsh; Kurt Lynn; Marc Collins; John Laming AFC; Ron Watts and Tom Teale-Sinclair, MAF Australia; Dave Black; David Inau and Sid O'Toole, PNGDCA Aviation Accident Investigators; Steve Saunders, Rabaul Historical Society; Peter Edwards; Peter Wilkinson; Tony Skelton; Richard Leahy; Mike O'Byrne; Massimo Lombardo; Flying Officer Gareth Iremonger, Aviation Medicine Unit, RNZAF Base Auckland; James Russell, Dragon Brothers Books; Guillaume Calloud; Rick Smits; Dave Phillips; Brian Lecomber; Rhys Nicholls; Andrew Gormlie; Peter Korugl and Lydia Veali, Post Courier newspaper; Colin Hicks; Eric Carpenter, Australian War Memorial; Monica Walsh, RAAF Museum; Tom Bruss, 32nd 'Red Arrow' Veteran Assn; Amelia Meyer, National Guard Educational Foundation; Gary Peak, McCauley Propeller Systems; Dean Boatman; Mick Wilson; Grant Le Lievre; Andrew Drummond; Phil Parker; Geoffrey Luck; Russell Thomson, Clear Communications; Rachel Vella; Guy Buchanan; Rory Callinan; Barry Huff; Dave Webster; Shane Wedding; Giles and Shelly Rooney; Erin Leslie; Xavier McHugh; Daryl Chapman, flickr.com/photos/darylchapman; Nick Turzynski.

What follows is an account of my progression through the aviation industry, on the long road to a captaincy with an international airline. It is a tale of an ordinary young man experiencing extraordinary things. Somewhere along the way I realised that the journey was in many ways more satisfying than the destination. The focus of the book is on my formative years as a bush pilot in Papua New Guinea, 1992–95. I hope my narrative will give you an impression of what it was like to fly as a professional pilot in that beautiful, scary, chaotic, unforgiving land. As is the custom in warts 'n' all tales, selected names in this book have been altered, to protect both the innocent and the guilty (some of these characters still ply their trade in New Guinea skies). My version of events may differ from those who were in Papua New Guinea at the same time as me. Our different perspectives and the passage of time may help explain this. Historical facts and accounts are as accurate as I could make them. If errors have been made they are mine and mine alone, and are not intentional.

Before my story unfolds, it's important that I pay tribute to the many pilots who spent far longer than I did as bush pilots in Papua New Guinea, dancing along *the knife edge*, and let them know I am in no way trying to 'big-name' myself in this volume. These pilots have a collective experience far exceeding mine. In a way, my story is theirs too, except their exposure to the hazards of PNG flying was exponentially greater. I have nothing but respect for these aviators. You guys know who you are: *Bol bilong yupela em i bikpela tru!*

Finally, I apologise if it appears that I have trivialised some of the aircraft accidents and loss of life covered in this book, especially to those who lost family and friends in these accidents. This was not my intention. I trust that by the end of the book it will be clear to the reader that the only difference between their fate and the fate of those of us who survived was that they were less lucky, not less skilled, than the rest of us.

Contents

Prologue 9

Introduction 12

Chapter 1: **An Officer and a Gentleman** 14

Chapter 2: **Pilot Training Squadron** 27

Chapter 3: **"Joe Civvy is trying to kill you"** 59

Chapter 4: **The Missionary Position** 73

Chapter 5: **Of Golden Voices, the Ononge
No-Go-Around, and *Raskols*** 98

Chapter 6: **Crash Burn Die** 116

Chapter 7: **Fuzzy Wuzzy Triffids** 136

Chapter 8: **Misadventures in the Manumu Valley** . . . 162

Chapter 9: **Bent-wing Bastards, Kiwi losses,
and Armageddon** 173

Chapter 10: **"Nothing exciting ever happens to me":
The Death of P2–SEF** 189

Chapter 11: **In like Flynn!** 204

Chapter 12: **Needles and Haystacks** 226

Chapter 13: **Missionaries, Mercenaries and Misfits** . . . 241

Chapter 14: **Dodge City and the Cheshire Cat** 261

Chapter 15: **"The bus drivers want to cut his
head off"** 279

Chapter 16: **Cowboys and Dickheads** 306

Chapter 17: **Bagpipes, Blood, and Farewell** 331

Chapter 18: **Fate is the Hunter** 350

Chapter 19: **Rubber Dog Shit** 363

Endnotes & References 385

PROLOGUE

No one else was flying in the mountain airstrips of the Goilala country that day. The cloud was draped heavily over the Owen Stanley Range, discharging dark columns of drizzle on the already waterlogged jungle, and I'd had a hell of a time just finding Woitape airstrip. After I'd landed there, slipping and sliding across the boggy grass up to the parking bay, a few bedraggled villagers appeared from behind a tin shack and asked, unenthusiastically, to be flown to Fane. Given the atrocious weather this was highly inadvisable, but I'd made it this far into the mountains and was foolhardy enough to give it a go.

The wet season gave me stomach ulcers. I'd find myself in situations where the margins of safety were razor thin, and then professional pride would lead me to push it even more in an attempt to get the job done.

Fane airstrip was only ten miles to the west of Woitape and I knew the bad weather route well: there was a narrow valley that ran between the downwind position in Woitape's circuit area all the way to a base turn point for Fane. Terrain on either side of the valley averaged 6000 feet, and there were mountain peaks over 8000 feet high to the immediate north and south. After take-off from Woitape, with my four passengers strapped into the back seats, I turned to position the aircraft over the valley entrance. Providence had smiled on pilots servicing this part of the Goilalas — a large solitary fir tree stood on a ridgeline at the entrance to the valley, marking its position. We Moresby-based pilots called it 'the Christmas tree', and used it as a navigation aid. If you could see that tree, your position was confirmed and you could happily continue, even in absolutely shocking weather. Approaching the tree, I slowed the aircraft down and put out a touch of flap, setting the Cessna 206 up in a bad weather configuration so I could fly lower and slower and reduce my turn radius in case I needed to circle. The mouth of the valley was only barely open, choked by tendrils of cloud that snaked downwards from the solid overcast above. I could see about halfway down it, but not to the end. I was forced to orbit in my present position, craning my neck to look down into the valley with each pass over the Christmas tree, hoping that the visibility would improve. After several turns over the tree the weather appeared to be lifting — there was a gap in the cloud and a hint of sunlight peeked back at me from the far end of the valley. It teased me: *Come on in, the valley is open*. I made my move, descending to the treetops as I rolled into the valley, acutely aware there could be no turning back. Straightaway I was forced lower and lower in order to stay out of cloud.

This may have been a mistake.

The gap in the cloud became smaller and smaller as I descended, a shrinking tunnel twisting down the gorge. In a matter of seconds I was so low my wheels barely cleared the trees on the valley floor as I passed, and jungle-clad walls closed in on me until I was a mere wingspan from both sides of the valley. And then, in an instant, the gap was gone and I was flying blind. In cloud. In the bottom of a gorge. With terrain on both sides rising thousands of feet above me.

Time stopped.

The passengers started screaming, anticipating the aircraft smashing into the side of the mountain. And their deaths.

Shit.

Survival depended on my airspeed indicator and my compass. I fought back the rising panic and focused on these two parameters. Full power. Raise the nose. Hold a climbing airspeed. Hold the same course I was on when the world went white — a mosquito's dick to the left of east.

Airspeed, heading. Airspeed, heading.

I had the capacity for just one other thought:

Will I hear the sound of the airframe smashing into the trees as we crash, or will I be dead before it registers?

●

Introduction

When once you have tasted flight, you will forever walk the earth with your eyes turned skyward, for there you have been, and there you will always long to return.

ATTRIBUTED TO LEONARDO DA VINCI

I was lucky. At about 13 years of age I knew what I wanted to be when I grew up. When you know the destination, it's easier to plan the journey, and that's always been the way with me.

I'd had the usual boyhood daydreams — at age ten I was going to be an archaeologist, soon after that the Army was to be for me, and I'm sure racing car driver made an appearance at some stage too. Maybe even firefighter. But it was as a passenger on an Air New Zealand F-27 Fokker Friendship at age 13 that I contracted a serious case of the flying bug. I can still remember leaning right out into the aisle so I could look through the open cockpit door. The pilots were busy in their cocoon of lights, knobs, dials and gauges. We were on final approach into Gisborne's airport (my home town on the East Coast of New Zealand, population 30,000) and I could see them wrestling with the controls. The runway danced in the windscreen and the Captain was making adjustments to keep it central in his windshield. It seemed the aircraft had a mind of its own and was reluctant to go where he wanted it to. He was really working hard on the control column: pulling back, pushing forward, rolling left and right. When we were a few hundred feet above the ground the co-pilot pushed an engine control forward, and the propellers driven by the Rolls Royce Dart engines screamed into full forward pitch with their characteristic wail. To this day I love the sound of propellers going into fine pitch. It's my *smell of napalm in the morning.* As we descended, the runway became larger and larger in the windscreen; the view engulfed us until I saw nothing but sky as the Captain flared the aircraft to bring it down firmly on the tarmac. Wow, that looks like challenging stuff, I thought. And bucket loads of fun. Plus they get paid for it, they wear snappy uniforms and they are the bosses of their domain. There was also the not-so-small matter of the rather pretty girl working the cabin as air hostess, handing out snacks and drinks and sweets, although I was too young to appreciate exactly what kind of perk of the job this might turn out to be . . .

I was hooked.

Flying lessons were expensive and, although I'm sure my parents would have done their best to accommodate any request I had and help me fund some civilian flying training, that thought never entered my head. I knew I wanted to be an airline captain and it seemed the most obvious way to do this was to become an Air Force pilot straight after leaving high school, do my return-of-service commitment to the military, then transfer to commercial aviation. Why pay for flying training myself when the Royal New Zealand Air Force's coffers could do so?

So that was the plan.

It looks so simple written down like that, and I thought it would be. Of course, it wasn't. Ultimately, I was to achieve my goal, but there were more than a few hiccups along the way, and had it not been for my mix of strong-headedness and initial naiveté, I would never have made it. A good dose of *right place right time* also helped. Like I said, I was lucky. Just as well, for in my New Guinea years an absence of luck would have seen me with an absence of life in a very short span of time. As we shall see . . .

●

Chapter 1

An Officer and a Gentleman

A pilot candidate should be naturally athletic and have a reputation for reliability, punctuality and honesty. He should have a cool head in emergencies, good eye for distance, keen ear for familiar sounds, steady hand and sound body with plenty of reserve; he should be quick-witted, highly intelligent and tractable. Immature, high-strung, overconfident, impatient candidates are not desired.

WW1 **US ARMY** RECRUITING GUIDELINES[2]

I applied to join the Royal New Zealand Air Force (RNZAF) in 1988, halfway through my last year of high school. I was 17 years old. I passed the first stage of screening (being able to fill out the application form in vaguely legible and coherent handwriting) and received an invitation to attend an initial selection interview.

It was held in the local Army Hall, and I was one of half a dozen interviewees. We were ushered into a classroom and handed IQ assessment-type problem-solving worksheets, mathematics and English comprehension tests, and an aviation aptitude test. In the aptitude test we were presented with a series of pictures of cockpit instruments and a selection of silhouettes of aircraft in various flying attitudes. We were asked to match each cockpit picture with the aircraft picture that best represented what the aircraft was doing, based on the instrument indications. I found the maths test quite hard (there was a time limit for this test, and there wasn't enough of it), but the English and aviation aptitude tests seemed fairly straightforward. Immediately after these tests we were transferred to an adjoining room and told to wait for our one-on-one interview with the RNZAF Recruiting Officer. At the end of my interview an assistant handed the Officer the results of my tests and, after he examined them, he told me I'd be progressing to the next stage of the selection process: a four-day selection board to be held at RNZAF Base Hobsonville in Auckland. My scores were good enough for me to be considered for the position of Officer Cadet Direct-entry Pilot. I had hoped to join the RNZAF as a University Officer Cadet (under this scheme the RNZAF would sponsor cadets through a three-year degree course at Canterbury University in Christchurch before they began their pilot training) but my maths test marks were not high enough for this to be an option. Still, I was over the moon with the news that I was on track to join a military pilot's course and train as an RNZAF Officer. Over the next few weeks I eagerly awaited the arrival of the envelope containing my tickets to Auckland and the details of the selection board at Base Hobsonville. I wonder if the postman knew how keenly I watched him on his daily cycle past our house as I waited for the day he deposited the magic envelope marked *Confidential: RNZAF* in our mailbox.

It arrived. A few months later I found myself at the Air Force Base in Auckland, undergoing more intelligence and aptitude testing, problem-solving exercises with the other candidates, psychological evaluations, medical examinations (my first exposure to the rather intimate 'turn your head to the side and cough' testicles/hernia examination), plus a link trainer-type flying aptitude test. This contraption was a very basic cockpit mock-up in an enclosed box, like a 1970s version of today's arcade game flight-simulators. Using the joystick inside the box you could 'fly' a blue light around a grid on the computer screen in front of you. The blue light moved randomly and you had to counter its movements with the joystick to keep it in the centre of the grid. While I struggled to keep the errant dot in the middle (it wandered all over the show like a drunk driver) one of two light bulbs on the top of the computer screen (a red one and a green one) lit up at random intervals. There were two push buttons on the console below the screen, and these had to be pushed as quickly as possible with a free hand (reaction time was measured) in order to extinguish the lights: the left button killed the red light, the right button the green. This while trying to keep the crazy blue dot centred in the middle of the grid. It was a bit like the old 'rub your stomach and pat your head' coordination exercise, with a test of one's reflexes thrown in for good measure.

The officer selection process also included an afternoon of impromptu speeches. Aside from putting us on the spot and testing our public speaking abilities, this no doubt served to assess candidates' levels of self-confidence. I do not remember what I was asked to speak about that day, but I have vivid memories of one of my fellow candidates. He was asked to speak for three minutes on the topic of police brutality. A rather geeky chap, with nervous eyes and a banjo-on-the-patio grin, he stunned us all when he opened his speech in total seriousness with the line, "The problem with police brutality . . . is that there is not enough of it." His attempt at humour was received like a bad case of haemorrhoids. That very afternoon he was informed that his attempt to join the military had been unsuccessful and was removed from the selection process.

At the end of the second day of tests and interviews I was feeling a bit off-colour. I informed the RNZAF staff and was sent to the base doctor, who discovered I had just come down with bronchitis. I had recently returned from my first-ever skiing holiday and must have contracted the illness during the trip. Talk about bad timing. The RNZAF personnel were most understanding though, and after I spent two days recuperating in the Air Force Base Hospital, they allowed me to finish the selection process before I flew on an Air New Zealand F-27 Fokker Friendship back home to Gisborne.

I was reasonably happy with how it had all gone, and was confident that I would be accepted. I felt I had prepared well, and I did believe (perhaps too confidently, but without being arrogant about it) that I was the sort of person they were after.

A few weeks passed. I still remember getting the phone call in

November 1988 from the Recruiting Officer who had done my initial interview at the Gisborne Army Hall. He told me that I had been accepted for pilot training and that I would start in early January 1989. What awesome news! I was home alone that afternoon and ran around the house doing a Tom-Cruise-on-Oprah's-couch routine: yelling and screaming and hooting and punching the air etc. Suffice it to say I was very, very, very happy.

The day for me to join the RNZAF arrived — 10 January 1989. I had been sent Air New Zealand tickets to get me from Gisborne to Christchurch, where I was to be picked up by Air Force staff and driven to RNZAF Base Wigram. That base is closed now, and what was once a hive of accommodation blocks, training schools, parade and sports grounds and an active runway with a parachute training school and a rifle range, is now a suburban sprawl of new streets and townhouses. In 1989 Base Wigram was the primary RNZAF Base for officer training, ab-initio[i] pilot training, navigator training, and mechanic and engineer training.

I arrived at Christchurch Airport and made my way to the baggage claim area. I met a couple of guys who were also joining the RNZAF that day and we soon spotted the uniformed driver who was to take us to the Air Force Base. He was accompanied by Flight Sergeant Dave Crail, who seemed a reserved and quiet chap as he sat in the van next to the driver, neither of them saying a word. First impressions are not always accurate: we were soon to learn that Crail was a hard man, far from quiet, and we came to fear him and the influence he had on our grades at Officer Training School.

Once at the base the vehicle pulled up outside an accommodation block that was to be our home for the next 13 weeks of officer training. We were instructed by Flt Sgt Crail to drop our luggage there and walk about 200m down the road to the Command Training School (CTS). This was a group of buildings where most of our training would take place and

---

[i]   The first stages of flight training.

where the administrative offices were located. More new recruits had joined us — there were now about eight of us — and we ambled along in a loose group down the base road, excitedly chatting away. We were the kings of the world — "Hey there, we're the new batch of Air Force Pilots!" I'd seen *An Officer and a Gentleman,* and *Top Gun;* I thought we must be 'the best of the best of the best'. We were so naive — "OK, I'm here, give me my Queen's commission and my wings!" — and saw Base Wigram as a place where our dreams were to become reality. The dream was soon shattered.

Crail stormed up next to us and with a furrowed brow and no-nonsense bark let us have it: "STOP! What the FUCK do you think this is, a PICNIC? Put your shit in your left hand, form into two lines, no talking, look straight ahead, and MARCH!"

He had morphed into Louis Gossett Junior's drill instructor from *An Officer and a Gentleman,* but a lot taller, thinner, and Caucasian. Crail was 6 foot 4, built like a rake, and a bit like the loo paper in public toilets: he was rough and tough and took no shit. He was a walking war-movie cliché — I wouldn't have been surprised that day in 1989 if he had launched into his own version of the Gunnery Sergeant's classic lines in Stanley Kubrick's *Full Metal Jacket*:

"Where in hell are you from, McLaughlin?"

"Um . . . Gisborne, Flight Sergeant."

"HOLY DOGSHIT! GISBORNE! Only STEERS and QUEERS come from Gisborne Officer Cadet McLaughlin, and you don't much look like a STEER to me . . . so that kind of narrows it down!"

I realised with a knot in my stomach that Wigram was a place where dreams could be absolutely crushed. What I didn't realise was how politics and personalities could come into play to derail the best laid career plans and aspirations. I was to learn this many years later, looking back on the experience.

In one of the CTS classrooms we were introduced to the staff and given a lecture on base life and the way our officer training was structured: the location of all the facilities we would be using, details of some administrative items that needed to be attended to, and an introduction to our first week's CTS schedule. I also met the rest of the trainees on my course. There were 28 cadets on RNZAF #189 Officer Training Course: ten of us who would go on to train as pilots; eight who, after partially completing officer training, were to begin three-year university degrees sponsored by the RNZAF before beginning their training as pilots, navigators or engineering officers; ten who hoped to graduate as Air Force officers with ground jobs in administrative roles. Later that afternoon we marched back to the accommodation block (Flt Sgt Crail didn't have to yell at us this time: if nothing else we were quick learners) and unpacked. Over the next several days we were issued with our uniforms (summer, winter, normal dress and formal) as well as kit bags, shoes, socks, stationery, hats and caps, a greatcoat and a raincoat, brown leather gloves for winter parades and many others bits and pieces that now escape memory.

It didn't take long to settle into the CTS routine: up at 0500; a 30-minute morning run with Flt Sgt Crail at 0600; wolfing down breakfast in the Non-commissioned Officer's Mess (NCO's Mess) between 0645 and 0715; a mad rush back to the barracks to finish preparing our rooms for the daily white-glove inspection by the duty Officer at 0730. This was the stereotypical search for dust, for items out of place, and for less-than-gleaming shoes and less-than-perfect creases in shirts and slacks and shorts and jackets. Oddly, we were also required to have our socks aligned perfectly in military rank and file rows in our sock drawer, all rolled up into balls done with the prescribed technique so they looked like smiling faces. Smiley socks were important if you wanted to become an officer in the RNZAF.

There was never enough time in the morning to achieve all the tasks that needed doing: morning ablutions; the ironing of uniforms; the spit-shining of shoes; the polishing of belt buckles; and last-minute study for exams later in the day — the list was endless. Somehow I managed. We also had to cope with the daily construction of the bane of any military recruit's existence — bedpacks. The bedpack concept must have been dreamed up by some particularly sadistic military man as a way to inflict daily stress on the hapless recruit. A bedpack is made up of four blankets and two sheets and has to be folded in a certain way with exact dimensions so it winds up looking like a blanket-and-sheet sandwich. The proud cadet then places it at the foot of their bed. It took several minutes to fold and construct one that would pass inspection and we were always short of time. A crappy looking bedpack was a sure way to fail your morning inspection and you didn't want that. A single failure led to a loss of privileges (LOP), which entailed a loss of access to the TV room in the NCO's Mess and the loss of a weekend pass (meaning you could not leave the base during the weekend — our only chance to escape). Several fail grades in succession could lead to failing the officer training course altogether.

My bedpack preparation time was cut to almost zero a few weeks into the course when those of us in my wing of the accommodation block (all ten soon-to-be pilot trainees) 'acquired' some extra blankets and sheets, so we could hide pristine ready-prepared bedpacks in the roof space in one of the hallways, only bringing them out a few minutes before the daily morning inspection. Most of us also hid sleeping bags in the roof space, choosing to sleep in these rather than use our blankets and sheets so we didn't ever mess up our beds. These two cheats made the daily pre-inspection preparation a great deal easier and freed up vital minutes that could be spent doing something else. Once the inspection was complete, one of us would monkey up into the roof space and the still-assembled bedpacks would be handed up and stowed away until the next morning when the deception would be repeated. In the last few weeks of officer training the cadets in my wing had the system down to a fine art — every timesaving tactic we could come up with had been employed — and I found myself with plenty of time to spare before morning inspection.

Not all of my #189 course mates were utilising these timesaving tactics: most mornings the cadets in the other wings were still running around like blue-arsed flies right up until the moment Flt Sgt Crail and the Duty Officer arrived to start the inspection. One morning, during a week in which I was the designated course leader, I asked one of my fellow cadets to help me out with one last task before inspection (stacking ironing boards in the communal laundry room). He wasn't very impressed, as he was busy enough just getting himself ready. He reluctantly agreed to help, rolling his eyes, and saying with a sigh, "Yeah sure, McLaughlin, I'll give you a hand. Why don't you put a broom up my arse and I'll sweep the floor while I'm at it!"

Lectures and the other exercises at CTS began at 0800. There was a short break for coffee mid-morning, an hour for lunch and then we worked through to 1700. We were given instruction, practice, and examination in: Command and Leadership; Interpersonal Relationships; Service Law and Offences; Drill and Ceremonial; Service Customs and Traditions; Weapons Handling (9mm pistols for aircrew; rifles and submachine guns for ground staff); Survival, Safety and First Aid; Active and Passive Defence; Health and Fitness (we had gym sessions several times a week, plus the daily run with Flt Sgt Crail); Written and Oral Communications; Meetings and Chairmanship; Study of Political Systems and International Relations; Military History; RNZAF Organisation, Roles and Operations; Etiquette; and Administration Procedures.

It was such a busy time and so much was crammed into the 13 weeks that, looking back on it now, most of it is a blur. Without my graduation certificate to refer to (it lists the topics we covered in 1989) I would not have been able to tell you what we studied.

At the end of each hectic weekday, dinner was served in the NCO's Mess from 1800 to 1930 and we spent the rest of the night cramming for exams and tests as well as getting uniforms ready for the next day and, of course, preparing for the next morning's room inspection. We were busier than a one-legged man in an arse-kicking competition.

Soon after starting at CTS we were introduced to Flt Sgt Crail's sidekick, Sergeant Robinson. Robinson was British, crass, arrogant and overweight. We nicknamed him 'BFR': Big Fat Robbie. He had a sadistic streak and liked nothing better than picking on someone who was having problems with their drill moves on the parade ground (some of the cadets who were slated to become non-flying officers in the RNZAF had two left feet) and subject them to a barrage of insults and criticism. One of my course mates, Ozzie Mansor, was a diminutive softly spoken doctor from Mauritius. He was a top bloke, but his marching and rifle drills were entirely atrocious. BFR loved yelling at poor Ozzie. A typical BFR tirade went like this:

BFR: "Officer Cadet Mansor, your rifle drill is FUCKING HOPELESS!"
Mansor: "Yes, Sergeant Robinson."
BFR: "What is your rifle drill, Officer Cadet Mansor?"
Mansor: "It's fucking hopeless . . ."
BFR: "I can't HEAR you, Mansor."
Mansor: "It is FUCKING HOPELESS!"
BFR: "FUCKING HOPELESS . . . WHAT?"
Mansor: "FUCKING HOPELESS . . . SERGEANT ROBINSON!"

I never had much respect for BFR. He would make a huge show of pointing out any less-than-perfectly polished shoes, a badly ironed shirt, or an askew double Windsor, and yet he himself was a real slob. His own uniform looked slept in and his shoes hadn't been anywhere near a tin of polish in ages. Most of the time he looked like the cat had just dragged him in. Backwards. Through a hedge. I resented BFR's hypocrisy. Flt Sgt Crail on the other hand commanded respect. Crail's uniform was always in top-notch condition and we all wondered how he got such an incredible glassy shine on his black drill shoes. Crail carried himself with style and exuded confidence. BFR carried himself with indifference and exuded body odour.

Highlights of the 13-week course included the time we spent on the base rifle range with our submachine guns, rifles, and pistols; a parachute jump training course where we learned the correct landing technique after a jump (sadly we didn't get to jump out of a plane — we were strapped into an open parachute and towed behind a jeep on a cable and released from 200 feet, a poor man's version of the training); being allowed into the garden bar of the Officer's Mess one weekend to stage our own 'Bavarian Night' (a colossal piss-up complete with a live oom-pah brass band and compulsory German-style fancy dress for attendees); and the leadership exercises, during which all officer cadets took turns being group leaders. Some of the leadership exercises were day trips; some involved tented camps away from Base Wigram in the New Zealand wilderness. The best ones were the multi-day exercises. I particularly remember an exercise when I was the leader. We were camped in the pine forests of south Canterbury and my small group was tasked with moving by night, undetected, from one end of a valley to the other, a distance of only ten kilometres or so. We had to arrive at a predetermined point before a midnight cut-off. Moving as silently as we could, we followed a firebreak in the trees, stopping often to take cover in the saplings at the edge of the forest. Senses were sharpened, as we knew that we were being tracked by Flt Sgt Crail and BFR. If they found us (and they did), they would appear out of the inky night and lob tear-gas grenades at us while firing submachine gun rounds (blanks, we presumed) over our heads. It was incredibly exciting gung-ho stuff for an 18-year-old: dressed in full camouflaged fatigues, with army boots and steel helmets, gas masks, black face paint, a field radio, maps, and with a backpack full of rations and gear strapped to our backs. I also remember a daytime exercise where we again moved with stealth in small groups towards a designated pick-up point. Before we were extracted by the waiting Huey helicopters back to camp, the area was dummy-strafed by two RNZAF McDonnell Douglas A-4K Skyhawk fighters — they came rolling in out of the big blue and screamed past us with two deafening treetop-level passes over the pick-up point. It was awe-inspiring stuff.

The leadership exercises were great fun. Fun that is, until a team leader didn't achieve their objective, and/or didn't impress the CTS Staff with their leadership style (one staff member always tagged along with the groups, assessing the performance of the designated leader). When this happened the cadet would be put under the microscope during their next assigned leadership task. If this also went badly, the cadet could be cut from the course. We lost a few course mates this way.

A few weeks into the training the nine pilot-to-be officer cadets of #189 decided to follow a long-established Air Force tradition and purchase a course car. These were generally large, old, cheap vehicles, ideally a model that would accommodate all course members at once. We sourced a 1951 Chevrolet Styleline Deluxe from a friend of a friend in the southern town of Timaru, and dispatched a couple of the boys with

$2000 to purchase it. It was a proud day when it arrived on base. The massive Chevy (no doubt held together by body filler and paint after its long, hard life) was painted glossy pink and its chromed grill, bumper, mag wheels and rear gravel shields sparkled in the Christchurch sun. We christened it Floyd. It must have been one of the finest course cars Wigram had ever seen.

The Commanding Officer (CO) of CTS at this time was Squadron Leader Jim McMillan. He was an ex-navigator and was a great guy. We took Floyd around to CTS to show McMillan our purchase and he was so impressed that the next day he presented us with a Squadron Leader pennant, like the mini flags you see fluttering from the bonnets of diplomatic cars. His wife had sewn the pennant for us and we proudly attached it to Floyd's front aerial. Over the next few days, young NCOs would stand to attention and give Floyd a snappy salute as we drove past, all nine of us on board, crammed into the two bench seats. We thought it was hilarious. The Base Commander got wind of this, however, and decided it wasn't so funny having his junior ranks saluting a fake Squadron Leader pennant on a 1951 Chevy driven by officer cadets, and we were instructed to remove it immediately. Thank you, Mrs McMillan, we had a blast.

Before I give the impression that the 13 weeks of officer training was all work and no play, I must admit that during the weekends we let our hair down and hit the beers pretty hard; both within the base, and in the bars and bazaars of Christchurch. The officer cadets in my wing tended to stick together and we got up to all sorts of mischief. The age-old cocktail of testosterone, alcohol and outrageously high levels of self-confidence resulted in considerable collateral damage amongst the young female population of the city. I was the second youngest of the group and observed in awe as my worldlier colleagues worked their magic in the bars and nightclubs. Cadet Clark Malone, now Wing Commander Malone, was the ringleader. An extrovert of legendary proportions, he did everything with class, style and an air of dignity. Even the really dirty stuff. A top-20 hit at the time was a song by 'Was (Not Was)', *Walk the Dinosaur*. It was a crowd favourite at local nightclub The Firehouse. When the house band launched into that song Clark would attack the dance floor (and any hapless maidens within a 20-metre radius) and do his own 'Dinosaur'. We looked on with jaws agape as he unleashed his signature moves: 1. Begin with seductive and rather over the top hip waggle. 2. Roll upper torso forward into a hunch, holding arms close to body like a dinosaur's stunted forelimbs. 3. Snap thumb and middle fingers to beat, circling the dance floor like hungry predator. 4. Make eye contact with cute girl. Or her friend. Or both of them. 5. Gyrate body like lust-crazed T-Rex. 6. Repeat steps 1–5 as necessary until aforementioned girl/girls are pulled.

It worked!

As final exams were passed and all leadership exercises completed, we began preparing for our graduation parade. Our physical training (PT) sessions also wound down: the climax of the course was a ten-mile/16 km running race from the Air Force Base out to the Taitapu Tavern in the South Canterbury countryside. Much to my surprise I was first across the finish line and celebrated with a cool ale at the bar while waiting for the tail-enders to arrive.

When the day of our graduation parade finally arrived, out of 28 original course members, #189 Officer Training Course had 22 graduates. During the parade, our seven colleagues who were assigned to ground roles were commissioned as fully fledged RNZAF Officers. The nine pilot trainees (myself included) and the six cadets who were off to begin their three years of study at Canterbury University, were not. This seemed unfair, as we had all passed the same training course. It was simply a cost-saving measure by the RNZAF: we were to stay in the rank of officer cadet (with the associated lower salary — the below-average-wage sum of NZ$15,741 per annum) until we graduated with our wings at the end of our pilot training course. Our university-bound colleagues would remain officer cadets until their degrees were completed and they too had obtained their pilot, navigator or engineer qualifications.

As the next batch of officer cadets arrived on Base Wigram to begin their own 13-week odyssey at CTS (fresh meat for Crail and BFR), we packed our things and moved across the road to No. 2 Officer's Mess. Besides me, there was Jason 'Easty' Easthope, Clark 'Clarky' Malone, Grant 'Reidman' Reidy, Tim 'Robbo' Robinson, Grant 'Tommo'

RNZAF official

#189 Officer Training Course graduation. Seven ground officers and nine pilots.

Thompson, Logan Officer, Kevin 'Walshy' Walsh, and Rob 'Flu' Fluit. One could only pray that our aptitude for the next chapter of our training would prove better than our aptitude for creating unique nicknames.

Cheesy monikers aside, it was an exciting time. We had survived officer training, we were no longer the junior CTS course on base and, most importantly, we were about to get our teeth into the phase of training that was the real reason we had joined the military: to train as pilots.

●

Chapter 2

Pilot Training Squadron

Lieutenant George: "Crickey, I'm looking forward to today!
Up-diddly-up, down-diddly-down: whoops, poop,
twiddledeedee! A decent scrap with the fiendish Red Baron;
bit of a jolly old crash landing behind enemy lines;
capture, torture, escape — and then back home in time
for tea and medals!"
BEN ELTON AND RICHARD CURTIS: "BLACK ADDER GOES FORTH"[3]

If we thought officer training had been hectic, we were in for a shock.
The initial workload as the pilot training began was worse.

We were now the junior course at Base Wigram's Pilot Training Squadron (PTS) and faced 12 months of flying training, flight checks and exams before graduating with our RNZAF wings and being posted to one of the operational squadrons. PTS was housed in a row of classrooms and briefing rooms that had been tacked on to the front of Wigram's hangar #1, on the northern end of the airfield, near the base's main gate. At any one time PTS hosted two wings courses, a junior and a senior course, as they worked their way (under a strict timetable) through three phases of training.

The ground school phase was first: four weeks of exams preparing us for the flying stages. We had lectures and exams on aeroscience (the physics and mathematics of flight); mental dead reckoning;

meteorology; principles of flight (aerodynamics); aircraft instruments; aircraft performance; navigation; and aircraft engineering. The information wasn't hard to digest — it's just that there was a hell of a lot of it. It was like trying to drink from a fire hose. We struggled to keep up and avoid information overload, but there was some good news. The focus was very much on the nitty gritty of the business of flying and for the most part the military stuff like inspections and parades had taken a back seat. We were only subjected to a room inspection at No. 2 Officers Mess by the duty officer once a week; this was more of a formality than anything else. The theatrical search for dust we had experienced while under officer training was a thing of the past. Happily, bedpacks were no longer required.

Our move across the road to 2 Mess was a welcome change. It was a sprawl of weatherboard buildings facing the base sports pitch. There were four two-storey accommodation wings, a formal dining room, a reception room (the anteroom) with fireplace and small library corner, a TV room and, of course, a bar. Our single rooms, although much older and well worn than the CTS accommodation, were fairly large, with a single bed, side table, built-in desk and bookcase and a spacious wardrobe. There was also a sink and mirror in the room and each accommodation wing had its own communal showers and toilets. One hundred dollars per week was deducted from our salary for the privilege of living in 2 Mess. This was a bargain by any standards. Meals in the mess were silver service, with à la carte dining for lunch and dinner and attentive service by starched white-clad waiters and waitresses. Cheese, crackers and port were served nightly after dinner in the anteroom. The 2 Mess meals were excellent. On top of the cheap food and board, drinks served in the bar were priced ridiculously low: about half-price compared to the civilian world. Because of this, and the tendency for officer cadets to get rather carried away, our bar tab was monitored by CO CTS. Any officer cadets seen to be overspending on alcohol were called in for an interview and asked to tone it down. The only #189 pilot trainee I recall getting called in to explain a weighty bar bill was our poster boy for fast living, Clark Malone.

As in any military setting, there was a pecking order and hierarchy at play within 2 Mess. At the top were the senior university officer cadets (known as 'pukes' — a reference to their penchant for pissing it up until they were physically ill). Some of them had been living in 2 Mess for over three years. Lower down the ladder of seniority were the pilot and navigator trainees in their intermediate phase of training and last, and certainly least, was us. Ruling the roost, with an appropriate measure of arrogance and a sense of superiority, was the President of the Mess Committee (the PMC). A senior puke, he was the top dog and the direct link with the COs of the training wings, the CO of CTS, and the Mess Staff. The PMC was in charge of day-to-day discipline at 2 Mess. If anything untoward happened in the mess (and it did, regularly!) he was responsible for handing down in-house punishment. He was also responsible for the apologies that had to be offered to the relevant people in the wake of officer cadet mischief.

There were by now 12 trainees on #189 Pilots Course — three officers from other services had joined us hoping to earn their RNZAF wings: Lieutenants Colin 'Tan-Man' Tan and George 'Chewbacca' Chew from the Republic of Singapore Air Force; and Lieutenant Bruce Grant from the Royal New Zealand Navy. All three were a bit standoffish, perhaps as they were officers already and looked down on us lowly non-commissioned officer cadets.

The excitement was palpable the day we were fitted out with our zoom bags (flying overalls), flying boots, gloves, SPH4 flying helmets, Mae West life jackets, parachutes and flying jackets. Predictably, the boys got dressed up in all the flying gear and paraded around the accommodation wing of 2 Mess that night, quoting cheesy *Top Gun* lines and generally behaving like kids on a sugar high at a fancy dress party. *That's right Iceman . . . I AM dangerous!* It was immature, shallow and behaviour inappropriate for an officer. It was fantastic.

Our numbers reduced more quickly than we could have imagined. As the examination dates for the various PTS ground school subjects approached we lost Kevin Walsh — he decided that the RNZAF was not for him and he resigned before we even got to the flying stage. The rest of us scraped through the exams OK, and finally the day of our first flight arrived. At the time the RNZAF was using the Pacific Aerospace CT4-B

Airtrainer for the basic and intermediate phases of the wings course. The Airtrainer is a single-engine side-by-side aerobatic military trainer, powered by a 210 horsepower fuel-injected Continental piston engine. The CT4-B has a cruising speed of 120 knots, a top speed of 207 knots, a range of 500 miles, and an aerobatic rating of +6/−3 G. While not a stunning performer, it was well suited to its role and is still used by several of the world's air forces as a basic trainer.

The Pacific Aerospace CT4–B Airtrainer over RNZAF Base Wigram.

Unlike some of my course mates, I had never been up in a small aeroplane before. I distinctly remember my first mission in the CT4-B: the wings course introductory flight. I strapped into my seat next to instructor Flt Lt John 'Benny' Benfell and we departed for the Lake Ellesmere training area south-east of Christchurch City. It was all so new to me: the smooth growl of the engine as she fired up; the flicker of the cockpit's electronic gauges; the wavering of the needles on the HSRMI; the distinct purring of the altimeter's vibrator. Benny's fireproof nomex glove-clad hands moved with practiced precision over the myriad of switches, knobs and dials in the busy cockpit. He turned this on, adjusted that, changed the subscale here, and tested annunciator lights there. These pre-flight and post-engine start procedures seemed complex and they were all performed from memory. I felt more than a little apprehensive knowing that before being sent solo in a few weeks time I would have to perform them as soundly as Benny.

After take-off he showed me what the Airtrainer could do with a snappy aerobatics routine. In classic ex-fighter pilot style he was allergic to straight and level flight, and the sky and the earth merged in a blur as he looped, rolled, pulled, spun and yawed the small aircraft far above the Canterbury countryside. I loved every second of it and couldn't wait for the flying training to begin. I was the kid; PTS was the ultimate candy store.

A couple of days later we were paired with our instructors for the first phase of the flying training. I was assigned to Flt Lt Steve 'Chook' Morrissey. On meeting him, the origin of his nickname was obvious. Mad keen on helicopters and prone to waving his arms about when he got all excited about something, Morrissey strutted about like a rooster in a hen house, his jerky body movements reminiscent of a 1970s *Thunderbirds* marionette. Eccentricities aside, he was a great instructor, and I enjoyed flying with him.

Twenty-one years after we flew together, Chook Morrissey made international headlines in the most tragic of circumstances. In 2010 he was a Boeing 777 First Officer with Air New Zealand and, on a Hong Kong layover, went hiking in Hong Kong's New Territories with a fellow Air New Zealand pilot. It was the height of summer, and the Hong Kong Meteorology Service had issued a hot weather warning for that week: temperatures had soared to 34 degrees Celsius (93 Fahrenheit) with humidity over 90%. The two separated towards the end of the hike, with Morrissey walking to the trailhead alone while the other pilot stopped to rest. Morrissey failed to show up the next morning for his scheduled work duty, and his alarmed colleagues notified the Hong Kong police that he was missing. After an extensive search involving over 100 emergency services staff, with tracker dogs and helicopter support, his body was discovered seven days later, on 11 August, 200m off the path in the Pat Sin Leng country park. It appeared that he had tried to take a shortcut, only to lose his way and become disoriented, severely dehydrated, and ultimately incapacitated by Hong Kong's intense heat and humidity. I had not seen Chook Morrissey since my Air Force days, and was very sad to hear of his untimely death.

Monday to Friday, half of each day was taken up with ground lectures and a never-ending series of exams; the other half of the day was for a massed pre-flight briefing in the operations room at PTS, a flight (sometimes two), and a post-flight debrief. As long as the weather cooperated we flew every day, learning the basics, so after 11 sorties we could pass the first major milestone in any pilot's career — being sent solo. During weeknights we were busy studying for upcoming flights and exams, and we would make trips from 2 Mess across to hangar #2 after dinner and sit in the Airtrainer cockpits learning and practising the drills and procedures we were required to perform from memory. Thursday evenings were spent dusting and cleaning our rooms, as the Duty Officer carried out 2 Mess room inspections on Friday mornings. On weekends, especially Sundays, I'd shut myself in my room in the mess and study and prepare for the flights scheduled for the coming week. Most guys on the wings course did the same.

The RNZAF flying training syllabus was similar to that followed by civilian training organisations, but it was compressed and concentrated to fit it into the 12-month window afforded by the training budget. There was little or no extra training made available if a student fell below the required standard and the failure rate was high. There was a stark reminder of this in the hallway between the PTS operations room and the briefing rooms. Here the wall was adorned with the official RNZAF photos of all current wings courses, including the course that had moved on to Base Ohakea (in New Zealand's North Island) for the advanced phase of the training. When a cadet was cut from the course ('chopped'), instructors would draw a large black triangle over the head of that cadet. Ominously, on most photos, many of the cadets wore these black hats before their course was complete. We all had high hopes we'd emerge at the end of #189 wings course as RNZAF pilots, but the statistics indicated that half of us probably wouldn't make it (the black hats always seemed an odd indicator of failure. This practice might have originated in the Royal Air Force, where "he got his bowler hat" was RAF-speak for a pilot trainee failing and being discharged. This may have alluded to the chopped officer having to hand in his service uniform and cap and return to the civilian dress of a gentleman — a suit and bowler hat).

The tonic to the pressure-cooker environment of PTS was the Friday night drinks in the Officers Mess bar. Friday's beers were the highlight of our week, and we partied hard. The bar was at the end of the central corridor in 2 Mess, adjacent to the entrance to the eastern-most accommodation wing. Two guys with the same name tended it. Young Chris was an easygoing man of conspicuous happiness, while Chris senior was a crusty, grumpy old git. He grunted and snarled at us across the bar like a demented old-age pensioner, reluctantly serving us pints of beer as if the amber fluid belonged to him and he was paying for it himself. The grizzled dwarf inhabited an alternative universe, one in which people employed as bar staff never actually had to serve drinks to their patrons. The best response was to ignore him — we refused to let him put a damper on the serious business of getting drunk.

Friday night mess booze-ups almost always led to late-night missions into downtown Christchurch, where the partying continued. I shudder to think of the irresponsibility of it now, but back then drink-driving laws were largely ignored and the least intoxicated of us would take the helm of Floyd and drive the rest of the #189 boys into town. This weekly binge drinking was such an important part of the Air Force culture that all base personnel were released early on Friday afternoon so they could head to their respective drinking holes and hit the beers ASAP.

The 2 Mess drinking was heaviest when there was a special occasion or a milestone to be celebrated. My introduction to the carnage was 189's initiation night, soon after we started at PTS. In a ritualistic setting not dissimilar to that found in university halls of residence, college fraternity houses and surf-lifesaving clubs, we made our first official appearance in the No. 2 Officer's Mess bar. We were following in the footsteps of countless officer cadets who had traipsed the same halls and beer-engrained carpets since 2 Mess's completion in 1939 (the year the RNZAF was formed). The bar's wood-panelled walls housed a shrine of sorts. The northern wall, along the picture rail, was peppered with dozens of stickers. Known as 'course patches' (designed and printed by the course members themselves) they represented every CTS course that had ever passed through the mess and had been ceremonially affixed to the wall during each course's initiation night down through the years. Trainees wore an embroidered version of their course patch with pride, over the right breast of their flying overalls and jackets, until a squadron patch replaced it once they had been awarded their wings and joined an operational squadron. The stickers had become central to a long-standing 2 Mess tradition — the challenge was to affix them in the most outrageous and unexpected locations. In Christchurch there were course patches on trams, buses, street signs and in shop windows; at the beach, the airport, and in Hagley Park; in ladies' rest rooms in bars and nightclubs. The best effort was that of course number 888 — some daring bugger had climbed 15 feet up onto the awning by Christchurch's Sockburn roundabout and placed a sticker on the town clock.

Our patch depicted the winged lion of St Mark (the symbol of CTS) superimposed over a white cloud on a field of blue. From behind the cloud the silhouettes of three fighter jets burst into the cerulean sky, their contrails blending with the rays of a rising sun. Our course number, 189 (representing January 1989, our CTS course commencement date) was prominent across the top, while a loose Latin translation of our tongue-in-cheek motto — *Work Hard, Play Hard, Stay Hard* — scrolled across the bottom. It was a proud and poignant moment when we hoisted one of the 189 boys high atop our shoulders to place our patch on the hallowed wall on initiation night (it would be there still had the mess not been demolished by unscrupulous property developers in 1998). This formality achieved, the drinking games began. The master of ceremonies for the proceedings was preppy PMC Logan Cudby, the senior puke. He took the floor and presided over a number of games where the object was clearly to get everyone as drunk as possible, as quickly as possible. There were sculling competitions, a team yard-glass, carrier landings, raw egg eating contests, blindfolded wrestling matches where combatants beat the bejesus out of each other with rolled-up newspapers, and a party trick performed by PTS instructor Flt Lt Mark Woodhouse, who inhaled a condom through his nose and pulled it out through his mouth!

The days and weeks at PTS and 2 Mess rolled by. Sorties I had now covered, all under the watchful, if eccentric, eye of my instructor Chook Morrissey, included all the basics: straight and level, climbing, descending, turning, stalling, engine failures, glide approaches, and circuits (a circuit is when an aircraft takes off, climbs to 1000 feet above the ground, does a reversal turn to fly parallel to the runway, then descends and lands back where it started. The circuit presents a good test of all basic piloting skills). On 13 June, five weeks after we had started at PTS, I landed after my 11th training sortie with Flt Lt Morrissey. He told me to taxi off to the side of the runway. This was a good sign. "OK,

#189 course patch.

McLaughlin", he said, "fly three circuits by yourself then park her at the flight line. I'll be waiting for you in the briefing room. Cheerio!" With that he undid his five-point harness, unplugged his helmet, opened the canopy and climbed out onto the wing and down to the grass. As I moved off Morrissey gave me a big grin and a thumbs-up, then he turned and began his long walk back to the PTS buildings, his helmet cradled under his arm. I was alone in the cockpit. It was surreal. After carrying out my pre-take-off checks and obtaining a clearance, I took off and talked myself through the first circuit, verbalising all my actions over the intercom as if Morrissey was still strapped in next to me in the Airtrainer's cockpit. It was so strange to be alone. After the first circuit and touch-and-go I applied power and became airborne for my second circuit. This time I relaxed, stopped verbalising everything, and actually started to enjoy myself. It was a great feeling to be trusted with the aircraft as solo pilot for the first time, and (as for most pilots) remains an important and vivid career milestone. After the flight I climbed out of the cockpit of the CT4-B Airtrainer no longer a junior wings course student, but as a solo student, past the first hurdle of the flying training and eager to progress to bigger and better things. All of my #189 course mates were similarly successful, although the odd one needed some extra flights, and by the end of that week all 11 of us had been sent solo.

That Friday night the 2 Mess bar was our stage, as the senior pilot's course, the PTS instructors, some CTS Officers and our university cadet colleagues helped celebrate our successful solo pilot status. Our PTS instructors presented us with our solo certificates. I still have mine:

It's a big day when McLaughlin takes off on his own. Instructor's proud, but there's a knot in his stomach. Flight Commander's pleased but kinda wonders if Matt will make it — he's such an unco. But holy moly just look at him. He's right on centreline, never a swerve or a bounce. Anyone can tell that he's a PTS stud — see those white epaulettes, shiny shoes, and that willingness and GENEROSITY in the bar. Now the CO is more sure than ever that he will keep right on with the safe, confident, "experienced" style that he has displayed 'til now!!!

Needless to say, another epic booze-up ensued.

I was loving the training and the life at 2 Mess. There was such a great sense of adventure and a bond of camaraderie between the lads. I have nothing but happy memories of that time — we were young, enthusiastic, highly motivated and passionate about what we were doing. I was living my dream and had to pinch myself some days to make sure it wasn't just some wild illusion. Cecil Lewis, a British WWI pilot, summed up our mood as young PTS students in describing his own pilot training: "My hope, my belief in myself and in life, was boundless, vague and vast as a cloud horizon before sunrise . . . everything you did should be the best possible. You should live gloriously, generously, dangerously. Safety last!"[4]

Even the daily routine of prepping for a flight was a ritual to look forward to: we'd stride out from the PTS buildings across to the Airtrainer hangar in our flight suits and flying boots. Inside the safety section we'd zip on a Mae West life preserver and then tightly strap on our parachutes. Flying helmets were collected, nomex flying gloves slipped on, then we'd inspect the Form 700 maintenance logbook and sign it to indicate we'd accepted the aircraft from the engineers. Walking out to the flight line we'd look for the tail number of the aircraft assigned for that sortie and begin a pre-flight inspection and cockpit prep. As cheesy as it sounds, I could not wipe the smile off my face. I felt like Clint Eastwood striding out to his trusty steed. The only thing missing was the Colt 45.

Halfway through the first Airtrainer phase we took part in a Survival Training course. We were driven into New Zealand's rugged Southern Alps and dropped off in the wilderness in two groups, with no food, wearing only our flying suits and carrying only a parachute. This was a simulation of bailing out of an aircraft into inhospitable terrain. We were left in the mountains for three days and were expected to construct shelter, keep a fire burning (in order to signal any passing aircraft) and forage for food. The first two tasks were straightforward, but New Zealand's South Island was on the cusp of winter and food was scarce. We found nothing edible.

Some of the flying and survival instructors were staying at a campsite a few kilometres away and arrived in their jeep unannounced at random intervals during the three days to assess how we were doing. On the second night I sat with my group, huddled together in the cold around our feeble fire. We felt more than a tinge of envy knowing that the instructors were somewhere nearby, warm and cosy inside their cabins, their tummies full of good food. Our stomachs churned — we hadn't eaten since breakfast two days earlier. The 189 boys decided to do something about it. We hiked for a couple of hours, following the gravel track the instructors had been driving on, until we stumbled on their camp. Jason Easthope and I volunteered to break into the kitchen and steal some food. As we edged nervously into the camp my heart pounded, and I listened for any sign that the training staff had stirred. Easty and I did a quick snatch-and-grab in the pantry and came away with an armful of goodies, our veins bursting with adrenaline. We hiked the two hours back to our campsite and shared the spoils. There were two cans of beer, two eggs, some fruit, bread, and a tin of condensed milk. Such an eclectic menu never tasted so good and, after frantically consuming it all, we were careful to conceal the evidence of our feast. We knew the instructors would be back soon after daybreak.

On the last day we were separated into even smaller groups. I was partnered with the two Singaporeans, Tan-man and Chewbacca. We spent the afternoon constructing lean-to shelters out of fallen logs, bracken and ferns. That night we heard the unmistakable *whop-whop-whop* of an approaching RNZAF Huey (UH-1H Iroquois) helicopter. It made a low pass over the forest canopy and dropped us a frozen chicken! It had been gutted, but not plucked. The Singaporeans had not been in on the late-night mission to raid the instructor's food stores, so were by now absolutely ravenous. We split the carcass into three, drooling like madmen, and boiled it in a jerry can over the fire. *Le poulet surgelé a la Iroquois! C'est magnifique!* I can still taste that boiled chicken over 20 years later.

On the morning of day four, after a restless night in our leafy solo shelters, we were picked up and transported in the back of a Mercedes Unimog truck back to Base Wigram. We stopped off at a remote country tavern near Hanmer Springs for a toilet break, and I saw with great amusement a #188 course patch stuck high on the wall at the exit to the garden bar. Wow, those boys really got around. Back at base, a hot shower and a real meal were heavenly. A few days later we were given our grades from the survival exercise. #189's hotshot course commander Flt Lt Ricky Smits told me that I had become quiet and introverted and it was felt that I had contributed little to the group's survival effort. He assessed me as a 'low average survival risk', meaning the instructors didn't think I'd make it if faced with the real thing. I had to bite my tongue and not blurt out that I had hiked for four hours and poached *his* food in order to survive. I was fairly certain that was an *above average* effort.

Another training exercise was an open ocean helicopter rescue. We were told to don our full flying gear and board two RNZAF Huey choppers. They flew us to Christchurch's Akaroa Harbour, on the far side of Banks Peninsular. The helicopter's doors had been removed, and we lined up along the doorsills, sitting on the floor with our legs dangling over the side. The choppers descended to low-level over the water and we were told to jump at ten-second intervals. This we did, dropping some 30 feet into the icy water. As I pin-dropped into the harbour I pulled the ripcord on my Mae West lifejacket and shot back up to the surface. I bobbed in the frigid water, watching as the Hueys flew a racetrack pattern around us and returned to winch us back on board one by one. The chill of the water, added to the blast from the rotor's downwash as we were winched back into the Hueys, made for some frozen officer cadets. We flew back to the base and defrosted with hot showers and coffee.

Once a year there was an RNZAF parade in Cathedral Square, the heart of the city of Christchurch, where the mayor handed the Base Commander the keys to the city. It was a symbolic gesture — an annual reaffirmation of the strong ties between RNZAF Base Wigram and the people of the city. Over 1000 uniformed personnel took part in a parade through the city streets, including all of the cadets from No. 2 Officers Mess. We were kitted out in full winter uniform, replete with dress caps, brown leather dress gloves, and mirror-finish shoes (thanks to layer upon layer of spit polish and generous lashings of elbow grease). The silver buttons of our dress jackets glinted in the autumn sun and the front creases of our dress pants were like knife edges (if Air Force basic training taught you anything, it was complete mastery of the art of ironing). We clattered into the western side of Cathedral Square in a massive marching formation and were brought to a halt by command-barking ceremonial sword-wielding officers and stood obediently at attention as the formalities began. Parades were always a test of willpower, as there was a temptation to glance around, but I resisted and kept my stare fixed on the hexagonal walls of a police kiosk in front of me. Peripherally, I was aware of the Gothic bulk of the Anglican cathedral to my right, the square's most iconic structure (destined to be largely destroyed by the terrible earthquake of 2011), and the wind teasing the branches of the trees on the western edge of the square to my left. City loop trams ting-tinged their way along Worcester Street to our immediate north, their passengers seemingly oblivious to the military spectacle unveiling itself in the heart of the city. Luckily it was a cool morning, as it was not uncommon on hot parade days to see new recruits unaccustomed to standing still for long periods faint and topple to the ground like felled trees. At the end of the ceremony we were dismissed and I walked with my course mates back towards the RNZAF buses that would shuttle us back to base. We strode through the central city streets like we owned them, jaunty and full of *joie de vivre*. I have never been more proud of being in uniform than I was that day, as a member of my nation's defence forces in her most fair southern city. Daydreams of my own self-importance were short-lived — they were dealt a fatal blow by an old lady who stood hunched over the top of a parking meter on Colombo Street, smacking it with her handbag like it was an errant schoolboy. She saw me approaching and broke into a smile. I prepared myself for a compliment from her regarding how impressive I looked in full formal mess kit. "Oh, thank goodness you're here," she croaked, "this is jammed, can you fix it for me, young man?" Talk about getting shot down in flames — she thought I was a city council meter man!

Back at PTS, we had moved from the basics on to more advanced training: aerobatics, spinning, navigation, and instrument flying. In the air, our instructors hammered home the importance of aviation's favourite mnemonic: P A P (power + attitude = performance). For each combination of a specific engine power setting and a specific aircraft attitude (the orientation of the aircraft in relation to the horizon, both in pitch and roll) there is a corresponding performance outcome. For example, in the CT4-B Airtrainer, with a cruise power setting (25 inches throttle and 2500 prop rpm) and the nose held steady two degrees below the horizon, the aircraft will fly at a constant altitude, i.e. level flight, at 125 knots. With a climb power setting (30 inches throttle and 2700 rpm) and an attitude of 15 degrees nose-up, the aircraft will climb at 100 knots. If the military flight training was good for anything, it was hammering home these fundamental concepts of flight, and it was only later in my career that I realised just how solid my RNZAF training had been.

Another great aspect of the military flying was the rate at which we were given responsibility for our own missions and the speed with which we were introduced to more advanced phases of flight. We were on a much more accelerated learning curve than that I experienced later in civilian flying. This was because of the tightness of the wings course schedule, but also because firstly we had been selected as candidates with an aptitude for flying who should be able to learn quickly and, secondly, because the RNZAF wanted graduate pilots who could be entrusted from day one as commanders of military aircraft in critical high-stress situations. We were handed large dollops of responsibility very early on in the flying syllabus. It seems incredible to me now, looking back, that I was flying the CT4-B solo and practising spins and an aerobatics routine when I only had 25 hours in my logbook. That's just the way it was and we rose to the challenge.

Not all the students made the cut. The first to be chopped was our Navy trainee Lt Bruce Grant. He left us soon after he was sent solo. Singaporean Lt George 'Chewbacca' Chew was chopped after we returned from the survival course. Nine of us remained.

As seriously as we took things during the week, we continued to pursue opportunities for R & R with vigour. One Friday night one of the guys in the 2 Mess bar said he'd heard that a big group of trainee nurses would be meeting up at a local nightclub, The Palladium. We didn't need to hear any more. Battle stations! Out the door we went, a cloud of beer fumes and dodgy aftershave. Eight of us piled into Floyd for the trip into town, four vs four in the front and back bench seats. Clarky took the helm and gunned the big Chevy around Wigram's roads, turning aggressively into the corners and narrowly missing the sentry post at the main gate as we exited the base. As he threw the mighty beast around a sharp left-hand corner, the driver's door opened. In slow motion, with the car still slewing around the corner, centrifugal force pushed the front seat passengers towards the open door and Clarky was ejected onto the road. Jason Easthope (Easty), sitting next to him in the front seat, had a Coke can in his hand. As Clarky tumbled out the door, Easty calmly handed his drink to the guy sitting next to him, grabbed the wheel as he slid across to where Clarky had just been and, cool as a cucumber, took over the steering, plonked his feet on the pedals, gunned the gas pedal, and kept driving! He did a u-turn and returned to where we expected to see Clarky's motionless body lying bloodied on the asphalt. The mood turned sober as we drove back to see how badly injured he was. We underestimated the bugger's resilience. Clarky was calmly standing at the side of the road, albeit slightly bent out of shape, with his trousers ripped all down one leg, his shirt in tatters across one shoulder and with blood beginning to seep from his grazed skin. We were torn between taking him straight to the base hospital and laughing. Beaming with a maniacal grin, he pulled a stunned Easty out from behind the wheel and took his place: "Piss off, Easty. I was driving!" he snapped. And off we drove.

The nurse-hunt proved unsuccessful. You can't win them all.

One weekend there was a rash of mess pranks. I returned to my quarters after dinner to find that everything in my room that wasn't nailed down had been turned upside down. My bed frame and mattress, the side drawer, all the books in the bookshelf, my clothes folded in the wardrobe and the drawers — everything had been inverted. I was pretty peeved and it took hours to get my room back in order, but must admit that I admired the perpetrator's attention to detail. Even the posters and photos on my walls had been carefully removed and reaffixed upside down.

One cadet returned to his room to find it as bare as Mother Hubbard's cupboard. The entire contents of his room had been relocated to the grassy area between the accommodation blocks. It was a classic — his room was there, perfectly replicated, alfresco.

The pranksters hadn't stopped with that. Senior University Officer Cadet Marcus Graney was running around the mess in a panic. His prize possession, his Jaffa-orange Fiat Bambina, was missing from its spot in the mess car park. After a quick search we located it — enterprising cadets had manhandled it indoors and it sat on the carpet in the corner of the anteroom, next to the tea and coffee trolley!

At PTS there was an endless stream of exams, check flights and challenges. During the weekends there was an endless stream of parties: 2 Mess Bavarian night, toga nights, solo nights, and mixed dining-ins. A mixed dining-in was a formal dinner in the Officers' Mess, and we could bring a date. It was a sure-fire way to impress the Christchurch lasses. I have memories from one party where a near-naked officer cadet ran through the bar with a burning length of toilet paper hanging from the back of his undies, his pace picking up as the flames got closer to his nether regions. It was like something out of a Guy Ritchie movie.

2 Mess Toga night 1989 was another standout. Officer Cadet Dane Fea, a legendary boozer and all-round wild man, patrolled the halls of the accommodation block in full costume (sandal-footed, sheet-clad and sporting a plastic laurel wreath atop his head), encouraging the troops with his loud battle cry of "Toga! Toga! Toga!" Fea bore a uncanny resemblance to John Belushi in *Animal House*, staggering around the mess with a half empty crate of beer in one hand and an open bottle in the other. His dedication to the cause was impressive: the toga party was scheduled for Saturday night, yet he was doing his promo work for the piss-up the Friday night before — a full 24 hours early!

One dreary Christchurch morning, flying was cancelled due to low cloud and poor visibility and I found myself with some free time. I wandered back to 2 Mess and poured myself a coffee in the anteroom. Just then CTS hard man Flt Sgt Crail halted a marching formation of neophyte officer cadets right in front of 2 Mess. He'd just finished yelling at one — "Harris! You are a CRIPPLE!" — when he glanced into the anteroom and saw me watching the scene. His back to the cadets, Crail looked over at me and winked, his mouth creasing into a sly smile. I couldn't believe it! His smile disappeared as he turned to face the cadets, raising his voice to bollock them again. It turns out Crail's tough guy routine was all just a big show, to help him mould the fresh cadets into Air Force officers. I never noticed it during my time at CTS, but a fellow trainee pointed out to me years later that Flt Sgt Crail had worn a Mickey Mouse watch. This incongruous accessory probably summed him up. He didn't take himself anywhere near as seriously as we thought, and neither was he the hard man he seemed at the time.

At PTS the months rolled by. Our course grew smaller. Grant Thompson, the big-hearted ever-smiling Southland man was next on the chopping block. We also lost Tim Robinson, who I admired for his burning ambition to become New Zealand's first astronaut. It was sad to see the boys go, but those of us who remained didn't dwell on the losses — we had to focus on the job at hand and believe that we were destined for success.

By this time we had come to realise that only one of us stood out: Jason 'Easty' Easthope. Easty was the youngest member of 189, a quiet unassuming 18-year-old from the town of Rotorua. Easty oozed outrageously high levels of confidence and at times seemed reckless in his quest for adrenaline, but unlike some others he definitely had the natural ability to back it up. He had a magic touch — whether it was flying an aeroplane, riding a motorbike, driving a car or playing sport. I once saw him throw three bullseyes in a row during a pub darts match at Christchurch's Bush Inn Tavern. His course mates wrote of him[5]: *Easty aspires to fly Skyhawks, or otherwise Skyhawks, and as a final choice, Skyhawks. He's the one with the aggressive nature in the flying sense, but easy going in personality. When executing a loop in the Airtrainer it's normal to pull about 3.5 G. Easty was surprised to hear this, as he had been pulling 6 G each time! When he was asked why he uses 6 G, his reported answer was, "because that's all the Airtrainer is allowed to pull!" — typical.* Jason Easthope was easily the most gifted student of 189, and he got his wish, going on to fly A-4K Skyhawks with the RNZAF, SEPECAT Jaguars with the RAF and the FA-18 Hornet with the RAAF (although he was busted a few times along the way for unauthorised low flying!). He was featured in ABC Australia's television series *Real Top Guns*, filmed in 2007.

On 24 October 1989, in the midst of our attempts at working hard, playing hard and staying hard, we were reminded that being an Air Force pilot wasn't just a game and that there were grave consequences when things went wrong. That day the New Zealand Air Force's premier display team (a six-ship formation of RNZAF A-4K Skyhawks, known as Kiwi Red) was returning to Base Ohakea after a training sortie. As each jet peeled off the formation to come in to land, performing a manoeuvre known as a roll-under break, two aircraft collided. The pilot of Red 4, 24-year-old Flying Officer Graham Carter, had no chance to eject from his stricken jet as it descended in a fireball to the ground and was killed. The mid-air collision shattered Kiwi Red's accident-free record and reminded us all of the seriousness of the job at hand.

As I look back on my RNZAF logbook, my most vivid flying memory from this period is of a solo low-level cross-country navigation flight. Low-level nav sorties ended with a simulated bombing run on a target. We had to adjust our speed and track en route to arrive over the designated target as close as possible to a predetermined time. It was amazing how the application of the appropriate techniques (that we had learned in ground school and practised in the aircraft with our instructors) could lead to split second accuracy over that target, even some hours after we took off. My flight saw me at 250 feet above the ground, traversing the wide fertile expanse of Canterbury's alluvial plains before turning into the mountains and flying up tight riverbeds between the towering snow-capped peaks of New Zealand's Southern Alps. As the flight progressed the greenery of the plains gave way to the muted brown tones of the high country grasslands and the jade green of boulder-strewn alpine tributaries. All under a dome of flawless turquoise sky. It was breathtaking. At one point I dithered while looking down at the map strapped to my lap, and when I looked up I had to pull back on the stick to avoid a collision with a towering power pylon. Some two hours later I rolled in on the designated simulated bomb drop site, a small rural town in the Otago hills, only 20 seconds late on target.

One holiday weekend a few of us travelled south to the city of Dunedin, the home of Otago University, for some R&R. This of course involved drinking copious amounts of alcohol and chasing the girls of the university halls of residence. We crashed varsity parties, pissed it up at local pubs and did our best to sweet talk the southern ladies. I was mildly successful, and returned happily to Base Wigram at the end of the weekend nursing a slight hangover and fond memories of a most accommodating Physiotherapy Department student. What I didn't know until later was that I was also nursing a developing case of glandular fever; a.k.a. mononucleosis; a.k.a. 'the kissing disease'. It presented itself a couple of weeks later as a raging fever, swollen glands in my throat, a loss of appetite, an overwhelming sense of lethargy and all-over body aches and pains. It was not a good look for a pilot trainee halfway through his wings course. I spent ten delirious days in the Base Wigram military hospital and after my release had a meeting with the CO of the Flying Training Wing, a bigwig officer who had a palatial office in the same building as Wigram's control tower. He explained that the tight wings course schedule made it impossible for me to make up for the flying I had missed, so I had been removed from #189 pilots course with immediate effect. On hearing this I had a horrible feeling that my military career was over before it began, until he explained that I was to be given two months paid leave and sent to my hometown to fully recover. Once healthy again, I was to return to RNZAF Base Wigram and join the next wings course: #589 pilots course. This was quite a setback, but as it was out of my hands I accepted it and soldiered on. I was not alone. Clark Malone came down with the same illness and was to be re-coursed onto #589 with me. Had we chased and caught the same girl in Dunedin? I can only hope that if we did, I got to her first!

After about six weeks of recuperation, during which time I stayed with my family back in the town of Gisborne, I saw a local doctor and was given a medical clearance to resume flying training. When I got back to Base Wigram and 2 Mess the junior course had not quite reached the stage in their syllabus where I could rejoin them without me repeating a lot of flights that I had already done, so no doubt to keep flying training costs on budget, I was not allowed to join them straightaway. Instead I was sent to work as a general dogsbody at the RNZAF Museum hangar (Base Wigram's Hangar #6) for three weeks. My duties included helping museum staff make fibreglass mannequins for a new static display, welding a set of storage shelves out of steel beams and putting the cowls on the wreck of a WWII-era F4U Corsair fighter that sat in the back of the hangar. It was an extremely frustrating time for me. From my workstation in the hangar I could see out onto the airfield, and watched as my #189 course mates taxied out twice a day, launching their training sorties. They were nearing the end of the second phase of the training, and would soon be moving to RNZAF Base Ohakea in the North Island of New Zealand to begin the last phase: on the BAC 167 Strikemaster Mk.88 jet trainer (essentially an armed version of the British Jet Provost). I was happy for them, but it was hard to see my 189 friends progressing while I was stuck, wings clipped, in the hangar. I felt totally detached from the flying. My break, a total of three months in the end, had not been good for me.

Finally the day came when I joined #589 pilots course and got back into the training. The attrition rate within 589 had been just as high as 189 before it — 589 had started with 12 trainees. When Clarky and I joined them there were only six left: Wally Thompson, Glen 'Dog' Davis, Colin 'Heff' Heffer, Jon 'Prettyboy' Harris, Carl 'Mexican Bandit' Brightwell and Rob 'Sack' Curtis. The best nickname of the bunch belonged to Sack. Cadet Rob Curtis had picked up this doozy from Flt Sgt Crail when 589 were undergoing basic officer training at CTS. One day Rob had come out from the barracks a little late for the morning run, with his running gear un-ironed and his hair awry. Flt Sgt Crail had looked him up and down, and yelled at him: "Curtis, you are a SQUARE peg in a ROUND hole. In fact . . . you are a SACK OF SHIT!" It stuck.

One of the first things on the schedule when I joined 589 pilots course was a trip to an aviation medicine (AVMED) course in Auckland.

In February 1990 we were flown in the back of a C-130 Hercules to Wellington, then transferred to an RNZAF Boeing 727 for the sector up to Base Whenuapai. Over the next three days we attended lectures on the medical aspects of aviation at the RNZAF Aviation Medicine Unit near Base Hobsonville. Topics included the composition of the atmosphere; how this changes as altitude increases; the effects of acceleration in flight on the human body; the limitations of visual and vestibular orientation; how to operate aircraft oxygen systems; and human risk factors in aviation (stress, fatigue, decision making, situational awareness, and crew dynamics). The seriousness of the threat of subtle incapacitation due to a lack of oxygen at altitude was reinforced graphically when we spent an afternoon in an altitude chamber. In our first drill we were seated in rows inside the chamber and instructed to don oxygen masks. The chamber environment was then raised to 25,000 feet, meaning that it contained 60% less oxygen than air at sea level. We then removed our masks and performed a simple pre-briefed task: we took a pad and pen from a central table and wrote down the number 250. We were to subtract seven from this number, writing the answer below, then continue subtracting seven while signing our name next to every fifth calculation. Sound easy? Not at 25,000 feet, where the normal useful time of consciousness (the time before you pass out due to a lack of oxygen supply to the brain) is only 3 to 5 minutes. Initially, I thought I was doing well, but soon felt light-headed and vague and it became very hard to stay awake, let alone concentrate on the maths and the signatures. As I struggled with the task, I looked around. A few of the 589 boys already had their masks back on, meaning they'd reached the point where they had started losing consciousness. One was reaching out with one hand, snapping his fingers closed as if he were catching imaginary butterflies. Another slumped into unconsciousness right next to me and mask-clad attendants rushed to him, placing his mask back over his face and reviving him. As my peripheral vision closed in and the world started to fade, they did the same to me, and I 'woke up' as the oxygen mask was placed back over my face. Once outside the chamber and fully revived, we huddled together and compared our scraps of paper. Mine was an illegible scribble, looking like a toddler had tried to copy my signature, and the mathematics was way off. It was quite a learning experience. The next chamber run was a simulation of a rapid depressurisation, with the chamber raised from 5000 feet to 35,000 feet in 10 seconds. This relative atmospheric pressure reduction caused a sudden and dramatic drop in temperature and the moisture in the chamber condensed, enveloping us in instant cloud. Air escaped explosively from every place in our bodies where air resides — the lungs, the sinuses, the teeth (from poorly constructed dental work; this can be very painful) — and some other unmentionable places. Not for nothing is the hypobaric altitude chamber also called the *fart chamber*. A rapid depressurisation is not pleasant. I was glad to experience it first hand, but even more glad to get out of there afterwards and get away from some of my internally fragrant course mates. The AVMED course complete, we spent a Sunday afternoon at Auckland's iconic Mon Desir Hotel, a hotspot of bacchanalian shenanigans near the Takapuna waterfront (the perfect place for eight trainee Air Force pilots on R&R).

The next week saw us back at Base Wigram, where we continued with the second phase flying syllabus. I soon started feeling settled at PTS again. But it wasn't to last.

Not long after getting back into the flying and the ground lectures I attended a 2 Mess formal dining-in. My 589 friend Marc Collins (who had recently been chopped from his navigator's course and was awaiting a discharge from the RNZAF) and I decided it was the perfect time to attempt to break the No. 2 Officer's Mess record for the number of sherries consumed before dinner. The Air Force doctors had advised me not to drink alcohol for six months after recovering from glandular fever — something to do with the disease affecting normal liver function — but I was 19 years old and bulletproof so of course ignored their advice. The record for pre-dinner sherries was 15, set by an infamous party-animal-of-an-officer-cadet named Ian Smith several years prior. Marc and I knocked back the sherries with great gusto as we milled about in the anteroom, hobnobbing with the other cadets and officers. By the time we were called in for dinner, we'd polished off at least ten sherries each. I must have been hit soon thereafter by a wave of alcohol, as the amber liquid was unleashed on my system and I don't have clear memories of my actions for the rest of the night. My hazy, pissy recollections include me devouring my main course before the top table officers began theirs (a no-no), setting fire to a menu to see how quickly it disappeared in a fire ball (also a no-no) and yelling a boozy long distance greeting to Flt Lt Peter Mount (one of the PTS instructors) on the other side of the dining hall: "MOUNT!" To top it all off I went to the bathroom mid-meal (another no-no), slurring, "I'm just going for a piss, sir" as I walked past the big brass at the top table — and made a fuss when I got back from the toilet and discovered that the boys had hidden my chair: "Where's my bloody chair, you tossers!" Chair-hiding was standard practice if anyone was silly enough to leave the room during the evening.

I put on quite a performance.

I woke up the next morning with the mother of all hangovers to Clarky banging on my door: "Matty, I don't believe what you did!"

"What do you mean?" I asked, my head a throbbing, pounding mess.

Clarky had let himself into my room. "You vomited down the sleeve of your jacket!"

"Are you sure?" I asked. I was shocked, knowing that that sort of extreme behaviour would not go down well on a wings course. I knew I'd had a skin full but thought I would have remembered doing that! He looked in my wardrobe and there on a hangar was my jacket — clean as a whistle. There had been no down-the-sleeve vomiting as part of my performance the previous night. The rumour was out there however and it was much better gossip-fodder than the truth. The story of the officer cadet who threw up down the sleeve of his jacket spread around the base like wildfire.

On Monday morning I was summoned to CTS to explain myself to the CO. Even though we, as Senior Pilots Course, had nothing to do with CTS any more, we were all still technically under CO CTS's control as he was ultimately responsible for discipline at No. 2 Officers Mess. Unfortunately our friend Squadron Leader Jim McMillan was no longer the CO: McMillan had moved on to bigger and better things and had been replaced by the sullen Sqn Ldr Dally. Dally was a dick. To borrow a great descriptive phrase from English actor David Niven: Dally was "thin, sandy and weedy. He exuded an aura of defeat".[6]

I was ushered into Dally's office, thinking that I was in quite a bit of trouble. I sure was. Dally's punishment was extreme. I was not given the opportunity to explain myself, nor did Dally attempt to establish which of the rumours about the evening's events were based on fact and which were fanciful fabrications. As he was new to the job, he leapt at this opportunity to make his mark and impose his will on the officer cadets by making an example of someone. Unfortunately I was that someone. Like a megalomaniac headmaster with a big stick he laid into me, ordering me to:

1. Write letters of apology for my behaviour to the 2 Mess kitchen staff, to him and to the senior officer present at the dining-in.
2. Move out of No. 2 Officers Mess immediately and move to the NCO barracks on the other side of the base. I was to take all my meals in the NCO's Mess, as well as (worst of all) take part in the daily morning run and room inspection with the brand-new CTS cadets.

This was at a time when the workload during the later stages of the wings course was high enough as it was without additional pressure being applied. I was suddenly faced with the normal demands of the flying training as well as having to take part in the daily niff-naff basic officer training stuff like runs and inspections; niff-naff I had lived through one year previously. It was not a good look.

As the second phase of the training came to a close, the focus was on night flying, low-level navigation, an introduction to formation flying and, most importantly, the final instrument flying check on the CT4-B Airtrainer. My instrument check flight was on 8 March 1990, and the check pilot was the CO of PTS, the gruff Squadron Leader McWilliam. He was a man of few words, little humour and the only PTS face that we never saw at the 2 Mess Bar. He did not mix with us socially and was always stern and aloof. I found him *very* intimidating. He strapped in next to me in the Airtrainer cockpit, saying nothing. I was determined to give him what I thought he wanted (a mistake you can make when you have spare capacity and are looking to impress your superiors). Prior to take-off, it was standard procedure for me to give a lengthy brief about the flight we were about to undertake, including the instrument aids I would be tracking on, the altitude I would be climbing to, and the emergency procedures in case of various system failures during the flight. Knowing McWilliam's fighter pilot background, I decided to be gung-ho about it all and not bother with the brief: "Sir, I'm supposed to brief you on this flight before we launch," I said. "But you and I have both done this flight many times before, so I'm not going to brief it. Let's just go and do it!"

And off I went. I thought he'd be really impressed with my confident *lets-kick-some-arse* no-nonsense approach. I was wrong. After a frosty post-flight walk from the flight line back to the PTS classrooms he let me have it in the debrief, barking that he had never EVER heard of a student forgoing the briefing, especially on a check flight, and that this was simply NOT acceptable. He seemed most upset, but my instrument flying was too good for him to fail me, so he reluctantly gave me a minimum pass mark.

The stage was set however for my stress levels to go through the roof.

At the time I had an additional responsibility as Entertainments Officer for 589's upcoming away-from-base camp (the final navigation phase of the Airtrainer stage of the wings course: Exercise Wise Owl), which was to be held in my hometown of Gisborne. My role involved sending official RNZAF in-house minutes (memos) to various departments organising logistics for the social activities I had planned. Sqn Ldr McWilliam was one of those on the minute distribution list. Every time I sent him one he'd send it back, with red pen all over the 'errors' I'd made in the format of my letter. There were no errors in the content or the spelling or anything of any substance that needed to be corrected: just minor and inconsequential errors in the format as prescribed by one of the RNZAF manuals (there was a manual for absolutely everything — talk about bureaucratic overkill). His red-penned scribblings were things like: *TWO spaces after this line*; *INDENTATION required here*, etc. It was really petty stuff, but acutely stressful for a young officer cadet and this, added to his obvious displeasure with my instrument check flight, convinced me that he had decided that I was not RNZAF officer/pilot material.

I was right. I reviewed my PTS records in 2011 after they were released to me by the New Zealand Defence Force Archives. After my IF19 check with McWilliam he wrote in a confidential in-house report: "Following IF19 OCDT McLaughlin's Officer qualities have been reviewed by me, and assessed as unsatisfactory . . . two weeks ago his behaviour at a No.2 Officers Mess dining-in was disrespectful and disgusting . . . on IF19 he showed a total lack of respect for me, and the course he is undergoing . . . twice OCDT McLaughlin has submitted the same minute to me and neither have been anything like examples of service writing . . . I do not have to tolerate this arrogant, disrespectful or flippant behaviour and will not. If I have to speak to him again about Officer qualities he will be recommended for suspension." This was in marked contrast to what was written about my Officer qualities when I successfully completed Initial Officer Training (qualifying me to receive a Queen's Commission) the previous year. The commanding officer of CTS had written: "(OCDT McLaughlin) should prove to be an asset to the RNZAF." In a fortnightly summary of my progress just one month before my IF19 check flight with McWilliam, Sqn Ldr Duxfield wrote: "OCDT McLaughlin is a polite, well presented young man whose cheerful manner enables him to relate well with his course and the staff." McWilliam clearly disliked me, and his words were to have their desired effect soon enough.

The minutes bouncing back to me from McWilliam's office, the daily grind of early morning runs and room inspections, and being banished to the NCO's barracks and NCO's Mess combined to really ratchet up the pressure on me. Apply enough pressure and you can break anyone, like the CIA applying enhanced psychological interrogation techniques (waterboarding) to coax (beat) confessions out of suspected terrorists in Guantanamo: *Yes, yes, alright, I admit it — I'm an Al Qaeda operative working out of RNZAF Base Wigram!* My flying started to suffer. My circuit work had never been the strongest aspect of my flying and the quality of my circuits deteriorated to the point where I failed a flight.

It was a night flight and I'd had the misfortune to be paired with the extremely and inappropriately domineering instructor Flt Lt Gordon Snow. It's hard to shine when you are being bullied and yelled at, shoulder-to-shoulder, in the cramped cockpit of a CT4-B Airtrainer.

The decline in the quality and consistency of my circuit flying happened very quickly and I remember feeling quite detached from it all. It was like a stranger had taken over my body, a stranger who was not as good a pilot as I had been before the dark clouds of stress engulfed me. Up until then I had never been a star, but I was a good average student, and had passed every stage of the training without any dramas. I was told years later by instructor Flt Lt Neil Kenny that the general feeling among the PTS staff was that I shouldn't have had any major problems getting through the course and graduating with my wings.

When a pilot trainee failed a flight the normal protocol was to be put on *doubtful* status (not a very encouraging label at a time when the last thing you needed was yet more stress), and given one or two remedial flights before a *chop ride*, which was pass or fail. A pass removed the doubtful status and the student continued on with the wings course syllabus. A fail meant just that — your wings course was over (and you'd have a black triangle drawn over your head on your course photo). It's fair to say that in most cases being placed on doubtful status was the kiss of death.

Ideally, a wings course trainee was supposed to have one instructor per phase, i.e. two different instructors for the two Airtrainer phases at Base Wigram. I had by now (mostly as a result of being re-coursed with glandular fever) flown with eight different instructors during eight months of flying training. There was little or no continuity for me: as soon as I got used to one instructor's style I found myself flying with a new one. Instructor number eight, Flt Lt Coulter, did the two remedial flights before my chop flight and taught me absolutely nothing. I had only flown with him three times previously and had hardly established a rapport with him. Perhaps my fate was already sealed, but having so many different instructors certainly didn't help.

I flew my chop ride with Sqn Ldr John Duxfield the following day. He was a lovely chap. Bubbly, friendly, empathetic and actually human, unlike some of the instructors I'd flown with. But it was too late for me, too hard for me to pull myself up from the downward spiral of stress and a loss of confidence in my own flying ability. I wasn't even in the cockpit with him: it was like I was looking down on this guy sitting in my seat — he looked like me, he sounded like me — but he was the one flying the plane, and he was making all sorts of silly mistakes I'd never made before.

The flight went badly and I knew I was going to be chopped. Based on my performance that day Duxfield had no other option. Downwind in the circuit for what was supposed to be my last landing, he asked me how I thought it had gone. "Not so good," was my reply. "OK," he said, "let's fly back to the training area and do some aerobatics and you can re-join with a buzz-and-break for your final landing." He was such a gentleman: he was offering me a final few minutes of fun in the CT4-B Airtrainer before my RNZAF career came to its premature end. Maybe he felt bad for me. Only 12 days had elapsed since my check flight with the gruff and unimpressed Sqn Ldr McWilliam. Things had unravelled so very quickly.

I remember my last rejoin to land: a steep dive at 200 knots to zero feet on the non-traffic side of the runway, then an almighty pull and roll through 180 degrees to 500 feet on the downwind and a close-in base turn. I sideslipped to my final landing on the end of Wigram's bitumen strip and taxied to the hangar in silence. After a short post-flight debrief (it doesn't take long for someone to say, "Sorry, McLaughlin, you're chopped.") I made my way back to the accommodation block of 2 Mess. I avoided speaking with any of my course mates, but they would have known just by looking at me how my flight had gone. The chop didn't feel real until I called my family in Gisborne that night and told them it was all over. It was a really tough phone call to make. There were tears. I felt that I had failed them more than I had failed myself: they had been so proud of me when I joined the RNZAF.

The next day I went to PTS to collect my things and to clean out my locker. I took my last look at the graffiti scribbled in large letters on the locker formerly used by Sue Smith, one of the first females to graduate as a pilot in the RNZAF, some two courses ahead of me: JET NOISE MAKES ME HORNY. Evidently this was very much the case as it came out after she graduated that she'd been banging so many guys around RNZAF Wigram that instead of asking, "Have you been for a ride in the Sioux lately?" (the Bell 47 Sioux was the training helicopter based at Wigram), a common question on the base was, "Have you been for a ride in the *Sue* lately?" She had been a busy girl.

As I walked one last time through the Pilot Training Squadron Operations room I saw my nametags on the magnetic board they used for assigning our daily flights to particular aircraft tail numbers. I'd seen people chopped before and knew the instructors would peel MCLAUGHLIN off and discard it, reapplying the name of a new trainee and recycling the magnet. I remember thinking, *You're not going to throw my name in the bin, you arseholes.* I couldn't stop them drawing a black triangle over my head in the #189 course photo in the hallway, but I sure as hell wasn't going to leave my nametags there to be discarded and recycled like so many chopped pilots before me. In an act of defiance I took my magnetic nametags with me. I still have them.

As a part of the post-chop admin procedures, I had an interview with the CO of the Flying Training Wing. I knew that it was at this interview that chopped pilots would sometimes be offered a navigator's course to keep them in the RNZAF. This was not offered to me, and I wouldn't have accepted it if it had been. I was determined to become an airline pilot with or without the Air Force. I accepted a discharge from the RNZAF, and my 15-month military career came to an end. It was 30 March 1990.

Plan A had ended in tears. How had this happened? How did the wheels fall of my finely engineered plan to become an airline captain via a few years as an air force pilot? The standard of my flying and my progress through the syllabus had been adequate until I was ordered to move out of the Officer's Mess, and I began feeling that Dally and McWilliam and the system were out to get me. A major contributing factor to my demise was alcohol, more precisely institutionalised alcohol abuse. Sqn Ldr Dally hadn't had me removed from 2 Mess because he didn't like me. He didn't even know me. He had done so because of the story circulating around base about a drunken officer cadet vomiting down the sleeve of his jacket during a dining-in. For him, a line had been crossed, and someone had to be held accountable. I take full responsibility for my behaviour that night in the mess, but I had been led astray. I was mature enough to handle the demands of the flying syllabus and seemingly possessed the skills necessary to be successful as a military pilot, but I was not mature enough to find the right balance between *working hard*

and *playing hard.* In my youthful exuberance and naiveté I had signed up enthusiastically to the Armed Forces culture of binge drinking: a strong and embedded culture fuelled and encouraged by the instructors and senior officers. Getting drunk and ending up lying comatose on the floor of the 2 Mess bar during solo night celebrations was considered par for the course. That sort of behaviour was expected and encouraged. If a cadet didn't partake of the Friday night boozing sessions in the 2 Mess Bar, questions were asked about his ability to fit in and be one of the boys. Alcohol was a major part of Armed Forces life. But there were limits. Getting intoxicated at a formal dining-in was frowned upon and could put one's career in jeopardy. If you pushed it too far — had too much fun, got too intoxicated at what was deemed an inappropriate setting or time — then the same system that aggressively promoted the binge-drinking culture in the first place would turn around and chop you off at the knees. Talk about double standards.

There had been a bit of bad luck for me also — contracting glandular fever and being forced to take a three-month break in the middle of intense and focused training like a wings course didn't do me any favours. I feel now that perhaps fate decreed that I would need an ample store of luck later in my career — good juju that would keep me alive in my Papua New Guinea years — so my luck deserted me as I neared the end of my time in the RNZAF.

The New Zealand Air Force's motto is *Per Ardua ad Astra*: through adversity to the stars. I'd experienced the bit about adversity all right, but was no closer to the stars.

After my departure from 2 Mess and the RNZAF the vomit-down-the-sleeve story snowballed, becoming much more elaborate and amusing. My flying skills may not have been legendary, but the story of me being kicked out of the mess was. Seven years after I was discharged from the military I was in Sydney on a layover (by then I was a first officer flying Boeing 747-400s for Cathay Pacific Airways) and met up with an RNZAF C-130 Hercules crew at a pub downtown. They were in Australia (staying at RAAF Base Richmond) to participate in a tri-nations precision flying exercise, Operation Bullseye, and one of the Hercules pilots was my 189/589 mate Clarky Malone. As Clarky introduced me to his crewmates over a few cold beers, a junior pilot's eyes widened as he heard my name. He shook my hand like I was a rock star: "Wow, Matt McLaughlin! You're the guy who got kicked out of the Mess for puking down the sleeve of your jacket!" There's no stopping a good story . . .

●

Chapter 3

"Joe Civvy is trying to kill you"

Nulla tenaci invia est via
(For the tenacious, no road is impassable)
SPYKER AUTOMOBILES' MOTTO[7]

I was discharged from the RNZAF and caught a flight back to my hometown. Although I was upset, it was hardly the end of the world. I firmly believed that my ultimate goal of being an airline pilot was still more than achievable, so I made a conscious decision not to dwell on the extreme shortness of my RNZAF career and just get on with it.

The very next day I drove down to the flying school at my local airport (Air Gisborne) and asked them what I needed to do to obtain my Commercial Pilots Licence (CPL). Chirpy and knowledgeable Air Gisborne instructor Nigel McDonald explained that I would need a total of 200 hours of flying experience, and would also need to pass several examinations. On my release from the RNZAF I had a total of 122 hours in my logbook, comprising 92 hours of dual time (time spent in the aircraft with an instructor), 26 hours of solo flight experience and four hours of flying with fellow students. I was hoping that my RNZAF flying experience and the exams I had passed at Base Wigram would be taken into account by the New Zealand Civil Aviation Authority (NZCAA) and permit me a fast-track to a CPL, but after I contacted them it became clear

I'd receive little credit for my Air Force experience (I was only issued with a private pilot's licence). The area where I was most lacking the required experience was solo time. The commercial licence called for 100 hours total solo time, so I was over 70 hours short. It was brutally obvious that becoming a professionally qualified pilot in the civilian world was going to take considerable time, effort and money. At that time flying a small four-seater single-engine aircraft cost $99 per hour solo and $117 per hour with an instructor. Nigel estimated it was going to cost me well over $10,000 to obtain a basic CPL. I only had about $2000 in the bank, so this was money I didn't have.

I formulated a new plan: get part-time work, ideally afternoon and night shift work, so I could study and fly during the day and earn money at night to pay for it all. Once I earned my CPL I hoped to pick up a bit of part-time flying work for Air Gisborne while studying for the next steps in a civilian pilot's career path — learning to fly twin-engine aircraft, gaining an instrument rating (enabling a pilot to fly in cloud and reduced visibility conditions as well as on clear days, and conduct instrument approaches to land in bad weather), and becoming qualified as a flying instructor. With these credentials, a young civilian pilot could reasonably expect to follow a well-trodden path to a slot with the national airline (Air New Zealand). Pilots following the civilian route into Air New Zealand would generally work as a flying instructor and charter pilot with a small company for a few years, then interview for a position with the flag carrier as a first officer on the Fokker F27 Friendship. From that foot in the door would come a first officer (co-pilot) position on the Boeing 737, and one day a command on a wide-body international airliner, like the Boeing 747-400 (perhaps 15–20 years later). This is the path most half-decent non-military pilots took. Even though I was new to the game of flying, and despite my recent setback, I knew I was at least half-decent, so I fully expected this to be the route I would follow.

My first flight at Air Gisborne was with instructor Nigel McDonald. It was a reality shock. Gone were the armies of ground staff preparing the aircraft for me: uniformed mechanics, engineers and re-fuellers. Gone was the *Top Gun* style nomex flying suit, the parachute pack, the Mae West and the bug-eye visor-equipped flying helmet. Gone was the top-of-the-line avionics and instrumentation of the CT4-B's aerobatic cockpit. In their place was a tired old Cessna 172 that I would have to pay to fly. And me in jeans and a T-shirt and a borrowed aviation headset. Nigel talked me through the start-up of the entirely underwhelming 160 horsepower Lycoming engine and we taxied out and departed for my first flight out to the training area south of Gisborne's Midway Beach. First impressions were not good. After the Airtrainer the Cessna seemed dangerously underpowered, and I didn't like flying with a control yoke (like a F1 car's steering wheel) — having become used to the Airtrainer's control stick. The cheap moulded plastic of the Cessna's control panel housed dinky plastic instruments that looked like they'd fallen out of a cereal box: *Free Artificial Horizon in this week's box of Cornflakes! Next week get your very own Directional Gyro Compass!* As the Cessna reluctantly climbed and I levelled her off at 3000 feet, I wondered if I could ever get excited about civilian flying. There would be no more aerobatics, no more inverted flight, and no more aileron rolls all the way from the training area back into the circuit like I used to do when rejoining for a landing at Wigram. I was a real greenhorn and had much to learn about the aviation industry. Soon enough I realised that civilian flying training was simply different, not inferior, to the military way. I even came to enjoy flying the Cessna 172.

My progress in the aviation industry was to be much slower in civvy (civilian) street than it had been in the RNZAF. Having mapped out my new career plan of attack, I focused all my energies on getting some work. For the next 18 months, while I obtained all the necessary qualifications and flying experience as a part-time student at Air Gisborne, I ran myself ragged shuttling between different shift jobs. I did whatever I had to do to earn money to put towards my flying training. These jobs were far removed from the privileged life I'd experienced as an officer cadet and a pilot trainee at RNZAF Base Wigram. I worked part-time as a barman at a nightclub, as a weekend sales assistant in a local brewery, and at Pizza Hut as a kitchen hand and a driver. Pizza Hut's employee uniform — a gingham shirt and baby-poo-brown trousers — wasn't quite as sharp as my RNZAF 2 Mess kit. I worked as a part-time lawn-mower, as a dag-crusher in a wool store (yes, collecting the shit-encrusted fleece from the back end of a sheep and separating the wool from the shit), and as maître-d' at an up-market restaurant on the banks of Gisborne's Taruheru River. I also worked an afternoon shift at the public bar of the Sandown Hotel. This job was a real eye-opener. It was a rough and ready old tavern, with chipped Formica tables, sticky carpets, a wall of dog-eared beer-brand posters and a line-up of cancer-vending machines. The sharp vinegar smell of stale beer met customers at the door and escorted them to their tatty barstool. My patrons were a mishmash of ages and ethnicities but occupied the same rung on the socio-economic ladder: the bottom. The regulars would sit there all day, drinking themselves into a stupor, staggering out only when their pockets were empty. Benefit day was the worst (every Wednesday, the day on which Government unemployment, sickness and childcare allowances were paid). On Benefit day the public bar was an orgy of alcoholism, domestic violence and parental negligence: customers soiling themselves at the bar; husbands and wives slapping each other around; young children left unattended in the car in the Sandown's car park for hours as their parents stopped by for 'just a quick drink'. Although most of the regulars were happy drunks, I found the place quite sad and depressing. Watch Lee Tamahori's visceral 1994 film *Once Were Warriors* to see what I'm talking about.

Soon after I started as a student at Air Gisborne, as a peculiar kind of torture, my #589 wings course colleagues arrived in a large gaggle of Airtrainers and based themselves at Gisborne Airport for the final navigation phase of their CT4-B Airtrainer flying: exercise Wise Owl. This tented camp was their last phase of flying in propeller aircraft — after Wise Owl they would transfer to RNZAF Base Ohakea and begin the last phase of wings course training on the BAC 167 Strikemaster jet trainer. Nigel McDonald didn't realise that these were my old course mates and sat me down to warn me about their imminent arrival. He told me that the military CT4-B pilots would be oblivious of any civilian aircraft's position as they joined the circuit for a landing, and that their gung-ho manoeuvres could lead to a mid-air collision. "Be careful, Matt," he said. "The Air Force guys will try to kill you." I'd heard this line before, months earlier at a briefing in the RNZAF when we were about to fly into the civilian airport of Dunedin in the far south of the country. Then, I'd been told that the 'inexperienced' civilian pilots would be the ones oblivious of their surroundings. The duty Ops Officer had warned us to keep a good lookout for them, especially in the circuit area, saying: "Guys, be careful out there — Joe Civvy is trying to kill you." This state of mutual disrespect and ignorance was strong between civilian and military pilots. I continue to see this *us vs them* mentality to this day. Having had the opportunity to see both sides of this coin, I know that the mutual animosity is entirely unnecessary. There is no 'best' way to learn to fly, and no group of pilots is naturally better or more talented than any other group. Nigel McDonald was an excellent instructor, as was John Slaney, the no. 2 man at Air Gisborne. They were as good as the best RNZAF instructors I'd flown with, and head and shoulders above some of the more mediocre trainers I'd had, or my #189 and #589 course mates had trained under. Now I had experienced civilian flight training standards I had something to compare the RNZAF instructors with. Most of the air force instructors were top-notch, really excellent, but there are bad apples in every barrel. In the RNZAF in the 1980s and early 1990s those at the rotten end of the scale were most likely to be ex-fighter pilots. This isn't to say they weren't good pilots — they wouldn't have made it through the rigours of their operational training if they weren't switched-on units — they just weren't always good *teachers*. There was no middle ground with the fighter jocks — they were either really nice laid-back professionals, or cocky immature hotheads (a young 75 Squadron flyer was interviewed in the 1990s and asked what it felt like to be an operational strike pilot on the RNZAF's A-4K Skyhawks. He was infamously quoted as saying it was such a buzz he felt like "masturbating in the main street"). Rudi Drummond, a pilot trainee on course number 888, was paired with one of these characters. After one of Rudi's check flights with the CO didn't go as well as expected, his instructor — who felt Rudi's test result reflected badly on his capabilities as a PTS trainer — lashed out during their next flight together, castigating him with a firm head butt, helmet to helmet in the cockpit of the CT4! Any flying instructor acting like this in today's world would be suspended from teaching duties immediately. My #189 course mate Jason 'Easty' Easthope flew with another bad apple who would push the sharp end of the CT4-Bs canopy-breaker into his leg whenever Easty made a mistake while flying. Nice one. Good instructional technique. This clown went on to become a training captain on the de Havilland Canada Dash 8 with the ill-fated airline Ansett New Zealand, and had to be told by management to tone it down after reports filtered back of his haranguing and intimidation of trainees under his care. He's now a senior captain with an international airline in the Middle East, no doubt still full of his own self-importance and oblivious to his inappropriate and counterproductive approach.

Thankfully, the generation of pilots since those days, both military and civilian, have had the importance of teamwork, crew resource management, and communication in aviation drummed into them from day one, so there are fewer and fewer of these counterproductive personalities within the system.

The RNZAF detachment of Airtrainers and their support crews descended on Gisborne, pitching their ops, accommodation and mess tents on the northern perimeter of the airport. The #589 boys knew that their Wise Owl camp was in my hometown, and they tracked me down and invited me to the Friday night booze-up in the main mess tent. This was a party I had planned when I was camp Entertainments Officer a few weeks earlier at RNZAF Base Wigram. I was being invited to a party that I had been responsible for organising. The irony was not lost on me, but I happily joined them and we had a great night. I even managed to rustle up a few local girls to come out to the party and brighten things up.

A few days later the RNZAF personnel packed up and headed south for Wigram, leaving nothing but a mountain of empty beer cans and a patchwork of yellow tent-sized voids in the grass behind Air Gisborne. I continued with my work, study and flying. I had a number of CPL exams to sit: principles of flight and performance; general aircraft technical knowledge; aviation law and publications; flight navigation general; and meteorology. I had the most difficulty with the meteorology exam, and had to sit it a soul-destroying three times before I made the 70% pass mark. It seemed such an imprecise science, and some of the exam questions seemed utterly pointless: *Question Five: An occluded front sits off the western coast of the South Island of New Zealand. Describe the wind and weather conditions you would expect to see during the next 48 hours at Westport and Christchurch airports. Will the wind back and increase, or veer and decrease?*

Did I really need to know this? Was I studying to be a pilot or a weatherman? If I was flying to Westport or Christchurch, why wouldn't I just obtain pre-flight 24-hour forecasts and real-time aerodrome weather reports from the aviation weather service, like all pilots do before they go flying?

Three months after starting my civilian flying training I had my last contact with my former colleagues from #189 pilots course, who were nearing graduation and close to earning their wings. I phoned the Base Commander of RNZAF Ohakea and obtained permission to visit them in a rented Air Gisborne Grumman Cheetah (a four-seater low wing single-engine aircraft). Ohakea was the base for the advanced phase of the wings course as well as lead-in and operational training for New Zealand's fighter squadrons, flying the BAC Strikemaster and the McDonnell Douglas A-4K Skyhawk. Civilian aircraft were not normally seen at Base Ohakea. I did my best to arrive in style, contacting Ohakea tower when about 10 miles out and requesting a buzz-and-break join to land. The buzz-and-break join (also called a run-and-break) is normally only flown by high performance military aircraft and originates from WWII, when it was found to be the most expeditious way to get an aircraft (or formation of aircraft) on the ground. It involves a dive at max speed to the runway threshold followed by an aggressive 180 degree reversal turn at high G to wash off speed, configure the aircraft and land as soon as possible. By doing this inbound aircraft spend minimum time at slow approach speeds, a time when they are most vulnerable to being bounced by enemy aircraft. Skyhawks and Strikemasters put on a great show in a buzz-and-break, thundering over the end of the runway at dot feet at over 400 knots (740 km/hr) and executing steep low-level turns before touching down on the tarmac. My buzz-and-break that day was probably the slowest and crappiest Base Ohakea had ever seen. I wound up the Cheetah to its maximum speed in a dive — a pathetic 140 knots — and rolled and pulled as hard as I dared without overstressing the non-aerobatic aircraft through a continuous low-level reversal turn for the landing. James Turner, a junior fighter pilot who had been two courses ahead of me at Base Wigram, was on the airfield that day, and when I ran into him in 2009 he actually remembered my 1990 buzz-and-break. It was so slow and crappy and hilarious it made an impression. A bit like watching a 1961 Morris Minor drive the F1 circuit at Monte Carlo. I spent one night at Ohakea and boozed it up with my former course mates. We got pretty rowdy in the Officer's Mess bar that night, but were altar boys in comparison to behaviour exhibited there in the past. One night in the late 1970s Ohakea's fighter pilots left their mark on the joint. They'd been politely requesting a replacement for the bar's ancient out-of-tune upright piano for some years but the Base Commander repeatedly turned them down, probably due to budget constraints. One Friday night, full of piss and wind and tired of off-key ivory-tinkling, they loaded the elderly piano onto a trailer and drove it off-base to a nearby one-way bridge. The boys (after downing a million beers) had decided the best way to get a new one was to see the old one fall to its death in the river bed. As they manhandled the piano up and over the bridge's guard rails civilian traffic backed up behind them, with drivers down the line becoming irritated as they wondered about the reason for the hold-up. One intoxicated officer put on his hat and marched up and down the line of cars, informing drivers that there had been a suicide and the delay would continue until the police recovered the body! The Ohakea boys were a wild bunch (and they got their new piano).

Air Force pilots the world over have a strange relationship with pianos, a relationship often involving pyromania. In the UK in the 1980s a visiting RAF squadron was drinking in an Officers Mess. After a few too many, someone tried to play the piano only to discover it did not have any internal workings. The chaps decided it was non-operational and proceeded to set it on fire. Unknown to them, the innards were away in London being professionally refurbished! This turned out to be a very expensive mistake for the visiting squadron.

After the Ohakea piano euthanasia-via-bridge incident, the RNZAF issued an order banning the burning/destruction of base pianos.

Ohakea's pilots got around the official ban by pooling a few dollars and purchasing a ratty old upright piano from a second-hand store. The next Friday night it was wheeled outside the Officer's Mess, attached to a car's tow bar and ceremonially set alight. Booze-fuelled onlookers cheered the driver on as he drove in ever-faster loops around the Mess roundabout, whooping and hollering like a rabid bunch of Lord-of-the-Flies schoolboys as the piano's fiery carcass traced a flaming circle before them. Suddenly the towrope broke, catapulting the wheeled fireball up against the Mess steps. The driver, a determined bugger, then tried pushing the blazing instrument around the roundabout using the front of the car, but wound up driving right through it, engulfing his vehicle in flames! Fortunately the Base Fire Brigade was on hand to extinguish the blaze, and no one was hurt. I'm told the resulting melted patch of tar on the roundabout was visible for years afterwards.

The owners of Air Gisborne, John and Margaret Reid, were very good to me. As soon as I obtained my CPL, and as I continued working towards my twin-engine endorsement and instrument rating, they employed me as a part-time charter pilot. John was one of New Zealand's best known fish spotters, meaning he was employed by fishing companies to find large schools of fish from the air and direct their fleets of purse-seine fishing boats to the catch. John was in such demand as a fish spotter he'd often run out of hours well before the end of the year (commercial pilots were only allowed to fly a total of 1000 hours in a 12-month period) and needed one of the Air Gisborne pilots to fly with him and act as aircraft commander. I was sometimes given the job and spent many hours with John at low level over the water. We'd fly in large lazy search patterns well off the coast, eyes peeled for the distinctive discoloured patches on the ocean's surface that indicate a large school. John could tell by looking at the colours in the school and its characteristics not only how large it was, but also the composition. I was always amazed at his accuracy. One day we were fish spotting between Gisborne and Napier when we found a school. John was in constant radio contact with the boat captain and told him what he thought of it: "Yeah, mate, it's about 35 tonnes, 20 miles off the coast on a southerly bearing from Mahia Peninsular and bearing 080 from Cape Kidnappers — 20 tonnes of trevally, 15 tonnes of mackerel."

This particular day we'd already been looking for schools for two hours, so we flew to the closest airport and refuelled while the fishing boat set course for the coordinates we'd passed them. John timed our arrival back over the school to when the purse-seiner was approaching the fish and ready to drop its nets. It was fascinating to watch. A small skiff popped off the back of the mother ship, towing a large net behind it and made its way in a wide orbit around the school. There were two escape routes for the fish: to sound (dive) and swim under the net, or to stay on the surface and make a run for the gap in the net before the skiff looped around to the mother ship and cut them off. There were two ways to stop them. As the net encircled the fish, a rope that passed through rings at its base was pulled, closing it from below like a purse (giving the fishing boat its name). This stopped them sounding. To stop them running for the gap in the still-closing net involved us. We watched the movement of the school from above and let the driver of the skiff know which way the school was turning. If they ran for the gap he could tighten his circle accordingly and try to cut them off. On this day, the school made a turn towards the narrow gap just as the skiff was about to complete his circle. I'd seen this before, and following John's advice ducked down to 50 feet over the water and ran the aircraft's shadow between the fish and the gap. This could be quite challenging, at low level in a Cessna 172, especially in windy conditions. But it worked, and my airborne corralling turned the fish back into the net. With the purse-strings of the net drawn closed and the fish safely inside, we returned to Napier Airport for an hour or so, returning after the boat had its catch on board and was ready to head off in search of the next school. These were big boats, with below-decks cold storage for 100 tonnes of fish. As usual, John's estimate of the size and composition of the school was spot on. We heard from the boat's skipper: "Thanks for that, John. Nice school, it was 34 tonnes. Two thirds trevally, one third mackerel." It was just as John had predicted when he first spotted the school. This sort of accuracy was the reason for his immense success as a fish spotter, and the money from this work must have been a major part of Air Gisborne's revenue.

Other part-time work I picked up from Air Gisborne included forestry surveys for the NZ Forestry Corporation, aerial photography flights for the Lands Department, drug-spotting patrols for the local Police (looking for hidden cannabis plantations in the State forests between Gisborne and East Cape), ad hoc charters, and on-call medivacs for Gisborne Hospital.

In May 1991 I began working towards qualifying as a flying instructor. With John Slaney as my mentor, I spent weeks and weeks learning the classroom briefings and in-the-air flying lesson syllabus as prescribed by the NZCAA. It was a lot of work. A high standard of flying was expected and Slaney pushed me to achieve it. As we got airborne during each of the practice 'lessons' (I was the pretend instructor, he acted as my student) he would balance a box of matches on its end in the centre of the aircraft dashboard. It was my mission to fly so perfectly in balance for the whole flight that the matchbox stayed there, even during steep turns and engine failure drills. John's hard-man push for precision flying ensured that I passed the flight test with the CAA examiner with no problems on my first attempt.

I was now able to pick up more part-time flying at Air Gisborne working with their new crop of students. This was great, but I hadn't been busting a gut with all the restaurant and bar shift work, the building of flying hours, and the studying for my exams and flight tests just to get *part-time* flying work. As soon as I became fully qualified I started searching for a full-time flying position. The age-old aviation paradox was about to reveal itself to me: you need flying experience before anyone will give you a flying job, but you need a flying job in order to build up some experience. To make matters worse, at about this time Air New Zealand shut down its Fokker F-27 Friendship fleet and laid off a lot of pilots. Highly qualified F-27 drivers[ii] flooded into

---

[ii] An industry term for 'pilots'.

the domestic aviation market, snapping up all the jobs that I had been suitable for. With them circling in the pond, and me a low-time CPL, I couldn't get any job interviews. New Zealand's flying scene was dead to me. I needed a new plan if I was going to get a job as a commercial pilot.

Actors Mel Gibson and Robert Downey Jr presented me with a solution.

Some time in 1991 I settled down in front of the TV with a bowl of popcorn to watch *Air America*. The movie follows the exploits of a group of pilots flying covert operations in and out of Laos for an arm of the CIA (Air America) during the Vietnam war. Before I saw this film I had always believed that the only way to get an adrenaline fix in aviation was to be a military pilot. I was wrong. Eighteen minutes into the film, Robert Downey Jr's character is on a familiarisation flight with Mel Gibson in a Pilatus Porter. As the blue-and-white Porter flies between jungle-clad mountain peaks, Gibson tells Downey to prepare for a landing.

"Landing where?" asks a shocked Downey.

Gibson points out a scratch of bare dirt amongst the vegetation ahead. It's a poor excuse for an airstrip: less than 100m long and impossibly steep.

"Oh come on!" exclaims Downey. "That's not a strip, that's a mountain!"

Incredibly, the Porter lands there, touching down firmly right where the dirt strip meets the jungle and disappearing in a cloud of dust as Gibson's character selects full reverse pitch. It's a spectacular scene and a gutsy bit of flying. Wow! A seed was planted in my mind as I watched. Perhaps I could become a volunteer pilot with one of the overseas aid agencies and fly into some gnarly challenging terrain and service airstrips like those in the movie. Where could I fly? South America? The South Pacific? I started looking into the 'hows' and 'wheres' of volunteer work. I contacted an organisation called the Catholic Overseas Volunteer Service (COVS) through my local church and told them I'd be willing to work as a volunteer pilot wherever I was needed. Having done so I went back to the grind of the shiftwork and the part-time flying, not sure that I'd ever hear back from them.

Be careful what you wish for.

A few months later COVS contacted me and said I'd been accepted. They had a volunteer position for me: I'd been assigned to fly a Britten-Norman BN-2 Islander for a church mission station in a place called Kerema, in the Gulf Province of Papua New Guinea (PNG). I was very excited, but there were two things I needed to look into. Not only did I not know what kind of aeroplane a BN-2 was, I didn't know anything about PNG (I wasn't even sure where it was). "P N *what*?" Lucky I didn't know the history of the place or how dangerous it was to fly there in those days or I would never have gone.

Younger readers will be shocked to learn that there was no internet in those days (that's right — no Google, no Wikipedia . . . Shock! Horror!), so I went to Gisborne's public library and found information on PNG and a map showing where Kerema was located in an encyclopaedia and an atlas. A weighty volume of *Jane's All the World's Aircraft* provided some technical information on the BN–2. I made photocopies of it all and studied it at home. The Islander looked like a big machine: A ten-seat twin-engine utility commuter aircraft first manufactured in 1967, suited to operations from short and rough airstrips. At 6600 lbs (2994 kg) MCTOW (Maximum Certificated Take-off Weight), and with two 300 horsepower Lycoming IO-540 engines, it was more than twice the size of anything I'd flown so far in my career. I also took out and read *Into the Crocodile Nest* by Benedict Allen, a first-hand account of an Englishman immersing himself in a local tribe in PNG's Sepik River region in the 1980s. PNG sounded like a wild and woolly place — remote villages; traditional subsistence living; inaccessible terrain.

Getting a one-year volunteer position in PNG turned out to be the easy part. Getting a PNG visa was not. There were months and months of delays as my visa was sorted out by COVS and the PNG consulate in Wellington, New Zealand's capital city. Finally it arrived and I had a departure date — Easter 1992. On the Sunday before I left my local parish priest dedicated the mass to my overseas service, and there was a morning tea for me in the church hall afterwards. I'm not an overly religious person, despite having been raised as a Catholic and attending Catholic schools, but it was a really nice farewell. Parishioners milled about, sharing cups of tea, scones and biscuits:

well-wishers all. Some asked me what my flying would involve and what it would be like living in PNG as a mission volunteer. I chatted away, explaining that it would be a wonderful adventure and that I was sure the flying wouldn't be too different from the flying I had done so far in the military and at Air Gisborne. I'm not sure if my confident waffling was meant to reassure them or me. I really had no clue what I was talking about.

●

Chapter 4

The Missionary Position

*"Do not follow where the path may lead. Go instead where
there is no path and leave a trail."*

RALPH WALDO EMERSON[8]

**The landmass of Papua New Guinea sits above Australia's far
northern shores, its geographic outline giving the impression that
it is balancing there on Queensland's Cape York Peninsular like a
giant roosting bird, a massive fowl pointed westwards towards the
archipelago of Indonesia.**

This giant island, the world's second largest, is shared between two
nations: the western half is Papua, a province of Indonesia (known until
2002 as Irian Jaya), the eastern half is Papua New Guinea. The island has
a complicated history: a pawn of British, Dutch and German colonial
governments. Pre-WWI, the western half of the island was Dutch New
Guinea, with the eastern side split by a gentleman's treaty into northern
and southern sections — the top administered by Germany (German
New Guinea), the bottom by Australia (the Territory of Papua). In the
aftermath of The Great War the League of Nations stripped Germany
of its colonial powers and handed control of German New Guinea to
Australia, at which time it was renamed the Mandated Territory of New
Guinea. Australia continued to govern both eastern-half territories until
the Second World War, when a swift Japanese invasion claimed many of

the northern coastal ports and the large islands of New Ireland, New Britain, and Bougainville. The Australians, and later their Allied partners the US and New Zealand, staged a gallant resistance, primarily from their military installations in and around the capital city, Port Moresby, and ultimately defeated the Japanese invaders. Post-war the territories were combined — renamed 'Papua New Guinea' — and the nation was given self-rule in 1973.

I arrived in Port Moresby on Easter Sunday 1992 on a Solomon Islands Airways Boeing 737 via Auckland, Port Vila in Vanuatu, and Honiara in the Solomons. First impressions tend to stick, like my shirt did to my back that day as soon as I walked out of the aeroplane into PNG's burning tropical air. The heat! Two words best describe my arrival: culture shock. The landscape was dry and dusty and uninviting. Sunburnt hills crowded around the airport, dotted with thin stands of anorexic trees doing a poor impersonation of vegetation. The airport facilities were tired, dirty and run down. The terminal was packed solid with people milling around actively engaged in the pursuit of doing absolutely nothing. Waiting. Watching. The airport fence between the aircraft parking stands and the car park was jam-packed with people ogling the new arrivals — a technicolour explosion of bright floral dresses, caps, shirts, and dark faces peering through the chain link. I felt like the new animal in the zoo — hundreds of necks craned and twice as many eyes tracked me as I made my way through the arrivals hall to the spit-stained curb to find my church-arranged greeter.

A smiling Caucasian man in his early 60s approached me. "You must be Matt. Welcome to Papua New Guinea!" He had a shock of curly grey hair, intelligent eyes behind bifocal glasses, a Hawaiian-style tropical shirt, long trousers, and leather sandals. He introduced himself as Brother Damian Keane. I liked him at once. He guided me out to the car park (the necks and eyes still on me) to his waiting jeep, a small faded green Suzuki 4WD, and drove me to his mission transit house in the Port Moresby suburb of Gordons. En route, the suspension of the Suzuki squeaking and bouncing as we passed over innumerable potholes on the maintenance-starved Hubert Murray Highway, the cabin swirling with the dry dust that seemed to coat everything in this city, Br Damian filled me in on the plan that had been laid out for me. Details of my training and the 'hows' and 'wheres' of me being checked out and released to fly the mission plane solo in Kerema had been sketchy prior to my departure from New Zealand (I hadn't let this bother me, deciding to stick with the Antipodean mantra 'she'll be right!'). The only thing I knew was that the Catholic Church was to provide me with food and board during the posting, and I'd receive a missionary wage of 20 kina per week (US$80 per month; when I lived in PNG 1 kina = US$1). Straightaway the news was bad. Damian explained that the BN-2 Islander I was expecting to fly, Kerema's mission plane, had been sold (the Islander's running costs had become too high), and they were looking to purchase a smaller aircraft. The clergymen running the mission station, Bishop Paul Marx, and his administrative assistant Brother Michael Nolin, had neglected to pass this somewhat vital piece of information on to COVS in New Zealand prior to my departure. Before the aircraft's sale Kerema had been without a mission pilot. Now they had a pilot (me), but no plane. Damian continued: Brother Michael had arranged for me to be trained by a commercial aviation company here in Port Moresby, Air Manubada, using their aircraft, and once the Diocese of Kerema purchased a new plane, and presuming I was released as competent to fly solo in PNG, I would then move to Kerema to take up my missionary pilot position. As it turned out, this never happened, but it was certainly the plan.

Within minutes of arriving at Damian's house and dropping my bags in the guest room, I sat with him on his verandah, cradling an ice-cold local beer. The man's hospitality could not be faulted. We chatted as the sun disappeared on the western horizon, not as it did in mid-latitude New Zealand — a long laboured graceful descent — but tropical style, in a sudden surrender to the night, like someone had turned off the lights. At the clunk of darkness I was introduced to Port Moresby's unrelenting nocturnal soundtrack — barking dogs, the frantic drone of cicadas, and the thundery death knells of distant storm clouds. I asked Damian about his role in Port Moresby. He was a member of the Order of St John of God, a Catholic Brotherhood engaged in the provision of youth welfare services and rural health care. He'd spent years in a mountain village called Kamina in the Gulf Province, helping his Order run the local health centre, but now ran the St John of God transit house and acted as a Mr Fixit for the mission stations. Damian was a coordinator of transport and accommodation arrangements, a go-to man for visa renewals and Immigration Department hiccups — a general but vitally important dogsbody for PNG's Catholic clergy and missionary volunteers. He spent a total of 18 years in PNG and retired to his Order's rest home in Sydney. In his later years he became an active member of Mensa Australia, as well as working *gratis* for aid agency 'Palms'. He passed away in 2009.

The next day Damian gave me a tour of Port Moresby. Its appeal as a coastal trading port, going back to the first contact with Portuguese explorers in the 16th century, was clear: a wide and sheltered natural harbour, pristine tropical waters, a bountiful coastal strip resplendent with orchids, coconut palms, spiky pineapple bushes, and hedgerows of vibrant purple bougainvilleas. It was also a city haunted by the ghosts of World War II, with reminders of Moresby's military history at every turn: abandoned gun emplacements on Paga and Touguba Hills near the CBD; weathered sections of PSP (pierced steel planking — interlocking metal sheets used by US Army engineers as a ready-made surface for airstrips and roads) making an appearance as a component in many a suburban gate and fence; a war-era causeway across Fairfax Harbour to Tatana Island, site of a long-abandoned deep water anchorage; the rotting steel carcass of a wartime merchant ship, the *Macdhui*, lying on its side on the reef in Port Moresby's inner harbour, its watery grave courtesy of a Japanese bomb attack in June 1942[9] ; Wards Airstrip, a 1940s runway used by RAAF and US Army Air Force (USAAF) cargo planes, recycled as Wards Road, a major artery linking the Poreporena Freeway with Boroko.[10]

I had never before seen a city of such jarring contrasts. Moresby was a third-world sprawl of impoverished squatter settlements and traditional villages, with corrugated iron shacks clinging to dry hillsides and stilt houses clustered in sheltered coastal inlets. But here and there, and always on prime slivers of land, were glass and steel clutches of luxury apartments; swimming pools and member's clubs and 24-hour security patrolled compounds; mini fiefdoms encircled with high walls and razor wire and electrified fences, like glam fortresses parachuted in from the pages of *Condé Nast Traveller*. Here a Waikiki Beach condo shared a fence line with a Rio de Janeiro favela. It was incongruous, grating, unpleasant. How could these two worlds coexist when the haves lived such a privileged existence within spitting distance of the have-nots?

As we drove past the Boroko shopping centre, a clamour of *meris* (women), open-air markets, scruffy public buses, and dilapidated taxis, Damian gave me a rundown on the nation's social and political scene. He explained that PNG society was still based on a tribal structure, and this meant the concept of nationhood was one that was neither understood nor embraced. A PNG national first and foremost feels allegiance to his or her tribe, to his family, to his *wantoks* ('one-talks': literally, those who speak the same dialect, which in linguistically diverse PNG meant any one of over 800 different languages). The *wantok* system, where clansmen look out for each other, is at the same time PNG's greatest asset and its most toxic curse. It serves as a de facto social welfare system, with members of the same tribe responsible for housing and feeding each other and sharing in the community's assets. But when the *wantok* system is transferred to democratic politics and the free market it becomes nepotism and corruption.[11] Damian explained that, politically, the nation was a basket case. Loose political loyalties dominated by tribal groupings rather than party ideology or policies inevitably lead to dysfunctional democracy.[12] There was widespread unchecked use of 'electoral development funds' (slush funds) by parliamentarians to reward the kinship groups who supported their election bids[13], a high turnover of politicians and chronic political instability with an overabundance of no-confidence motions and a revolving door of prime ministers. Tongue-in-cheek, Damian said the endemic you-scratch-mine-I'll-scratch-yours corruption could see the country renamed Papua 'You Give Me'.

Tied closely with the *wantok* system was the concept of 'payback'. Any real or imagined wrongdoing by one tribal group against another was immediately and unreservedly avenged. Retribution was seen as the only way to maintain societal balance. Damian gave me some grim advice regarding payback: "If you accidentally run someone over, don't stop. Drive to the nearest police station quicktime and have yourself locked up. If you don't, within five minutes there will be hundreds of bystanders baying for your blood. You'll be dragged out of the car and beaten to death." He illustrated his warning with a chilling tale. One day two government employees — one a doctor, both of them PNG nationals — were driving down a road next to the aerodrome in the Highlands town of Goroka. The driver lost control in some loose gravel and skidded off to the side, striking and killing a six-year-old girl. The villagers in the area had been in contact with Europeans for almost 40 years, they were Christians, there was a mission station within 150 metres of the accident site, and many men in the village held jobs in Goroka. But this veneer of civilisation was paper-thin. At the death of the child witnesses to the unfortunate accident reverted in an instant to their tribal ways. They rushed, enraged, at the occupants of the car, who tried to escape by running up onto Goroka's airstrip. The crowd of avengers caught them and stoned them to death, smashing their skulls with jagged rocks, hacking and kicking at their bodies in a brutal frenzied attack.[14] Damian's cheery conversation held one more titbit of advice:

"Oh, and never walk around alone in the suburbs of the city, especially after dark: you will be held up at knife or gun point, and bad things will happen to you."

Later that day Damian dropped me off at the airport so I could meet the owner and chief pilot of one-man-band Air Manubada, Mack Lee. His aviation charter company was based in a back room of the South Pacific Aero Club, where the International Terminal stands today. I walked through the aero club's car park to find him standing at the back of a light goods van, unloading bags of flour, rice and cartons of sugar. He was not at all what I was expecting. Thirty-something-year-old Mack Lee was of Chinese stock, born and bred in PNG. He was tall and tubby, and wore a white, short-sleeved pilot's shirt, too-short shorts and light sneakers. His dark hair was combed into a collegiate side part and he squinted through Elvis Costello nerd glasses. Mack did *not* look like a pilot. He turned to me, held out his hand, and threw out a warm "gidday!" in a shrill North Queensland Aussie drawl, large dimples cleaving his jolly face. I'd just met the greatest stereotype-buster ever, and (I didn't know it at the time) one of PNG's best known and respected pilots. One fellow aviator said of Mack: "He had a generosity of spirit that was huge and unquenchable . . . (he) was not only the best pilot I ever shared the skies with, but also one of the nicest people I was fortunate enough to meet."[15] I was in good hands.

The process of being trained as a bush pilot was to be a slow one. Within a couple of days of meeting Mack he'd taken me up in his Cessna 206 Stationair, the *Goilala Kekeni* (a sturdy six-seat 300 horsepower single-engine high-wing utility aircraft, wonderfully suited to PNG's flying environment) in the Port Moresby circuit area, and we'd done a bit of upper air work so I could get a feel for the machine, but then he'd departed for Australia on a two-week holiday. I was left alone in Port Moresby, staring at the wall of the transit house. Br Damian suggested I hang out at the aero club and meet a few of the commercial pilots. He thought I could soak up a bit of knowledge via osmosis, sitting and chatting with them at the club bar after work. They were wise words, and that's exactly what I did.

In the early '90s Port Moresby's airport, Jacksons International, was a busy hub. The main players were Air Niugini and Talair, with their multiple movements of jet and turboprop aircraft on international and domestic flights. Milne Bay Airways (MBA), a smaller turboprop operator, nipped at Talair's heels, and the airport tarmac buzzed with the light aircraft of the smaller charter and mission operators: Missionary Aviation Fellowship (MAF), Divine Word Airways, Simbu Aviation, Mapmakers, the Summer Institute of Linguistics (SIL), North Coast Aviation, New Tribes Mission, Wantok Aviation, Nationair, Christian Revival Crusade and Trans Niugini Airways (TNA). TNA was the largest of the charter operators based at Jacksons, with a handful of pilots and four aeroplanes. They were based out of a shipping container-cum-office at the back of the South Pacific Aero Club, next to Mr Yorke Mendoza's maintenance hangar. TNA was a Franco-Australasian affair, with owner-operator Frenchman Gerard Phillip, Australian ex-MAF missionary pilot Brian Cox, and New Zealanders John Levers, Johnathan Thomson, Dave Sarginson and Tony Froude. The company had a fairly high staff turnover and its ranks would later include Gerard Conron, Ian McCabe, Gerry Krynen and Cameron Gibbs. One Friday afternoon I introduced myself to Dave 'Sarge' Sarginson and Tony Froude, who sat cradling a sundowner in the aero club's garden bar. I was immediately impressed by these guys. They were experienced bush pilots, having already mastered the challenge that lay ahead of me, but there was no arrogance or bravado here. When I asked how they felt when they first flew into the PNG mountains they happily gave me their honest recollections. Tony said it was completely different to flying in New Zealand. So dangerous. So unforgiving. Always one to call a spade a bloody shovel, he said his first trip into the mountains had left him "fucking terrified". Sarge, the more experienced of the pair with a background of high country flying in New Zealand's Southern Alps, was more wordy. His first flight had been in a BN-2 Islander with TNA's Johnathan 'The Long Arm' Thomson, an all-ports tiki tour of the mountain airstrips north of Port Moresby (Thomson's nickname stemmed from his former life as a policeman — 'the long arm of the law'). Sarge said his brain "shut down" when he saw the sorts of airstrips TNA were operating into — there were no normal visual cues to judge approaches and landings into these high altitude short, steep, hairy landing strips, and he was initially at a loss as to how they should be 'attacked'. He also remarked on the rigours of the administrative side of the operation — the cargo unloading, the collection of airfares, the loading of the return freight and passengers — "for the two hours we spent flying that day The Long Arm spent three hours on the ground arguing with the locals!" Sarge had picked up an unfortunate nickname on his first PNG flight. Cheeky Thomson, who spoke the local tongue of the mountain communities, introduced Sarge to the village folk at every airstrip as *man bilong kuapim sipsip*, telling Sarge this meant 'man who works with sheep' (this seemed fair enough, as Sarge came from a sheep-farming background). The locals seemed to find this description highly entertaining — there was much laughter and slapping of backs and mirth at every port. It was only weeks later, when Sarge himself got a handle on the local language, that he discovered *man bilong kuapim sipsip* actually meant 'man who sexually violates sheep'!

Chatting with Sarge and Tony, seeing them bright-eyed and animated as they described their daily routine of launching into the challenging mountain airstrips north of Port Moresby, telling me the whole operation was fraught with risk, I itched to experience it for myself. It appeared PNG flying was going to open a Pandora's box of adrenaline and excitement and fear and danger — the very things I'd been seeking. Their stories had been illuminating, but nothing was to prepare me for the shock and awe of the real thing.

More than I remember my first solo in an RNZAF CT4-B Airtrainer, more than I remember my first flight as the captain of a wide-body passenger jet, I remember the first time I experienced an approach and landing at a Papua New Guinea bush strip. It was Fane (pronounced *far-nay*), a village airstrip in the Goilalas (*gwee-la-las*), a section of the Owen Stanley Range to the north of Port Moresby. I was on my first training trip with Mack Lee, soon after he arrived back from his holiday, and I sat in the front left seat of his Cessna 206, P2-CBL. We'd departed Moresby on a gin-clear morning and Mack had guided the aircraft from the right-hand seat, pointing the machine north-east towards a large inlet of mangroves along the coast, paralleling this soggy landmark (Galley Reach) for 25 minutes before turning up a river valley and plunging into the Owen Stanley Range. A few minutes later, level at 5500 feet AMSL (above mean sea level), amidst a jumble of alpine peaks, sheer ravines and thickly wooded slopes, Mack pointed beneath us to our destination. I looked down, but there was nothing there. Nothing that my brain registered as an airstrip.

"It's right there!" exclaimed Mack. "We're downwind for landing now . . . see the village and the smoke and the landing strip on the side of that hill?" I saw it, and my stomach tightened. *We can't land there! It's a scratch of dirt on the side of a mountain!* I was about to experience the Pilatus Porter scene from *Air America* . . . for real! Issues of the airstrip's slope and extreme shortness aside, Fane was located in a place where passenger aeroplanes simply should not be operating. The airstrip was in a cul-de-sac of tight valleys, a small C-shaped basin surrounded by 8000-foot-high peaks. A spider web of ridgelines fanned upwards from the valley floor, reaching up to the sky, looming over the cramped

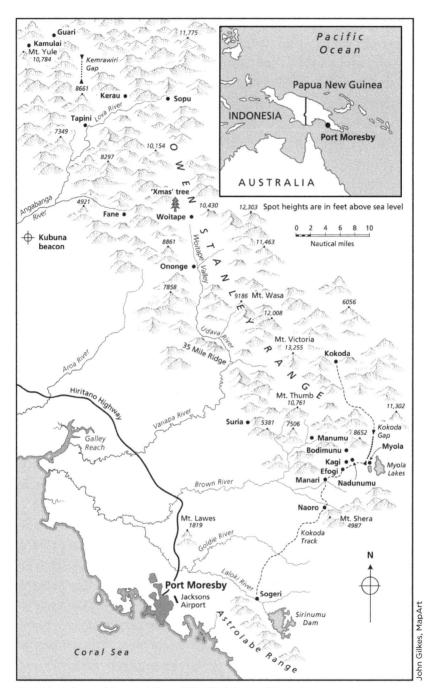

Port Moresby and the airstrips of the Goilalas and Koiaris.

basin like the forward pack of a titanic rugby team. The skidmark that was Fane's landing ground stood bare at 4400 feet above sea level on the upward slope of one of these ridges, a grassy line carved out of the hillside, bordered by white cone markers, angling up to a small cluster of huts and shacks. As Mack turned onto a final approach to land on this skidmark it bobbed in the windscreen like the postage stamp-sized landing deck of an aircraft carrier on the high seas. I still could not believe he was serious about landing here. *He's joking, right? We're air transport pilots, not bloody topdressing pilots!* There was a total absence of the normal visual cues for an approach and landing — the Cessna flew suspended over a void, with a gut-wrenching 1000-foot drop to the unforgiving river gorge below. *This is not normal.* With concentrated and focused precision Mack held the Cessna's speed at a firm 65 knots, modifying the power setting to maintain a constant approach angle to the end of the 12% sloping airstrip, holding the threshold steady in the same point on the aircraft's windscreen. Every cell in my being screamed, 'We are going to crash!' but Mack's calm demeanour indicated that to him at least, this experience was completely normal. As the end of the airstrip passed under us Mack didn't so much land, as *arrive*. It was rough and raw and agricultural. Landing on a steeply sloping airstrip required a totally unique flare technique (the flare is the last part of the landing, where the pilot pulls back on the controls to transition from the nose-down approach attitude to the nose-high landing attitude. In a normal landing this attitude is held and the aircraft allowed to settle onto the runway). Mack left his flare *very* late, and it seemed we would impact the end of the airstrip in the approach attitude. At the last millisecond he simultaneously cut the power and raised the Cessna's nose, timing his move perfectly so the nose got to its highest point precisely as the main wheels touched down firmly in the grass and dirt at the airstrip's threshold. The stall warning horn cried out at the same moment. *Holy shit, this guy is good. He's crazy . . . but he's good!* His technique enabled him to transition the Cessna from airborne to earthbound in one fluid movement and, although a risky and abrupt manoeuvre, it gave him great control, allowing him to throw the aircraft on the deck precisely where he wanted it. (I was soon to learn this was the key to ops into short airstrips — putting the machine on the ground right at the airstrip threshold. Mack was to hammer this into me as my training progressed — a PNG bush pilot had to touch down abeam the first cone marker. Land any later, any further into the strip, and you might not have sufficient runway remaining to stop.)

The aircraft rode roughly up the undulating surface, the undercarriage bouncing and crunching beneath us, Mack adding power to hold the momentum and get us up to the parking bay at the top of the steep slope. What an incredible display of control and precision flying. I was really impressed, and humbled, and realised my confidence in my own flying background might be a little overblown. I was 21 years old and had 467 hours in my logbook. I held a New Zealand CPL, a twin-engine aircraft endorsement, an instrument rating, and I was a qualified flying instructor. My all-important ab-initio hours had been at the hands of the RNZAF, New Zealand's preeminent pilot training establishment. Given this background, prior to that first PNG bush strip landing at Fane, I had felt like I was well on my way to being an accomplished pilot. Seeing Mack's approach and landing served as a wake-up call. It was very clear that Papua New Guinea was going to demand pure flying skill, heat-of-the-moment decision making and airmanship of the highest order. It didn't matter what I had done before, the hours padding my logbook, the aircraft types I'd flown: mastering PNG bush flying was going to be like learning to fly all over again, from scratch.

But there was much more to this bush flying game than just stick-and-rudder skills. I did as Mack did, exiting the aircraft at the top of the strip. We were instantly mobbed by villagers — small dark people with suspicious eyes and expressionless faces. I felt like I was on the set of *The Empire Strikes Back*, filming an Ewok supply drop! Their harmless appearance belied their fearsome reputation. The Australian colonial Government considered the tribes of the Goilalas 'uncontrollable' until the 1970s.[16] Until then their contact with Western culture was characterised by resistance to the law, armed clashes, murder, and contempt for sentences handed out by the courts. A European observer who lived amongst the Goilala natives for two years wrote in a 1977 research paper that they were 'obsessed with power and aggression' and exhibited 'hatred and violence and a fierce joy in humiliating and destroying their enemies'.[17]

Mack moved to the Cessna's starboard cargo door and supervised the unloading of the freight — some dry goods for a local tradestore. This was my first introduction to PNG's lingua franca, Pidgin English (*Tok Pisin*). A tiny fuzzy-haired man with bright eyes, wearing a faded blue T-shirt that commemorated, bizarrely, *Born in the USA Tour* — *Springsteen 84*, introduced himself. "*Nem bilong mi Deva*," he said softly. Mr Deva appeared to be the tradestore owner, and he and Mack huddled over Mack's receipt book as other villagers moved boxes into piles under the aircraft's wing. Mack gestured at one of the piles: "*Dispela cargo bilong yu, nau yupela mas baim dinau.*" It was easy enough to get the gist of what was being said in this charming lyrical language ('dinau' meant debt — Mack was saying 'this is your cargo, now you have to pay for it'), but seeing Mack communicate this way I realised that I too would have to master Pidgin if I was ever to be sent solo in the mountain airstrips.

Ouch! I felt a sharp prick on the back of my leg and turned to see a group of snotty-nosed village kids crowded behind me. One of the dusky munchkins had just plucked a hair out of the back of my thigh! His face wide with a toothy grin he pinballed through the tight crowd and disappeared down a track behind the airstrip. Before I could react Mack laughed and explained that most of these bush *pikininis* (children) had limited or no contact with white-skinned, fair-haired Europeans, and compared to them (and to Mack) I was very hairy! Curiosity had got the better of my 'attacker' and he'd pulled on my leg hair just to see what would happen.

Now another man stood with Mack under the wing, marshalling bystanders with an outstretched arm, directing them away from the aircraft with the flick of a clipboard like he was shooing flies. He had an air of authority and was clearly a 'big man' in the village. His name was Alex Gusi. He sported a neatly trimmed Tom Selleck *Magnum P.I.* moustache and a smart red shirt with a logo and lettering prominent over the left breast pocket: 'Trans Niugini Airways'. I watched him pass money to Mack before escorting four villagers and their baggage into the back of our Cessna. I realised he was a double agent, playing both sides, transferring TNA's passengers onto our flight; no doubt carrying out the same deception in the other direction too. This was priceless — a bit of cloak-and-dagger in the wilds of Papua New Guinea! A delightful line attributed Franklin D. Roosevelt immediately came to mind: "He may be a bastard, but he's *our* bastard."[18]

The loading and negotiating complete, I climbed back into the aircraft's cockpit with Mack; the doors closed, the passengers strapped in ("*Pasim seatbelt, no ken simok, dispela balus em bai kirap na go long Port Moresby!*"), and followed him through his checklist as he fired up the engine and set the flaps and trim wheel for departure. The cabin was ripe with an acrid smoky scent, one I was to become very familiar with — everything in these mountain communities, including the people, was infused with smoke from the open cooking fires of traditional bush-material homes. I looked back to check that all was secure in the cabin before take-off, right into the eyes of the Goilala woman seated behind my right shoulder. She was clearly very excited to be on board and grinned at me through rotten red-stained teeth. Her questionable oral hygiene was the by-product of chewing betel nut (known locally as *buai*), a mild stimulant and a nationwide addiction. Now Mack demonstrated the bush strip short-field take-off technique. He taxied to the lip of the airstrip, the point where the level parking bay met Fane's 12% down-slope, and brought the aircraft to a firm stop with the foot brakes. Here he ran the engine up to full power, checking the temperature and pressure gauges in the cockpit before departure. The Cessna strained against the brakes like a leashed fighting dog, threatening to burst free and career down the precipitous slope at any second. With the control column pulled all the way back into his chest, Mack let her go. The aircraft accelerated nose-high down the steep strip, a 1600 kilogram winged slingshot, the undercarriage echoing the same bangs and crunches as when we'd landed, the machine braking free from the surly bonds of Earth after a ridiculously short ground roll. As the Cessna transitioned to flight Mack eased forward on the control column, allowing a build-up of airspeed, and the ground fell away beneath us as we catapulted out into the void off the end of Fane's airstrip. What a rush!

Over the course of the next month Mack schooled me in the ways of

The agents at Fane airstrip, Alan Kafua (left) and Alex Gusi (right), double agent.

PNG bush flying. He was an excellent training pilot — calm, professional, a clear communicator — and broke the process down into digestible chunks. Navigation came first. There was no point in mastering bush take-off and landings if you couldn't safely navigate your way out to the mountain airstrips. The key to finding one's way out to the most common point of entry to the Goilalas — the Woitape Valley — was a critical landmark Mack called the 35 Mile Ridge. If you departed Jacksons Airport and held a course to the north-north-east, a series of 'markers' would guide you there. But you had to know what you were looking for. First waypoint: an isolated peak bordering Port Moresby's inland floodplains, 1800 foot-high Mt Lawes. Then, at 16nm from Jacksons, a bridge where the Hiritano Highway (the sole road west of the capital) crossed the Brown River.

Twelve miles later, abeam track off to the right, the disused clay airstrip at a village called Suria. At this point your north-north-easterly course intercepted the Vanapa River, whose constricted turbulent waters emerged from deep within a narrow north–south canyon directly ahead of you. These were the waters flowing out of the Woitape Valley, waters that would lead you to the Goilala airstrips. At 35 miles from Jacksons, the Vanapa made a hard westerly turn behind a distinctive 5000 foot-high ridgeline — the '35 Mile Ridge' — and became the Udava River. After a five mile-long dogleg the Udava straightened up onto a north–south course, cutting through a deep ravine crowded to the left by a spur of peaks averaging 7000 feet; to the right by the imposing 12,000-foot-high wall of the Owen Stanley Range. This was the Woitape Valley. The only concept more mind-blowing than the immense scale of this formidable terrain was the fact that airstrips had actually been built on the side of some of these mountains.

On a blue-sky day the navigation out to the 35 Mile Ridge and the Woitape Valley was fairly straightforward — the markers and landmarks were hard to miss. It was a very different story when the weather closed in, when low cloud hung like a veil over the mountain tops, when passing showers reduced visibility to almost nil, when a pilot could easily make an error and turn into the wrong valley. Early in my training Mack pointed out two potential deathtraps. The first was halfway through the 90 degree dogleg on the 35 Mile Ridge. Here a minor tributary of the Udava River peeled off to the north, looking very much like Woitape Valley. But rather than leading to any village airstrips, four miles later this valley terminated abruptly on the southern flank of 9186 foot-high Mt Wasa. Any pilot flying up this valley at low level was doomed. The same trap awaited the unwary halfway up the Woitape Valley proper. Here, just before the ridge-top airstrip at a place called Ononge, the river split. The left fork would guide you to Woitape village. The right fork would lead you into a dead-end gorge in the lee of the towering peaks of the Owen Stanley Range. Again, this was a one-way ticket to disaster, and Mack cautioned me to *never* fly into any mountain valley in poor visibility conditions unless I was 100% certain it was the correct one. (In April 1995 private pilot Paul Messervy was on his way from Port Moresby to Woitape. He died in one of these valleys when his twin-engine Piper Seminole impacted the side of Mt Wasa at 8000 ft AMSL. It appeared he'd followed the wrong river, become disoriented and descended through broken cloud over what he thought was lower terrain. He'd done exactly what Mack had warned me not to do.)[19]

Mack exposed me to all the pieces of the Goilala navigation jigsaw as we flew daily missions from Jacksons Airport into the mountains north of Moresby. These included the back door route to take when the Woitape Valley was clagged in and impenetrable (a coastal run via the navigation beacon at Kubuna to the headwaters of the Angabanga River); the east–west saddle linking Woitape and Fane, with its distinctive solitary pine tree (the 'Christmas tree' described in the prologue); the Kemrawiri Gap north of Tapini, a bad weather umbilical cord between the Goilalas and the two airstrips in the lee of Mt Yule (Guari and Kamulai); the high country traverse of the Kosipe Plateau (a fine weather shortcut between Woitape and Tapini). Each part of the puzzle was characterised by distinguishing landmarks, geographic signposts, visual navigation markers so vital in the days before GPS. They were things as simple as a unique bend in a river, a distinctive rock formation on a ridgeline, or an oddly shaped cluster of village huts. An intimate knowledge of these quirky signposts helped cement a mental road map of the area, allowing a pilot to navigate visually in and around the Goilala mountain strips and be 100% sure of their position at all times, even in diabolical weather.

Fane (4400 ft AMSL, 451 metres long, grass, sloped 12%) had been my first, but Air Manubada also routinely serviced the strips at Ononge, Woitape, Tapini, Kerau, Sopu, Guari and Kamulai. Mack decided to check me into all of them, figuring they mimicked the airstrips I'd be servicing in the mountains behind the Kerema mission station.

Ononge (*oh-nong-ghee*, 5300 feet AMSL, 500 metres long, red clay, 7% slope), was a white-knuckle aircraft carrier deck, a clay scuff mark standing stark and isolated atop an exposed ridgeline in the Woitape Valley. Afternoon tailwinds and turbulence turned Ononge's circuit area and final approach track into a roller-coaster ride, making it at times one of the most dangerous of the Goilala strips. It wasn't overly steep, but real estate was so tight up here the clay runway was not straight! It was bent to follow the line of the ridge into which it had been carved. After landing you had to put in a bootful of right rudder to scoot the aircraft across to starboard to stop from tumbling off the side.

Woitape (*woy-tah-pee*, 4900 ft AMSL, 915 metres long, grass, sloped 1.6 %) was nestled in a narrow clearing at the headwaters of the Udava River, eight miles upstream from Ononge, 17 miles past the 35 Mile Ridge. It seemed like the easiest strip in the Goilalas — flat by New Guinea standards and long enough — but it had a couple of traps. Firstly, there was no option for a go-around (an aborted landing) here once you descended below 5200 feet (300 feet above the ground) on short final approach, due to the rising bowl of terrain all around the strip. Secondly, this airstrip tended to lull departing pilots into a false sense of security. It was easy to forget that Woitape was almost 5000 feet up, where the air is considerably thinner than at sea level, meaning aircraft take-off performance was diminished (less air into the engine, less air for the propeller to bite into, less airflow over the wing to produce lift). At the other Goilala strips the large downhill gradient for take-off (with aircraft sling-shotting down the slope) helped mitigate this high altitude performance penalty. At the other strips there was also the advantage of a void (a drop-off into a deep valley) at the end into which the aircraft could fall and continue to accelerate. At Woitape there was no such advantage. Woitape nearly caught me out soon after I was sent solo, when I took three off-duty US Navy personnel for a spin around the Goilala ports. Mack had drilled into me not to take any more than five passengers out of Woitape, warning me the aircraft was performance limited and the departure from the strip involved a climb-away over significant obstacles — a flat section of the Udava riverbed. On this day I thought I was being very professional and responsible, and I lined up for take-off and set maximum power with only the three Navy lads and one villager on board, plus some small items of luggage. *Maximum five passengers? Check.* The aircraft seemed very slow to accelerate to flying speed and I became anxious when we were still not airborne when over three-quarters of the way down the strip. I was too inexperienced to realise what was happening — the aircraft was overloaded, as the combined weight of the trio of burly Navy guys was equivalent to at least six villagers! The Cessna staggered off the end of the strip with the stall warning horn blaring and I had to turn at low level to avoid hitting a stand of trees. I followed the rocky course of the Udava riverbed, barely avoiding the vegetation on either side, and ever so slowly gained speed and eased gingerly into a shallow climb, setting course for Port Moresby.

It was a rookie mistake — forgetting that Westerners were almost twice the size and weight of the Goilala tribes folk — and not one I was silly enough to repeat.

Tapini (*tah-pee-nee*, 3100 ft AMSL, 915m long, grass, 4.5% slope) didn't appear overly challenging, but was the strip with the most daunting history. Tapini airstrip is wedged onto a sliver of land at a right-angled bend deep in the canyon-walled Lova River valley. The approach to Tapini necessitates a descending base leg into the canyon, with the aircraft headed straight for a mountain before a last-minute 90 degree left turn that brings you onto a very short final approach segment. The challenge here was that, some mornings, patchy cloud in the river valley obscured any view of the strip as you began your descent into the gorge. Flying blind while letting down over a river surrounded by mountains was not generally a good idea. Thankfully, help was at hand. There was a goat track on the flanks of the mountain immediately off your right wing as you descended, cutting its way at about five degrees from the horizontal down towards the river. The natives and livestock that had formed this path had done the pilots of the Goilalas a great service: if you tracked it with your wing tip you'd be set up at precisely the correct altitude when you made your late turn onto final approach for Tapini. We called it the 'Tapini ILS' (ILS stands for instrument landing system, a ground-based navigation aid found at major airports worldwide that provides inbound aircraft with precision lateral and vertical guidance all the way to touchdown). Weather issues and the tight turn onto final approach aside, Tapini was an easy airstrip: a wide grassy aerodrome, almost one kilometre long, only 3100 feet above sea level, and somewhat of a banana (in the landing direction the first 200m of the strip was flat; the rest was angled uphill). Most days I ignored the level bit, choosing to touch down at the base of the uphill section. I never had any dramas at Tapini, but there were some notable crashes here over the years.

One of the most often quoted statistics in popular aviation culture is based on a conversation between Raymond Babbit, the autistic-savant character played by Dustin Hoffman, and his brother, Charlie, played by Tom Cruise, in the 1988 movie *Rain Man*. The pair are about to board a domestic flight between Cincinnati and Los Angeles when a neurotic and panicky Raymond makes it clear there's only one airline he would consider travelling with — Qantas — based on their accident-free record. "Qantas never crashed," he says. There's no doubt that Qantas is a great airline, with an enviable safety reputation, and the coverage they received in the movie must have been beyond their PR Department's wildest wet dream. But Raymond Babbit's assertion simply isn't true. Qantas *have* had their share of accidents, including some in which crew and passengers died, especially in the years before 1973 when they operated domestic flights within Papua New Guinea. Two of Qantas's crashes were at Tapini.

In October 1949 a Qantas Fox Moth was caught in a downdraft on approach and landed short of the Tapini airstrip, ripping the undercarriage off.[20] Nine years later one of Qantas's brand spanking new DHC-3 Otters, VH-EAY, departed Port Moresby for Tapini. Geoffrey Luck, the Australian Broadcasting Corporation's senior PNG correspondent, was on board:

> *This (aircraft) crashed at Tapini on August 13th 1958 when under the command of Qantas chief pilot in TPNG, Ken Montagu. It's a nervy approach — up a gorge, banking hard to land over a hillock on a short strip sloping uphill . . . EAY had a 'heavy' landing and bounced up the strip before veering off to the left; its plunge into a ditch was arrested by a newly installed fence post. The starboard undercarriage leg came up through the floor, tearing the co-pilot's seat out of its mountings and moving it two feet to port. This allowed the propeller to hit the ground and fold its blades . . . The leg also tore out the main electrical junction box, causing short circuits and a small fire . . . Both Ken and I were apparently in shock — I ordered him to go back and put out the fire as it was only a small one; he then called for a pot of paint to obliterate the word QANTAS on the fuselage and wing. Bad publicity apparently.[21]*

While the Qantas pilot blamed this accident on windshear, claiming that the Otter was caught in a downdraft as it approached the airstrip over the gorge, it was suggested by other sources that a combination of a possible aircraft overload (the cabin was full of sections of railway line for delivery to a Tapini sawmill) and pilot inexperience (Montagu had never before landed at Tapini) were more likely responsible.

Ten years later, the Royal Australian Air Force lost a DHC-4 Caribou military transport aircraft at Tapini. In October 1968 a crew of seven (a trainee captain, a check captain, a loadmaster, and four Army personnel) departed Port Moresby for a training flight to Tapini, Menyamya, Aseki, Wau and Lae. The purpose of the flight was to 'check out' the left seat captain into these mountain strips. They had no difficulty finding Tapini — the en-route and destination weather were both fine, and they arrived overhead the aerodrome at 6000 feet. The windsock indicated a light southerly breeze. The check captain, who was not flying the aircraft but observing the trainee captain from the co-pilot's seat, later summarised the briefing he gave to the trainee: 'Because of the steep slope at the far end of the strip there was no problem in stopping the aircraft, therefore there was no requirement for a STOL (short take-off and landing) approach and it was not necessary to touch down close to the threshold.'[22] For some reason this briefing was subsequently ignored by both pilots, including the pilot who had given it! When the aircraft descended below a normal approach path for Tapini and looked like it was going to touch down short of the threshold, neither pilot took the immediately required action of adding power to arrest the rate of descent. Their initial reaction was to pull back on the control column. However without any attendant thrust increase the Caribou didn't respond. The main wheels struck a bank of loose earth approximately 50ft above the threshold and well short of the airstrip. The aircraft spun 180 degrees and came to rest on the aerodrome's southern edge. The loadmaster and three of the four Army personnel on board were injured to varying degrees; the aircraft was a write-off. The undercarriage was destroyed, the front section of the fuselage was buckled and torn, the left propeller was deformed, the rear fuselage was bent out of shape, and a wing tip was torn off. The post-crash report by RAAF investigators blamed the accident on an error of judgement on the part of the pilots involved: "They allowed the aircraft to strike rough ground 490ft short of the threshold on a runway with no

The RAAF Caribou wreck at Tapini.

RAAF Museum Point Cook

useable underrun, after briefing that there was no requirement to land close to the threshold."

Kerau and Sopu were the least serviced of the Goilala ports. Kerau (*key-rau*, 7100 ft AMSL, 579m long, grassed red clay, 2.5% slope) was only seven miles upstream from Tapini on a flat mountaintop above the Lova River gorge, but an impossible 4200 feet higher. Mack limited our load out of Kerau to three passengers and freight only — the Cessna's take-off performance at an airstrip this high was extremely poor (on a 20 degree day at Kerau, the equivalent density altitude for performance calculation purposes was a mind-blowing 9400 feet). Every take-off from Kerau was a heart-in-your-mouth stressfest. The aircraft was painfully slow to accelerate across the clingy red clay of the airstrip surface, and it was not uncommon for the Cessna to stagger off the end with the stall warning horn sounding. Thankfully there was a 3000-foot-deep valley to fall into.

Sopu (*soh-poo*, 6500 ft AMSL, 532m long, grassed clay, 12% slope) was further up the same valley, at the headwaters of the Lova River, cut out of a high altitude spur of the Owen Stanley Range. It was the steepest strip in the area. On paper it was 12%, the same as Fane, but the first fifth or so of Sopu was flat, before it went ballistic, curving steeply to the parking bay at the top. The grade of the sloped section was more like 15%. Mack didn't ever fly into Sopu after midday — turbulent tailwinds roaring up the Lova River gorge made landings here just too dangerous.

The last of the Goilala strips were Guari and Kamulai. These strips were geographically set apart from the rest of the ports and were normally accessed via the Kemrawiri Gap — an 8000-foot-high saddle 13 miles NNW of Tapini. Guari (*goo-are-ee*, 6100 ft AMSL, 600m long, gravel, 6.4% slope) was similar to the strips at Fane and Ononge, a sloped slab of a strip jutting out into the void, with drop-offs on three sides and a mountain ahead of you as you landed. Kamulai (*kah-moo-lai*, 5600 ft AMSL, 481m long, gravel, 11% slope) was Guari's sister strip, an evil sibling, a short, rocky, nasty excuse for a landing ground. Kamulai was nestled in the same basin as Guari, chiselled out of the sheer north-eastern flank of 10,700 foot-high Mount Yule. Kamulai was notorious for swirling crosswinds and turbulence, most especially in the afternoon when convective currents danced on the ramparts of the mountain above, sending treacherous downdrafts across Kamulai's landing threshold (TNA's Gerard Phillip crashed a BN-2 Islander here in 1991 after he was caught in one of these vicious currents just before landing. Phillip and trainee pilot James Okana were unhurt, but the aircraft was destroyed).[23]

The hardest thing to get my head around was the approach to land at all these airstrips where the visual references were so completely different. It was a mindfuck, a cognitive disconnect. If setting up for a landing at any 'normal' flat runway on a flat section of topography anywhere else in the world was primary school arithmetic, attacking one of the one-way upsloping mountain airstrips of PNG was university level calculus. At some strips you made your approach to land over a void, as if suspended in space, as if you were not moving at all. At others you were descending into a tight-walled canyon, claustrophobic and threatening, with close-proximity scenery chugging past you at a great rate of knots. The key was to ignore the off-putting and conflicting visuals and go back to basics. I imagined a wire coming from the end of the threshold out to a final approach course at 3 degrees from the horizontal, curving around the corner to a base turn position, then up onto a downwind leg 1000 feet above the strip level; a filament suspended in space like the smoke trail of a stunt pilot who'd just flown the perfect circuit. Arriving at a mountain airstrip all I had to do was intercept this imaginary wire in the sky and I could join the circuit at any point. As long as my power setting was the same every time on final approach, with the same attitude and target airspeed (65 knots in the Cessna 206), and the aim point (the threshold) stayed in a constant position in the windscreen, then I was flying a correct and safe approach path. I just ignored what the strip did after the threshold — it didn't matter if it sloped up the side of a mountain ridgeline at 15%, or it was a dead flat patch of grass on a coastal airstrip — if my power settings and aircraft attitude were 'in the ballpark', then my approach was good. Always falling back on a rigid set of parameters like this also allowed me to quickly pick up what was happening atmospherically in the vicinity of an airstrip. If my power settings were higher than usual I was caught in a downdraft; if lower, an updraught or a tailwind. As I became more experienced these changes weren't just picked up by glances at the cockpit gauges — they were sensed. Soon PNG mountain airstrip ops became a tactile and auditory affair: real, raw, instinctive flying.

At each of these airstrips Mack had me doing all the paperwork and most of the communicating. *Tok Pisin* (Pidgin) was the only way to converse with the tradestore owners and passengers in the mountains. It has its origins in the Pacific labour trade of the late 1800s, when thousands of New Guinea labourers were shipped to German plantations in Samoa. Here Pidgin had developed as the common language of a multicultural and multilingual workforce, and it was brought back to New Guinea when the indentured workers were repatriated.[24] The more familiar I became with the language, the more I appreciated how delightful it was, a playful tongue bursting with charming descriptive words and phrases. I was *boss-man balus* (balus = bird or aeroplane), or *kapten* (captain). A helicopter was a *mixmaster bilong jesus*. An aircraft crash was described as *balus i bagarap* (the aeroplane is buggered-up). The near-naked men of the remote villages wore *arse gras* (arse grass = leaves stuck in their belt to cover their backside). To start a journey, villagers would *throwim way leg* (throw away their leg = start walking). If you were sick, you were *dai lik lik* (a little bit dead). If someone in the village died, they were *dai pinis* (dead, finished), and to be buried was to be placed in a *hul bilong planim man* (a hole to plant a man = grave). And the pick of the bunch: a woman's bra was *kalabus bilong susu* (kalabus = prison, susu = breast; literally 'a prison for boobs'). The phrase I used most often in the early days was *yu tok isi isi plis, mi no save* (talk slowly please, I don't understand!).

Flying into the Goilala strips with Mack was supremely exciting. What had initially appeared frightening and foolhardy was slowly becoming the norm — I was acclimatising to the demands of this bush flying madness. Every approach to the short one-way high altitude mountain airstrips was a precision flying exercise requiring strict discipline. There was no room for sloppiness or error or inattention. Fear was ever present, but the mind was too busy with the acute concentration required to safely land your aircraft on the postage stamps of dirt that sufficed in these parts for aerodromes to acknowledge it. Bush flying in the mountains of PNG, fear and excitement were bound together as one. I was to lose count of the number of times I landed after particularly hairy approaches to see my hands shaking after engine shutdown. But there was no time to be fearful or afraid. You just did what had to be done. It was seat-of-the-pants flying where your life depended on sound visual navigation, strict airspeed and attitude control, precision landings, and always, always making sure you kept an escape option up your sleeve.

●

— Chapter 5 —

Of Golden Voices, the Ononge No-Go-Around, and *Raskols*

*The secret of reaping the greatest fruitfulness and the greatest
enjoyment from life is to live dangerously.*
FRIEDRICH NIETZSCHE[25]

**Within four and a half weeks of starting my training with Mack Lee
and Air Manubada, Mack had sent me solo into five of the Goilala
airstrips: Ononge, Woitape, Fane, Tapini and Guari.**

Six days a week I battled the Trans Niugini Airways lads at these
outports, launching from Port Moresby amidst a gaggle of Cessnas and
BN-2 Islanders; the aircraft peeling off in a bomb burst at the 35 Mile
Ridge for their ports of choice, me doing my darndest to outfox Sarge
and Tony Froude and the other pilots of 'the nasty opposition' and beat
them to the waiting passengers and freight. I had settled in well, and was
almost at the point where Mack was happy to send me off to fly solo for
the mission station at Kerema. But trouble was brewing.

Behind the scenes frustration levels were high. Bishop Marx and
Brother Nolin were upset that my training was taking longer than
they'd expected. They wanted me to move to Kerema as soon as possible
although, strangely, they still hadn't purchased a new mission plane.
Mack was frustrated because he wanted the training done right and

wasn't prepared to sign me off early. He knew the possible consequences of letting a pilot loose in the PNG mountains prematurely — a pine box lowered into a six-foot deep *hul bilong planim man*. COVS, the volunteer agency in New Zealand, got involved too, reminding all parties that the clock was running on my one-year commitment as a mission pilot. I was piggy in the middle, a *boss-man balus* missionary with no aeroplane. Just as things started to go really pear shaped, a compromise was reached. The Catholic Church of Kerema realised their timeframe didn't match mine and they released me. Mack Lee, realising that I wasn't too bad a pilot, and that he could do with some help, offered me a job. I took him up on his offer and said an awkward thankyou and goodbye to Marx and Nolin in Kerema. It was an unfortunate set of circumstances and, although the decision had been out of my hands, I did feel a touch of guilt having transitioned so quickly from *missionary* to *mercenary*.

My new role as junior Air Manubada pilot saw me working a very fluid flight roster, as unscheduled hops between Goilala ports were common. Often I'd land at one of the airstrips with a firm plan to pick up passengers and freight and fly straight back to Port Moresby only to find a huddle of people stripside wanting to be shuttled somewhere else: locals, missionaries and itinerant government health and education workers. They could purchase a ticket to fly with me for 20 or 30 kina, and be at any other Goilala port within 10 or 15 minutes. This was infinitely better than the alternative: an all-day hike along arduous village paths snaking through some truly horrendous terrain. One day, about to depart Fane on a Tapini shuttle, I saw Tony Froude loitering on the porch of a wooden house at the side of the strip. I wandered over to say gidday and he let me in on the Goilalas' best kept secret. This was the home of two elderly French nuns, Sister Martha and Sister Gerard of Our Lady of the Sacred Heart (their order had been serving the community here since 1915).[26] The old dears didn't have much interaction with Europeans and they were always happy to entertain visitors. Morning tea with these lovely ladies was to become a regular diversion. Whenever I could, I dropped in to see them for a quick chat, leaving Alex Gusi and his offsider Alan Kafua to arrange my passengers and freight as I sat down at the nun's squeaky wooden table and tucked into fresh-ground coffee, hot scones straight out of a wood-fired oven, and homemade guava jam. In return I'd carry their outbound mail and post it for them in Port Moresby. It wasn't much, but doing this tiny good deed helped ease the residual guilt I felt for dropping the mission job with the Church in Kerema.

The more I flew into the Goilala ports behind Moresby the more I got a sense of the wartime credentials of some of these seemingly insignificant villages. It was only after I left PNG I made an effort learn more about the nation's rich 20th century history. Far from being forever isolated from the real world, some of these clusters of tin shacks and bush-material lean-tos played a vital, if little-known, role in the defence of Port Moresby during the Japanese air raids on the capital during 1942–43. This was at a critical juncture in WWII, a time when the balance of power between Allied and Japanese forces was at its most precarious, a time when it seemed altogether possible that the Oriental invaders would one day march right on into Australia itself, grasping control of the supply routes across the entire Pacific Ocean.

Following the Japanese occupation of Rabaul on New Guinea's eastern island of New Britain in January 1942, Port Moresby was well within range of Emperor Hirohito's bombers and fighters. The Territory's military commanders realised the urgent need to expand the network of civilian coastwatching stations that had existed prior to WWII. The rapid Japanese advance necessitated the deployment of top secret radio signals detachments to the remote mountains around the approaches to Port Moresby, to give advance warning of Japanese air raids. To this end the 'Air Warning and Coastwatching System' was created within nine days of Rabaul's demise. The signals detachments (more commonly referred to as 'spotters') consisted of two or three volunteers, initially drawn from the ranks of the 39th Australian Infantry Battalion. Their training was supposed to include a seven-day course at Signals Camp just above Rouna Falls 18 miles out of Moresby on the Sogeri Road, but often the course was compressed into one day, or they received no instruction at all and were trained in the operation of their communications equipment while en route to their secret destination. Such was the urgency of their mission. One author wryly remarked: "All that most of the spotters had in common was an abysmal ignorance of anything to do with signals."[27] Despite this, the network quickly became extensive, covering the approaches to Port Moresby as well as many other areas of military tactical significance; in the first month alone 15 stations were established. By the end of 1942 there were over 180 signalmen operating from 61 stations throughout Papua and New Guinea. In October 1942 the air warning and coastwatching stations were incorporated into one company, the New Guinea Air Warning Wireless Company (NGAWW).

These men did more than just give advance warning of air raids: they collected ground intelligence; passed on weather observations; assisted with enemy target identification; and aided in the rescue of downed airmen. The Japanese soon learned of the presence of the spotters, which made their mission all the more dangerous, with the men facing torture and execution if captured. One 'Tokyo Rose' (the name given to any of several English-speaking female broadcasters of Japanese propaganda), in a characteristically caustic tone, dubbed them the *golden voices*.[28] In one unfortunate incident NGAWW operatives were betrayed by their own side. Spotters at Salamaua (a town on the north-eastern coast, in Morobe Province) had an expansive view of Salamaua's enemy-occupied airstrip, and had been providing invaluable intelligence reports on the movements of Japanese aircraft as well as reports on the damage caused by Allied bombing attacks. One day in July 1942 a villager came running to their hidden observation post shouting, "*Masta, man bilong Japan i kam, planti man i kam!*" (Lots of Japanese troops are coming!). As the three Australians made a hasty exit into the jungle an enemy grenade and machine-gun attack broke out behind them. The spotters had been extremely careful not to give away their position (never lighting fires; using the noise from a nearby river to mask the sound of their generator) and couldn't figure out how they'd been compromised. Had they been dobbed in by Japanese-friendly locals? This was not the reason for the enemy attack. Well-known war correspondent Damian Parer had visited their hideout and taken photos of their location for the Department of Information. Aware of the sensitive nature of the pictures, he'd left written instructions with the film that it was not to be used until he personally gave the OK. Some ignoramus at the department, confirming that the words 'military' and 'intelligence' shouldn't be included in the same sentence, released a picture from the reel to the Australian media. The Japanese had learned of the spotters' Salamaua hideout when their agents saw the picture and read about the location in the *Sydney Morning Herald!*[29]

In the mountains north of Port Moresby there were stations at Ononge, Tapini and at Goilala, a remote outpost three days walk from Tapini on the main spine of the Owen Stanley Range. Spotters Powderham, Marshall and Webb set up the station at Ononge. Setting out from Yule Island, 55nm west of Port Moresby, their journey took two weeks — transported by military launch, *lakatoi* (a large traditional tri-hull canoe), by truck and on foot. Signalman Webb described the last part of the journey: "We are a few thousand feet up and still climbing. The country is rugged in the extreme. The jungle seems impenetrable and the valleys and mountains are awe-inspiring. Knowing as we do how treacherous and wild these parts are, we pity any airman who crashes in this steamy unruly riot of nature which is at times veiled in cloud and mist . . ."[30]

Conditions were no less challenging once the spotters made it to their respective outposts. These men were often living among native tribespeople who had never had contact with Europeans. They lived in complete isolation, in fear of discovery by the enemy, in a hostile and alien environment. At the end of their secretive field posting they would return to HQ in Port Moresby sick with malnutrition and often plagued by malaria, scrub typhus and skin diseases of every variety. The 'golden voices' of the New Guinea Air Warning Wireless Company were yet more unsung heroes of PNG's defence against Japanese invasion.

In Ononge the spotters set up their Teleradio equipment and the aerial in a village hut (*haus wialas*). Spotters were generally dispatched with three months of rations as well as extra bags of salt, and cowrie shells, so they could barter with villagers for fresh produce. Soon after arriving the three Australians asked the local government police boy to set up trade with the locals. The story goes that within the hour the whole village turned up, with 48 *meris* each carrying a 10kg bag of sweet potatoes. The shocked spotters paid for the almost 500kg of starchy vegetables with salt. They had just finished stacking their weighty purchases under the *haus wialas* when they saw another 55 *meris* arrive with another 500kg of sweet potato! Webb wrote: "What do you do with a ton of sweet potato? We've had them boiled, baked, chipped, and stewed. Just as well they make very good eating."[31]

On one occasion the Ononge spotters were broadcasting a warning of inbound enemy aircraft to Port Moresby HQ when enemy fighters started circling overhead. They stopped transmitting and lay low. When I visited Ononge village in 1992 I was told a similar story, although it had a more dramatic ending. I was given a tour of the village behind the airstrip and shown into Ononge's church. The priest told me that one Sunday morning during the war, Japanese aircraft attacked the village, perhaps suspecting the presence of the Australian spotters. It just happened that as they swooped in low over Ononge on their strafing run the village folk were gathered inside the church, celebrating Sunday mass. Japanese bullets tore through the flimsy weatherboard walls, cutting a swathe of destruction precisely between the congregation, who occupied the main body of the church, and the priest, who stood at the pulpit. Not one Ononge resident was hurt in the attack. After such a convincing display of divine intervention I'm guessing attendance figures for Ononge's Sunday mass were at record highs for the remainder of the War years.

I had my own near-miss at Ononge just 12 days after Mack Lee sent me solo to the Goilala airstrips. On 8 June 1992 I was scheduled to fly two trips to the mountain ports north of Port Moresby. The first, a routine mid-morning flight to Woitape and Fane, went off without a hitch. The weather was fine and clear, there was little wind, and it was an easy mission. By the time I got back to Moresby and refuelled the aircraft and helped company cargo boy Jimma load the Cessna for the second flight, it was just after 1pm. On board were four passengers and their baggage, about 100kg of tradestore goods, and about 150kg of fuel (giving me an endurance of three hours, more than enough for the 25 minutes-each-way flight to Ononge and back). I had not had much experience with afternoon trips into the mountains yet, but did know enough to realise that conditions would be significantly more challenging in the pm. This was when the morning's katabatic (down-slope) winds would reverse, transforming into anabatic (up-slope) winds. This meant tailwinds for the critical approaches into the Goilala's short one-way uphill airstrips: making a tricky job trickier (the tailwinds would translate into a landing with a higher groundspeed, meaning more runway was required for the same landing speed — a strip effectively became shorter in tailwind conditions). It was also the time of afternoon build-ups — the massive convective clouds that would shroud the mountain valleys in cloud, punctuating them with microbursts and squally rain showers.

One USAAF pilot, posted to Port Moresby with the US 5th Air Force in 1943, gave a fine account of PNG's afternoon weather in his memoirs. His assessment of the scary pm weather was just as relevant for me in the 1990s as it had been when he wrote it during WWII:

We new pilots were warned: 'watch out for New Guinea's afternoon weather. It can become a sneaking bitch.' New Guinea's treacherous afternoon weather started in the early morning as tame fleecy-white clouds. All day these innocent puffs of white were heated by the tropical sun and fed moist sea air. Those puffs of cotton rolled, boiled, and grew into ominous iron-grey cumulonimbus banks which moved across the sky until they lodged on top of the 14,000 foot Owen Stanley Mountains. By late afternoon, they often formed into a vertical grey wall that reached up to infinity. When I first came to New Guinea and observed this daily weather phenomenon, I found it fascinating; but once I was in the air and forced to meet its challenge, my attitude changed. I looked upon it as a horrid, recurring nightmare. These cloud banks didn't just appear. They were sneaky. First they were mushrooming, picturesque, anvil-shaped, vertical columns. Then, like jaws in a trap, they moved together. If you were at the wrong spot at the wrong time of day, within minutes you could find yourself trapped, locked in their clutches, and surrounded by a solid wall with all visible escape routes sealed.[32]

As I climbed out from Jacksons Aerodrome towards the 35 Mile Ridge and the entrance to the Ononge–Woitape valley, I noticed conditions had become a lot more blustery since my first flight. Flying parallel to the 35 Mile Ridge at 6500 feet my aircraft was buffeted by severe turbulence in the lee of the Owen Stanleys to the north. The cloud cover was lower than it had been earlier, with a ragged 7000-foot base obscuring most of the mountains around me. Ononge's circuit area was still clear though, with the cloud 500–1000 feet above the level of the 5300 ft AMSL strip. I joined overhead and turned downwind at 500 feet AGL[iii], noting that the windsock showed a tailwind of at least ten knots. This was going to be interesting. Turning onto final approach the aircraft was hammered by choppy turbulence and lurched this way and that as I fought to maintain a steady aim point (the second cone marker on the 500 metre-long 7% up-sloping strip) and hold an initial approach speed of 70 knots. Mack had taught me to anticipate an updraught as I crossed a knoll about 100 feet before touch-down in Ononge, and with my stomach in nervous knots I waited for it. If not anticipated, the updraught would balloon the aircraft high on the normal approach path and could increase the indicated speed by 10 to 20 knots. This day the updraught came early and was much more vicious than normal. I was too slow to react. In a nanosecond I was pushed high and fast, and now faced landing about halfway up the airstrip. Ononge has a 10-foot-high embankment at the end and I knew if I persevered with the approach I would crash into this wall of earth and rock. I was in more hot water than a Japanese tea bag.

I had no choice. Go around. I applied full power and waited for the aircraft to respond. It didn't. Nothing happened. With my landing weight of 1400kg (15% below maximum weight), at over 5000 feet above sea level, and 15 degrees Celsius above ISA[iv], my normally aspirated Continental engine had limited power to give me.

Someone or something stopped the clock. Time slowed down. It seemed like each second became a minute and I became acutely aware of the smallest details of the scene (this effect, temporal distortion, is a perceptive phenomenon commonly experienced by people faced with sudden life-or-death situations). The aircraft kept descending and we bounced halfway up the strip. I should have turned right at this point, avoiding a shack at the top right-hand side of the strip and falling off to the lower ground of the Woitape valley to my immediate east. But I didn't.

[iii] above ground level

[iv] International Standard Atmosphere

I was fixated on the airspeed indicator. The aircraft was barely flying — the stall warning was blaring and she was very mushy on the controls. I held the aircraft on the edge of controllability, and as the embankment at the end of the strip started filling up the windscreen, the psychological shock of impending disaster manifest itself as a hot prickly rash, which swarmed like a clutch of centipedes from between my shoulder blades up the back of my neck to the top of my head. The prickly heat intensified on the top of my scalp, then crept down to my forehead, stabbing like a headband of electric needles. It is a sensation I will never forget.

The only escape route open to me was to fly to the left of the embankment and fall into the valley to the west, but to do this I had to nurse the aircraft in ground effect[v] through the vegetation growing on the side of the strip. As I gingerly rolled the Cessna to the left I heard an alarming whap-whap-whapping from my side of the fuselage: the aircraft had become an airborne lawnmower, chopping its way through the low patchy scrub where the airstrip met the jungle. My front seat passenger (a local man) undid his seatbelt in slow motion and started scratching around on the right side of the cockpit looking for his door handle. He was preparing to jump out of the aircraft before we crashed! With seconds still taking minutes, I had the time to ponder his actions — I understood his logic, but his plan was deeply flawed. There is no exit door on the right side of the cockpit in a Cessna 206. My only other thought was immense disappointment with myself that I was about to crash an aeroplane in New Guinea so soon after being sent solo.

As the stall warning horn continued blaring away I flew less than five feet above the deck, the Cessna still impacting grass and saplings as I aimed for the left side of the embankment. We finally fell away into the valley and I nosed the aircraft down a touch and slowly retracted one stage of flap, hoping to reduce my drag and outclimb the forest we were sinking into. This tactic worked and I picked up flying speed and stooged down into the valley, doing a 180 degree turn and making my way towards Woitape (by now I was well below the level of Ononge's

---

[v]   There is less drag on an aircraft, thus better performance aerodynamically, when it flies very close to the ground = *ground effect*.

threshold, and flew behind and below the knoll where I'd picked up the massive updraught). I remember 60 knots was the maximum speed I saw on the airspeed indicator throughout the entire go-around.

I don't remember landing in Woitape five minutes later. I do remember telling the passengers that conditions in Ononge were too dangerous, that I was going to leave them here, and that I'd pick them up the next day and shuttle them to Ononge. They didn't argue, and tootled off into the village. I got out of the aeroplane. My hands were shaking like a seismograph needle and I felt physically sick.

A quick walk around revealed just how lucky I'd been. The propeller and the front of the engine cowl were stained green from all the tall bush grass I'd flown through. The left-hand-side wing strut was also covered in grass stains, and foliage (sticks, grass, leaves) hung between the left main wheel and the sprung steel undercarriage leg. I soaked a rag in avgas from the underwing fuel drainage valve and scrubbed off all the stains, picked the vegetation from the undercarriage and unwound a couple of vines from the wing strut. Once my hands stopped shaking I saddled up and flew home, having decided I wasn't going to tell Mack about my misadventure.

Safely back in Port Moresby I secured the aircraft on the tarmac in front of the aero club and drove back to Br Damian's house. I had a mini nervous breakdown that night as I related my near-miss to Damian, some kind of post-traumatic hyper-arousal freak-out. His solution was to serve me a large glass of scotch. It helped. My diary from that day has one simple entry: *Bloody good lesson. Wind. Afternoon. Local knowledge. Nothing is predictable. BE CAREFUL!*

That Friday night over a few beers at the aero club I told the story to Sarge, Tony and the TNA boys. I told them that on landing in Woitape I'd had foliage in my undercarriage, and poopage in my pants. They thought it was funny. "Shit!" said Sarge, "you went to the LEFT in an Ononge go-around? Everyone knows the go-around is to the RIGHT, you silly bastard!"

After my Ononge near-miss I was acutely aware of the danger of flying in this new and foreign country, a country where pilots were rarely afforded second chances when bad decisions were made. I was aware too of the breakdown of law and order that had become a part of everyday life in Papua New Guinea, in the big cities in particular: corrupt police and soldiers, and roving gangs of youths and young men involved in petty crime, armed hold-ups, rape and murder. In PNG these gang members are known as *raskols* (rascals). The moniker sounds almost cute, like a mischievous child — "you naughty little rascal, you didn't eat your Brussels sprouts!" — but to think of PNG's *raskols* in these terms is like thinking of Stephen King's Cujo as an overweight puppy with a slight obedience deficit. The *raskols* had no respect for life or property — they wanted what you had, and would kill you to get to it. It mattered not if you were a man or a woman, a boy or a girl, local or expatriate. They were equal opportunity thugs.

A specific set of circumstances created PNG's *raskol* problem. Various experts point to changes in labour market policy in Papua New Guinea prior to the nation's independence in 1975 as the genesis of the law and order problem. At this time Australia-based unions lobbied hard for the introduction of a Minimum Wages Board, tasked with setting wages to supposedly ensure a good standard of living for those with formal employment. One commentator[33] said this was "both inappropriate and dangerous in the context of PNG". The resulting discrepancy between the earnings of those with formal employment (the minority in PNG) and those without (the vast majority) led to great inequity in the community and an ever-widening gap between rich and poor — a problem the country hadn't seen before. Urban unemployment and rural–urban migration became attendant problems. The drift of the have-nots towards the bright lights of the cities in the futile hope of joining the haves snowballed and the country's tribal history, coupled with a lack of income-generating work, led to the young and disaffected joining gangs. These *raskol* gangs gave the migrants the social and material support they couldn't get from their government (there is no social welfare in PNG) and operated free of the disciplinary influence of tribal leaders and the social controls that would normally restrain deviant behaviour in the village. To throw fuel on the fire, alcohol abuse and easy access to unlicensed firearms (in no small part due to the armed conflict on Bougainville from 1989 to 1998) exacerbated the law and order crisis.[34]

These issues continue to have a profoundly negative impact on the nation's social and economic development today. As noted by AusAID in Canberra, law and order problems "directly and substantially diminish the quality of life of all citizens, add to business costs, and deter foreign investors and tourists alike."[35]

I was aware of this social chaos, but had not realised the significance of the problem until the first Saturday in October 1992, five months after my arrival in-country. I parked outside the South Pacific Aero Club (SPAC) early that morning and walked into the Air Manubada office. I had a sparrow-fart Woitape–Fane–Woitape–Ononge–Moresby flight lined up, and expected that cargo boy Jimma was already at work on the tarmac, loading the Cessna. After picking up the aircraft logbooks and the tradestore order books, I walked out into the corridor and was just passing the sliding glass doors that opened into the aero club's bar when something stopped me dead in my tracks.

Blood.

Lots of it.

Blood was smeared on the glass doors of the bar; there were pools of blood and bloody footprints across the floorboards; bloody handprints on the walls and doors; and a trail of blood leading into the bar, across the carpet, and out into the covered barbeque area outside. It was something straight from a slaughterhouse, or a Quentin Tarantino movie set. As I stood frozen in the middle of the room the aero club's cleaning woman shuffled in from where she had been mopping up the sticky red mess in the bar, squeezing claret-red water from her raggedy mop into an old bucket at her feet.

I had been at the aero club less than 12 hours earlier for the Friday night barbeque. This weekly social get-together was the social highlight of my week. As was always the case on Friday nights at the aero club, some of the members had brought along their families, so there were women and children present along with the usual mix of expatriate pilots, aero club students and staff, off-duty policemen, local businessmen and private pilots. What the hell had happened after I left?

I watched the cleaning lady work her way across the bloodied floorboards with her mop, my stomach a clenched fist of knots. Just then John Close, SPAC's senior instructor, arrived and told me what had happened the previous night. Five *raskols* had burst into the beer garden through the corrugated iron gate at the back of the club. They were armed with knives, axes, machetes and homemade shotguns, and started attacking anyone and everyone at the barbeque. They swung their blades with equal contempt at locals and expats alike, waving their weapons around demanding cash, wallets and valuables from the aero club patrons. John explained that it had been a classic case of PNG 'payback'. Included in the group of *raskols* were a couple of disgruntled ex-employees of the club: they'd been fired some time ago for unsatisfactory performance as security guards. They came back that night with their *wantoks* with weapons drawn to teach the club members a lesson, to extract revenge for their loss-of-face after being laid off.

Australian pilot Sid Makary was also there that night — I'd been having a beer with him before my fortuitous early departure, prior to the carnage. He later described the attack:

I was having a beer with Dennis Hilditch, John Mowatt, Colin Cousten and Ian Parkinson, standing by the barbeque hotplate in the covered area next to the bar. Suddenly there was a commotion coming from the car park, outside the aero club's gate and corrugated iron fence. The security guard was having heated words with someone unseen. The gate burst open and a guy with a homemade shotgun walked right up and pointed the gun at us. He had a spare shotgun cartridge in his mouth, and he was yelling something, but we couldn't make sense of it. If I hadn't been so shit-scared this might have been funny — "I'm sorry, I don't understand what you're saying, would you mind removing that shotgun cartridge from your mouth so you can speak more clearly?" More raskols came into the club, one knocking the security guard at the main door to the ground while another swung at him with an axe, landing a blow in between the guard's legs. The guard screamed.

The axe man then ran over to John Mowatt, yelling, "Give me your money!" He swung the axe and hit John's shoulder. The rascal swung again at John's leg — blood spurted out and John screamed in pain.

The axe man turned to Ian Parkinson, yelling, "Give me your shoes!"

"Take my fucking shoes!" said Ian.

The raskol swung his axe at Ian, catching him on the side of his hand as he raised his arm in self-defence. The axe man moved behind Colin Cousten, ordering him to lie face down on the concrete. As Colin lay on the floor a raskol with a knife approached and demanded his wallet. Colin pointed at another raskol and said, "He took it already" (quick thinking Colin had in fact thrown his wallet into some nearby bushes when the raskols had first arrived on the scene). The axe man swung angrily at Colin from behind, landing a blow square in the middle of his back. While all this was going on I saw Dennis Hilditch and others pushing the women and children up and over the fence separating the aero club from the airport tarmac, to get them to safety. I moved so my back was to the fireplace so no one could attack me from behind. A raskol came up to me, and motioned with his knife towards my throat, saying, "Give me your wallet." I gave it to him. Soon after, the raskol with the shotgun came back, motioning for me to lie down on the ground. "Give me your watch," he said, so I did. "Give me your wallet," he demanded.

"I gave it already!" I yelled. He placed the shotgun to my head. I was scared the homemade gun might go off accidentally. He left me and went off to rob the others. Some of the raskols were now inside the bar. They went up to Franko in Franko's corner (Franko was one of those regulars in the seedy bars of the world you can set your watch by; always there at a certain time; always sitting in the same spot). One brandished a knife at him — "Give me your wallet!"

Franko, looking calm and collected, said, "You want what?"

"Give me your wallet!" the raskol screamed.

"You want WHAT?" said Franko. He pulled out a HUGE knife, a knife so big it made the raskol's one look like a potato peeler. The *raskol backed away, and left him alone.*

A raskol approached Simeon, the head barman, screaming, "Give me the money!"

Simeon said no. The raskol jumped up onto the bar and started swinging his axe around, but got hit in the face by a ceiling fan, and fell to the floor. Simeon produced a tomahawk from behind the bar and chased the stunned raskol away.

The raskols all had bare feet, so some of the patrons started smashing beer bottles on the floor of the bar. The raskols left. The last one made a run for the gate — a little bloke, unarmed. He ran past me so I grabbed him and tried to stop him leaving. One of his mates came back through the gate with a shotgun, yelling, "Back inside, back inside!" and "On the ground, on the ground!" I again found myself on the ground with a homemade shotgun to my head.

It got very quiet. The attack was over, and the raskols were gone. The whole thing had only lasted a few minutes. John Mowatt was sitting there white as a sheet. "John, are you OK?" I said. "I'm OK," he replied. "Look after the others". Blood was pissing out of his arm, so I got a rag and tied it over the wound.

When the attack was over, John Mowatt and about five others lay bleeding in and around the aero club bar, all requiring urgent medical attention. In typical PNG style the ambulances that were called never showed up, so the wounded were taken to Dr. 'Jabba' Jim Jacobi's medical clinic in Boroko on improvised stretchers: tabletops lashed to the flat decks of SPAC members' vehicles. The clinic was closed, so they were carried into the restaurant next door and eventually treated by an emergency doctor. While waiting for the doc to arrive John was asked by the restaurant manager if he wanted something to eat. He remembers saying, "Satay would be nice", then he passed out.

In a 2009 email John remembered that night:

From the corner of my eye I saw what I thought was a South Pacific Lager stubby heading towards me and ducked. Something hit my right shoulder and — splat — I went down. I can remember seeing blood everywhere and using my left hand I grabbed my right shoulder and tried to squeeze the wound shut. I can remember holding my shoulder and looking towards the entry gate where there was a man pointing a shotgun at me and saying, "Don't move!"... there was no chance of me doing that. After a while I heard a noise from my right side (towards the door to the club house) and glimpsed some movement, then there was a pain in my right leg, just above the knee. That got my attention real quick and I forgot about my shoulder, which was still bleeding everywhere...

Each of John's gaping wounds required over 20 stitches to stop the blood flow, and he needed eight bags of plasma to replace the blood he'd lost. It was a miracle no one was killed.

Charles (Chuck) Perry, a Talair pilot, was there that night too, with his wife and three-year old daughter. He sent me his recollections in 2012:

If memory serves, the raskols hit the club about 8:30pm. I had just gone into the bar from the BBQ area to get some more drinks and as I was standing there being served there was a large commotion outside — people were running from the BBQ area around the front of the aero club and through the bar area . . . as I turned Wendy Gerdes rushed past me saying, "We're in big trouble!" Wendy and a number of other women hid successfully in the ladies toilets.

I went to the door that led out to the BBQ area and among the rushing people were raskols with balaclavas and weapons — I remember seeing at least one shotgun — homemade variety. Through the running people I saw Joanne and Chelsea (Chuck's wife and daughter) standing looking at me from just the other side of the BBQ so I quickly ran to them and we went out on the grass area near where the old P-39 fighter was — by the fence between the aero club and Yorke Mendoza's maintenance facility. As my eyes became accustomed to the darkness I saw Dennis Hilditch

(President of the aero club) throwing children over the 10' high chain link and razor wire fence into Yorke's place . . .

At this point we lay down on the grass with Joanne saying to Chelsea, "Be quiet like a little mouse," and lying on top of her. Chelsea never made a sound. I kept my head up watching what was going on — I saw John Mowatt go down under a hail of axe blows. I saw Colin Cousten standing by the BBQ with one hand resting on it being screamed at to get down on the ground by a raskol with an axe. Colin was staring back at him defiantly and I remember thinking, "For fuck's sake, Colin, stop looking at him." I had in my mind the sort of advice given to hostages in a hijack to be as non-threatening and 'invisible' as possible. The look on Colin's face was 'How dare you, you bastard.' Eventually Colin got down on his hands and knees and that's when the raskol took an almighty swing with his axe and hit Colin in the back.

At this point all the club members/patrons were on the ground . . . many bleeding from grievous wounds . . . or on the other side of the chain link fence 'airside' with a few yelling at the raskols that the police had been called and were on their way. Chris Miles (Talair's ops manager) I particularly remember doing that — this was of course long before mobile phones.

All the baddies were walking around backlit by the clubhouse and I was thinking about my Glock 19 at home. At this stage I could have opened fire (and I would have) on the bastards with ZERO danger to anyone except the raskols. Laying near to me was Jean Kekedo's husband who usually carried a revolver — "Where is your revolver?" . . . "In my car." . . . "It's no good there." . . . "Where is your Glock?" . . . "At home." . . . He just looked at me. It was almost comical. On any other night there would have been at least six handguns scattered among the members . . . this night all had been left at home or were locked in cars.

Also lying near us on the grass was the child of a British couple whose names I forget. She was separated from her parents and was crying out for them. Joanne couldn't shut her up. Eventually a raskol heard her and walked out a bit from the BBQ area staring *into the darkness . . . then he took a few more steps . . . as his eyes became accustomed to the darkness he saw all of us lying there. He came over and held his shotgun to my head and demanded my wallet or he would "Blow your head off and fuck your wife." I remember distinctly it was a homemade shotgun. I gave him the cash in my wallet, then he turned his attention to Kekedo who did the same . . . A few minutes later with much heathen yabbering they all ran out the gate . . . then a few ran back in again just as we were getting up off the ground . . . then they all departed.*

I was told later, by both Sid Makary and Chuck Perry, that the Moresby police soon caught one of the *raskols* involved in the attack. He dobbed in his mates, and eventually all the culprits were behind bars. The expats involved were told that they wouldn't have a problem with these criminals again. The *raskols* probably wound up in the bottom of Waigani swamp with concrete shoes, or as Chuck put it: ". . . they all ended up croc bait face down in the swamps just outside Moresby from what we were told at the time."

As I walked out the tarmac to pre-flight the Cessna 206 that morning, the blood-soaked aero club behind me, for the first time I wondered if I'd done the right thing by coming to Papua New Guinea. Was it worth it, risking your life to get some hours in your logbook? The attack really made me feel that I was an outsider, a foreigner, and not welcome. It was a natural over-reaction, but I imagined a nationwide hostility and resentment towards any non-indigenous presence, and I felt afraid. The brutality and the rawness of the attack were unlike anything I had ever experienced. Images of the blood-soaked aero club haunted me for a long time.

●

— Chapter 6 —

Crash Burn Die

A straight line is not the shortest distance between two points in New Guinea. It is usually the quickest way to press headlines.
ARTHUR JACOBSEN[36]

My life was now ruled by the PNG mountain flying roulette wheel. All flights shared a common start point (take off from base, in my case Port Moresby) but there were parallel streams of outcomes.

The happy-ending stream saw a safe return home after an incident-free flight. The not-so-happy stream either ended with a bare-knuckle shit-your-pants scare and a lucky escape, or something far worse, perhaps fatal. Most days there was a razor-thin line between these outcomes; a line as sharp as the blade on a Goilala tribesman's bush knife.

Was the flying really that hard? A 1997 Royal Australian Air Force Flying Safety Special, an advisory circular to RAAF pilots, reinforced the dangers of PNG ops to their aircrew with characteristic military dryness: *There is no unusual blend of flying skills required for flying in tropical mountainous areas, nor is there any special mystique about operating in these areas . . .However, because so many of the more demanding aspects of flying — unpredictable and rapidly changing weather, rugged terrain, inadequate navigation aids, poor living conditions, marginal aircraft performance, demanding missions and long flying days — are often present (usually in combination), far higher standards of airmanship, supervision and plain professionalism are required . . . In every flight there is a requirement for sound decisions which are based on solid training and guarded by adequate supervision. This is especially so in tropical mountainous areas; where these factors are inadequate, the success of an operation in marginal conditions is jeopardized.*[37]

The advice given in the RAAF publication was something of an understatement for those of us doing the hard yards in PNG's small General Aviation aircraft. We didn't have the luxury of hooning around in a C130 Hercules or DHC-4 Caribou. Flying into the mountains in a Cessna 206 or 185, or a BN-2 Islander (all piston engine-powered aircraft with limited performance at high altitude airstrips in the tropics) was like rolling up for a gang fight armed with a BB gun. The aircraft we flew were marginal. The airstrips were marginal. The afternoon weather was marginal. We were asking for trouble just being there. On paper the basics were the same as flying in any other part of the world. Take off. Climb. Point aircraft at destination. Avoid terrain and inclement weather en route. Descend. Land. But the crash statistics were a clear indication that this was <u>not</u> just any other part of the world. Between 1990 and 1994, the period when I was cutting my teeth as a PNG bush pilot, the numbers were shocking. On average, there were two aircraft accidents per month, leading to the loss of ten percent of the country's aircraft inventory per annum. 129 pilots and passengers died in this five year period.[38] This was a diabolically high loss rate for civilian flying, aircraft crash statistics that cemented PNG's reputation as one of the most dangerous places in the world to be a pilot.

I'd been in Papua New Guinea for only six months and, as if the trauma of the aero club attack wasn't enough, three fatal aeroplane crashes had been reported in that period. The weekend I'd first arrived in Port Moresby I'd read newspaper headlines of a Talair EMB-110 Bandeirante crash in the Daulo Pass, west of Goroka.[39] Pilot Thomas Jay Cabrera, the Talair air hostess Dorothy Vincents, and nine of 13 passengers aboard were killed. Two months later Kiwi newbie Dean Hannah had killed himself and his nine passengers in the false Manumu valley (see Chapter 8), and one month before the aero club attack Australian Paul

Brown of Honor Egger Air Transport (HEAT) had crashed his Cessna 206 in the mountains near Kamina in the Gulf Province, killing two of his six passengers. Brown got away with broken vertebrae, three broken bones in his foot, a dislocated collar bone, and a severe head gash, and had to spend a night in the jungle before being rescued by helicopter the following day.[40] (Brown returned to PNG after a period convalescing in Australia and continued with his flying career, only to be killed the following year in the crash of an Island Airways BN-2 Islander he was piloting with fellow aviator Dieter Wirth). While disturbing, none of these accidents were close to home enough to make an impression on me. I didn't personally know any of the pilots involved, so it was easy to disassociate myself from these tragedies, hold them at arm's length, and adopt the mantra *accidents happen to others, not to me*. As crazy as it sounds now, I really was more concerned with building hours in my logbook than I was with the very real possibility that I would be killed or maimed in a crash in the rugged PNG mountains.

One month after the aero club attack, the danger of PNG flying was brought a lot closer to home. My daily routine in Moresby saw me up early and at the flight planning office at the base of Jacksons Airport control tower before 7am, lodging my flight plan for the day's scheduled runs up to the Goilala airstrips and checking the latest NOTAMs.[vi] My filed flight plan included the altitude I planned to fly on my way to the mountains, the routing for the day, the estimated flying time between airstrips, an approximate take-off time, and the fuel load I expected to have in tanks when I departed Port Moresby. These flight plans were used by air traffic control to coordinate aircraft departures and included vital information should an aircraft fail to call in after landing and should they need to activate a search-and-rescue phase. I'd park the company car, a beaten up old Subaru Leone sedan, in the car park and climb the noisy steel stairs up to the flight planning office. Many mornings I'd run into Peter Gill at flight planning, a 39-year-old missionary pilot who flew a Cessna 180J for the Christian Revival Crusade (an Australian-based Pentecostal

---

[vi] Notices to Airmen — notes promulgated by the local civil aviation authority detailing important changes to airstrips, radio frequencies, navigation aids etc.

protestant church). He was a nice guy, and we'd chat away, comparing our routes for the day and discussing the morning's weather and how much trouble we thought we'd have getting out into the mountains. He and I were almost always heading in the same direction: me to the Goilalas, him to the mission stations of the Central Province. I enjoyed my morning chats with Peter.

On 7 November 1992 the shrill sound of an emergency beacon whoop-whooping away on the emergency VHF frequency 121.5 became forever associated with death. These beacons, known as ELBA's or ELT's are mandatory equipment on all passenger-carrying aircraft. They can be activated manually by the pilot, or auto-activated in the event of a crash. The beacon's signal is used by search-and-rescue teams to help locate an accident site. That morning I was climbing out from Ononge when I picked up the sound of a beacon on my #2 radio. I reported this to Air Traffic Control (ATC) and continued on to Moresby, hoping that the beacon was an inadvertent activation rather than an impact-triggered activation. I found out later that day that the beacon I'd heard was coming from the wreckage of Peter Gill's Cessna 180J, and Peter was dead.

Peter Gill arrived in-country in 1985 with a bare commercial pilot's licence, but by the time of his accident had a total of 2029 hours under his belt: 1700 of them in PNG in the Christian Revival Crusade's Cessna. Gill was no PNG rookie. At 0730 that morning Peter departed Port Moresby for Kira, a mission strip that lies on the same track as Moresby–Woitape, but 30 nm further north, nestled on the opposite side of the Owen Stanley Range. It was a route very familiar to him: he'd been there 20 times before, with eight trips in the previous 10 months. At 0854 he called Port Moresby on HF radio, telling them he was departing Kira for Moresby for the return trip, with five passengers (a husband and wife, their two children, and a grandmother). Seven minutes later he called again, advising ATC he was climbing to 10,000 feet and that he'd call again over Woitape at 0916. That call was never received and at 0937 ATC initiated a search-and-rescue alert. Mack Lee was in the area that morning too, and picked up the beacon at 1044. He carried out a grid search over the mountains between Pete's departure point and Woitape, and quickly found the wreckage. Peter's Cessna 180J had impacted at

8800 feet on the almost vertical (70 degrees of inclination) western slopes of the Guimu River valley, equidistant between Kira and Woitape. It appeared that the aircraft was intact and Mack orbited overhead, hoping to see signs of life from the red-and-white Cessna. Sadly, there were no survivors.

In the weeks that followed, Accident Investigator Alan Yarnold tried to establish the cause of Peter's crash.[41] It was an odd one. The aircraft had impacted 250 feet above the floor of the steep valley, at low or idle power, with partial flap selected. The estimated groundspeed was 70 knots (130 km/hr), with deceleration forces from the extremely short ground roll (five metres) making the crash unsurvivable. Had Peter experienced engine trouble and elected to force-land on the mountainside? The throttle cable assembly and propeller governor were disassembled and inspected to see if they contributed to the crash, but neither showed evidence of malfunction or failure. Carburettor icing was discounted as a cause of engine power loss, as was water-contaminated fuel. The aircraft was in positive control up to and including the point of impact. Was there bad weather at low level in that valley that morning? Was he attempting a 180-degree reversal turn, only to run out of room and elect to land on the mountainside? The weather at the time had not been too bad. TNA pilot Ian 'Killer' McCabe was in the area on the morning in question, and described conditions as "2/8 to 3/8ths cumulus on ridges, base 10,500 feet, visibility OK, cloud tops 11,500 to 12,000 ft: Woitape–Kira gap open." This tallied with the clear weather I saw further south that same morning, in the Woitape–Ononge valley. Yarnold's final analysis was that for an unknown reason, Peter Gill was attempting a forced landing on the mountainside. Six lives were lost. We will never know the exact reason for this crash.

Pete's death was a little too close for comfort. For the first time the victim in a 'crash comic' (our term for the monthly post-accident reports released in magazine format by the PNG Department of Civil Aviation) was someone I knew. There was a face and a personality and memories of our interactions to go with the bland factual details of his death. I was still more concerned with gaining flying experience and fattening my CV than with the clear and present danger of PNG bush flying though, so I did what any PNG bush pilot would do: I blocked thoughts of Peter Gill, and kept on keeping on.

This was to be the pattern for the bush pilots of PNG in the 1990s: every few weeks you'd hear of another fatal crash involving one of your colleagues. Like a surgeon used to the sight of blood we grew numb to this, tuning out the visceral shock of it so we could continue going to work every day, flying in the same marginal conditions and into the same marginal airstrips where these pilots and their passengers had died. It's odd that, at the time, we hardly gave these dead pilots or their passengers a thought: they may have been the topic of limited bar talk soon after we heard about their fate, but then they were forgotten and not mentioned again. We were supposed to be Supermen. Their stories were our kryptonite, and we turned from them like a vampire recoils from sunlight. We could never let ourselves think *that could have been me*. If we'd dwelled on the dangerousness of it all, and the risks we were exposing ourselves to on a daily basis, we'd never have been able to carry out our duties as pilots. WWII correspondent Frederick Faust summed up this coping mechanism well when he wrote about US Marine Corps pilots losing colleagues in aerial combat: "If they let themselves go, thinking about what happened, it spoiled their flying. If a man went in, they simply had to X him out of their minds, the way you lose a piece in chess and the game must go on with what is left."[42]

I'd be lying if I said I wasn't troubled by the crashes of 1992, my first year in Papua New Guinea. I put on a brave face in front of Mack Lee and the boys at the aero club, but I was most definitely spooked by the death of so many pilots and passengers. I found out much later I wasn't alone. I spoke with one Port Moresby-based pilot while compiling stories for this book, and he told me that after a couple of years living and flying in PNG he'd become quite a fatalist. He knew "too many" of the guys who were killed, and he began feeling that he too might end up sharing the same fate. He had even stopped planning his post-PNG flying future, as he wasn't sure he'd live through it. Although this 'it's out of my hands' attitude now seems a bit wacky, I think he was one of the most objective and realistic of the PNG bush pilots I spoke to — like me he had come to realise that it didn't matter how good you were, or how careful, one day simply through the continued exposure to danger and those damn statistics, you were going to have an accident. You might walk away from it and you might not, and nine times out of ten it was the roll of the dice that determined the outcome, not your own skill and experience.

As soon as I had started working full time for Mack Lee I had transferred from Br Damian's house near Gordon's Market to a rented apartment at the Salvation Army compound behind the Boroko shops on Angau Drive. It was a shoe box, with barely enough room to swing a kitten let alone a full-grown cat, but it was nice to finally have my own digs. I was moving up in the world — no more was I the '20 kina pilot' — as Mack was covering my rent and paying me a wage of around 280 kina per fortnight, which worked out at the time to be about US$7000 per year. It wasn't much, but it was a lot more than the $20 per week stipend I'd received from the Catholic Diocese of Kerema. While my Air Manubada salary was on the frugal side (I was earning less than half as much as the TNA boys), Mack Lee was generous in other ways. On Fridays he would pass me some cash so I could buy beers and a meal ticket for the weekly aero club BBQ, and he'd often take me out to dinner during the week with his mates from Port Moresby's Chinese community. When I returned from my first solo bush-pilot mission he rang the bell in the aero club, signalling he'd shout all the patrons to a few drinks in celebration, and the following year, when I reached the milestone of 1000 flying hours in my logbook, he paid for a big booze-up and dinner at the Cathay Club on Waigani Drive (since renamed the Country Club) for all of my Port Moresby friends.

Finally I was a full-time pilot. I flew Monday to Saturday, with generally early starts and early finishes. Most days I was done flying by 2pm, and after putting the Cessna 206 to bed, and passing the money from the days flights to Mack (payments from tradestore owners and cash fares I'd earned at the mountain strips) and recording it all in the account books, I'd make a quick run to Jimm Trading, a Chinese-run mega tradestore at 6 Mile, to pick up the Goilala station dry goods orders for the following day. Some days I'd also do a covert run to Ling's Freezer in Gordons Industrial Estate and pick up a tray of frozen New Zealand lamb flaps (a low-grade fatty off-cut, known as lamb belly in the US and the UK). This 20 kg carton would be added to the aircraft's load the next day (but wouldn't appear on the manifest), and I'd sell it at a 100% mark-up at the mountain airstrips as a way of making a bit of extra cash. Jobs done, I'd generally be home by 5pm at the latest. Back at the Salvo's compound, I'd settle in for the evening — preparing a basic meal of tinned fish and rice, and indulging in my one treat — eating half a packet of Twisties (saving the other half for the following day) while watching the nightly re-runs of *MASH* on the local TV network. I had a very simple and modest lifestyle, but I was a professional pilot, I was building good solid hours in my logbook, and I felt like I was on my way to a future as an airline pilot.

Although I was no longer under his roof, and despite my hectic flying schedule, I did make an effort to keep in touch with Br Damian Keane, who had become a good friend. An interesting part of having Damian as a mate was the wide spectrum of Christian clergy and missionaries I met through him. Although I didn't always agree with their beliefs, or the way they foisted these beliefs on the local populace, I did have great respect for their selfless dedication to the cause. While the churches of the world, and religion in general, are responsible for some highly questionable acts throughout history, their overall record in a place like Papua New Guinea cannot be faulted. Since the arrival of the first European churches in PNG in 1874, they have been the bedrock of formal education for locals through the establishment of mission stations, often in remote rural communities. Hand in hand with the spreading of 'the good word' and education has been the introduction of Western medicine. Churches of various denominations have always had responsibility for a significant percentage of PNG's rural health centres, and trained nearly all of the community health workers and the majority of nurses. This influence has not diminished, with particular respect to schooling, and church-run institutions continue to account for a large percentage of all student enrolments. During my time in PNG the churches ran six out of nine national teacher training colleges and continued to play a vital role in delivering services to remote rural communities.[43] Today, even though the funding for these services often comes from PNG national and provincial governments, those at the coalface are still most likely to be a mix of church and other non-government organisation (NGO) workers.

The folks I mixed with through my friendship with Damian came from a wide spectrum. At one end were the short-timers, missionary lay-people — most often those with hands-on qualifications like teachers, builders, doctors, nurses — who were in-country for a one- or two-year volunteer contract, most often only passing through Port Moresby on their way to or from one of the isolated coastal or mountain communities. These people were fantastic: they'd taken time out from their normal first-world reality to live in relative poverty, far from home comforts, isolated from friends and family, giving their time and energy and skills to those in need. The world would be a happier place if we could all give selflessly like this.

In the middle were the long-timers: the old-school, formal, stiff traditionalists like Bishop Paul Marx of Kerema, his sidekick Brother Michael Nolin, and the senior clergy of Port Moresby's Catholic community. I take my hat off to those living out in the bush in the isolated communities (Br Damian himself had spent years living in a small village called Kamina in the mountains behind Kerema in the Gulf Province), those doing the hard yards, but I was never sure about the hierarchy camped out in the fairly lush accommodation and surrounds at HQ in Port Moresby. Theirs seemed to be a sheltered life; a life of comfort; a life of sermons and celebrations; an active social life with hearty dinners, port and red wine, and (to me anyway) a disconnect from their congregation, who lived in tin shacks, hand-to-mouth, and struggled for survival in the *real* Port Moresby, clinging to their faith to help them get through.

Off the far end of the scale were the wide-eyed evangelical bible-bashers, the overly cheery folks that seemed intoxicated with the boundless love of the Good Lord above, and singularly convinced that the rest of us needed salvation. Whether we wanted it or not. Thankfully, these crazies were thin on the ground, but one day, before I had moved out of Damian's house, a group from this end of the spectrum turned up on his doorstep. I buzzed them in, watching the razor wire gate open jerkily into Damian's steep concrete driveway off Henao Drive. The three of them, from Canberra in Australia, were preachers from the

'Missionaries of God's Love', a Roman Catholic congregation founded in 1986. They looked like 1960s rock stars — a scruffy, natural-fibre wearing, sandal-footed, long-haired, bearded, guitar-strumming trio — but were bereft of all the good bits (the drinking, the drugs, the free love, the hit records). I met them at Damian's steel-gated main entrance door and escorted them upstairs. It was a courtesy call: they were new in town and had stopped by to introduce themselves. I was peripheral to their conversation, but noticed very soon that they were way too happy to be taken seriously. They sported big grins, glazed eyes and one of them hammered away at a guitar while the other two sang way-too-happy happy songs. I thought they might be high on the wacky tobacky. "No way brother, we're high on the power of Jesus!" would be their response to this accusation from a heathen like myself. Damian couldn't stand them, and was dumbfounded by their lack of awareness of Port Moresby's law and order problems. He laughed after they left. "Those bloody fools! They walked here from their accommodation down the road. Walked!"

"They were lucky not to get held up! They'll probably get robbed on the way back!"

I didn't think I'd see them again (Damian was sure he would — he was convinced they'd end up in Port Moresby General Hospital with stab wounds). I was wrong.

A week later, flying my normal Goilalas run, I landed at Fane. I pulled up at the top of the strip as usual and clambered out, ready to offload the tradestore goods for Deva and Alex Gusi, and see if there were any passengers for Moresby. Suddenly I heard a shout from the verandah of the priest's house: "Praise the Lord, our chariot is here!"

And then: "Matt! Welcome brother!"

It was the Missionaries of God's Love rockers. Oh shit! They'd been in Fane for a couple of days, spreading the good word, and no doubt strumming their fingers raw and singing themselves hoarse with peppy, perky Jesus songs. They purchased tickets to fly with me back to Port Moresby.

I bundled them and their guitars and their irritating cheeriness into the middle and front seats of the Cessna 206. Fane's resident priest stood at the side of the airstrip, giving am I'm-glad-you're-leaving farewell wave — the wave you give your in-laws when they leave after staying at your house. For two months. I ran through my pre-start checklist and was just making a visual sweep of the strip around me to see that the prop was clear when I felt the pressure of an open palm on my shoulder. And then it began:

"Lord, we ask you and your son Jesus Christ to work through Matt's hands on this day and guide us safely through these clouds and mountains."

The other two chimed in with an "Amen."

"But Lord Jesus Christ in heaven above, if it is our time, and you chose to take us today, and we crash during this flight, we look forward to meeting you and all the choirs and angels in heaven, and experiencing the glory of God with you and the heavenly Father above."

"Amen!"

"Praise the Lord!"

Oh for fuck's sake, I thought, don't jinx it guys. These afternoon flights were worrying enough without fate being tempted by the prayers of idiots! I looked down the strip and over to the departure track, a right turn towards Woitape. The afternoon cloud boiled overhead and a gusty crosswind swept raggedy scud across the take-off path into the river valley below. If we had engine trouble after take-off we were dead — with or without the intervention of the Big Man upstairs.

Within a few weeks the Air Manubada flying schedule had become routine. As routine as flying in the bush in PNG could be. Near-misses were not infrequent. One day I departed Woitape airstrip bound for Ononge. At about 300 feet above the deck there was a loud metallic bang and the aircraft swung to the right, like we had been hit by something, then straightened up and flew normally. My already tight sphincter tightened further, clenching like an eyeball full of lemon juice. I made an instant scan of the engine instruments — all were in the middle of the green range. The fuel tanks were still half full. All indications in the cockpit were normal. The cause of the bang and yaw was a mystery. I flew on to Ononge with my heart in my mouth and landed there, gingerly reducing the power for the descent and approach, expecting at any moment for the engine to shit itself. It operated normally and the landing was uneventful. After coming to a stop in the red clay parking area at the top of the strip I jumped out and performed a thorough check of the exterior of the Cessna. I focused on the starboard side of the ship, as I was convinced I must have hit a bird on take-off: what else could explain the metallic bang and the lurch to the right? But there were no impact marks, no damage, and I couldn't find anything wrong with the aircraft. I loaded up a couple more passengers and freight for Moresby and carried out a further check before we departed: a full engine run-up. Again, all seemed normal. The flight from Ononge to Jacksons field was normal too. It was only when I went to put the aircraft to bed for the day (installing the wheel chocks, placing a protective cover on the airspeed sensor, popping the control lock in its place inside the cockpit) that I finally figured out what had happened.

I liked to leave the three-bladed propeller looking tidy when I left the aircraft for the day, with one blade pointing vertically down, and the other two splayed upwards. As I grabbed one of the blades to move it into position, I found it was loose in its hub, and moved two to three inches in either direction. There wasn't supposed to be any free play at all: the blade was supposed to be 100% rigid. On closer inspection I was horrified to see multiple deep gouge marks on its front and back surface. The damage to the propeller blade was the reason for the bang and the yaw, and engineers later explained what had happened. McCauley propeller blades are held in place by two metallic rings: a primary split-ring retainer at their base and a secondary retaining ring where the blade exits the hub. The secondary ring keeps the blade from falling into the hub when stationary. This retaining ring had come off during my take-off from Woitape, gouging lines in the blade surface as it departed at a great rate of knots off into the Goilala bush. It failed because either it was not seated properly, or it was installed back-to-front, or it had been stretched too wide during installation. If this failure had led to a failure of the primary split-ring, the whole propeller blade would have separated from the hub. The resulting thrust imbalance would have led to the engine ripping itself from its mounts almost instantly. Milliseconds later, due to the Cessna being grossly out of its centre of gravity range, we would have fallen out of the sky, completely out of control. Luckily for me and my passengers, the damaged propeller blade stayed in position. Once again I had had a lucky escape. It was not my fate to crash burn and die just yet.

It was however the fate of another Moresby-based bush pilot to crash. At the tail end of the wet season PNG national pilot James Okana departed Jacksons Airport in Wantok Aviation's BN-2 Islander P2-NAA, bound for Guari. The flight was a coffin charter, with the usual 'victims': ten grieving relatives, some light baggage and a coffin containing their dear departed. Forty-five minutes after departing Jacksons Airport, Okana called Port Moresby ATC on HF radio, reporting that he was holding in the Guari area, unable to make an approach and landing due to inclement weather. Five minutes later he called back giving his position as "abeam Mount Yule on climb to 10,000 feet". Okana held in this position for the next 49 minutes, looking for a break in the clouds so he could descend and land at Guari (which is at 6100 feet AMSL, in a horseshoe valley immediately north-east of 10,700 foot-high Mt Yule). He could not find a way through, and advised ATC that he was returning to Port Moresby. A further 36 minutes later he entered Port Moresby terminal airspace, and was transferred to the tower frequency. A few minutes after that he called the tower, advising that he was 10 miles from the field. The tower controller instructed him to track direct for a final approach for a landing on runway 14R. Okana acknowledged this, then said he was experiencing problems with one engine. Shortly after this, both his engines stopped, forcing him to execute an emergency landing in the Waigani swamp, four miles short of the runway. Okana chose a landing spot carefully, avoiding the trees, selecting a muddy clearing covered in patchy kunai grass. The aircraft touched down successfully but the nose wheel assembly collapsed during the deceleration, causing significant damage to the nose cone and the forward belly. James and his passengers exited the aircraft unhurt. The occupant of the coffin remained dead. No change there. Okana had made the best of a bad situation, but as the subsequent investigation would show, it was a situation entirely of his own making.

James Okana's BN-2 Islander in the Waigani swamp.

He had departed Moresby with a total fuel endurance of 170 minutes. This seemed a sensible amount, as it allowed for the 90-minute return trip to Guari, the 45-minute reserve fuel that aircraft were required to have in tanks at all times, and a 35-minute buffer. The problem was his total time from engine start until his forced landing was 150 minutes. This only left him a buffer of 20 minutes of fuel at cruise power before the tanks were dry. He had used up this buffer while climbing and descending between 6000 and 10,000 feet in the Guari area during his 49 minutes of holding: the BN-2 Islander's engines, like all aircraft power plants, use significantly more fuel when climb power is set.[44] His tanks had run dry four miles short of the runway, turning his aircraft into a glider. Okana had fallen victim to a common trap: holding for too long in shitty weather in the hope of getting to your destination, all the while chewing through fuel that you might need if you are forced to divert to an alternate.[vii]

None of us were particularly critical of James Okana after his Waigani swamp adventure. *Let he who is without sin cast the first stone.* The truth was, we'd all come close to making the same mistake, so it seemed

---

[vii] *alternate* is an aviation term meaning your second choice airport if you can't get to your intended destination.

prudent to keep our mouths shut. I remember one Goilala trip in the Cessna 206, where I too had loitered for far too long (in the vicinity of Tapini), trying every attack angle — low level, high level, via different valley systems — to get in. When I was unsuccessful I set course for a return to Moresby to find that, like James Okana, I had foolishly used up most of my fuel. On final descent into Port Moresby I had one hand on the control column and one hand on the fuel selector (the Cessna 206 fuel selector has three positions: left wing tank/off/right wing tank. Fuel is drawn from only one of the tanks at a time to feed the engine). The right tank was indicating zero and the left tank was indicating a few litres above zero. I planned to run the right tank completely dry, then switch tanks as the engine coughed and spluttered, and hopefully make the airfield on what little fuel remained in the left tank. Pucker factor high! I made it that day (sometimes E stands for *Enough*, not *Empty*), but it was a bloody close call, and I never got sucked into holding due to bad weather for too long ever again.

The day after Okana's swamp landing I heard a knock on the door of the Air Manubada Office. A small gaggle of timid Goilala villagers pitter-pattered through the door to see us and asked Mack if we could do a coffin charter to Guari. You guessed it, they were James Okana's passengers, still trying to get the coffin and themselves home. There was a mumbled exchange of quotes and offers for the flight, a price was agreed on, a dirty wad of notes changed hands, and Mack headed out the door to load as many of them and their precious cargo as he could into P2-MFX, Air Manubada's Cessna 185.

I saw Mack on the tarmac after he got back from the charter. He was a particularly cheery chap any day of the week, but on this occasion his smile just about split his face, it was so wide and beaming. He told me about his flight. He had departed from Jacksons runway 32L, and climbed out over the Waigani swamp as he set course for Mount Yule and the Kamulai/Guari basin. The cabin was packed with villagers down the port side of the Cessna 185, with the coffin in the place of the seats down the starboard side, and assorted bags and tradestore goods sitting piled on the cabin floor and strapped under the cargo net that held the coffin in place. Also present, sprigs of bougainvillea, the ubiquitous Port

Moresby flowering plant that served as a cheap stand-in for lilies at PNG funerals. A coffin charter always involved a few springs of bougainvillea. The subtle aroma of these blooms mixed with the sharp antiseptic smell of embalming fluid (often leaking out of the coffin and dripping to the floor, where it crept along the seat tracks and mixed with the rice grains, sugar crystals and other detritus from the aircraft's life as a cargo-hauler) was the classic whiff of a PNG coffin charter. It was like your grandma's perfume mixed with a dead grandma.

As Mack climbed out over Waigani Swamp, and the aircraft passed overhead James Okana's crippled Islander, the passengers became very animated: pointing to the outline of the aircraft in the mud far below and yelling to each other over the noise of the engine. They were reliving their traumatic experience from the previous day. With them gesticulating and chattering away, Mack had a sudden evil thought. A dark and mischievous idea that crept to the front of his mind, grabbed it and refused to let go. Mack was disinclined to resist. At that moment he closed the Cessna's throttle, bringing the engine suddenly to idle. The nose dropped and the aircraft descended towards the swamp. The cabin was instantly quiet as the aircraft entered a power-off glide, and the clamorous drone of the engine was replaced with the hiss of the outside airflow. The passengers started screaming, struck with utter disbelief and horror that they were again facing a crash landing in the swamp. *Aiieeee! Mama! Mama! Balus em i bagarap gen!?!* (Shit! Is our aeroplane buggered-up again?) Mack let this scene develop for a few moments before reapplying full power, pulling up from the dive and climbing back to his cruise altitude. Cruel? Yes. Fair? Clearly not. Amusing? Most definitely.

Mack was known for his mischievous streak. One day I arrived at Ononge airstrip a few minutes behind him. The locals had been spooked by something and crowded around my aircraft asking to buy tickets to Port Moresby. I wondered why they were approaching me, when Mack sat in the empty Cessna 185 at the top of the strip, with no villagers anywhere near him. He was strangely silent. Once we got back to Moresby he explained what had happened. As he flared for landing at Ononge, a pair of village pigs ran out onto the strip in front of him and he had a hell of a time dodging them while retaining control of the Cessna 185 as he careened up Ononge's right-hand dogleg landing run. He'd had this happen to him once before, and had warned villagers on that occasion to "keep the bloody pigs OFF the strip!" This second near-collision with the porcine runway invaders really pissed him off so, after bringing the 185 to a stop at the top of the strip and shutting down the engine, he leapt out of the aircraft wild with rage and hell-bent on revenge. Mack pulled out his handgun, a 9mm Glock 17 and ran down the strip in search of the pigs. They were snuffling around about halfway down, rooting around in the scrub off to one side of the strip, and Mack let the bastards have it. He opened fire and the loud report of the weapon and the bullets ricocheting off the red-clay strip soon saw the pigs disappear into the bush, screeching and squealing as they went. Mack plodded back up to the top of the strip, panting and sweating like a bugger after his exertion. He turned to the stunned crowd of Ononge locals sitting at the top of the strip, the still-smoking gun in his hand: "Any passengers for Moresby?" he asked.

Stunned silence.

I picked up a full load of passengers out of Ononge later that same afternoon. Mack's plane was empty for a week!

One December afternoon, with the day's flying safely behind me, I stopped by at the Gateway Hotel adjacent to the entry gates to Jacksons Airport. I was making arrangements for a Christmas function for the newly formed Papua New Guinea Surfing Association. I was the Social Director, tasked with organising piss-ups. As one branded by the RNZAF as a pisshead I was, on paper at least, well qualified for this post. I ran into pilot Dave 'Sloppy' Alsop at the Hotel's downstairs pizza restaurant and heard the sad news there'd been a crash. Images of another pilot and his passengers lying mangled in a crushed aircraft wreckage filled my thoughts. Bloody hell. Not again.

Earlier that day Milne Bay Airways pilot Richard Goddard departed Gurney in a BN-2 Islander bound for Misima. The flight was a charter for Coecon Ltd, a local construction company, and five of their staff were on board. Goddard had been in PNG for just over one year. He'd arrived with minimal experience (less than 300 hours, holding a private pilot's licence only) and first flew for a church organisation in Kiunga in the Western Province, joining MBA in late September 1992 with 523 hours total time. Goddard was hired by MBA on the assumption that he would pass his commercial pilot's licence (CPL) flight test with DCA examiner Mark 'Cowboy' Wilcox, scheduled four days after he joined the airline. He did not pass the test however, with Wilcox not satisfied with his performance: "Richard was generally prepared in the systems of the Islander, but showed errors in general airmanship and handling . . . requires more training." The senior MBA pilot who had trained Goddard (let's call him Captain X) refused to give further instruction, saying he didn't want to "submit himself to the hassles again". This was an entirely inappropriate attitude for a check pilot tasked with the training of new company pilots: a captain entrusted with the responsibility to ensure rookies could operate safely in PNG's dangerous flying environment (more on oddball Captain X in Chapter 13). Subsequent to this, Goddard received further instruction from DCA pilot Allan Yarnold, who soon passed him as competent to hold a PNG CPL. But there were strings: it was a condition of the CPL issue that Goddard must first fly 20 hours of ICUS (in command under supervision) with another MBA captain before being allowed to fly solo on commercial operations. Over the next month this ICUS flying was carried out, with Goddard flying with Captain X as well as with MBA pilot John Wild Jnr. At the end of his ICUS flying with Goddard, Captain X wrote in a training report: "(Richard) still requires more exposure with safety pilot prior to flying by himself." Captain X listed six points that he felt Goddard should pay attention to. Point number five was of note: "Do not enter clouds". The last of the ICUS flying was overseen by John Wild Jnr. The pair flew almost 18 hours together, and at the end of the ICUS, Wild said of Richard Goddard, "He seemed a very capable pilot and I don't remember him ever doing anything stupid or unsafe".[45] Goddard was sent solo on MBA's commercial flights in the BN-2 Islander in November 1992.

Six weeks later he was dead.

Gurney's WWII-era airstrip lies on the western shore of, and is aligned pointing directly at, the wide and elongated horseshoe of Milne Bay. The Bay is 20 nm long and 6 nm wide, opening to the Solomon Sea to the east, with its narrow coastal strip crowded on its other three sides by mountain barriers. Goddard's route that December afternoon in 1992 saw him taking off from Gurney and flying out into Milne Bay on a direct track to Misima, which is a small volcanic island in the Louisade Archipelago, 150 nm east. The navigation is not difficult and the flight shouldn't have presented much of a challenge, as there are ground-based navigation aids at both airstrips, and the whole flight is over water. John Wild Jnr, who was flying in and around Gurney that day, reported that, although there was low cloud on the ranges and extensive cloud cover higher up, the visibility in the bay was OK. John said that to get to Misima, Goddard could have chosen to fly "under or over [the cloud], no problem." What happened next was a perplexing change in Goddard's flight routing. For reasons unknown, soon after take-off he elected to turn north and flew straight towards the cloud-covered 3000-foot-high mountains of the Alotau Peninsula's Stirling Range, Milne Bay's northern barrier. There are three possible reasons he elected to do this. One: Coecon Ltd had been involved in feasibility studies on a possible road project which might cross the peninsular at some suitable low point. His passengers may have asked him to make a diversion to the northern side of the peninsular so they could view the ranges from that side. Two: Goddard may have been carrying out a diversion due to weather on the direct track over the water to Misima and decided to track via the northern side of the Alotau Peninsular to get into smoother flying conditions (this seems unlikely, given the not-so-bad conditions in the weather report supplied by John Wild Jnr). Three: there may have been a mechanical problem with the aircraft and Goddard may have started a turn back towards Gurney airstrip, only to become distracted and maintain his course to the north in error. Whatever the reason, the Islander flew into cloud headed straight for the tops of the Stirling Range. A witness at Ahioma village, on the northern side of Milne Bay, saw the aircraft disappear into murky weather and noted it was heading in an unusual direction. He lost sight of it but concentrated on the engine noise. He heard the noise diminishing for about 90 seconds, then heard the sound of breaking trees and a loud bang followed by a noise like thunder and then a few seconds of harsh metallic ripping tearing sounds. Then total silence.

The MBA Islander impacted nose first into a near vertical rock face, then fell 20 feet into trees below. The impact force was estimated at 120 Gs. It was not survivable.

Post-accident, three different experts examined the engines retrieved from the wreckage. One stated that he believed the right engine had failed prior to impact. The other two disagreed, arguing that there were no technical faults with the aircraft and it had hit the terrain with cruise power set on both engines. Engine failure or not, it was hard to understand what could have caused Goddard to maintain a track pointing directly at the Stirling Range, when the safer lower ground (in fact, no ground at all, just the wide open expanse of Milne Bay) was just off to his right. Like a lot of PNG aircraft crashes before it and since, it just didn't make any sense. The accident report was dry in its summary: "For reasons unknown the pilot executed a major diversion from his flight planned track and flew directly towards steeply rapidly rising terrain and into cloud conditions considerably less than the legal minima."

For a few years the wreckage lay where it had impacted the vertical face of the ridgeline, a metallic-white smudge clearly visible against the green and grey of the mountainside. It was yet another sober reminder of what happened when things went bad in PNG aviation: not that we needed reminding. It had only been five weeks since the death of Peter Gill.

●

Chapter 7

Fuzzy Wuzzy Triffids

We learn little from victory, much from defeat.
JAPANESE PROVERB[46]

It's August 1942. Deniki village, seven kilometres from Kokoda. A member of the Australian Army's 30th Brigade stands tense under the eaves of a grass hut, his rifle raised and his eyes focused down the barrel, scanning the dense jungle ahead for movement.

Reinforcements are on the way, but for now he is one of just 79 Australian troops holding back a Japanese force numbering over 2000.[47] For four days the Australians have been locked in a deadly cat-and-mouse with the enemy, engaging in guerrilla-style probing attacks to delay and frustrate the Japanese advance. The opposing forces are battling for control of the Kokoda Track, the now-famous dirt trail across the Owen Stanley Range that links Port Moresby with Kokoda township and the north coast beachheads of Buna and Gona.

The Japanese were busy in early 1942 — occupying Rabaul and Kavieng in January, and continuing their invasion of the Australian-administered Territory of New Guinea with conquests of Lae and Salamaua in March. By July the 144th Regiment of the *Nankai Shitai* (the South Seas Detachment)[48], an invasion force from Rabaul, landed at Gona Mission on the north Papuan coast and began preparing for an overland assault on Port Moresby. Within the month they had 13,500

Our course car, 1951 Chevrolet 'Floyd'.

The author and RNZAF CT4-B Airtrainer, 1989

#189 Pilot Training Course.
Back row left to right: Logan Officer, Tim Robinson, Bruce Grant, Rob Fluit, Clark Malone, Grant Reidy.
Front row: George Chew, Kevin Walsh, the author, Grant Thompson, Colin Tan, Jason Easthope.

RNZAF Airtrainers practice formation flying over the Canterbury countryside.

The author's alpha and omega: my first RNZAF flight was in tail number 39, my chop flight was in #48.

Three shots taken on approach to land at Fane airstrip: elevation 4400ft, slope 12%, length 451m.

The Qantas Otter crash at Tapini, 1958. The 'Tapini ILS' is highlighted in the background.

Geoffrey Luck

Lined up for takeoff at Tapini. Elevation 3100ft, slope 4.5%, length 915m.

Giles Rooney

Guari airstrip. elevation 6100ft, slope 6.4%, length 600m.

Georgie and Ron McKie

On final approach into Kamulai. Elevation 5600ft, slope 11%, length 481m.

On approach into Sopu. Elevation 6500ft, slope 12%, length 532m.

A Trans Niugini Airways Cessna 185 at Sopu.

Ononge airstrip. The church that was strafed by the Japanese in World War II is visible behind the strip.

The Air Manubada fleet at Ononge: Cessna 206 P2-CBL and Cessna 185 P2-MFX.

An Airlines PNG twin Otter at Ononge airstrip. Elevation 5300ft, slope 7%, length 500m.

A view of Fane airstrip, looking downslope, in the takeoff direction.

The papua New Guinea bush pilots' workhorse: the Cessna 206.

Efogi airstrip in the 'Jungles'.
Elevation 3800ft, slope 9.5%, length 487m.

Kagi airstrip in the Jungles.
Elevation 4100ft, slope 12.5%, length 447m.

Georgie and Ron McKie

PNGDCA archives

Spectacular photos of the 1984 Douglas Airways crash at Kagi. Incredibly the pilot and passengers survived.

PNGDCA archives

troops ashore,[49] including two transportation companies (equipped with light trucks, bicycles, and 500 horses) and an engineering unit tasked with building a road across the Owen Stanley Range, the imposing wall of mountains standing between them and their goal.[50] Despite having no intelligence assessments on the condition of the village track that wound up and over the range, they chose to believe it was a 'motor track'.[51] Their overland invasion force was issued with half rations for 16 days, as the Japanese believed that once Kokoda and the top of the mountain range was attained it would be 'an easy downhill walk to the far coast', and Port Moresby would fall within eight days.[52] If the reader knows anything about the Owen Stanleys, they will realise this to be a ridiculous presumption.

Both the Japanese and Australian military commanders grossly underestimated the harshness of the terrain and the difficulty of getting men and equipment across this formidable mountain barrier. The Australian military, for their part, displayed a confused duplicity with respect to the Kokoda Track. Soon after the Japanese landed at Gona, the Australian commander Major General Morris gave the media his assessment of the situation: there *was* some kind of track over the mountains; it was rare that a white man had traversed the range; there was no chance a battalion of Japanese could make it across intact; it was a *boong* track[viii] and nothing else.[53] If Morris had done his homework he would have learned that the first Europeans to traverse the Track had done so in 1904; since then it had been an officially recognised overland mail route for the Australian Administration.[54] Later, in complete contradiction to his earlier assessment, Morris asked a subordinate to investigate the possibility of building a road across the Owen Stanleys to Kokoda.[55] The Kokoda Track was never surveyed or reconnoitred however, and its true nature remained a mystery to the higher echelons of the Allied forces.

There was also confusion on both sides about the nature of the Kokoda 'Gap', with an idea existing that it was a narrow mountain pass, only an arms-width wide, that could easily be defended by a few men

---

[viii] a track made and utilised by villagers only.

who could hold a much larger force at bay.[56] Or simply blown up, with this suggestion coming from Allied Commander Douglas MacArthur's chief of staff: " . . . the pass may be readily blocked by demolition with TNT."[57] All this was complete hogwash — the gap is actually a 10km-wide plateau, 7000 feet above sea level, in between the towering 9000 to 12,000 foot peaks of the surrounding range.

The Track itself, between Owers' Corner near Port Moresby and the northern coast airstrip and village at Kokoda, is 96 kilometres long. Its brutal ups and downs add up to an incredible 10,000 metres of vertical terrain, an amount equivalent to scaling Mount Everest from sea level. The Kokoda Track is not for the faint-of-heart, nor the unsure-of-step. Even now, almost 70 years after the War, it is nothing more than a narrow dirt trail, snaking its way up and over the harsh jungle-cloaked mountains. I ran it non-stop and solo in 2011 (competing in the annual 'Kokoda Challenge' race), and can assure you its torturous length is still very much like it was at the height of the Kokoda Track campaign in 1942, when it was described by Australian Colonel Kingsley Norris:

Imagine an area of approximately 100 miles in length. Crumple and fold this into a series of ridges, each rising higher and higher until seven thousand feet is reached, then declining in ridges to three thousand feet. Cover this thickly with jungle, short trees and tall trees, tangled with great entwining savage vines. Through the oppression of this density cut a little native track, two or three feet wide, up the ridges, over the spurs, round gorges and down across swiftly flowing mountain streams. Where the track clambers up the mountainsides, cut steps — big steps, little steps, steep steps — or clear the soil from the tree roots. Every few miles, bring the track through a small patch of sunlit kunai grass, or an old deserted native garden, and every seven or ten miles build a group of dilapidated grass huts — as staging shelters — generally set in a foul, offensive clearing . . . About midday and through the night, pour water on the forest so that the steps become broken, and a continual yellow stream flows downwards, and the few level areas become pools and puddles of putrid, black mud. In the high ridges above Myola, drip this water day and night over the track through a fetid forest grotesque with moss and glowing phosphorescent fungi.[58]

The Kokoda Track saw some of the Pacific theatre's most bitter fighting, and marked what one writer called a 'pivotal point in Australian awareness,'[59] with Australians fighting for their homeland without the help of larger and more powerful friends. The battle for control of the Track raged for six months. It was a muddy, bloody, desperate tussle, with close-quarter fighting: neither side would yield, and every inch of the Track was a fierce tooth-and-nail struggle. Not only were Japanese and Australian troops facing off against each other, they had to deal with dysentery, pneumonia, all manner of skin infections, trench foot, and endemic tropical diseases such as scrub typhus, malaria and dengue fever. It has been estimated that for every battle casualty there were 4.8 tropical disease casualties.[60] The New Guinea jungle was a truly horrid place to be fighting; aptly described by author Peter Brune as 'a bastard of a place'.

The turning point came two months in, when the Japanese reached their furthest point of advance, the Ioribaiwa Ridge, just 46 kilometres from Port Moresby.[61] By this time they were a spent force, with the supply line weaving behind them all the way back to Buna and Gona on the north coast terribly overextended. Japanese troops were critically short of ammunition and food: they were rationed a mere four tablespoons of cooked rice twice daily, and only got this if it hadn't already been pilfered by troops further down the line.[62] On 18 September, after the Japanese captured Ioribaiwa Ridge from the Australian defenders, a Japanese officer wrote: "Transportation of rations reported to be difficult. How will we live in our present condition without any food? In another few days we will have to eat roots or tree-bark . . . Heard distant rifle shots, slept and dreamed of home".[63]

The South Seas Detachment was by now harassed from every angle, with stiff Australian infantry resistance, persistent Allied bombing runs on the Japanese beachhead at Buna[64], and daylight strafing of their positions on the Track by RAAF Kittyhawks out of Port Moresby. Reeling from military setbacks in parallel operations at Milne Bay (200nm east of Port Moresby) and Guadalcanal in the Solomon Islands, and unable to guarantee a robust supply line over the Owen Stanleys to their frontline troops, the Japanese high command at HQ in Rabaul was forced to order a withdrawal all the way back to Isurava and Kokoda on 23 September.[65] Australian newspaper reporter Geoff Reading passed through Ioribaiwa Ridge soon after the Japanese retreat, writing: " . . . the Jap column had withered in the mountains and drawn back, like a tentacle of a mortally wounded octopus."[66] Australian troops were delighted to see the Japanese finally on the back foot.

By the time the campaign was over, six months to the day since the Japanese landings on the north coast, Allied forces had prevailed and driven the Japanese all the way back to Buna and Gona. But the cost was high — 2019 Australians had been killed,[67] with many more wounded or sick. The US Army joined in at the closing stages of the campaign and lost nearly 700 troops.[68] The Japanese dug in at their north coast beachheads and, in the absence of a full evacuation option, chose to die fighting rather than face the humiliation of surrender. They dutifully followed the *Bushido* (warrior) tenet of *gyokusai* — honourable suicide. Japanese losses from all causes for the six month campaign have been estimated at a staggering 13,000.[69]

Today the Kokoda Track has a special place in Australian military history, and walking in the footsteps of the brave defenders of Port Moresby has become something of a pilgrimage. Guided hikes of the track (lasting from four to seven days) have become increasingly popular — in 2010 over 4000 made the journey. This popularity has been a boon to the villagers along the track, with tour companies employing locals as guides and porters as well as sourcing food and produce from them, and paying to use village land as camping sites en route. The Koiari people more than deserve this economic stimulus: their kinsmen made a significant contribution to the Australian victory — toiling as supply carriers up the track and returning as stretcher bearers, manhandling the sick and the wounded to rear-area aid stations. More than a few Australian diggers owed their lives to the Papua New Guinean labourers enlisted in this work by the Allied war machine, carriers who earned the proud nickname *Fuzzy Wuzzy Angels*. These men were immortalised in a poem, written by Royal Australian Engineers Private Bert Beros. Here is an excerpt:[70]

> *Bringing back the badly wounded,*
> *Just as steady as a horse,*
> *Using leaves to keep the rain off,*
> *And as gentle as a nurse.*
>
> *Slow and careful in bad places,*
> *On the awful mountain track,*
> *The look upon their faces,*
> *Would make you think Christ was black . . .*
>
> *May the mothers of Australia,*
> *When they offer up a prayer,*
> *Mention those impromptu angels,*
> *With the fuzzy wuzzy hair.*

Approximately 3000 local carriers were involved in the campaign,[71] employed by ANGAU — the Australian New Guinea Administration Unit — a military organisation which replaced the Australian civil administration during the War.

The most famous of the carriers was Raphael Oimbari, who was photographed by combat cameraman George Silk on Christmas Day 1942. That day Oimbari was one of five PNG nationals assisting Private George Whittington, an Australian soldier wounded in the battle for Buna. The photograph of Oimbari and Whittington has become the definitive image of the Fuzzy Wuzzy Angels.

Oimbari, a quiet unassuming villager from Hanau, near Popondetta, was one of the few Fuzzy Wuzzies to receive official recognition for his wartime efforts. He received the Order of the British Empire in 1993 and was given a state funeral on his death in 1996.[72] There are monuments to him and to all the Fuzzy Wuzzy Angels at several locations in PNG and Australia, including the Museum at Kokoda, Remembrance Park in Port

George Whittington and 'fuzzy wuzzy angel' Raphael Oimbari, December 1942.

Australian War Memorial

Moresby and at ANZAC Square in Brisbane.

The renewed interest in all things Kokoda, and the addition of a hike of the Kokoda Track to Australians' bucket list has not been without drama. It is a wonderful thing to tread in the footsteps of the Kokoda campaign troops; to see what they saw; to experience the hardship they faced as they trudged up and down the muddy track in that 'bastard of a place'; to see some of the village airstrips and WWII battlegrounds en route; to see Kokoda village. But an exposure to the Owen Stanley Range, its jagged peaks and swirling mists and unforgiving dead-end valleys, comes with risk. Perhaps aware of this, perhaps not, 11 passengers (nine

Australians, a Japanese businessman, and a Kokoda local) boarded a DHC-6 Twin Otter in Port Moresby on 11 August 2009 for a scheduled flight (Airlines PNG Flight CG4684) to Kokoda. Journalist Rory Callinan later wrote about the passengers and crew:

> The Australians were a diverse group, but all were heading to Kokoda, united in their desire to walk the rugged trail to honour the sacrifices of Australian troops who died there fighting the Japanese during World War II. There was dairy farmer Max Cranwell and his daughter Leanne Harris, a mother of two. Bendigo bank manager Peter Holliday and his cousin Euan Comrie, an actor and social worker, were walking in memory of Pete's uncle, the late commando Edward "Ted" Holliday. There were also two young women who planned to walk the track and then finish off their holiday with a relaxing few days of scuba diving: occupational therapist Kelly Weire and her friend Hannah Kinross, who had just received word she had been accepted to act as a refugee youth worker in local schools. June Canavan, a sports medicine doctor, and Keith Gracie, a construction company owner and father of two, were doing the trek to raise money for a school in Tanzania. Their guide for the tour was a fit young fireman, Matthew Leonard, doing his first trek as leader of the group for the Victorian-based No Roads tour company. Perhaps wondering at the irony of his presence, given Kokoda's place in his country's military history, was Japanese jeweller Katsuo. And sitting in the back of the plane was well-known Kokoda local Kingsley Eroro, postmistress Grace's husband. Kingsley was returning from a stint working at the mines. Responsibility for these 11 lives lay with two young PNG pilots, Captain Jannie Moala, 26, and co-pilot Royden Sauka, 33.[73]

At 1052 the Airlines PNG Twin Otter departed Port Moresby, setting course for the Kokoda Gap, 38 nautical miles to the north-east. The planned route, scheduled to take just 28 minutes, followed the Kokoda Track all the way to the Gap, climbing to an altitude of 9000 feet AMSL before an immediate descent into the Kokoda Valley on the other side of the Owen Stanley Range. Weather at the departure end was fine, with a light southerly breeze rolling in from Bootless Bay, a few broken clouds at 1500 feet AGL, and a visibility in excess of 10 km. The weather forecast for the Kokoda end was not fantastic (significant cloud layers down to 500 AGL, isolated thunderstorms, and areas of reduced visibility in showers and drizzle), but was typical for a late morning flight over the Owen Stanley Mountains, and typical for Kokoda, an airstrip in the lee of the ranges well known for experiencing regular substantial rainfall. There are no navigation aids at the airstrip at Kokoda, so the last part of the flight was to involve a visual descending segment where the pilots would be expected to use a combination of their GPS (satellite navigation) position and the mark-one eyeball to stay clear of the significant terrain around Kokoda and safely descend from 9000 feet in the Gap to the strip (elevation 1270ft AMSL) and make an approach and landing.

Nineteen minutes into the flight the crew made a call on the Kokoda area pilot-to-pilot VHF radio frequency, reporting they were inbound to " . . . Kokoda via the Kokoda Gap on descent now through the Gap." Actual weather reports from pilots in the area at the time indicated that there was a solid bank of cloud situated at the junction of the Kokoda Gap and the Kokoda valley, making visual flight (staying clear of cloud) difficult. Eight seconds later the Airlines PNG crew received a cautionary call from the pilot of P2-KST, a Hevilift Twin Otter departing Kokoda on climb for the Gap and the track to Port Moresby (the reciprocal flight path of the inbound Airlines PNG flight). The pilot of P2-KST replied to their call: "Copied, climbing to 10,000 feet will be maintaining 10,000 feet, *just be careful*." (author's emphasis).

Careful they were not.

Just 90 seconds later the Airlines PNG Twin Otter hit the heavily timbered eastern slope of the Kokoda Gap at about 5700 ft AMSL, 11km south-east of Kokoda airstrip. The aircraft was destroyed by impact forces.

There were no survivors.[74]

Almost immediately a team of accident investigators from the PNG Department of Civil Aviation and the Australian Transport Safety Bureau began working at the wreckage site, hoping to shed light on the reason for the crash. They looked closely at the Twin Otter's airframe and flight controls, engines and propellers, fuel system, and the on-board flight instruments and electronic components able to be recovered from the debris. They looked at medical and pathological information passed to them after the recovery and identification of the flight crew, and the grim business of their respective autopsies. Neither pilot exhibited any abnormalities in terms of general health (the co-pilot had coronary artery heart disease, but it was considered unlikely this was a factor), and toxicological testing (for drugs and alcohol) came up negative. The aircraft systems that could be inspected were found to have been serviceable at the time of the crash and not to have contributed to the accident.

The investigation concluded that the accident was probably the result of controlled flight into terrain (CFIT): that is, an otherwise airworthy aircraft was unintentionally flown into the mountainside, with little or no awareness by the crew of the impending collision. The final report stated: '. . . it was probable that during the descent, the crew was required to manoeuvre the aircraft to remain clear of cloud, or regain that status, and in doing so, impacted terrain.'[75]

Flying in the mountains of PNG is like balancing on a knife edge. Sadly, on that day in 2009, the dreams of the nine Australians to walk the famous Kokoda Track came to an sudden and tragic end when they fell from the knife edge into the abyss.

My association with the area began in 1992, when Mack Lee checked me into the Koiari (*coy-ya-ree*) airstrips of the Central Province. Most of these strips are actually on the Kokoda Track itself — servicing the villages that dot the serpentine vein of the Track. They were known collectively as 'The Jungles' by the Moresby-based bush pilots. In October of '92 Mack and I strapped into the Air Manubada Cessna 206, P2-CBL, departing Jacksons runway 14R with a wide reversal turn over the blue-green waters of Bootless Bay. We set course to the north-east, climbing to 5000 feet and passing over the Varirata National Park lookout, a sheer bluff on the western extremity of the Astrolabe Range. Beneath me I could see the Sogeri Road twisting up the gorge to our east, and the white explosion of spray and wispy vapour downstream of the Sirinumu Dam, where the Laloki River leaps down a rock face to form the double-tiered Rouna Falls. The patchy scrub-covered hills rose to meet the Sogeri Plateau, the landscape highlighted here and there with the grey-black scars of dry season burn-offs and orderly stands of army-green rubber plantations. It wasn't long before I could make out the first of the Jungle strips (airstrips are plentiful in the Koiaris — there are eight different village landing grounds within a 5nm radius, centred just 30nm NE of Port Moresby). In 1942, with the Japanese advance stretching from the northern beachheads across the Owen Stanley Range and creeping ever closer to their prize — Port Moresby — Royal Australian Air Force and US Army Air Force aircraft strafed and bombed the Kokoda Track. Seen from the cockpit of the Cessna, the Jungle airstrips appeared as if they too had been scattered haphazardly, higgledy-piggledy like bomb scars on the rugged terrain beneath us: Naoro in a dead-end river valley on the eastern shoulder of 5000 foot-high Mt. Shera; Manari four miles to the NE, perched on a sliver of land at a jungle-choked three-way river junction; a further four miles out the trio of Efogi, Kagi and Bodinumu, each on different spurs within the same tight valley, menacingly hemmed in by the towering peaks of the Owen Stanley Range; on the same ridgeline as Kagi but 1000 feet higher up — Nadunumu; just above these four strips, on the 7000 foot-high grassy plateau between Mt Bellamy and the Kokoda Gap — Myola; and finally, just five miles north-west, but in a completely different valley system, Manumu.

The Jungle strips were a gnarly bunch. All were short, averaging 480 metres long. All were one-way airstrips, with slope varying between 2.5 and 12.5%. All were hot 'n' high, with elevations between 1800 and 6700 feet AMSL. All were surrounded by significant terrain, and at four of the strips (Bodinumu, Kagi, Efogi and Manari) you were committed to land once you turned onto final approach 400 feet above the level of the strip. These four were *no-go-around* airstrips — if a pilot attempted to abort a landing below this critical point, turning away in the hope of climbing and returning for a further landing attempt, they would impact the terrain encircling these airstrips. The aircraft simply wouldn't be able to outclimb the surrounding mountains. Finally, the Jungle airstrips were all in such close proximity, especially Kagi, Efogi, Bodinumu and Nadunumu, there was a significant risk of aircraft colliding when in their respective circuit areas. Strict and careful adherence to standard radio calls and procedures and an eagle-eyed lookout were vital in the Jungles.

One of the common sector pairings on Jungle runs was a flight between Kagi and Efogi. This sector was reputed to be one of the shortest Regular Public Transport (RPT) flights in the world. Mack observed me as I flew the sector on that day in 1992: I lined the Cessna up at the top of the strip, ran through my before take-off checks, called Moresby on HF radio, made a quick call to possible circuit traffic on the VHF radio, and applied full power while standing on the brakes. A check of the Ts and Ps (temperature and pressure readings from the aircraft engine gauges), full back stick, and brakes release. The Cessna, with a light load of me and Mack and two passengers and their bags, leapt down Kagi's 12.5% down-slope like Usain Bolt off the blocks. In the blink of an eye the Cessna hit flying speed (about 55 knots) and jumped into the air. I released the back pressure on the stick and held her close to the deck as the speed increased, and we launched into the void off the sheer end of Kagi's threshold. Kagi and Efogi are so close (less than 2 nm apart), as soon as we were airborne from Kagi we were already on a base leg for Efogi. Things were going to happen *very* quickly.

The airspeed was increasing towards 90 knots and I set cruise power to rein it in. I also levelled off, holding 4200 feet on the altimeter and trimming forward to take the pressure off the stick. Now, less than 30 seconds after take-off, I eyeballed the threshold of Efogi airstrip, just coming into sight out the left window, 400 feet below us, one mile to run. Power back, speed below 100, select flap 30, quick call on VHF telling area traffic I'm turning final for Efogi, trim for a slight descent, and turn 90 degrees left to align with the strip. Propeller pitch lever full forward, power back, attitude for 70 knots; full flap, push and trim forward to cancel balloon from flap 40. Precision flying now, maintain aim point at second cone marker in on the 487 metre-long undulating grass strip.

Check windsock. It's calm today. Approaching the threshold, nose up, power back, speed target now 65 knots. The ground rises to meet us, filling my peripheral vision left and right. Trees and banana palms flashing under the nose as we approach the threshold. About to make contact, fly the aircraft to the grass abeam the second cone marker. No margin for error — if I float, missing the aim point, we'll skid off the end of the strip into the jungle. Flare. Power off, hold nose up to arrest rate of descent. Stall warning horn sounds as we touch down. Flaps to zero, hold nose off, modulating pitch attitude to ride the bumps. Moderate braking, counter resulting nose-down pitch with more back stick. Speed under control as we come to the end of the strip, keep up momentum sufficient to pull into parking bay, staying clear of the welcoming villagers gathered stripside. Park brake on, cowl flaps closed. Throttle to idle. Call on HF radio to Moresby cancelling SARWATCH. Avionics switch off, fuel master to cut-off, master switch off. Prop stopped, sector complete. Headset off, look across at Mack. We both smiled like kids at a carnival. From take-off to landing the whole thing had taken about two minutes.

Mack showed me all the Jungle strips over the course of several combined revenue/training flights over the next week or so, and signed me off to operate into all of them solo. While Air Manubada's bread and butter remained the strips of the Goilalas, I was to fly a couple of times a week into the Jungles too, mostly on charter flights and vege-runs when we flew vegetables and fruit back to Port Moresby.

One odd thing about operating into the Jungle strips was the stark contrast in the village temperament between communities that were so geographically close (and so small — none of the Koiari villages held more than 300 people). When the Australian Administration had first proposed an overland route between Port Moresby and Kokoda, in 1900, one official said of the Koiari (Jungle) locals: "They are treacherous, truculent, aggressive, cruel and cunning. They are cannibals from a sheer love of human flesh, and hunt each other simply to gratify their carnivorous desires. They fight treacherously and lie abominably."[76] Thankfully, this was no longer the case in the 1990s, but the reception pilots received on arrival at each Jungle strip was very different, based on each village's innate character. Bodinumu and Kagi were ghost towns

— there was hardly ever anyone at the side of the strip, and I operated into these ports many times only ever seeing my own passengers. These villagers were either not interested in the comings and goings at their airstrip, or they stayed out of sight. Efogi, just two miles away, was the polar opposite. There was always a large welcoming committee at the top of the grassy strip, with smiling tradestore owners, random villagers, youths and children. The place had a real family vibe. I felt like a rock star arriving in Efogi, they were that warm and friendly. The Manaris were the oddest bunch. Here it was neither deserted nor crowded. The villagers were there alright, but they were shy and withdrawn. No smiles. No welcome. Adults avoided eye contact like I was a modern-day Medusa; toddlers hid behind their mother's legs, peeking out at the white stranger climbing out of the *balus*.

The standard Jungles load was people and tradestore goods into the mountains, people and produce back to Moresby. Mondays and Thursdays were vege-run days, with the Koiari villagers stacking bags of fruit and vegetables strip-side. It was not uncommon to fly several tonnes of produce back to Moresby on these days, involving multiple trips to multiple airstrips with a gaggle of aircraft from both TNA and Air Manubada. After unloading their cargo at Jacksons Airport the villagers would truck the fruit and vegetables to Port Moresby's markets, to be sold at stalls run by their *wantoks*, then fly home to the Koiari strips to repeat the process a few days later. The subsistence crops taken to market included kaukau (sweet potato), plantains, yams, taro, bananas and cassava. The produce was presented to the pilots in one of two ways at the Jungle airstrips: either in hessian sacks, or in large banana-leaf-wrapped bundles held together by vines or string. We called these organic green parcels 'Triffids,' as they seemed to swarm and multiply once they had been loaded onto the aircraft (and had the same air of malevolence as their 1960s silver-screen namesakes). How was it that there were always more unloaded after landing in Moresby than you had allowed to be loaded prior to departure? The Koiari villagers had no appreciation or care for aircraft performance of course, and wanted to get as much produce as possible to the Port Moresby markets to maximise profits. So they would sneak extra bundles of Triffids (and vege-filled hessian sacks) on board when the pilot wasn't looking. This could easily lead to a near-death experience, when an aircraft refused to fly at the critical point during a take-off roll due to being well above maximum certified take-off weight. I'm sure all of the pilots of the Jungle runs know what I'm talking about. TNA's Dave 'Sarge' Sarginson, master of the understatement, had an article on PNG flying published in *NZ Wings* magazine in mid 1993. In it he related one of those *'I have a friend who did something stupid'* stories, a thinly disguised self-incriminating tale of Triffids:

"To avoid overloading pilots estimate the load by lifting each bag. Failure here can result in a really nasty experience. Recently 1100kgs instead of 800 was mistakenly loaded on an Islander at a marginal one-way strip, the error becoming very apparent during the final 50 metres. Fortunately the aircraft was able to make it over the threshold and sink down the valley to gain flying speed, leaving its pilot much more experienced."

I chatted with Sarge in New Zealand 15 years after his article was published, and got the *real* story. The airstrip concerned was Efogi: "I nearly bought it that day! The take-off roll was sluggish. Over the hump down the hill and was not looking good. It was too late to stop. Had 60 knots at the bottom but she did not want to fly. Made the big break at the last second and was good to clear the high grass at the end. Fucking banana tree in the windscreen! No chance of over it, no speed to bank and go round, so I skidded to get it out of the window and cleaned it up with the left main gear. Some of it stayed there 'til Moresby. She staggered over the rest of the grass and I poled forward down into the gully. Lost some height, gained some speed and flew off to Moresby where I weighed it . . . I had 1400 kg of Triffids on board: 500kgs over!"

There was a long history of pilots having fun and games in the Jungles. When I flew there the still-visible wrecks of three BN-2 Islanders, a Cessna 172 and a GAF Nomad were a constant reminder that the job was not to be taken lightly. In 1984 Douglas Airways pilot A S Shaw became one of the few PNG bush pilots to have a crash recorded on film. His fun and games took place at Kagi.

Shaw was new to Douglas Airways and, although an experienced BN-2 Islander pilot (with almost 1000 hours on type), he had never flown the BN-2 into the Jungles prior to joining the company. One morning he made an approach into Kagi, with six passengers on board and a load of supplies for some Australian Army reservists who were waiting for him at the airstrip. On short final approach Shaw later reported the aircraft experienced substantial sink rate and height loss, and when the application of full power didn't seem to help, he elected to carry out a missed approach. He made a very steep turn to the left at low level towards the Bodinumu Valley, but the aircraft stalled (an aircraft stalls when the wing is no longer producing sufficient lift to sustain controlled flight) and continued to descend, with the bank angle increasing towards an alarming 80 degrees. Shaw had put his aircraft into a state of flight that was simply not recoverable. The aircraft fell out of the sky, impacting a tree and crashing into a scrub-covered slope left wing first, abeam and 35 metres below the level of the strip. Luckily for the seven occupants of the aircraft, the Australian Army personnel waiting and watching strip-side at Kagi were able to run to the accident site within a few minutes and pull them from the smouldering wreckage. Three passengers were unhurt, three had serious injuries, and pilot Shaw had sustained a broken left leg and ankle. The Army reservists moved them to the airstrip and administered first aid. Soon after this the wrecked aircraft exploded in a fireball, destroying all of the cargo and 60% of the fuselage.

As usual, the details of the accident flight, including a statement from the pilot, were subsequently passed to the PNG Department of Civil Aviation (PNGDCA), whose Safety Department was tasked with establishing cause, and making recommendations to try to prevent such a crash in the future. The accident investigator's job was made a lot easier when it was discovered one of the Army reservists had snapped photos of the Islander as it crashed. The photos are spectacular, yet disturbing. They show the aircraft just prior to impact, with full flap, full back elevator, and full right rudder. With a bank angle of 80 degrees and an estimated indicated airspeed of 60 knots, the stall speed was calculated to be 96 knots. Once Shaw made his steep left turn at low level, a crash was the only possible outcome (Kagi is one of the Jungle *no-go-around* strips). Looking at the shocking pre-impact photo sequence, you realise how lucky the occupants were to survive. It's a testament to the rugged design of the BN-2 Islander that they got away with it.

Using the photos as well as all the other data at hand, the accident investigators gave the following opinion as to cause: 'Because of a lack of proficiency the pilot failed to maintain the correct approach profile and he incorrectly decided to discontinue the approach by attempting a steep turn at low airspeed.'" While investigators agreed the presence of windshear (rapid changes in wind speed and direction, in this case from a very strong wind on approach to almost zero wind at the airstrip) may have been an environmental factor, they pointed out that this is a normal aspect of operations into mountain strips. The report was critical of 'inefficiencies in the check and training and strip endorsement systems as practised by the company' (Douglas Airways), adding that an in-depth assessment of Shaw's abilities did not appear to have been made, particularly in regard to short-field operations. An inspection of company training files revealed Shaw had only flown three Jungles training flights (with landings at Bodinumu, Manari, Kagi, Efogi and Manumu) before being sent solo on Douglas Airways' commercial flights. When the Douglas Airways training captain who had overseen Shaw's training attempted to argue that Shaw had extensive prior experience in the Jungle strips through his previous job with Central Air Services, it was pointed out to him that Central Air Services did not operate BN-2 Islanders (Shaw had been operating the single-engine Cessna 206 into the Jungles in his last job). Investigators felt that Douglas Airways should have given a pilot unfamiliar with operating the BN-2 Islander into the tricky Jungle strips much more training prior to letting him loose on the travelling public.

Two weeks after I was checked into the Jungle strips I flew a charter from Moresby to rarely used Myola, the highest of the Jungle ports, to drop off a pair of Australian trekkers who were going to hike from the Myola Plateau all the way back to Port Moresby, exploring the southern half of the Kokoda Track. While this is commonplace nowadays, in the early 1990s it was a rare thing. I got them there safely, dropping them off at Myola's soggy parking bay, and helping them disgorge their load of backpacks, sleeping rolls, cooking utensils and boxes of food and supplies. A local guide and a team of porters waited for them strip-side.

All of the Jungle strips dripped with WWII history, but especially Myola. The location for the strip was discovered by ANGAU Lieutenant Bert Kienzle, who was a rubber planter and a miner at Kokoda prior to his enlistment.[78] He recalled seeing some dry lake beds behind Kagi on pre-war flights between Kokoda and Port Moresby, and in August 1942 decided to reconnoitre the area. His diary recounts the exploratory patrol: *3 August — We broke camp at 0700 hrs and arrived at the first dry lake at 0725 hrs. It presented a magnificent sight — a large patch of open country right on top of the main range of the Owen Stanley Range. It was just the very thing I had been looking for to assist us in beating the Japanese.*[79] Kienzle had discovered a clear and flat area suitable for supply drops, although the lake beds were covered in sharp reeds and very wet and boggy. He named the area Myola after the wife of a friend. It was an important find, with author Peter Brune going so far as to say that 'Kienzle's Myola discovery was the logistical turning point of the campaign'.[80] Myola soon became a major Australian advance supply depot, with most troops diverted from the original Track north of Kagi (the pre-war mail route), instead following Kienzle's new trail across and up to the 7000 foot-high Myola Plateau 8 km to the east. Initially, there was no airstrip here, so food, weapons, ammunition, mail, and medical stores were dropped from super low level by 'biscuit bombers' (Douglas C-47 cargo planes). The retrieval rate of goods delivered in this way was only 50%, as most were dropped without parachutes, and supplies were often lost in the jungle or badly damaged on landing. Actual film footage of these daredevil drops feature in Australian Damien Parer's 1942 Oscar-winning documentary, *Kokoda Frontline*. In grainy black-and-white, a C-47 releases packages out of its left rear door over the clearing at Myola. Koiari villagers point to the sky, a mix of fear and excitement on their faces as they observe this strange metallic beast ejecting its load. The C-47 finishes its low-level run, with the last of the supply packs impacting the earth, and barely pulls up over the trees at the far end.

Once the Japanese had been turned back at Ioribaiwa Ridge and retreated as far as the Kokoda Gap, two field hospitals were set up at Myola, and Australian engineers began to work on an airstrip. It was hoped that medivac flights would soon be possible — allowing the air evacuation of the wounded and the sick direct to Port Moresby. The strip was ready in October 1942, but was too short for large military transporters. Two small Red Cross planes made the first landings at Myola, but they could only evacuate one patient at a time.[81] The first landing of a large aircraft was made by civilian pilot Tom O'Dea, in one of Guinea Airways' Ford 5-AT Trimotors (more on Guinea Airways and the Trimotors in Chapter 11). O'Dea departed Myola carrying eight patients, with bystanders watching nervously as his aircraft staggered off the end of the soggy runway, reluctantly crawling into the sky, and disappearing behind the plateau's western ridge. His aircraft's performance was severely limited by the high elevation of Myola's runway (6,700 ft AMSL). O'Dea completed the medivac flight, delivering the patients to Port Moresby and bravely returned to Myola, but this time his wheels bogged during the landing run and the Trimotor flipped onto its back. The aircraft was pushed to the side of the airstrip, where it lay for the next 37 years. It was recovered by the RAAF in 1979,[82] when it was slung underneath a powerful Chinook helicopter and moved to its current resting place at the Modern History Museum on Ahuia Street in Port Moresby.

A present-day point of interest at Myola is the wreckage of a US Army Air Force Curtiss P-40E Warhawk (this single-engine fighter/ground attack aircraft was known by British Commonwealth forces as the Kittyhawk). I visited the wreck in 1992, the day I dropped off the two trekkers at Myola. Their local guide invited me to join them to check it out, and we hiked a short distance to the tree line. This was my first time in the PNG jungle, and I remember more about that part of the hike than about the WWII aircraft remains. We left the bright, open Myola lake beds behind us and plunged into the thick forest. It was like entering another world. Within a few short steps there was nothing but green — no sky, no noise — just an eerie quiet, a clammy darkness beneath the

The Guinea Airways Ford 5–AT Trimotor that crahed at Myola, 1942.

heavy canopy, our muted footfalls and the oppressive embrace of the jungle. Soon enough we stopped at pile of twisted metal near the base of a rain tree. One wing stood vertical against the tree, the other lay flat some yards away, the R M and Y of its 'ARMY' markings still bold against the faded green of the wing undersurface.

The engine lay on the ground nearby, completely torn from the fuselage. A part-buried propeller blade pointed skywards between the engine and the rain tree, reaching up from the dank soil like the arm of a drowning man. This P-40E Warhawk is probably the one flown by American Robert Howard of the 49th Fighter Group on 8 November 1942. Howard had engine trouble over the Kokoda Gap and elected to make an emergency landing at Myola. He was unable to stop his aircraft in the short confines of the Myola runway, and overran the strip, crashing into the jungle at the far end.[83] Howard survived, but with severe injuries to his face. Soc Kienzle, son of Bert, the man who discovered the Myola Plateau, told me the story that, as the concussed

American airman was wheeled into the operating room, he passed a pre-crash photo of himself to the doctor and asked, "Can you make me look like this?"[84] There are a further five or six WWII Warhawks/Kittyhawks still missing in the Myola area.[85]

December 1992 heralded the end of my first calendar year in-country, and also brought the annual north-west monsoon. This annual cycle, Port Moresby's wet season, would prove to be a bitch, with six months of extensive cloud cover, heavy rainfall, and ragged weather from passing cyclonic weather systems. It was a frustrating time of the year to be a bush pilot. At least once a week the weather would be so clagged in around Jacksons airport that none of us could venture into the mountains. The bigger operators — Air Niugini, Talair, and Milne Bay Airways — weren't affected as much, as they had fully IFR (instrument flight rules) certified aircraft and flight crew, and simply launched into the soup on an instrument flight plan. This was generally not an option for the General Aviation piston aircraft operators on the field — Air Manubada, Trans Niugini Airways (TNA), Simbu Aviation, North Coast Aviation and the missionary flyers — so we sat around the airfield waiting for the weather to lift.

One morning, the third in a row where none of us had launched, I got sick of the waiting game and decided to try to get up to the Jungles. It was a really miserable day, with low scud almost down to the ground, and limited visibility in light showers. There was a tiny break in the cloud in the Moresby circuit area and I could just make out the base of Mount Lawes, five miles to the NNE. It was worth a crack. Jimma and I loaded up the Cessna 206 and I taxied out to the runway, obtaining clearance for a departure climbing on the 050 radial from the Port Moresby VOR (VFR route golf). I was licensed and approved to operate under VFR conditions only (staying in sight of ground or water at all times, and navigating by visual reference to ground features), but this flight didn't stay VFR for long. Soon after take-off from runway 14R, as I completed a reversal turn and picked up the 050 radial at about 1000 AGL, I encountered thin wispy layers of cloud and then, almost immediately, the cloud closed in around me. My frustration at having been grounded for two days got the better of me, so rather than turn back I kept climbing, completely blind and now outside the bounds of my licence. What I was doing was technically illegal, but I still considered it safe enough, as P2-CBL was equipped with a VOR CDI (course deviation indicator) display, and a digital DME (distance-measuring equipment) readout. I was able to fly on instruments alone, closely tracking the 050 radial and keeping an eye on the DME. I knew that as long as I stayed on this course and climbed to at least 3000 feet by seven miles, and 6000 feet by 25 miles, I would be above the terrain. This was the theory anyway. As I left the Moresby tower control zone I was handed to the area controller, who instructed me to continue tracking via VFR route golf and climb to 7000 feet. As the altimeter needle passed 4000, 5000, 6000 feet, and I focused on tracking the radial to the north-east of Moresby, I became more and more uneasy that I had still not broken out of the cloud. What if the weather went all the way up to 15,000 feet? I'd never break visual, and never know exactly where I was: having experienced seven months of PNG flying, I knew that putting myself in this situation was asking for serious trouble.

A couple of minutes after I had checked in on the area VHF frequency, I heard another aircraft making initial contact with the controller. It was TNA pilot Sarge, climbing out in a BN-2 Islander right behind me. I found out later that he was being followed by newbie Cameron Gibbs in TNA's Cessna 185 P2-TAC. The TNA lads had seen me launch and figured that if I was stupid enough to give a Jungles run a go, they would too. *Monkey see, monkey do.*

Sarge called me on the VHF: "Charlie Bravo Lima, this is Charlie Bravo Tango."

"CBT, this is CBL, go ahead."

"CBL, how is the weather up ahead?" Shit on a stick! — I couldn't tell Sarge the truth — I'd be incriminating myself.

"CBT, I'm visual *in between layers.*" This was my secret squirrel way of saying — *it's shitty and I'm fully IMC and I recommend you turn back.*

Sarge didn't get it, and continued upwards and onwards, as did Cameron behind him. It really was the blind leading the blind, with me up front feeling my way through the clouds. By now I was very uncomfortable with the state of affairs. Fanged butterflies performed aerobatics in my stomach as I trimmed forward to level off at 7000 feet, approaching 25 DME Port Moresby. I knew that the 12,000 foot-high wall of the Owen Stanley Range lay obscured by the cloud just 10 miles ahead. Just as I was about to give up on this madness and do a tail-between-my-legs reversal turn for Port Moresby, I popped out on top of the cloud layer. I quickly gained my bearings, with the Brown River to my left, Mt Shera and the airstrip at Naoro to my right, and the cloud-filled Kagi/Efogi valley visible off the nose. Phew.

I landed at Efogi and Kagi that morning, modifying my circuit patterns and approach paths to avoid the patchy stratus dotting the valley and, as I was the first aircraft to visit for three days, I easily solicited a full load of punters for the return flight to Moresby. My 5-seat capacity hardly made a dent in the crowds waiting strip-side, and there were more than enough scraps for Sarge and Cameron, who had persevered in the nasty weather and also navigated their way out to the Jungles behind me. I prepared to depart, making a call to Moresby HF as I lined up at the top of the strip at Kagi. Kagi's sloped runway points down the valley almost exactly at Port Moresby, and on a clear day you can see 20 miles to the lower country around the Brown River, where the foothills of the Owen Stanleys melt into the uneven terrain of the Moresby coast and the swamplands of Galley Reach. On this day there was nothing but a shroud of scud between me and Moresby. I'd have to climb back into the same soup in order to get home. Sure enough, within 20 DME Moresby I was fully IMC again, and I realised that there was only one way to get back: to fly to the runway on instruments, using the same technique as I had during the departure. The danger here was hitting 1800-foot-high Mount Lawes on descent into the Port Moresby circuit area. I transferred to the tower frequency at 10 miles, and requested a *practice* twin-locator instrument approach for runway 14L. This was a devious plan — the approach wasn't for practice at all — it was for real. It worked, and I descended in the cloud while tracking Moresby's twin

NDBs (non-directional beacons) Parer and Jackson, braking visual just below 1000 feet, three miles out on the extended runway centreline. I was extremely relieved to make a safe landing back at home base and taxied in and parked outside the aero club. Outwardly, I was proud that I had beaten the weather, but just between you and me I was also very much aware that the whole experience had bordered on foolishness, with my actions setting me up for some sort of calamity: either getting lost in the extensive cloud and being unable to let down safely, or mistaking my real position and making contact with some *Cumulus Granitus* in the heavy overcast.

Within the hour Sarge was safely back too, and ambled over to the aero club apron to have a word. "You arsehole!" he protested. "Visual in between layers!"

We grinned at each other.

"That was bloody pea soup out there!" continued Sarge, feigning anger. "I didn't see anything until I popped out of cloud at about 8000 feet over Manari! You arsehole!"

Sarge and Cameron had both had a hell of a time finding their way out there, having to rely as I had done on their instrument flying skills. It had been a stressful experience for them too (that's what happens when you play follow the leader with a dishonest leader).

The conversation soon turned to Cameron — he had not returned and we were worried about him, as his Cessna 185 had nothing but a ratty old AH (horizon indicator), a compass, and a turn and slip indicator. He was flying on bare-bones instrumentation: there was no chance for him to cheat as we had done and fly an instrument approach procedure to get home. The weather in the Moresby area was now worse too, with the cloud right down on the deck, and no clear patches anywhere. There would be no more VFR flying today. Jonathan 'The Long Arm' Thomson, TNA's chief pilot, soon joined us at the aero club with the good news that Cameron was safe on the ground in Efogi, and due to the inclement weather had decided to stay the night in the village. This information had been passed on by the TNA agent at Efogi via HF radio link (Cameron turned up in Moresby at noon the following day, with a captivating tale of an uncomfortable night spent in a bug-infested grass hut with generous offerings of burnt village food, dodgy water from the Elome Creek, and the close companionship of the head man's daughter! He assured us he turned down all three.)

With the day's flying now cancelled, Thomson, Sarge and I retired to the aero club bar and ordered a round from Simeon, the perennially happy head barman. Soon we were joined by TNA pilots Ian 'Killer' McCabe and Gerry Krynen, and moved to the plastic chairs and tables overlooking the airport apron. We sat down and did what groups of pilots do — shooting the shit about our recent flights. As one round of drinks rolled into the next, and the pile of empty SP lager stubbies grew at table centre, the flying stories became more and more incredible. The boys started loosening up about their near-misses and scares, sharing things we'd ordinarily keep to ourselves. These sessions were cathartic — you'd realise that you weren't the only one scaring yourself on a regular basis in the mountains (I thought I was the only one who sometimes landed with my hands shaking) — and offered an opportunity for us to learn from each other's mistakes and benefit from the pool of collective experience.

"Now there's a dodgy looking bunch of characters!" Jaunty PNGDCA Director of Air Safety Mike Feeney had dropped by the club and joined us for an early tipple. He wasn't wrong. We were a scruffy bunch. Our shirts were stained with dirt and sweat from cargo loading on multiple Jungle sectors; our boots caked with mud from the dirt runways. Some smoked, some gnawed on chips and nuts; all drank. We sat there smug and satisfied, like an artist after the last brushstroke of his masterpiece. In a different time we might have been USAAF C-47 Dakota or B-25 Mitchell pilots, dissecting the day's mission, raving about our low-level biscuit bombing sorties over Myola, or our bombing runs on Japanese positions at Gona and Buna, with ground fire beneath us like starbursts on Guy Fawkes Night, and Zeros hovering around us like flies as we lined up on target. These roles we did not perform, but the adrenaline freight-training through our veins after our PNG bush flying missions sprang from the same well: a well of excitement; a well of fear; a well of mortal danger. Membership into our club did not come easy — it had to be earned. Outsiders, pilots not experienced in our area of operations, pilots with less PNG time up than us — newbies, and military pilots who flew in-country for but a few days each year (and even then only in good weather) — were viewed as inferior, as liabilities, as unbaptised and unworthy. Having survived hundreds of hours of bush-strip ops was our badge of honour, and we held it close, guarding it like a fat kid guards cake.

●

Chapter 8

Misadventures in the Manumu Valley

It isn't particularly difficult to pilot a small plane, but it is terribly easy to make a monumental cock-up of it, and the consequences can be very untidy. There's a limit to what you might crash your car into, but from the air, everything has potential.

JAMES MAY, BBC TOP GEAR PRESENTER[86]

One fine Port Moresby morning I took off from Jacksons in the 'Goilala Kekeni' Cessna 206 (P2-CBL) for a quick Jungles mission: tradestore goods to Naoro, two passengers for Efogi, and with a loose plan to stop in Bodinumu and Kagi prior to my return home to see if there were any vegetables (Triffids!) to be brought back to Moresby.

After taking off to the south-east, towards Bootless Bay, I turned left in the climb and set course for Naoro. As it is only 27 miles north-east of Moresby, I expected to be in the Naoro circuit area in about 15 minutes. Jacksons tower handed me off to the area controller, and I informed him of my track and destination, and that I was climbing to 6000 feet. *Roger, Charlie Bravo Lima, maintain 3000 feet due inbound traffic.* I acknowledged the clearance, and wondered how long it would be before

I was able to continue my climb. A few minutes later, level at 3000 feet, this thought became more urgent, as I could clearly see (and knew from my awareness of the significant terrain in the Moresby area) that in about five miles I would fly straight into the western end of the Astrolabe Range. I asked the controller for a further climb. *Negative, Charlie Bravo Lima, maintain 3000 feet until advised.* He must have been having an off day. Deciding that staying alive was a better option than following his dud clearance, and with the mountain in front of me looming ever larger in my windscreen, I called him back: *Charlie Bravo Lima is now climbing to 6000 feet on track to Naoro. Cannot maintain 3000 feet due imminent collision with Varirata Bluffs.* He didn't argue.

This was the only time in all my years in PNG that I received such a dubious clearance and for the most part I found the local controllers to be very friendly, helpful and competent.

It was not the only time that a Moresby controller had issued such a clearance though, and in two cases an instruction to maintain 3000 feet was part of a sequence of events that ultimately led to tragedy . . .

In August 1976, 24-year-old pilot David Looker arrived in Port Moresby in a Piper PA23 Aztec. It was his first time in PNG and, after flying the Aztec all the way from Cairns, Australia, he planned to fly with his three passengers onwards to Lae after two days of sightseeing in Moresby.

On the morning of his departure for Lae, Looker attended the briefing office at Port Moresby airport. He submitted a VFR (visual flight rules) plan indicating that he would track via the Kokoda Gap at 7000 feet. The meteorological forecast he obtained indicated that there was fairly extensive cloud cover, but that it was broken cloud and that VMC flight (flight clear of cloud and in sight of the ground or water) should be possible. While at the briefing office he spoke with two staff members who, recognising that he was new to flying in PNG, went out of their way to brief him on his planned route and warn him of the potential dangers his flight presented. They warned him that 7000 feet across the Gap was *barely sufficient and that most pilots planned at 8000 feet to 9000 feet,* and that the Gap *was not a chasm through the mountains but merely a saddle a little lower than the surrounding mountain tops.*[87] Later, in their witness statements, they mentioned that David Looker had expressed surprise at the extreme terrain of Papua New Guinea shown on the Port Moresby Visual Terminal Chart, and that he had commented that it was hard for him to imagine there being mountains as high as his planned cruising altitude of 7000 feet (most terrain in Looker's native Australia is well below this level). The briefing office staff also pointed out the airstrips in the vicinity of the Gap: Manari, Efogi, Kagi, and the Lakes of the Myola plateau, explaining to him that these could be used as navigation points to aid him in successfully identifying the Kokoda Gap. The briefing officer's witness statement ended: *I concluded the briefing by telling him that one of the most dangerous aspects of Papua New Guinea flying was continuing flight into deteriorating weather conditions, and that if he had any doubts at all he should not hesitate to turn back . . . The pilot appeared to me to be quite cheerful and confident.*[88]

Soon after take-off Moresby Air Traffic Control instructed Looker to track outbound for the Gap on the 051 radial, which is the same as today's VFR Route Golf, the same track I was paralleling years later when I was instructed to maintain 3000 feet. Looker must have encountered cloud on the foothills of the Kokoda Trail en route, and he called ATC back: *We'll be staying below seven thousand due cloud at this stage.* The Tower then instructed Looker to maintain *not above 3000 feet* and to report when requesting further climb. It was a request they were never to receive from him.

Seventeen minutes after take-off, the area controller called Looker asking for his present position. He replied: *We're still trying to find a way through up here at the moment . . .* He was then asked to confirm that he was tracking towards the Kokoda Gap, and he replied *Affirmative, but it looks clagged in.* When he was asked to give his altitude he reported, *We're at three thousand.* The young man was very much out of his depth. He was now within 10nm of the Kokoda Gap, with terrain rising directly ahead to well over 7000 feet, yet he was still maintaining only 3000 feet. One can speculate that the cloud in the foothills from 3000 feet up forced him to track slightly to his left, NNE of his planned track, taking him towards Manumu airstrip. Manumu, a relatively flat grassy strip at 1800 feet AMSL, is about seven miles north-west of Kagi and Efogi, the airstrips he should have been overflying on his approach to the Kokoda Gap. Residents of Manumu confirmed Looker's drift to the left of his planned track soon after, when they observed an aircraft approaching from the south. Witnesses said the aircraft was below an extensive cloud cover and was very low. Manumu is situated at the mouth of a dead-end north–south valley: behind Manumu the valley narrows significantly and terrain rises extremely quickly (to 7000 feet within five miles and to 10,000 feet three miles later). The Manumu Valley is not a valley you want to fly up, ever.

After flying over Manumu the aircraft turned to the east, but after a short time it returned to the area and proceeded up the dead-end valley to the north. David Looker was lost, and was no doubt trying to make sense of the confusing picture presenting itself in the aircraft's windscreen: the geographical features and the airstrip beneath his aircraft did not match what he expected to see. Forgetting the warnings of the briefing office staff, he continued on, not realising the dire situation he and his passengers were in.

Looker's Piper Aztec went out of sight as it entered the Manumu valley heading north. Soon afterwards Manumu residents saw thick black smoke rising from behind a hill. The Aztec struck steeply sloping heavily timbered terrain on the eastern side of the blind valley, at an elevation of 4200 feet. The wreckage was spread over a 70-foot area between large trees, and the aircraft was destroyed by the impact and a post-impact fire. All four occupants were killed instantly.

A camera was found near the wreckage and the film recovered. Seventeen frames had been taken and were developed by PNGDCA Safety Investigation Department staff. They were shots typical of a tourist's stay in Port Moresby, and when I saw them (while researching this book in 2007) it saddened me to see that they were the same shots I too had taken when I first arrived in-country: pictures of suburban Port Moresby; of a visit to the Bomana War Cemetery; pictures of DC3's at Jacksons aerodrome; pictures of friends enjoying their holiday. The last four shots were snapped during the doomed flight. The last picture on the roll is chilling. It was taken as the aircraft turned north into the Manumu Valley and shows the view out the front windscreen. In the picture you can see the Aztec is hemmed in to the left and right by the steep valley walls. Just visible under the solid cloud base ahead is the dead end, a steep wall of rock and earth rising to over 7000 feet, just one mile straight ahead of them.

In 1983 this accident with its horrible and tragic waste of life was, incredibly, repeated. Thirty-nine year old John Smyth, like David Looker before him, arrived in Port Moresby having flown his aircraft, a Piper PA32 Lance, up from Australia. On 12 May 1983 Smyth and his four passengers departed Moresby for Popondetta, on the northern side of the Kokoda Gap. Like Looker seven years before him, Smyth had received a pre-flight briefing from an experienced PNG hand: he had a conversation with a RAAF pilot from the Australian High Commission in Port Moresby in the days before his departure.

In his witness statement, the RAAF pilot said: *I told him that mornings are the best time to cross the Owen Stanleys as cloud builds up during the day. I gave him a rundown on airstrips in the area, the main thing I tried to get over was don't ever fly in cloud.* The interviewer asked him: *Did he make any comment to that statement?* The RAAF pilot responded: *He said, 'Oh that means I won't be able to use my instrument rating.'*[89]

On the day of their departure, just before noon, Smyth and his passengers boarded their aircraft, which was parked in front of the PNG Air Services hangar, a local engineering workshop. The owner/operator, Yorke Mendoza, was the last person to talk to John Smyth. Yorke remarked that midday was not the best time to be crossing the Owen Stanley Range, to which Smyth replied, *It's no problem. I have an instrument rating.*[90] Alarm bells should have been ringing. This was Smyth's first time flying in PNG, and it seemed that his confidence in his ability to fly safely in Papua New Guinea in IMC (instrument meteorological conditions) was unshakable, despite being specifically warned to stay out of cloud.

Smyth's Piper Lance was cleared for take-off and instructed to track 045 from Port Moresby and to cruise at 9500 feet. A further transmission from the Moresby Air Traffic controller instructed Smyth to maintain an amended level of 3000 feet, as there was a Talair Twin Otter inbound from the Kokoda Gap area on descent to 4000 feet. The Otter pilot passed weather information to Smyth, telling him *the false gap is closing in. However if you have any difficulties penetrating you should have no trouble at about 11,000 feet, the ridges on the other side of the Kokoda valley are starting to cloud up, but if you are proceeding Popondetta you should have no problem.*[91]

The exact track followed by Smyth after this is unclear, but people at Manumu sighted his aircraft soon thereafter. Like David Looker before him, Smyth had drifted left, off the direct track between Moresby and the Kokoda Gap. The Manumu witnesses estimated his altitude at 3000 feet. They observed his Piper Lance proceeding towards the False Gap (which lies eight miles north-east of Manumu) but it returned a short time later, spiralling to gain altitude overhead Manumu before heading north, up the dead-end valley. Witnesses said the cloud base at the time was 1500 feet above the airstrip, making the base approximately 3300 feet AMSL: almost identical weather conditions to those on the day David Looker crashed in 1976.

Soon after the Piper Lance climbed into the cloud-choked blind valley behind Manumu, the underside of the aircraft clipped the top of a forested ridgeline causing Smyth to lose control and crash into the southern flank of Mt Thumb at 7800 feet AMSL. All on board were killed. It was determined by Air Safety investigators that the cause of the crash was Smyth's decision to continue in *flight conditions of poor visibility to the extent that he was unable to detect the terrain intercepting the aircrafts flight path.* In layman's terms, while flying in cloud he flew into the side of a mountain.

Smyth's 1983 wreck lies only 1.5 miles from Looker's 1976 wreck. Both were brand-new to PNG flying; both were killed on their first flight. They took seven people with them.

Sadly the Manumu Valley, or rather its imitator, the Manumu 'false-valley', was to claim another set of victims. This time I was involved, and the death toll was a lot higher.

On 11 June 1992 I flew passengers and tradestore goods on the mid-morning milk run from Moresby to Woitape, Fane, Ononge, and back to Moresby. It was typical weather for that time of year: by late morning there was a 3000–4000 foot cloud base, isolated showers in the mountains, and a high overcast. I had no problems navigating my way out to the 35 Mile Ridge and onwards into the Goilalas. On my return to

Moresby, as I stepped out of Cessna 206 P2-CBL, John Leevers of Trans Niugini Airways (TNA) approach me on the tarmac. He told me that New Zealander Dean Hannah had gone missing in P2-AWM, Charles Perry's Cessna 185, and asked me if I would join the search-and-rescue efforts.

Dean had only been in the country for a matter of days, and had been trained in and around the Koiari airstrips (the Jungles) by Richard Rowe. The Cessna 185 was under lease to Richard Rowe's company, Simbu Aviation.

Richard Rowe was something of a colourful character. He had many years of experience in PNG, most of it as an owner/operator, but he was known for pushing it — pushing his luck when flying and also pushing his luck with DCA with his lax approach to the application of aviation rules and regulations. In 1991 he had crash-landed a Cessna 206 short of the runway in Goroka when its engine failed as he came in for a landing. The subsequent DCA investigation revealed that Rowe had taken off from Chimbu with a hole in his oil cooler, a hole he had patched up himself with epoxy filler prior to take-off. His temporary repair had fallen off after departure and the engine had lost all oil pressure and seized. His do-it-yourself repair job was of course highly illegal, as well as being pretty stupid, and he was formally cautioned by a DCA official: *I would suggest that you re-familiarise yourself with the items of maintenance that may be carried out by a pilot and in the future not allow commercial considerations to outweigh legality and or common sense in your operations.*[92] Richard was a cowboy (we all were to some extent) and had checked Dean Hannah into the Koiari 'Jungle' strips after only three days of flying. Those of us on the airfield working for other flying companies were shocked that Hannah had been sent solo in PNG so soon. It had taken most of us several weeks, if not months, of flying to be sent solo. (I had flown 38 sectors over 32 days for a total of 27 hours in the Goilalas with Mack Lee before my first solo mission.) Although Hannah had arrived in-country with approximately 1000 hours in a Cessna 185, which is a challenging machine to master, we felt that his experience in New Zealand was largely irrelevant, as he had no experience of the terrain and airstrips and weather of Papua New Guinea. It really was such a different kind of flying: PNG flying demanded respect. If you didn't pay that respect by putting in the long hours of route-training; seeing the airstrips in different weather conditions; with different all-up-weights; with high level and low level approaches into all the valleys; and memorising critical landmarks — then PNG would make you pay. Sometimes with your life. Dean wasn't given the training he should have been given: we really felt that his checkout had been ridiculously quick. On top of this, he had exhibited a worrying over-confidence as soon as he arrived in PNG. When he had first met TNA's Dave 'Sarge' Sarginson (an accomplished Cessna 185 pilot with plenty of PNG hours under his belt) Dean had said, "I'm going to show you what I can do in a 185." An overabundance of confidence paired with a dearth of knowledge and experience is a deadly combination in PNG flying.

On the morning of Dean Hannah's departure for Manumu, TNA pilot Tony Froude saw him walking out to his Cessna 185. The weather early that morning was not great: low cloud in and around Moresby, which meant there'd be more of the same out in the Jungle strips. Tony asked, "Where are you going?" Dean said he was off to the Jungles. Tony, who was also scheduled to fly to the Jungle strips that day, said that he was going to wait for an hour or two and see if the weather improved before launching (which it did). Dean, ignoring the hint from a more experienced PNG pilot to remain on the ground, told Tony that he was not going to wait, but would fly now. He acted like he already knew what the weather was like that morning in and around the Jungle strips, telling Tony, "I have inside info."

Hannah took off soon after that, and when he failed to cancel his SAR watch after his scheduled arrival time at Manumu, Port Moresby ATC initiated the search-and-rescue phase. At about the same time other aircraft in the area reported picking up an intermittent ELT signal on VHF frequency 121.5.

After unloading my Cessna 206 and seeing my passengers on their way, I joined John Leevers in a Trans Niugini Airways Cessna 185 and we departed Moresby for the Manumu area to assist in the search for Dean Hannah and P2-AWM. By now it was early afternoon.

Once we got up there the weather in the Jungles wasn't so bad: just a typical shitty afternoon in the mountains with a low cloud base and fingers of mist running down off the ridgelines into the treetops. The valleys were navigable as long as you knew exactly where you were and kept an escape route open. These were two things that Dean Hannah had failed to do, and I felt bad that his training had been so poor. As John Leevers flew low-level up the valleys between the Brown River Bridge and Manumu, I scanned the terrain below for signs of Hannah's Cessna. I remember wanting to find the wreckage so we could get a chopper in there and rescue any survivors but at the same time I didn't want to be the one to find Hannah's aircraft: I didn't want to see an aircraft all crushed and mangled up against the side of a mountain somewhere. It wasn't an image I wanted to have burned into my mind.

Our search was unsuccessful, and Leevers and I returned to Port Moresby. The wreck was found later that day, when three Talair pilots searched the area in a Twin Otter. The owner of the missing Cessna 185, pilot Charles Perry, who had just returned from a morning Gurney–Misima run in a Talair Bandeirante, was one of them:

> I got back to Moresby a few hours later and he (Hannah) was still missing. Chris Miles (Talair's Port Moresby Operations Manager) had a Twin Otter standing by with Frank Halbauer and Mike Butler waiting to help me search. Frank flew it with me in the right-hand seat and Butler sitting in the cabin with a bunch of ground staff. The weather was stable that day with a high overcast limiting development of cloud so we flew direct to Manumu in the knowledge that we were searching under near identical conditions to that which existed at the time he crashed.
>
> I said to Frank that in the 185 he would have tracked via Brown River so we started flying back down the Brown River valley from Manumu. As we passed the entrance of the next valley west from Manumu I said, "Frank, if he is anywhere he is up here," so we turned up that valley and flew slowly (flaps 20/80 kts) up the right-hand side of the valley hard against the trees . . . at the dead end Frank turned and when we were about 2/3rds of the way through that turn Mike Butler spotted AWM (Hannah's Cessna 185). Frank did an orbit and I confirmed the ID.

To get to Manumu when there is low cloud on the ranges your best bet is to follow the Brown River until you are 28 DME (distance-measuring equipment, an onboard instrument giving distance in nautical miles from a ground-based station) from Jacksons Airport, at which point the river splits. You turn onto a compass heading of north to follow the left fork of the river and three miles later you will be right smack over Manumu. But there is a nasty trap waiting in this area for the inexperienced. If you turn from the Brown River at a different fork, some two miles earlier than the *correct* fork in the river, you are setting yourself up for disaster. This valley has the same compass orientation as the Manumu Valley, it looks identical to the Manumu valley at low level, but instead of seeing Manumu beneath you three miles later, you will be trapped in a narrow dead-end gorge. From the valley floor at 1500 feet AMSL, the terrain rises to well over 7000 feet within six miles. Mack Lee had warned me about this valley during my comprehensive training in the Jungles, saying: "Stay out of this valley, Matt, unless you've learned how to back-up an aeroplane." This is the valley that Dean Hannah flew into. Dean, who had somehow packed nine passengers into his six-seat Cessna 185, realised his mistake too late and the aircraft crashed into the treetops while attempting a reversal turn. All ten occupants were killed.

The bodies were shuttled to Manumu in a chopper and brought back to Moresby in a BN-2 Islander a few days later. Sarge was there the morning the body bags arrived in Port Moresby and is still trying to forget the assault on his senses as they were unloaded. Hannah's 1992 accident site was less than five miles as the crow flies from the crash sites of Looker (1976) and Smyth (1983). The whole affair was thoroughly unpleasant.

Richard Rowe, the man who had sent Dean Hannah solo after only four days of flying training, was killed seven and a half months later when his Cessna 185 crashed into a ridgeline at 7000 feet AMSL between Chimbu and Karimui in the rugged Central Highlands. His company's charter and aerial-work license had been suspended in the wake of the Dean Hannah crash, due to 'irregularities in the pre-operational training of the pilot concerned'. He had also had his check and training approval suspended by DCA due to 'several breaches of Civil Aviation Orders'.[93] On the day of Rowe's death Mike Feeney, PNGDCA Director of Air Safety, received an anonymous phone call informing him that Richard Rowe had departed Chimbu without a flight plan, and that Richard intended to operate the aircraft without reference to Air Traffic Control or any other aircraft. He was a cowboy to the end. Rowe and one of his passengers were killed when the aircraft was caught in a large downdraft while attempting to cross a 7600 foot-high mountain pass. DCA Accident Investigators travelled to the area to investigate Rowe's crash. By the time they got to the crash site local villagers had pillaged the wreckage. The wings had been hacked off with axes and bush knives, their aluminium skins carted off to be used as roofing and fencing material. The Cessna's engine was removed and hauled by 40 industrious men in relays up 600 feet of steep hillside and taken 3km to Komgale village. The investigators noted in their report that 'with the aid of money, cigarettes and sweets the people were persuaded to guide the team to the house where the engine had been taken. The motor was essentially being held hostage.' It was like dealing with children. The final report into Rowe's crash found the primary cause to be his 'failure to ensure that a safe margin of airspeed, height and manoeuvring airspace was present at all times.'[94]

●

Chapter 9

Bent-wing Bastards, Kiwi losses, and Armageddon

*You only live twice: Once when you're born
And once when you look death in the face.*

IAN FLEMING[95]

Soon after I started working full time for Mack Lee, a client booked a charter from Port Moresby to Rabaul. Mack was leasing a Cessna 402 at the time (Chee Air's P2-CBC), and he asked me to tag along with him and a pilot he had employed part-time to fly the 402, Joe Zahra.

Rabaul lies on the island of New Britain, some 440 nautical miles north-east of Port Moresby. I will never forget the views as we descended into Rabaul after the two-and-a-half hour flight. Back then Rabaul was one of the prettiest coastal towns in the world: a horseshoe harbour of vivid turquoise encircled by rugged green hills; nestling along its slim northern shores a town of some 30,000 residents. The most dominant peak was 2000-foot-high Mount Tovanumbatir, to the immediate north of the township. East and south-east of the town, and directly ahead and to our left as we came in for a landing on the easterly runway, were the volcanic cones and craters of Rabalanakaia and Tavurvur. Standing sentinel on the opposite side of the bay was another volcanic crater, Vulcan. It was breathtaking.

Rabaul lies on a fault-line at the junction of the north and south Bismarck microplates, and the stunning scenery owed its origins to the explosive forces of violent eruptions thousands of years ago. The whole harbour was actually the caldera of a giant submerged volcano, one that been relatively quiet since the last major eruption in 1937. Unfortunately Mack, Joe and I were only there for an hour or so, as we unloaded our freight and refuelled, and all too soon we departed for Port Moresby. Straight after wheels-up Joe rolled the 402 into an early right turn to avoid the quietly smoking cone of Tavurvur.

I didn't know it at the time, ignorant as I was of the rich WWII history of Papua New Guinea, but Rabaul town played an important role during the war years. Prior to WWII, Rabaul was the capital of the Australian-administered Territory of New Guinea. In early 1941, with Japanese forces steamrolling south (having had few problems conquering Burma, Malaya, Singapore, Borneo, the Philippines and the Dutch East Indies) a British-Dutch-Australian conference agreed to beef up Rabaul's defences. Beautiful Rabaul Harbour provided a superb protected anchorage capable of sheltering many ships, and the Allies realised the town's military potential. If the Japanese hoped to establish a major naval base within striking distance of the New Guinea mainland, Port Moresby, and northern Australia, then Rabaul would be ideal. The conference produced plenty of talk, but was short on any real beef. By December 1941 the Australians had sent only 1400 troops there including a modest RAAF detachment of four Hudson bombers and ten Wirraway aircraft. The Wirraways were touted as fighters, but in reality were a training aircraft, and were to prove worthless when up against the Japanese aircraft of the day.

The Japanese had indeed been coveting Rabaul. At 1248 on 20 January 1942 Rabaul was attacked by over 100 Japanese aircraft: bombers and their Zero fighter escorts. Eight gallant Wirraway crews scrambled, and in a ten-minute encounter three aircraft were lost in combat, one wrecked in a crash just after take-off, and two damaged in crash landings. Six Wirraway crewmen were killed and five wounded.[96] RAAF historian Douglas Gillison said of the Wirraway vs Zero dogfights that day: "the engagement was brave but hopeless"[97] (ironically, *wirraway* is an Aboriginal word meaning 'challenge').[98]

Two days later a Japanese invasion force of over 5000 troops[99] arrived. At dawn on 23 January a Japanese aircraft carrier and more than 50 ships arrived in Rabaul's Simpson harbour. The situation was clearly hopeless for the Australian forces. When the RAAF Squadron Commander was ordered by superiors in Australia to stay and fight it out he famously replied with a message ending *Nos morituni te sautamus*: a loose translation of the Roman gladiator's cry, 'We who are about to die salute you.' Rabaul fell that same day, when soon after 10 am the Australian Army's Commanding Officer issued the order 'every man for himself'. Escape plans in the event of an enemy invasion were not in place, and a hasty and confused retreat ensued. The Japanese captured over 800 Australian troops and many civilians.[100] Approximately one week after the invasion, 170 captives were marched to the nearby Tol and Waitavolo plantations. Private William Cook was there, and had guessed he was to be executed:

> *Three of us were tied together and we stood up. It's funny to walk to your death with two fellows whose names you don't know and will never know. We walked three abreast down the hill and I could see three Japs waiting for us at the bottom. The man on my right was praying quietly and the chap on my left was saying over and over to himself, 'God, what a way to die! What a way to die!' . . . The Japs were coming up to meet us and as they got in behind us I knew suddenly we weren't going to be shot. My stomach shrivelled and muscles went stiff, waiting for something to happen. Then it hit me, a stabbing burning pain in the middle of my back, and I fell forward on my face, dragging the other two on top of me. The Japs stood over us, lunging at us, and I felt the blade another five times in my back. I felt like screaming but my mouth was buried in the dirt, my head pressed down by the weight of the man on top of me, and no sound came.[101]*

Cook was one of only five or six survivors of what became known as the Tol massacre. It was hardly the first time the Japanese had carried out such atrocities. Their behaviour on the battlefield was governed by an ancient code of conduct known as *Bushido*: the way of the warrior. Central to this code was the principle that it was better to die or commit suicide than to fall into the hands of the enemy. This abhorrence of surrender meant that Japanese troops felt nothing but contempt for captured Allied troops; they were to be punished for their cowardice with brutally hard work, starvation diets, physical abuse or, as in this case, execution.[102] A document captured later in the war shed light on their attitude towards captured civilians and POWs. In a 'Notes for Unit Commanders' booklet, Japanese Officers were instructed: *To eradicate the sense of fear in raw soldiers, carnivals of bloodshed (or) human sacrifices to the war god are most effective. Killings with the bayonet should be carried out wherever an opportunity occurs.*'[103]

The Japanese troops soon established a formidable base in Rabaul, making it their major stronghold in the South West Pacific. They improved the two airstrips left behind by the Australians and built more, eventually operating out of five airstrips in the area: at Vunakanau, Tobera, Rapopo, Keravat, and Lakunai. At its zenith in 1944, fortress Rabaul accommodated some 550 Japanese planes, including 390 fighters.

Although they had been slack in their initial defence of Rabaul, the Allies were now determined not to allow Japanese fighters and bombers easy access to southern strategic targets, and accordingly, Rabaul was subjected to one of the longest Allied bombing campaigns of the Pacific War. The Japanese responded by ringing Rabaul's harbour with over 300 light and 76 heavy anti-aircraft guns and placed spotters on strategic approaches to give early attack warnings. Many of the guns were camouflaged and housed in reinforced tunnels. These bristling defences put up some of the most formidable flak in any WWII theatre, and Allied pilots tasked with Rabaul bombing and strafing missions were only too aware of the threat posed by the deadly curtain of anti-aircraft fire. Celebrated US Marine Corsair pilot Gregory 'Pappy' Boyington recalled in his autobiography that the Japanese gunners in Rabaul "put up bursts almost thick enough for us to walk on."[104] The true extent of the Japanese fortifications for their great base was only discovered after the war. During their three-and-a-half-year occupation of Rabaul they had constructed a 300km-long network of tunnels and underground bunkers. The subterranean complex included command posts, communications facilities, power generators, ammunitions dumps, food stores, vehicle and landing craft storage, repair facilities, hospitals, and air raid shelters to accommodate the tens of thousands of Japanese Army and Navy personnel stationed there.

Towards the end of 1943 Rabaul came within range of US carrier-borne aircraft and Allied aircraft operating from bases on northern Bougainville. With the movement of Japanese aircraft now severely hampered by the Allies, the Japanese Commander chose to withdraw his carrier group and most of the aircraft from Rabaul to prevent their destruction, although up to 100,000 Japanese troops still manned the base.[105] Rabaul ceased to be an offensive threat after this time, and by February 1944 the last of the Japanese fighter planes had left Rabaul for the northern Japanese base at Truk, in the Caroline Islands. This move by the Japanese Commander allowed the Allies to change their strategy on Rabaul: the effective stifling of Rabaul's offensive ability meant they could bypass Rabaul completely, leaving it to rot on the vine, and focus on a northwards push towards Truk, and eventually the Japanese mainland itself.

As the Japanese aircraft left their Rabaul base for Truk, New Zealand forces established a base on Green Island, 120nm east of Rabaul, from where they operated two F4U Corsair squadrons and a Lockheed Ventura squadron. The RNZAF received 364 Vought-built Corsairs during WWII from the USA under the lend-lease program, which had come into being before US forces joined the war. It was created to circumvent America's then neutrality and laws forbidding the export of weapons to the Soviets and Britain and her Commonwealth allies. Aircraft were assigned US designations and serial numbers and then 'leased' to the Allied Air Forces in need rather than sold to them.

The Corsair is my favourite aircraft of WWII, and I would sell my soul to get my hands on one. I worked on a Corsair airframe during my days recovering from glandular fever in 1990, when I was resident fibre-glasser and general dogsbody at the RNZAF Museum hangar at Base Wigram. In the Corsair, the Allies finally found an aircraft that could take on the Japanese Zero. 1st Lt Kenneth Ambrose Walsh was a member of the first squadron in the Pacific to go into action in the beefy Vought F4U Corsair:

> I learned quickly that altitude was paramount. Whoever had altitude dictated the terms of the battle, and there was nothing a Zero pilot could do to change that — we had him. The F4U could outperform the Zero in every aspect except slow speed maneuverability and slow speed rate of climb. Therefore, you avoided getting slow when combating a Zero. When we were accustomed to the area, and knew our capabilities, there were instances when the Zero was little more than a victim . . . the Zero, like most Japanese aircraft, had no armour plating or self-sealing tanks. So, if you hit them, they'd burn, with their aluminium construction including magnesium parts, which added further fuel to the fire. You can imagine what would happen if you got 30 or 40 hits on them.[106]

The Corsair was a far chunkier aircraft than the Zero. The F4U-1 model stood 16 ft 1 inch high, with 41-foot wing span, a 2000 hp Pratt & Whitney engine, and a maximum take-off weight (MTOW) of 14,000 lbs. The Zero was diminutive in comparison: only 10 feet high, with a 39-foot wingspan, a 1130 hp Sakae 21 engine, and a MTOW of only 6,164 lbs. The Corsair was a beast. Another US pilot said of his first encounter with it:

> . . . of all the aircraft I had seen, these were the most wicked-looking bastards. They looked truly vicious . . . They were damnably big fighters for their day. They had a vast length of fuselage between the cockpit and the propeller . . . It was pretty long-legged in the undercarriage department in order to give clearance to the great propeller, said to be the biggest ever fitted to a single-engined fighter. To increase the clearance — the undercarriage alone could never have achieved sufficient — the wings were of an inverted

RNZAF F4U Corsairs.

gull format, dipping downwards for about 4ft from the wing root at the fuselage, then rising sharply to the wing tip. Not for nothing was it called the bent-wing bastard from Connecticut.[107]

Allied pilots quickly grew to love the aircraft. One Kiwi pilot said the Corsair was *"the easiest aircraft I had flown to date . . . with everything laid out perfectly . . . the ultimate in 'arm chair' flying — for piston engined aircraft."*[108]

The Kiwi Corsair and Ventura squadrons at Green Island shared two crushed coral airstrips with a squadron of US Marine B-25 Mitchell bombers and a US Navy PBY5A Catalina flying boat squadron. In his book on the Vought F4U Corsair, Martin Bowman called the Kiwis the "forgotten squadrons" of the South Pacific campaign.[109] They were relegated to mopping up the remaining pockets of enemy forces left behind after the main Allied forces bypassed Rabaul.

A typical patrol undertaken by the Kiwis was a four-hour flight, with eight Corsairs per sortie, involving dive-bombing strikes on ammunitions dumps and gun emplacements in and around Rabaul's

Simpson Harbour. Other missions included coordinated attacks on the areas of Bougainville still held by the Japanese, who were now being fought by Australian troops. These were operations against an enemy who had lost all offensive capability, but this did not make the missions any less dangerous. The RNZAF's heaviest losses of the campaign came not at an earlier time when they were involved in aerial combat with Japanese aircraft, but during this period when they were operating from Green Island, a time during which their operations book noted a "complete absence of contacts".[110] It was the natural elements and pilot inexperience, rather than any Japanese action, which caused the RNZAF's blackest day of the campaign, 15 January 1945.

That morning two RNZAF Corsair squadrons carried out a combined bombing strike on Toboi Wharf on the Rabaul foreshore. Flying Officer Frank Keefe of Auckland piloted the second to last aircraft on target. After his bomb drop Keefe's Corsair took a hit from anti-aircraft fire in his wing root. The aircraft climbed steeply to 3000ft, rolled over on its back, and descended vertically into Rabaul's Simpson Harbour. Keefe managed to bail out of his stricken steed, safely descending to the water. He started swimming towards the middle of the bay, out of enemy artillery range, hoping to be picked up by a Catalina. Three NZ Corsairs had been overhead the field at 10,000 feet as part of a routine dawn patrol, and they stayed on station to keep watch overhead Keefe. These three aircraft were relieved by others during the day as fuel levels ran low so the watch could be maintained. After several hours Keefe managed to reach safe waters, only to have the tide turn against him and wash him back towards the Japanese guns.

The area was too hot for a Catalina rescue, so a back-up plan was put into action. A Ventura PV-1 bomber was launched from Green Island tasked with dropping two bamboo rafts to Keefe so he could paddle out of the harbour during the night and be rescued by a Catalina the following morning. Twelve more Corsairs accompanied the Ventura.

RNZAF Corsair pilot Bryan Cox, who had only arrived at Green Island for his first operational tour of duty 25 days earlier, was there, celebrating his 20th birthday that day. What a birthday it would turn out to be.

The 12 Corsair pilots were tasked with strafing the Japanese coastal guns, to draw their fire away from the Ventura as it made a low pass to drop the rafts. Bryan Cox wrote about the raft drop in his 1987 memoir *Too Young to Die:*[111]

> *With the Ventura and our two Corsairs in open line astern and the Ventura in the centre, we dived to ground level some miles down the coast out of sight of the Japanese in Rabaul itself, then in a wide arc we proceeded to fly behind Vulcan crater, hopping over the low hills onto the harbour. The Ventura's two Pratt & Whitney R2800 radial engines working overtime and developing a maximum of 4000hp meant that I had to open my throttle fairly wide to keep it in sight. It disappeared several times behind high trees or low undulations and when I noticed ominous wisps of blue smoke emerging from the trees and plantations a few feet below I instinctively employed the evasive tactics which we had been taught at Woodbourne a few months earlier skidding violently from side to side. I was conscious that the first two aircraft were conveniently alerting the Japanese guns which made me more determined than ever not to celebrate my twentieth birthday as their guest. As we flew over the harbour at water level, the other Corsairs from Nos. 16 and 14 Squadrons continued to strafe the surrounding waterfront areas.*[112]

The rafts were dropped successfully from the Ventura but Keefe was motionless. He had now been in the water for nine hours and was lying across a floating log, in the words of the gunner in the Ventura, "perhaps unconscious."[113] It was now approaching last light, so the RNZAF pilots had no choice but to set course for home and leave Keefe in the water. Seventeen aircraft left Rabaul for Green Island: 15 Corsairs (the three that had been overhead at 10,000 feet plus the 12 extras), the Ventura, and a Catalina that had been in the area.

The 15 Corsairs split into four groups: one three-ship formation and three four-ship formations. The four-ship formations had call-signs Onyx 25, Onyx 26 and Onyx 27. Cox later described the weather they encountered over the open ocean that night as "a jet-black tropical front, stretching from horizon to horizon, the type of which I had never witnessed before, nor have ever witnessed since. It was even blacker than a school blackboard.'"[14] There was a dirty line of rainstorms between them and Green Island, with visibility in heavy showers practically nil. Contacting Green Island Tower, the inbound aircraft were advised the cloud base was down to 500ft. The only aid to navigation at Green Island was a manually operated loop aerial mounted on a mast. Inbound formation leaders transmitted a number count call ("one, two, three . . .") on the radio and an operator on the ground zeroed in on their position with the aerial and gave them a magnetic bearing to steer to the aerodrome. The Corsair pilots followed their formation leaders, concentrating so hard on staying in close formation that they didn't have spare capacity to monitor their own position relative to the ocean below. They trusted that their leaders would provide terrain clearance in the challenging conditions. They were wrong. The combination of atrocious weather, darkness, fatigue, multiple aircraft and inexperienced pilots set the stage for disaster.

Birthday boy Bryan Cox was flying in the three-ship formation. As the trio of Corsairs descended into the inky darkness of the storm front he saw his leader's navigation lights disappear under his own left wingtip, a far from desirable state of affairs, and Cox became aware in an awful instant that he was in a 45 degree banked turn to the right, with his altimeter indicating zero feet! He instinctively pulled back on the stick, climbing to a safe altitude. Now bereft of his formation leader's guidance Cox realised he had no idea of the exact location of Green Island. To add pressure, he had only 30 minutes of fuel remaining. If he didn't find the airstrip soon he would have to bail out of the aircraft before it ran out of fuel and descend by parachute into the dark void beneath: not an attractive prospect. But fate smiled on him that night in the dark over the water. As he desperately searched for home in the reduced visibility of the storm, a lucky lightning flash illuminated Green Island airstrip directly beneath him. He was able to make an approach and safe landing. Incredibly, this was the first time he had ever landed a Corsair at night. Both of the other Corsairs in this formation made it back to Green Island, but only one made a safe landing: the other went into a diving turn while circling the lights of the base and crashed.

The 12 other Corsairs in the main group had flown into the same storm front. The lead four-ship formation (Onyx 25) entered the foul weather at 300 feet above the water while trying to find a way under it. As the formation descended, the pilot at the back, Don Walther, saw the two aircraft in the front of his formation collide with each other and hit the water in a ball of fire. The third Corsair in the formation took evasive action but he too hit the water. Don Walther made it back to Green Island and landed safely. In 1988 he spoke of his landing that night, having seen three of his colleagues crash and burn right in front of him: "I wasn't fussy which way I was going to put her down — front, back or sideways as long as it was land."[115]

The second four-ship formation (Onyx 27) fared no better. Just before the three crashes of Onyx 25, two Onyx 27 Corsairs crashed into the sea in a sheet of flame. The two remaining aircraft of this formation climbed immediately to 7000 feet, found Green Island thanks to a searchlight beam and the illuminated strip, and landed safely.

The last four-ship (Onyx 26) had become separated from the others, but also set course for Green Island at 400–500 feet above the ocean through the storm front. All four aircraft made it successfully into the circuit area but one Corsair was observed shortly thereafter climbing steeply above the rest of the formation, disappearing into cloud. It was never seen again. The other three Corsairs made successful landings.

Tragically, but perhaps not surprising giving the limited experience most of these pilots had flying solely on instruments, especially at night, seven of the 15 Corsairs had crashed while trying to find their way back to Green Island. A US Navy Catalina was scrambled to search for survivors in the water. There were none. The Catalina Commander said of the atrocious weather that night: "It was raining to beat hell, and as dark as a Zulu's ass."[116]

Only one body was ever recovered, that of the pilot who crashed while circling the lights of the base. To add to the tragedy the original downed Corsair pilot, Frank Keefe, was picked up by the Japanese only to die 15 days later, succumbing to an infection from a deep arm wound. A Japanese soldier, Minoru Fujita, recalled Keefe's capture in a 1987 letter:

. . . he was picked up by one of our small landing boats . . . I notice the upper part of his left uniform sleeve is tattered and the flesh is torn . . . it is a serious wound . . . I imagined how he felt being stranded in the midst of hostile forces, wounded, and having to watch his would-be rescuers flying away. I felt sorry for him.[17]

It was the greatest loss of aircraft and flight crew the RNZAF had ever seen in a day, and remains to this day their blackest hour: eight pilots and eight aircraft lost in one mission. A *New Zealand Herald* article dated January 1945 summed up the tragedy: *To those who had seen the Corsair squadrons taxi out in the morning, the day's tally was stunning — one Pilot shot down by the Japanese, and seven young men who did not come back after a gallant attempt to rescue their comrade.*

The official report into the incident noted that although the weather was very poor for some 40 minutes in the vicinity of the aerodrome, at no time was it bad enough to preclude normal aircraft operations, stating 'the weather was not sufficiently poor to cause such large scale loss as this.'[18] Simply put, the Kiwi Corsair pilots had found themselves operating in conditions for which they had not received adequate training. How much training did wartime fighter pilots have? Twenty-year-old Bryan Cox had a mere 198 hours total flight time in his logbook when he first flew the massive Corsair with its 2000hp Pratt & Whitney 18 cylinder twin-row radial engine. His initial conversion flying on the type was just eight hours and 45 minutes. He told me of his Corsair experience in a 2009 email: *. . . by the time we arrived at Green Island for operations I had flown 44 hours 40 minutes in Corsairs but no night flying! All operational flying was normally conducted in daytime, and neither Corsairs nor P-40's or most other fighters had landing lights fitted as are today standard. We also didn't carry torches, which are fairly standard during night flying in light aircraft today.*

It would be inconceivable, under normal circumstances, that a pilot would have his first night flight in an unfamiliar aircraft type in an operational theatre (as Cox did on Black Monday), but this was wartime, and the fighter pilot sausage machine was churning them out as quickly as it could. Losses were high, and they were not restricted to combat. The New Zealand Government archives hold the RNZAF's WWII Corsair squadron accident reports, and statistics from these accidents illustrate this point: of the 262 Corsair accidents recorded, almost half (117) were recorded during training flights, the taxi/takeoff/landing phase, and during formation flying. A high percentage of these accidents took place in New Zealand rather than in overseas operational theatres. Of the 38 Corsair pilots killed in the war years, 27 deaths were attributable to training flight mishaps, landing and take-off accidents, and mid-air collisions with other RNZAF Corsairs.[119] Unsurprisingly, the official report into Black Monday suggested more attention be paid to training pilots in night flying, instrument flying, and bad weather penetration by large formations.[120]

Forty-nine years after Black Monday I flew into the Rabaul area in the co-pilot's seat of a Milne Bay Airways Dornier 228. It had been two years since my first and only other trip there: with Mack Lee and Joe Zahra in the Cessna 402. As I flew abeam Rabaul's airport, the town was once again under attack. Attacked not by the invading Japanese fleet, nor by New Zealand Corsair squadrons, but by a force much more powerful, and one that was to wreck a different kind of havoc on the town and its surrounds. One from which Rabaul would never recover.

On 19 September 1994, after an intensifying series of precursor earthquakes (*gurias* in Tok Pisin), the Rabaul caldera erupted. Although it was reported that up to five separate vents from the Rabaul caldera discharged, most of the volcanic activity was centred at the Vulcan and Tavurvur vents. At 0730 Vulcan exploded, sending an ash plume 60,000 feet into the air. Deadly pyroclastic flows (fast-moving currents of superheated rock and gas) raced down the volcanic cones, and smoke and ash and debris as large as trucks spewed forth from the craters, raining down on Rabaul and its surrounds. One onlooker reported that Rabaul's Simpson Harbour was boiling, that most of the bay was covered in floating pumice and part of it was filled in with volcanic detritus. Sections of Matupit Island, linked to the south-eastern end of the airport by a causeway, subsided into the harbour, as did parts of the airport itself. Rabaul town was covered with up to two metres of ash and pumice, and black muddy rain falling from the ash cloud caused mudflows and flooding in surrounding areas. Within hours, downpours caused by massive eruption-induced storm clouds soaked the thick blanket of ash on the town's rooftops: the extra weight of the rain and the ash led to the collapse of an estimated 80% of buildings. Volcanic forces had unleashed their Armageddon on Rabaul.

Fortunately the Rabaul Observatory and the Government had the foresight to declare a state of emergency the previous night, ordering an immediate evacuation. More than 30,000 people had been transported well clear of the volcano zone and housed in mission centres, plantation buildings and schools. Only two deaths were ever attributed to the eruption: a child hit by a fleeing car and a man hit by lightning generated by the volcanoes.[121] At that time, two General Aviation companies were based in Rabaul: Islands Aviation and Airlink. Thanks to the early evacuation order most aircraft were flown out of Rabaul before the eruption, with company pilots ferrying them to the safety of nearby Namatanai on New Ireland and Hoskins on central New Britain. Only four airframes were left behind to face the wrath of the ash clouds: an Airlink Beechcraft Baron that was under restoration and had no pilot seats, an Airlink Cessna 402 under maintenance that had no engines, an Islands Aviation Cessna 206 that was in pieces in their hangar, and a perfectly serviceable Pacific Helicopters Eurocopter AS350 Squirrel (Pacific Helicopters' Rabaul-based pilot was out of town on leave and there was no one else available to ferry it to safety).[122] The last flight out of Rabaul was Air Niugini flight PX207, a Fokker F-28 jet service to Port Moresby on the morning of the eruption. Captain Barry Huff and First Officer Naime Aihi prepared the jet for a quick getaway at first light on that fateful day, having spent an uneasy night at an evacuation centre in nearby Vunakanau, rocked by increasingly frequent and violent earth tremors, with Huff later saying their accomodation shook all night "like a ship at sea." He described their pre-takeoff preparations in a 2014 email: ". . . a most incredible sight presented itself through the cockpit windows. Tavurvur volcano — situated only a short distance from the end of runway 12 — began erupting right in front of us. I transmitted a

An Airlink Cessna 402 after the 1994 Rabaul eruption.

(distress) call . . . and we hurriedly completed our pre start checks and boarded all passengers. The airport was now deserted, and by engine start the ash plume was about 3000 feet (high) and drifting towards the town . . . As we lined up on the runway, another unbelievable sight — a fully loaded truck with about 30 people on board crashed through the airport perimeter fence at high speed and drove straight across the runway in the direction of town . . . desperation and panic clearly evident on their faces. These were anxious times for all."

Port Moresby-based Milne Bay Airways (MBA) operated one of the first flights into the area after the eruption: to Tokua airstrip, 14 miles to the south-east. Captains John Wild Junior and Clive Morgan brought in Civil Defence staff, reporters and a photographer. In the pictures taken during this trip, Rabaul is a monochromatic void, the air still thick with ash; their yellow vehicle and their clothing provide the only colour in the drab and desolate landscape. Unfortunately, these sorts of calamities bring out the worst in people as well as the best. With many shops and warehouses partially collapsed under the weight of wet ash and mud, hundreds of opportunists made off with food, clothing and electronic goods. As the first official relief convoys entered the town a company of 100 armed police officers were under orders to shoot looters after only one warning. The local Police Commander made the zero tolerance policy crystal clear: "If people will not listen to you at roadblocks, you fire . . . any new cars or looters' vans seen driving out of there, you shoot the wheels out."[123]

My flight to Tokua airstrip was two and a half weeks after the initial eruption. When I was 200 miles out, I could already see an ominous curtain of darkness blotting out half the sky over northern New Britain. Rabaul's volcanic craters were still belching detritus high into the atmosphere and the heat carried far into the tropical sky was creating some violent and dirty weather: towering ink-black clouds of smoke and ash reached up to at least 30,000 feet; lightning popped like flash photography deep within sooty malevolent cumulonimbus cells. We descended on the southern side of Simpson Harbour, careful to stay clear of the ash plume, and set up for a landing on the grass strip at Tokua. On board the Milne Bay Airways Dornier 228 I co-piloted, with Captain Joe Kumasi in command, were emergency food supplies and equipment. The rescue operation was still underway, with thousands still homeless in the aftermath of the natural disaster. Tokua had become the de facto main airport in the wake of Rabaul's destruction, and had seen a flurry of aviation activity with the arrival of charter flights for government officials, international aid workers, scientists, the media, and church and mission volunteers. As the clean-up began, damage was estimated at 100 million Australian dollars.

In the years after the 1994 eruption there were attempts to move people back to Rabaul, but in the end the townspeople built anew at Kokopo, about 20 kilometres away, between Rabaul's old airstrip and the new airport at Tokua. Although Rabaul's wharf is still in use today (it's deep water anchorage is without equal in New Britain) the town remains largely deserted. It was a sad end for one of the most beautiful harbour towns on earth, and an inglorious end for a town that had played such a major part in the World War II years. My flight to Tokua that day was my first and last, and I have not been back to New Britain since.

●

Chapter 10

"Nothing exciting ever happens to me": The Death of P2–SEF

An aviator's life may be full of ups and downs,
But the only hard thing about it is the ground.
CHARLES KINGSFORD-SMITH[124]

Sometimes aircraft, like pilots, are destined to die in PNG. So it was with the Cessna 206 with the registration markings P2-SEF.

In mid 1991, 21-year-old Australian pilot Tim Johnston arrived in Papua New Guinea hoping to get a flying job. He approached Honor Egger Air Transport (HEAT) with his resume, figuring he was in with a fighting chance: *They had a high turnover of pilots and were considered the worst company in PNG, so I thought I'd have a pretty good chance of getting hired!* Ms. Honor Egger, the owner and operator of the small Lae-based charter company, was a standout in PNG flying circles, as female bush pilots were extremely rare. She was known around the traps as 'Captain Nipples' — this dodgy nickname came about because Honor was in the habit of going to work *sans* bra, and her 'headlights' were always on high beam, two beacons stage front. The classic nicknames didn't stop there. Her husband, Herman, was an aircraft engineer, and was known as 'Herman the German'. He hated this, and was always quick to correct anyone mistaking him as a citizen of *Das Vaterland*: "I'm not fucking German! I'm Austrian!" was his standard outburst. It was worth asking him which part of Germany he was from just to see the guy explode (HEAT pilot Colin Hicks took the art of needling Herman to the next level. When Herman gave a particularly firm "I'm fucking AUSTRIAN!" response, Colin retorted, "Austrian? Yeah, so was Hitler!" That one went down like a cup of cold sick). At the time of Johnson's arrival HEAT had four Cessna 206s, the PNG workhorse, covering bases in Nadzab (Lae), Menyamya, Vanimo and Aitape. Tim was hired, and did a two-week familiarisation period, flying with the chief pilot, before being let loose in the hairy strips of the Finisterre Range, on the Huon Peninsular north of Lae. When I interviewed him in the mid 2000s, he recalled his first impression of solo PNG mountain flying: *I remember thinking, 'I can't do this!' The weather was shit and there were things looming out of the cloud — like fucking big mountains!*

One morning in January 1992, he launched in HEAT Cessna 206 P2-SEF out of Nadzab, with a standard load of villagers and tradestore goods bound for the strips of the Mongi Valley. He stopped first at Ogeranang, a 550-metre-long grassed clay strip at 5500 feet AMSL, nestled at the bottom of a 9000-foot-high spur off the south-eastern end of the Finisterres. From there he ducked across to Mindik, the next stop on the milk run, a 665-metre-long strip at 4000 ft AMSL, five miles away in the next valley over. The weather was deteriorating:

> *I was groping my way around the main valley. The weather was ugly but I pressed on as I had excellent local knowledge having been operating in the area for about 6 months.*

He made it to Mindik and picked up two more passengers and a *liklik pikinini* (a small child), bringing the total souls on board to seven. As he lined up at the top of the sloping one-way strip for departure, he tried to raise Lae ATC on HF radio. It was his duty to inform them of his movements as part of the normal SAR (Search and Rescue) procedures. He couldn't get through (the radio had been playing up all morning), so decided to depart anyway and try to contact them once airborne. He kept trying to contact them during the eight minute sector to his next port, Masa — still with no luck. On arrival overhead Masa he realised not having contact with ATC was the least of his problems that day. Masa was a rarely used strip — short and challenging — approximately 380 metres long, 5400 ft AMSL, with a 10% uphill slope. It was a rough red clay and grass village airstrip, with rising terrain ahead: the only escape route for a go-around was a reversal turn into a parallel valley that offered descent to lower ground. This day a bank of cloud lay like a shroud over 90% of the strip and extended into the escape-route valley, meaning there was no go-around option. The same cloud prevented a normal straight-in approach. This was going to be tricky.

When the weather around the strips was bad, Tim had taken to flying what he called a "Baa-baa-black-sheep approach", a curving base turn to a very short final approach inspired by a 1970s TV series of the same name. The show was about the exploits of Pacific Island-based US F4U Corsair pilots in WWII (based on the wartime experiences of Maj. Gregory 'Pappy' Boyington). Visibility was so poor out the front of their Corsairs, with its long forward fuselage and nose-high attitude, that pilots could only align themselves with the runway by looking out the cockpit side window: thus the curved approach to landing. This was the style Tim adopted this day flying into Masa. He said later he was *'hugely overconfident'* at this early stage of his PNG flying experience. Tim saw no problems with flying a curved approach, swooping in offset to the strip along the edge of the cloud bank, starting to flare with a bit of bank still on, and straightening up at the last second. The first few months of solo ops in the mountains was a dangerous time for any PNG pilot, a time when they had a little bit of experience, but not enough to have seriously scared themself, and certainly not enough to learn their limitations. Tim was to find his limitations that day.

After an orbit over the top to assess the visibility and plan his approach path, he decided that he could just see enough of the strip to give it a go. He could see a tin shed that he believed was abeam the bottom end of the strip through a hole in the cloud, so planned his Baa-baa-black-sheep approach to land next to the shed (*When I got to the shed I should be able to see the strip and I would just hook it to the left and flare*). The strip above and below the shed was invisible to him, enveloped in cloud. He aimed at the shed at a 45 degree offset to the airstrip orientation, to stay clear of the cloud, and slowed up the aircraft so much that intermittent stall warning horn was sounding. As he descended parallel to the cloud bank, he became fully visual with the strip a couple of hundred feet off the deck and realised to his horror that the shed that he had been aiming to touch down next to was not at the bottom of the strip, but was actually halfway up! This left him less than 200 metres of airstrip to play with. He was now way too high to make a safe landing, and there was no VMC escape route open to him. Just to make things really exciting P2-SEF's cockpit instruments did not include a functional artificial horizon, so attempting instrument flight in an IMC go-around wasn't an option either. In a split second Tim came up with a new plan. He would land the aeroplane halfway up the strip and ground loop it before the embankment at the end (a ground loop is a desperate manoeuvre when a pilot purposefully slides the aeroplane through 180 degrees after landing, dissipating its forward energy and bringing it to an emergency stop). Given the situation he was in it was highly unlikely that he would get away with this (a ground loop often ends badly, with significant collateral damage such as a propeller strike, undercarriage collapse, or worse), but his self-confidence was such that he *100% thought I was going to pull this off*. He said later: *I had been doing a lot of crazy stuff like this, really stupid stuff, and pulling it off. I was pushing it harder and harder to see how far I could take it. I loved pushing it.*

He selected flaps up — *for the suck* — put the nose down, sideslipped the aircraft, and anticipated the ground contact with an exaggerated flare and a burst of power, to reduce the massive rate of descent. This was about as effective as trying to fertilise a 40-acre field with a fart.[125] The aircraft hit *very* hard — BOOM! In his peripheral vision Tim saw the main undercarriage struts splay, flexing up towards the wings, and in the impact the nose wheel was violently sheared from its attachment points and forced up into the engine bay. CRACK! The cargo pod was torn from the bottom of the fuselage, leaving a trail of rice, tinned fish and other tradestore goods scattered behind like Hansel and Gretel's breadcrumbs. The aircraft slid about 70 metres up the strip, with the propeller churning into the ground and dirt showering up over the windscreen — *like a tunnelling machine*. It came to a stop at a 90 degree angle to the runway. All was eerily silent. Tim sat there for a few seconds, and the passengers sat stunned, speechless. For a moment time stood still, then Tim screamed *–Fuck it!* — and lashed out at the top of the dashboard glare-shield with his fist. It fell off, and landed in his lap. *I just sat there staring at it.*

The six passengers climbed out of the aircraft. Incredibly, there were no injuries. Two of the passengers ambled off straightaway, to where Tim does not know, and he never saw them again. The others, for whom Masa was not their final destination, hung around for a while, until Tim refunded them their airfare and, for want of a better suggestion, told them to *walk*.

He tried to raise the Company HQ, or any aircraft in the area, on HF and VHF radio frequencies, but there was no contact. This was a problem. His inability to contact Lae ATC on departure from his previous strip, Mindik, meant that as far as they were concerned, he was still there. When they failed to hear from him and a SAR phase was activated, the first place they would look for him would be Mindik, not Masa where he and his buggered aircraft now sat. On top of that, even if they widened their search, which was likely, Masa still sat under a cloud blanket, and they would be unable to spot him from above due to the inclement weather and poor visibility. He was in a pickle. Tim spoke with one passenger who said he intended to walk to Pindiu, the nearest airstrip. Pindiu was near a road and was used as a collection point for coffee beans from the region's small airstrips, from where it was transported by truck to the largest town in the area, coastal Finschhafen. Tim decided to walk with the passenger to Pindiu.

They left at around 10am and followed village paths through the jungle, arriving in Pindiu just before sunset, some seven hours later. Tim found the HEAT agent in Pindiu village and stayed the night in his house: a bush-material hut. Meanwhile, with no SARWATCH cancellation, and no news from Tim, ATC had indeed begun a search-and-rescue phase. As soon as the Nadzab-based HEAT staff realised Tim was missing, Paul Brown in a HEAT 206 and Richard Lae in his own Beechcraft Baron had began searching for Tim, but the weather had closed in at all of the Mongi Valley strips soon after lunch and they were unable to locate his aircraft.

The next morning Tim walked to the road and hitched a ride in a coffee truck to Finschhafen. The ride took three to four hours. En route he remembers he used some of the company takings to buy two bags of mangoes, nibbling at them as the truck bounced its way to the coast. The truck dropped him off at Finschhafen's Harbour, where he found that he had just missed a boat to Lae. He waited a few more hours and took the next one, swimming off the jetty with dive-bombing local kids while he waited. Tim paid for the boat ticket with the HEAT takings, and remembers watching a video *Weapons of the Gulf War* in the boat's TV room, as it chugged its way along the southern coast of the Huon Peninsular towards Lae (Gulf War I had been raging on the Iraq–Kuwait border the previous year). He arrived in Lae at 1am, exhausted, and made a beeline for the Lae International Hotel, checking in and going straight to sleep in what must have seemed like luxurious surroundings after the tribulations of recent days.

The next morning, the second since the crash, he caught a PMV (public bus) to Nadzab Airport and made his way to the HEAT office (unbeknownst to him, P2-SEF had been discovered the previous afternoon by aerial searchers, Tim-less. He was feared dead, lost in the jungle). He strolled in to the office with a grin and a cheery 'Gidday!' like he always did. The HEAT office staff just about shat themselves. With his messy blond hair, grimy uniform and mud-crusted boots, he looked like something the cat had dragged in. To the HEAT staff there that day he was a phoenix from the ashes, a scruffy Australian Indiana Jones risen from the dead.

One week later Herman the German worked his magic on P2-SEF at Masa. The aircraft had a temporary nose wheel fitted along with a new propeller, and was flown back to Lae. Tim meanwhile had to face the music with the investigators of the PNGDCA. They suggested that his Baa-baa-black-sheep swooping offset approaches probably weren't a good idea in poor visibility conditions into short mountain strips. They also concluded that he should have stayed with his aircraft at Masa and continued to try to raise help using his HF and VHF radios until rescued.

I'm glad he didn't, as his Bear Grylls-style tale of walking through the bush makes for much better reading.

Tim didn't fly for about a month after the crash. After that he was based at Vanimo with HEAT for another six months until his one year work visa expired. He then returned to Australia, picking up a job flying a Tiger Moth out of Hamilton Island. He later gained employment on a freight run out of Mackay, Queensland, with Jetcraft, and joined Cathay Pacific Airways in Hong Kong in 1995, gaining his command on the Airbus A330 in 2005. He said of his one year of PNG bush flying: *Nothing came close to flying there. We were lucky to have participated in that period of aviation in PNG — before GPS and mobile phones.* Tim is still to be heard on the radio throughout the world's air-routes, with his distinctive high-pitched voice and Aussie accent. Whenever he is on the airwaves, some cheeky bugger (or several, all on board different aeroplanes) will cut in mimicking his voice with a "G'day, Tim!", "Morning, Tim!", "On ya, Tim!"

P2-SEF had survived it's conversion to a tunnelling machine at the hands of Tim Johnston, but its days in PNG were numbered. At around the time Tim left the country, New Zealander Tony Froude returned to PNG to take up a job with Lae-based charter company North Coast Aviation (NCA). Tony already had approximately eight months of PNG flying under his belt after his stint with Sarge and the Long Arm and the other reprobates at Trans Niugini Airways (TNA) in Port Moresby. On his return, he was either blessed or cursed by the flying gods, depending on your perspective. Tony Froude was to experience more than his fair share of aircraft incidents and accidents in PNG. Statistically speaking he took on dramas that perhaps should have been destined for some other poor bastard (possibly me), so we were most grateful for his generosity and valour in taking on these 'extra' misadventures. 'Froudy' survived two total engine failures in the Cessna 206, one partial failure in the 206, one partial failure in a Cessna 402, and one precautionary shutdown in a BN-2 Islander. Two of these episodes are worth a closer look.

His first major incident was a total engine failure during a training flight in NCA's Cessna 206 P2-AAC, with chief pilot Geoff Thiele in early 1993. The pair started the day with a betel nut (*buai*) charter from Wau to Kamulai, routing over the Kudgeru Gap. A solid layer of cloud hugged the Gap, but they climbed high enough to see that the other side of the pass was clear, and pressed on to Kamulai. After a routine stop in Kamulai, during which they dropped off the *buai* and picked up a few passengers, they departed for the next leg of the flight, to Tekadu. Tekadu lies 30 miles north-west of Guari, in the upper floodplain of the Gulf Province's Lakakamu River. The direct track between these airstrips involves an oblique transit of the southern ramparts of 11,700 foot-high Mount Strong. Approaching Tekadu, they could see most of the floodplain was blanketed in wispy stratoform cloud layers, but thankfully could still make out the strip through a hole in the broken cloud. Tony, who was flying the aircraft, began to slow up the 206 and spiral down through the hole. As he went to close the throttle to further decelerate, he noticed the oil pressure gauge drop to zero, and before he could say, "Shit, this ain't good, I hope the propeller doesn't stop," the propeller stopped.

The passengers started screaming, aware that being airborne in a Cessna 206 with a dead engine was not a great look.

Tony could still see the strip and manoeuvred to stay out of the cloud and stay visual with the threshold while trouble-shooting (the standard FMIP drills; a check of fuel, the mixture control, the ignition system, and a check for partial power). Entering cloud in this situation would have a been a one-way ticket to a crash in the swampy jungle. The engine did not respond, so Tony concentrated on positioning for a glide approach and landing into Tekadu. He would only get one shot at this, so it needed to be a top effort. He kept the speed up a bit higher than usual, and also approached the strip at a higher angle than normal: better to be too high than too low. Once he knew he could make the strip he selected flap (the flaps are electric, so worked off the aircraft battery even though the engine was dead) and sideslipped to lose a bit of excess height. Although a bit hot and high, he touched down in the normal landing zone and kept the aircraft rolling up the 5% sloping strip, even managing to taxi off the side of the runway into the parking bay (Tekadu is 430 metres long, at an elevation of 1200 feet). It was a sterling effort.

Fellow NCA pilot Brian Hoskinson was dispatched in another aircraft to pick up Tony and Geoff at Tekadu. After returning to Wau, their base camp at that time, the NCA pilots got pissed celebrating Tony's successful dead-stick landing. They would have got boozed anyway that weekend, but Tony's scrape gave them an excuse to hit the SP stubbies especially hard. Tony said the post-incident buzz was *pretty awesome*, adding: *perhaps that's why we flew in PNG, that combination of being young, flying . . . and shit loads of adrenaline!*

The scariest part of this engine failure was yet to come. Company engineers were flown in to repair the engine while the 206 sat crippled at Tekadu. Once it was ready to fly another NCA pilot, Fred Vanderol, was dropped there to fly it back to Nadzab. As Fred did his pre-take-off checks at Tekadu, he carried out the standard 'full and free' check of the flight controls: the ailerons and elevator. When he pulled the control column fully aft to check the 'up' elevator position, the elevator control cable snapped. The cable was later inspected and was found to be improperly seated in one of its pulleys. It was half-on-half-off, and had been chaffing, thus weakening, for a long time. There had only been a few strands of steel cable left intact. Had the cable failed one flight earlier, as Tony flew downwind during his engine-out approach and landing into Tekadu, he would have lost elevator control. The Cessna 206 would have crashed into the jungle, killing them all.

Tony's near-misses flying in PNG were like an advert for a Ginsu steak knife on late-night cable TV: *But wait, there's more!* It's here that P2-SEF, Tim Johnston's tunnelling machine from Masa airstrip, makes its reappearance.

In June of 1993 Tony was operating a series of North Coast Aviation coffee bean charters on the northern side of the Huon Peninsular. He had allowed a passenger to tag along with him for the day: Darren Hawthorne, the teenage son of NCA's Ops Manager at Nadzab. The freight runs involved shuttling between Sapmanga in the mountains and Wasu on the coast, transporting half-tonne loads of coffee beans that were to be shipped from the collection point at Wasu to the town of Madang, 160km to the west.

At about 5pm Tony prepared his fully loaded Cessna 206, P2-SEF (by now owned by NCA), for his fourth departure from Sapmanga strip. The take-off weight of 1545 kg put him 88 kg below maximum take-off weight. In Chinese culture, 88 is a wildly auspicious number. Tony and Darren weren't Chinese, and this lucky number wasn't to help them on this day at Sapmanga.

Sapmanga is a grassed grey gravel strip, 465m long, approximately 25 mins flying time from Nadzab. It's one-way, with a slope of 8.5% downhill to the north, shoehorned at 3000 feet above sea level onto the exposed flanks of a 10,000-foot-high peak on the western end of the Saruwaged Range. The departure out of Sapmanga involves taking off over some scrub and village gardens at the end of the strip then turning away from the mountainside and following the Urawa River valley down to the coast, some 15 miles away. As the light was fading, Tony decided this was the last flight of the day. The plan was for him and Darren to overnight in Wasu and continue with the coffee bean shuttles at first light the next morning.

As Tony taxied the 206 into position for take-off at the top of the strip, Darren made a casual remark: "Nothing exciting ever happens to me." Talk about tempting fate! Young Hawthorne was reaching out and tweeking the nose of Chance; giving the Grim Reaper the finger. Sometimes you're better off keeping your mouth shut.

Tony applied full power and the Cessna lurched forward, the 300-horsepower Continental engine roaring through the firewall, the Hartzell propeller biting into the mountain air, the undercarriage banging and crunching its way down the rough gravel strip. Everything was normal until just after the aircraft became airborne. As Tony felt the aircraft weight come off the wheels he eased forward on the controls to keep the aircraft in ground effect as it completed its acceleration to full flying speed. Just then the engine stopped. No bang, nothing dramatic, just a near-total loss of power accompanied by a hint of smoke coming from the engine. He estimated he was about 10 feet above the level of the airstrip when this happened. There were limited options, in fact only one: crash straight ahead into the garden at the bottom of the strip and hopefully come to a stop before hitting the mature trees beyond. Temporal distortion kicked in.

The aircraft descended back to earth like a wounded bird, and careened off the end of the strip in slow motion. The Cessna's left wing hit a pawpaw tree, tearing a section off. Sliding forwards, it ploughed into the loose dirt and low foliage of the garden. For a moment Tony thought he was going to get away with it unscathed — a bloody miracle. Unfortunately the boundary between the garden and the jungle was marked by a drainage ditch, and the aircraft still had forward speed. It nosed into the ditch, hit the opposite bank, and flipped onto its back.

Deathly silence.

The *drip drip* of fuel leaking from the damaged wing.

And then, the crackle of fire and a shockwave of heat.

The engine was burning and a grass fire began spreading around the upturned aeroplane. Tony and Darren hung upside down in their harnesses and Tony could see fuel pooling in the roof of the aircraft directly below his head.

"Fuck! Let's get out of here!"

This thought occurred simultaneously with flames creeping into the roof of the cockpit beneath him. Tony undid his harness and fell into the low blue flames head first, protecting himself with his forearms. His door was half open and he squeezed through the gap, crawling out through the grass fire that now surrounded his side of the inverted aircraft. There is no passenger door on the co-pilots side of a Cessna 206, the side where Darren was hanging in his straps. Darren was screaming, *"Get me out! Don't leave me!"* He was freaking out and couldn't undo his harness. Tony ran around to the other side of the Cessna and opened the right rear door — a double door that is used for cargo loading. There was no fire on that side yet, but it was creeping that way, and soon enough both sides of the 206 would be engulfed in flames. Their predicament was like a cheesy American TV car-crash sequence: the panic to get out before the cliché of the vehicle exploding in an orange fireball milliseconds after impact. Tony got to Darren in time, and pulled him out. Darren escaped without so much as a scratch, but Tony had not been so lucky. He had sustained second-degree burns on his face and neck, and third-degree burns on his forearm and chest. When he fell into the flames and then crawled through the grass fire his hair and eyebrows were singed off, and his nylon pilots shirt melted and stuck to his chest. The bottom of his ear was torn and bleeding from when his headset had come off in the initial impact.

The two of them staggered up to the village at the top of the airstrip, where Darren tried to raise the NCA office on Sapmanga's HF radio. Tony went into shock. With nightfall fast approaching Darren was advised by NCA staff that they would be picked up the next morning. Tony later said that coordination here was poor — pilot Dave Shute was working in an Islands Aviation helicopter only 10 minutes from Sapmanga that very afternoon, but was never contacted and asked if he could rescue Tony and Darren.

They spent the night in a thatched hut in the village, lying on a dirt floor next to an open fire. Tony's burns were blistering badly and he was in a lot of pain. He said the hut smelled like a BBQ and that this was vaguely enticing until he realised he was smelling his own burnt flesh. The pain was extreme: Tony got no sleep that night.

At first light the next day, 12 hours after the accident, a helicopter arrived from Nadzab carrying only the pilot and NCA's chief pilot Geoff Thiele. Strangely, no medical personnel were brought along to attend to the gravely wounded Tony. As Geoff came into the hut and saw Tony the first thing he said was, "Man, it got you good." The helicopter took Tony straight to Lae Hospital, where he was wheeled into a bare dusty room with a tiled floor, a metal-framed bed hanging from chains attached to the wall, prison style, and no hint of medical equipment. The facilities didn't inspire confidence. As luck would have it, Dr Emma Hucker, the wife of another NCA pilot, Jeffrey Hucker, worked at the hospital. She was a real-life Florence Nightingale here: discharging Tony and taking him back to the Hucker household, where he spent the next two weeks recuperating. Despite the discomfort, and the heavy cocktail of painkillers he was now on, that first night at the Hucker's place he remembers downing an ice-cold SP lager. Old habits die hard!

Tony settled into a daily morning routine of 2–3 hours with Emma, watching her picking dead skin from his wounds. This painstaking process was necessary to mitigate the risk of further infection. His worst wound was his right arm, where he fell into the fire.

He probably should have been flown to Australia or NZ as soon as possible, but he didn't have a passport as he was in the process of renewing his old one. The New Zealand High Commission in PNG expedited a new passport and when this was sorted, he flew to NZ to see a plastic surgeon at Auckland's Southern Cross Hospital. He was admitted to surgery right away, receiving grafts from his own thigh tissue onto the wounds on his arm and chest. The surgeon heaped praise on the way the wounds had been tended so well in the initial post-trauma phase in PNG: a testament to the professionalism and dedication of Dr Emma Hucker. Tony spent just one day in hospital then went home, spending a further three weeks recuperating. In an impressive act of generosity, a doing-the-right-thing approach that you don't always see from General Aviation charter companies, North Coast Aviation paid for his airfare to and from NZ and all his hospital bills.

While Tony was recovering in New Zealand, the PNGDCA Safety Investigation Department looked at all the data from the crash. Safety Investigator Mike Feeney headed the investigation. Performance figures from the Cessna 206 manual showed that the aircraft was not overloaded for its afternoon take-off from Sapmanga. The power plant had behaved normally at pre-take-off engine run-up, and all pre-take-off checks were normal. Feeney established that the aircraft had became airborne at the expected point down the runway for the take-off weight and the prevailing conditions. P2-SEF's engine was removed from the crash site and installed in a test rig at the Summer Institute of Linguistics aviation engineering base. It ran normally. A note from the head of the Missionary Aviation Fellowship (MAF) was passed to Feeney's team, for a time looking like it might explain Tony Froude's power loss. MAF had seen similar events with their Cessna 206 fleet. Their spate of take-off accidents had been caused by blocked engine exhausts. Baffles in the exhaust pipe had broken loose and moved into a position over the muffler outlet, blocking exhaust gasses. P2-SEF's engine was examined again, this time with a specific focus on the two exhaust pipes. Only one had been recovered from the accident site and was found to be operating without baffles. Unfortunately, in the absence of the other exhaust pipe, it could not be determined if a blocked exhaust was a contributor to this accident.

The remains of Cessna P2-SEF in a tree at Sapmanga.

Ultimately, the cause of the accident proved elusive, with Feeney stating in the final DCA report: "No conclusion can be reached as to the cause of the loss of power." The report made special mention of the post-accident actions of the high school student passenger, Darren Hawthorne: "The young man behaved particularly well under traumatic circumstances."[126]

Tony returned to PNG with an *Oh well, shit happens* attitude regarding the crash and his injuries. He said he had no fears or phobias about returning to PNG skies: but he did request to fly only twin-engine aeroplanes! He went on to become the deputy chief pilot of NCA in Nadzab. I remember when I heard that he was back in PNG and flying again how impressed I was that he had the balls to get straight back into it after such an ordeal. Balls of steel. These days he is a captain flying wide-bodies with a major international airline.

It had taken two pilots and two attempts, but this time P2-SEF was dead. Most of the aircraft lay as a burnt tangle of unrecognisable black shapes in the garden at the bottom of Sapmanga airstrip. The only component left relatively untouched was the tail section. A villager with a flair for installation art (PNG's answer to Damien Hirst?) somehow managed to carry the empennage section up the side of the strip and into the village. Here he perched it in a frangipani tree outside his grass hut, where it remained for some time as a weird totem to the efforts of Tim Johnston and Tony Froude, Cessna-killers extraordinaire.

●

— Chapter 11 —

In like Flynn!

I can resist anything except temptation.
OSCAR WILDE[127]

By early 1993 things at Air Manubada had changed considerably. Mack Lee's business had expanded, and now operated four aeroplanes on mountain runs and charters from his Port Moresby base.

His fleet included the single-engine Cessna 206 and a Cessna 185, and two twin-engine commuter aircraft — a Cessna 402 (previously with Richard Rowe's Simbu Aviation) and an ex-Royal Flying Doctors Service Piper Navajo from Australia. Mack hired Australian pilot Sid Makary to fly the 206, and I was doing my ratings on the Cessna 402 and the Navajo while still flying the occasional Goilala or Jungles milk run in the 206. I'd also moved out of the Salvation Army compound in Boroko and now shared a flat at the back of the Cathay Club with Sid. Our area of operations had expanded too. As well as servicing the mountain communities of the Goilalas and the Koiaris, Air Manubada operated a twice-weekly Cessna 402 charter on behalf the Ilimo chicken farm at 14 Mile out of Port Moresby, flying 16,000 day-old chicks per week to the Highland ports of Mendi and Mount Hagen; returning with a full load of fresh vegetables for the Moresby markets. We were also flying regular freight and passenger runs to the dive resort at Tufi in Oro Province, and ad hoc charter destinations included Tabubil, Kiunga, Nadzab, the Trobriand Islands, Gurney, and the hunting and fishing lodge at Bensbach in the Western Province.

Out at the coalface — the harsh terrain, intimidating weather, and dodgy airstrips of PNG — the accident rate remained stubbornly high. The list of incidents and accidents in '93 was long: Richard Rowe was killed when his Cessna 185 crashed into a ridge on a flight between Chimbu and Karimui. Pilot S. Kale crashed a BN-2 Islander while attempting a single-engine take-off at Kiriwina. As described in the previous chapter, Tony Froude crashed a North Coast Aviation Cessna 206 off the end of Sapmanga airstrip after an engine failure. Paul Crozier slid a Cessna 414 off the end of the short PSP-covered runway at Kikori. Dieter Wirth and Paul Brown and two passengers were killed when their Island Airways Islander crashed in the Simbai Valley near Madang. Airlink pilot R. Groves stalled and crashed an Islander after take-off from Namatanai on New Ireland, the result of an out-of-limits aft centre of gravity. Peter McGee wrote off Rimbunan Hijau's Islander in a take-off accident at Mount Hagen. Island Airways' bad run continued when Morris Konai destroyed a BN-2 in a landing accident at Bamboo airstrip in Madang Province. I had an engine failure after take-off in Mack Lee's Cessna 206, pulling off a fluky partial power landing on runway 32R at Jacksons Airport (my passenger, Bensbach Lodge's Brian Bromley, disembarked and made a beeline for the aero club bar to calm his shot nerves with a stiff drink).

Amidst this chaos and carnage the one great constant of expat life in PNG was the social scene. Port Moresby's social calendar was almost religious in its conformity to routine: Thursday night discos at the Yacht Club; Friday night drinks at the aero club, or downtown at the Travelodge Hotel (now the Crowne Plaza); Saturday night raves at the Firehouse nightclub at the Ela Beach Hotel, or fundraisers in the ballroom of the Islander Hotel (now the Holiday Inn); lazy Sunday afternoons at Crystal Rapids, or poolside at the Bluff Inn on the road to Sogeri. These weekly booze-ups served the exact same purpose as the 2 Mess bar sessions from my days as a pilot trainee in the RNZAF — they allowed the boys to let off some steam, facilitating a release of the pent-up stress from our continued exposure to PNG's dangerous flying environment. The

Peter McGee's BN-2 Islander crash at Mount Hagen.

unfortunate (or fortunate, depending on your perspective) consequence of this liquid PTSD therapy was roaming mobs of jacked-up expatriate pilots behaving badly in the city's bars and bazaars.

If we were going to kid ourselves that any of our watering holes were classy, the lobby bar at the Travelodge Hotel would have been the top pick. Port Moresby's social circles were extremely small, and at this venue it was not unusual to be surrounded by prominent local businessmen, mining executives, national politicians, and PNG celebrities. One Friday night I was there with the usual suspects: RH Trading pilots Massimo Lombardo, Paul Walsh and Dave 'Sloppy' Alsop; TNA pilots Dave Sarginson and Gerry 'Quickdraw' Krynen; Talair pilots Barry Brown and John 'Disco' Everett; and Government Flying Wing pilot Rob Cronin. As we stood in a circle, downing our SP draughts, growing pleasantly anesthetised as the alcohol worked its magic, Giles Rooney (a North Coast Aviation pilot based in Kerema) arrived with his Australian girlfriend in tow. A petite curvy blonde with an impish smile, she was wearing a short dark dress and high heels and was truly a sight for sore eyes. We were all white-girl starved, as there were so very few 'silverbellies' in-country, and I'd be lying if I said that we didn't all salivate as she sashayed into the bar on his arm. With Giles and his lady ordering drinks from the bartender, our testosterone-fuelled conversation turned to whether she was wearing a G-string, or had gone full Arnold Schwarzenegger — commando. She had no VPL (visible panty line), and the thought that she might be *sans* knickers was almost too much for us to handle. After some discussion, pilot Dave Alsop made a wager that he could find out the truth. We watched, captivated, as he strolled across to her. He started with a little chitchat, before leaning in to her saying, "That's a lovely skirt you're wearing. My girlfriend would love to have one like that. Tell me — is it silk?" As he spoke he ran his finger down one side of her torso, from the bottom of her ribcage to the very top of her thigh. It all looked perfectly innocent, as if his interest was solely on the fabric of the skirt. It was beautiful to watch. He returned to where we stood with a big smile on his face. "Houston, we have a G-string!" he exclaimed. "Right, someone owes me a beer!" Only Dave Alsop could have pulled that one off — he was one hell of a smoothie. But as lovable rogues go, he was hardly the first PNG had seen. The king of them all was Errol Flynn.

Flynn, for readers allergic to black-and-white movies, was an iconic Hollywood star of the 1930s and 40s. He was an overnight sensation in his first starring role; the 1935 Warner Brothers film *Captain Blood*. Dashingly handsome, with a twinkle in his eye and a swagger in his step, he went on to appear in over 60 films.[128] These included *The Charge of the Light Brigade*, *The Adventures of Robin Hood* (with Olivia De Havilland), *Objective, Burma!*, *The Private Lives of Elizabeth and Essex* (with Bette Davis), and my favourite, *The Dawn Patrol*. Flynn, an Australian by birth, was a serial womaniser, brawler and drinker of heroic proportions, described by his friend and fellow actor David Niven as a *magnificent*

specimen of the rampant male.[129] When his autobiography came out posthumously in 1960, the *Guardian* newspaper reviewer said of Flynn, and of his book: . . . *perhaps it is not the book to leave alone in the house with your daughter. But Flynn was not the man to leave in the house with your daughter.*[130]

Flynn honed his wicked, wicked ways during his early years, when he lived, worked, scammed and shagged his way through New Guinea.

He left his native Australia in 1927, aged 18, drawn north by news of New Guinea's Morobe district gold rush. He arrived in Rabaul, the capital of the Mandated Territory of New Guinea, and quickly talked himself into a job as a trainee government officer. This position was short-lived, after a background check revealed that his previous employer (in Sydney) had fired him for theft — he and a workmate had 'borrowed' from the company petty cash tin, spending their spoils on the horses at Sydney's Randwick Racecourse. His vaguely criminal past excluded him from government service, and he was dropped like a hot sweet potato. Next, he talked his way into a job as the manager of a copra plantation. In the job interview he was asked what he knew about copra: *M-mm, what do I know about copra? Only everything. I've been raised on copra. Spent all my life around copra*, he exclaimed confidently.[131] Flynn's Irish roots had left him endowed with more than a touch of the Blarney Stone. In fact he knew nothing about copra, and even less about running a plantation. On day one of the job, with no clue about how to proceed, he followed the advice he had received from an old New Guinea hand on working with the locals: *You just get hold of the Boss Boy . . . you call for him and just say to him, 'Boss Boy, carry on!' Just give the Boss Boy the impression you know more than he does — and the plantation will run like a clock.*[132] This worked for a few months, with Flynn standing before the assembled labourers each morning, shouting, "Boss Boy, carry on!" but eventually the plantation's owner discovered Flynn's lack of experience, and he was fired again.

Flynn lived and worked in the Mandated Territory of New Guinea and the Territory of Papua for the next four and a half years, with the occasional trip back to Australia. He was variously employed as the master of a Kavieng-based schooner (engaged in passenger and freight charters), as a gold prospector in Morobe (more about the goldfields later), and in the rather distasteful business of recruiting, aka 'blackbirding.' Flynn, always one to call a spade a spade, knew this work was unsavoury, admitting recruiting was in fact "slave stealing."[133] Despite being in decline elsewhere, the capture and trade of indentured labourers was thriving in New Guinea during the late 19th and early 20th centuries. Workers were often tricked into leaving their villages and, once sold by the recruiters to mining bosses, they had no way of getting home unless they completed a one- to two-year contract. Although they did receive a minimal wage, the labourers sold into the goldfields of Morobe and elsewhere were subjected to a tough and unforgiving existence. Heavy physical work, little rest, and poor nutrition led to illness and high mortality rates.

Two years after first arriving in Rabaul, Flynn took a trip south to Australia, in part to have a rather bad case of gonorrhoea seen to. He left behind many unpaid bills, broken promises, and the odd broken heart. Aside from his shady business dealings, Flynn had been extremely busy chasing and catching as many young ladies as possible during his first stint in the Mandated Territory. His father reminded him in a letter of the taboos of the early 20th century: 'My boy, always remember a man who has anything to do with a native woman stinks in the nostrils of a decent white man.'[134] Flynn was quick to confess: 'Dad, I stink.' He'd been an unprejudiced womaniser, later describing his first conquest of a mixed-race girl (who happened to be married to a local government official): *Maura was one of the most beautiful women I ever saw; honey-skinned, with freckles, long wavy hair, and a waist you could span with your two hands. Naturally my ambition was to spend as much time spanning it as I could.*[135] In 2007 I spoke with Paul Chue, whose father lived in Rabaul in the 1920s and 30s and remembered Errol Flynn well. This was both because Flynn owed him money (just proving how smooth Flynn was, to be able to separate a Chinese businessman from his coin!), and because of Flynn's rampage through the local female population. Chue Sr used to say that Flynn was so busy with the ladies, 'he needed a holster for his dick.'

Flynn returned to New Guinea in 1930, at the helm of a 54-foot cutter-rigged yacht, the *Sirocco*. He and three shipmates sailed her from Sydney to Port Moresby, taking seven months to complete what should have been a six-week trip. Biographer Lionel Godfrey said of Flynn's Australia–New Guinea voyage: *Not all the delays were attributable to amateur seamanship . . . the main holdups having been caused by inexperience, the temperamental engine — and the lifestyle of the mariners, which included large measures of carousing and wenching.*[136]

For a time Flynn ran a tobacco plantation on the Laloki River, 18 miles out of Port Moresby (very near the future site of the Spotters' Signals Camp, mentioned in Chapter 5). Ever the red-blooded rogue, he described in his autobiography the first time he laid eyes on his Boss Boy's daughter: *She wore a grass skirt, and that was all. Above her lava-lava garment, her little up-pointing breasts were so symmetrical and perfect as to have been attached by some means I didn't stop to explain to myself. Her skin was like shining satin, a colour of light mahogany, and as I stared at those up-pointing breasts my breath held — or must I resurrect the cliché that my heart stood still? I just stared at her and could only gulp . . . I had to have her.*[137]

It was during one of his several trips home to Australia that Flynn found his calling. In Sydney Errol was spotted by a casting director and eventually landed himself the role of Fletcher Christian in the Australian film *In the Wake of the Bounty*. The filmmaker's wife said of him: "Errol was a male butterfly . . . He breezed into all our lives, caused trouble with the girls in the studio, then left." In early 1933 he returned to New Guinea, sold his tobacco plantation, tied up some loose ends in the goldfields of Morobe, and left for England to pursue his dreams of becoming an actor.

Just two years later, after a stint working with the Northampton Repertory Company, his dreams came true, and he found himself on Hollywood's silver screen. But his links to New Guinea endured. Flynn still had outstanding debts with more than a few New Guinea businessmen, and these creditors followed his Hollywood career with interest. Several of them wrote to him, congratulating him on his success and politely reminding movie star Flynn that he owed them money. A brazenly immodest Flynn replied to them all, sending an autographed photo of himself with a note saying "This should cover it". Writer Malum

"This should cover it". Errol Flynn sent autographed photos like this to his PNG creditors.

Nalu, a prolific chronicler of all things PNG, relates a story from the picture theatre in Rabaul in the late 1930s. At the close of the latest Errol Flynn blockbuster, with the credits rolling on screen, a dentist to whom Flynn owed a considerable sum of money jumped up at the front of the theatre and shouted, "and teeth by Eric Wein!"[138]

Errol Flynn has been described as one of the most charming, engaging and self-destructive personalities to ever come out of Hollywood.[139] He achieved notoriety in 1942 when he took on a starring role he could have done without — as the defendant in a statutory rape trial, where he was accused of having had sexual relations with 15-year-old Peggy Satterlee and 17-year-old Betty Hansen.[140] He was eventually acquitted of all charges, but not before details of the court proceedings had become front-page headlines around the world. News of the trial had even reached the backwaters of the Pacific War, where US marines were fighting the Japanese from their South Pacific island airstrips. Pappy Boyington, a Corsair squadron commander based at the time in Espiritu Santo, Vanuatu, remembered Flynn's impact on the troops:

> We flew by day if weather permitted, and the evenings were taken up by outdoor movies . . . A public-address system would come on during intermissions at the movies, and we would hear newscasts from the rest of the world as well as home. The actor Errol Flynn was having a lengthy session in court concerning his amours at the time with some young things aboard his yacht. And a blow-by-blow account of the trial was woven into the newscasts. I'll never forget those few hundred lonesome lads under the coconut trees at Espiritu, chanting as one "Get that god-damn war news off the speaker. We want to hear about Flynn!" I wonder if Flynn realized how much entertainment he was providing the troops overseas.[141]

Errol Flynn's wicked ways gave us an expression still in use today. A wartime serviceman went out one night on the booze, and the next day reported to his colleagues, who asked him how he made out with the ladies. The fellow said with a sly grin, "I'm in like Flynn!"

Flynn died in 1959, a shadow of his former self: beset by alcoholism and illness, with his career in a tail slide (he lost his Warner Brothers contract in 1952), and with a series of failed marriages and relationships behind him. His obituary, from the pages of the *International Herald Tribune*, showed that despite his dramas and disappointments he still possessed his greatest attribute — style:

> Vancouver, B.C.: Matinee idol, Errol Flynn, 50, one of the last of the gallant screen heroes of two decades ago, died here today (Oct 15). Mr. Flynn, paunchy and graying but still exuding charm, was stricken last night in an apartment where he had dropped in for a drink. A coroner later ruled that Mr. Flynn died of heart attack. He said degeneration of the liver was a contributory factor in the

death. His life ended in the surroundings he liked best — with good liquor on hand and a beautiful young protégée nearby.

The following Monday, with happy memories of Friday's beers and smoothie Dave Alsop's Flynnesque G-string episode, I took off with Mack Lee in the Piper Navajo from Port Moresby on a charter flight for a local bank. Mack took the opportunity to use the flight to check me into some new airstrips. Our first stop was Errol Flynn territory — the airstrips at Wau and Bulolo, where Flynn worked a claim during the Morobe gold rush of the 1920s and 30s.

On a clear day PNG's landmarks make the navigation from Moresby to Wau and Bulolo fairly simple: you take off from Jacksons and set course just to the right of Mt Yule, head NNW to parallel the Owen Stanley Range, keep a lookout for the distinctive waters of Lake Trist on your right-hand side, and descend when abeam the Lake via the Kudgeru Gap to the Wau-Bulolo Valley. The valley stands out like the proverbial dogs bollocks — wide and grassy, with a landmark running through it that few PNG valleys possess — a partially sealed road. Unfortunately on this particular day Port Moresby was socked in under a gunmetal grey overcast, with the en-route landmarks obscured by mist and drizzle, so we did the next best thing and climbed up through the cloud to 14,000 feet (to avoid hitting all the hills) and tracked on the instrument route from the Port Moresby VOR to the navigation beacon at Tsile Tsile, which is situated just to the west of Zenag and the Lae-Bulolo-Wau road. Our weather forecast indicated that the northern side of the Owen Stanley Range would be CAVOK (clear of cloud and visibility OK), so we expected the weather to clear halfway along the route. This was a common early morning PNG weather pattern — a uniform cloud layer sat over one side of the ranges while the other side was completely clear. Only in the afternoons would things get more challenging, with the heat of the day brewing monster cumulonimbus clouds that would mushroom up to well over 40,000 feet. The turbulence, windshear and poor visibility from the accompanying rain showers that were part and parcel of these afternoon clouds made flight and navigation in the mountains very difficult.

Ten minutes into the flight, as we climbed through 12,000 feet, we finally punched out of the soup. To this day, even after a quarter of a century of flying under my belt, I never tire of the sensation as an aircraft pierces through the top layer of cloud into the bright sunshine above. Despite what land-bound mortals are experiencing below you on terra firma, it's always a nice day above the weather. Always. When you are climbing up through a solid overcast, deep within cloud, the cockpit is dim and sombre. All the pilot's attention is focused on their instrument scan, making sure that the aircraft is heading in the right compass direction, tracking the navigation aids precisely, climbing at the correct speed, and that the engines are operating normally. In cloud the body's ability to sense which way is up, and which way is down, and whether one is accelerating or decelerating or turning is severely limited due to the loss of external visual cues. The pilot must rely on the aircraft's primary instruments (the artificial horizon, the compass, the airspeed indicator, the vertical speed indicator, and the turn and bank indicator) to keep their aircraft in a steady, controlled state. The concentration is intense and absolute. When the aircraft bursts up through the top of the cloud into the clear air above it's like a rebirth into a safe and familiar environment. The cockpit fills up with bright sunlight, the top of the cloud layer falls away beneath you as the aircraft continues its climb, and the atmosphere cheers with the return of the pilot's full clique of senses.

Halfway along our route that morning, with the cloud layer a marshmallow blanket some 2000 feet below us, we could see that the weather forecasters had got it right — the northern side was indeed clear, and Mack pointed out the dogs-bollocks road snaking through the Wau-Bulolo valley as I began my descent. Far above us the sky was marked by the twin contrails of a northbound jetliner, white scratches in the big blue. I keyed the microphone when three minutes out: "All traffic in the Wau/Bulolo area, this is Piper Navajo Echo Golf Kilo, ten miles inbound via the Kudgeru Gap, descending through 10,000 feet, will be joining overhead for a landing at Wau." I overflew the airstrip at 5000 feet, descending downwind to position the Navajo on a two-mile final approach to Wau's runway 04. Wau (elevation 3,500 ft AMSL, 815 metres in length), like so many PNG mountain strips, is a one-way strip, sloping a considerable 8% up to the north-east. And like so many PNG mountain strips, in bad weather and/or with a large load on board, it is a strip to which you are committed to making a landing once you have descended and turned to make your final approach. The chances of a successful go-around are minimal due to the rising terrain at the top of the strip, and the mountains crowding in on the Wau-Bulolo Valley from all sides. An RAAF C-47 Dakota pilot had not had this pointed out to him, at his peril, when he made an approach to land in Wau in October 1960. It was the first time he had flown into the strip. He misjudged his approach, coming in too steeply, and after a heavy bounce decided to attempt a go-around. A witness described the ensuing chaos:

> As fast as (the aircraft) rose, the strip rose faster . . . I heard the tormented scream of Pratt and Whitney engines in fine pitch, and I saw the aeroplane briefly through the trees, nose-up at an impossible angle, just as it stalled and slammed on to the drome with a heavy thud that echoed through the valley. Greasy black smoke rolled upwards; the aircraft was burning. I was there in seconds, and it was a sight to behold. The fuselage had broken in two, just aft of the trailing edge of the wing, and through the flame-slashed smoke I saw men jumping from the break, rolling over and over through the inferno.[142]

Fortunately the 11 occupants of the aircraft survived, although several were badly burned. The civilian pilots based in Wau and surrounding ports were in an uproar when they learned that the RAAF had permitted pilots unfamiliar with Wau to fly unsupervised into such a challenging airstrip. Civil Aviation rules in the Territory prohibited this — civilian pilots had to make familiarisation flights into challenging airstrips with training captains before they were allowed to operate solo — but the RAAF was not under the Civil Aviation's authority so was exempt from this rule. One angry civilian pilot vented: *It's all right for the Air Force to be so darned sure of itself as long as the people flying their aircraft are the only ones who get hurt. But this latest crash shows just how big a danger is created for civilians when Air Force pilots, who, while they are highly competent, are unfortunately unfamiliar with Territory flying conditions . . . what is deplored is Air Force policy which permits men to fly into airstrips with which they are not familiar.*[143]

I did not share the fate of the RAAF C-47 pilot, and landed and taxied up to the top of Wau's airstrip, where bank staff waited to meet us. They began loading what looked like mail bags and a strongbox onto the aeroplane, and we were joined by two armed security guards who were to accompany us for the rest of the trip. While we waited Mack told me about the history of Wau and Bulolo.

In 1926 a gold prospecting syndicate known as the 'Big Six' followed a tributary of the Bulolo River up to a wide mountain ledge at 7000 feet. Here they discovered wildly rich deposits of alluvial gold on the upper reaches of Edie Creek. The gold rush that was spawned was one of the reasons that Errol Flynn left his native Australia, joining the hordes of adventurers flocking to New Guinea to find their fortune. Flynn described the scene at Edie Creek in his autobiography: *By day the natives and the white men chopped at the hillsides like termites, tearing up the soil and panning the earth.*[144] As is the case in most gold rushes, only a few men became rich. Flynn was not one of them: *Within a few days I heard all around the cliché of the gold field. 'There is too much New Guinea in the gold, they said, meaning that the earth was thin on gold, thick on soil.*[145]

On top of this, Edie Creek was not an easy place to get to. Although only 35 miles as the crow flies from the small town of Salamaua, the closest coastal port, getting there involved an eight to ten day hike. The route snaked up and down harsh jungle-choked mountain trails, and hiking parties were subjected to attacks by unfriendly tribesmen along the way. All supplies had to be carried in, with native labourers providing the muscle. They hauled packs weighing up to 25kg, which included their own food for the trip, and frequently consumed half the load during the multi-day slog through the mountains. It was a given that it was too costly to construct a road from the coast to the goldfields, but there had to be a better way to service the mining settlements of Edie Creek and the Wau-Bulolo Valley. A man of incredible vision, Australian Cecil John (C J) Levien, decided that the answer lay in the utilisation of air transport. This was at a time when global air freighting was in its infancy. His company, Guinea Gold No Liability (GGNL), constructed airstrips at Lae and Wau in 1927. The new airstrips were soon put to use by GGNL's first aircraft, a De Havilland DH37 (a single-engine bi-plane with room for a pilot and two passengers, who sat in tandem in a small forward cockpit), which was used to ferry in passengers and supplies. A sister company, Guinea Airways, was formed the same year to take care of the aviation side of the operation. The impact the first flights (between Lae on the coast and Wau in the mountains) had on the development of New Guinea was not lost on James Sinclair, an accomplished PNG aviation historian: "Life on the goldfields — and in the interior, the islands, and the remote outposts of New Guinea — would never again be the same."[146]

C J Levien and GGNL soon turned their attention to the Bulolo River flats, suspecting that over past centuries gold had been washed down from the mountains to the valley floor. Mining surveys confirmed the presence of alluvial gold there, with an estimate of gold-bearing deposits to a depth of 15 feet. What happened next was truly remarkable. Levien and his partners formulated an ambitious plan to conduct wide scale dredging of the Bulolo River bed in the Wau-Bulolo Valley. Contemplating this in the 1920s, in such a remote region, with zero road access, was no less outrageous than imagining a man walking on the moon. The logistical challenges facing them were considerable. They needed to carve more airstrips out of the jungle; source the manufacture of dredge components with dimensions and weight suitable for transport by air; and most importantly find an aircraft capable of carrying the components into short rough bush airstrips.

In addition to the two airstrips at Lae and Wau, more were eventually built — at Bulolo, Salamaua, Slate Creek and Bulwa. Dredge components were manufactured in the USA and transported to New Guinea via ship. The aircraft chosen by GGNL and Guinea Airways was the German Junkers G-31: a three-engine low wing all-metal aircraft in use at the time on Lufthansa's European routes. In consultation with their New Guinea-

A Guinea Airways Junkers G–31 is loaded at Lae aerodrome.

based clients, Junkers adapted the plane for its cargo role by adding a large hatch in the roof through which freight could be loaded by crane. The G-31 was at the time the largest freight-carrying plane in the world: with fuel for three and a half hours flying time it had a useful payload of 5800 lb (2600 kg), and with a reduced fuel load could carry up to 7100 lb (3200 kg). It was also well suited to New Guinea's hot and humid climate — its all-metal construction meant it did not need to be stored in large and costly hangars, as it was immune to the mildew and rot that afflicted its plywood and fabric predecessors.

With airstrips ready, and the first G-31 in service by early 1931, the transportation of dredge parts began. Dredge components were shipped to Lae's Voco Point wharf, situated half a mile from the mining company's freight shed at Lae aerodrome. Each section was designed so that it was not too large to fit into the G-31's hold, and no parts were heavier than what the Junkers could carry. The dredge components were unloaded by a 10-ton locomotive steam crane and hauled on flat top rail cars on a purpose-built railway line to the airstrip. Here another crane transferred the cargo directly into the belly of a waiting G-31. With the pilot strapped into the open cockpit, a cargo boy climbed up alongside the centre engine and cranked a handle to engage the inertial starter that would bring each of the three 525 hp Pratt and Whitney A2. Hornet engines to life with a splutter and a burst of smoke.[147] G-31 pilots, braving the elements in their noisy, draughty open cockpits, were busy chaps: their 35-minute flight from Lae saw them fly west up the Markham Valley, turning to the south to follow the Wampit Valley, then turning to the SSE at the junction of the Snake and Watut rivers and onwards to the grassy Wau-Bulolo valley. Unloading would have taken about 30 minutes, and a return trip about two hours. Pilots usually did four or five such trips a day.

The first dredge was completed and went into service on 23 March 1932. Visionary C J Levien didn't live to see his ambitious plans come to fruition — he died in Melbourne, Australia, two months earlier — but he was there in spirit. On opening day his ashes were spread over the river flats.

The area was soon buzzing with activity, with giant insect-like dredges crawling, snorting and crashing their way up the Wau-Bulolo Valley. Australian John Cooke was working for the mining company in Bulolo at the time and described the process as each dredge was put into service:

When the site was selected for the dredge a large rectangular pit was excavated. Into this pit the hull of the dredge was built and when completed water was diverted to fill the pit and float up the dredge. The superstructure was then assembled. The completed dredge was then ready to start digging its way up the valley with an escalator-like line of buckets digging deep below the water, gouging out the gold-bearing gravel. As the buckets reached the top, each load was tipped into the hopper and passed onto a moving screen where strong jets of water played on it, washing the smaller material onto finer screens. After passing from one process to another the gold was extracted and the fine gravel, sand and earth was washed back into the pond. The tailings, which are the larger stones and boulders, were carried on a conveyor belt high above out over the stern of the dredge to be deposited back to mother earth. As the dredge dug its way up the

A gold dredge in action next to Bulolo airstrip.

valley, floating in its own pond of water, it left behind ugly piles of rock tailings in place of what was once a lush green valley. A large gang of natives worked ahead of the dredge clearing the vegetation and felling the trees.[148]

GGNL's hunch that the Bulolo flats would be rich in alluvial gold proved spot on. Gold was dredged down to a depth of 120 feet, much deeper and in much greater quantities than the surveys had forecast. By 1938 there were eight dredges working the area, and mining and associated companies were operating a fleet of 14 aircraft into the region's airstrips, including Guinea Airways' four Junkers G-31s and two Ford 5-AT Trimotors. The Trimotor, nicknamed the 'Tin Goose', was an all-metal high-wing transport aircraft powered by three 420-horsepower Pratt & Whitney Wasp radial engines. This simple and rugged corrugated aluminium alloy aircraft was 50 feet long, had a 77-foot wingspan, and could carry a load of 3500 lbs (1600 kg) at a modest cruise speed of 80 knots. Although it only carried half the load of the G31s, it also had a large overhead hatch behind the wing for ease of loading, and was the perfect aircraft to service the goldfields airstrips that were too short to accommodate a G31. The Tin Goose was popular with Guinea Airway's pilots — unlike the noisy and draughty open cockpit of the G31s, the Trimotor had a fully enclosed and comfortably fitted cabin.

Gold output and cargo figures from that era were stunning. In the years 1931–40 over 25% of the total revenue of New Guinea's governing Administration came from gold royalties and associated charges — 70% of that gold came from the gold dredges that had been flown in, piece by piece, by air transport.[149] The volume of freight, including but not limited to the dredge parts, flown into the Wau-Bulolo Valley airstrips was mind-blowing. Freight figures illustrate the incredible contribution the New Guinea mining and aviation companies made in those pioneering days of air transport: in 1931, more freight was flown between Lae and Wau-Bulolo than the freight carried by all the air services of the United Kingdom, France and the USA combined.[150]

The dredging operations ran smoothly until the outbreak of war in the Pacific and the arrival of Japanese troops in New Guinea in January 1942. Two days before their capture of Rabaul (see Chapter 9), Japanese aircraft attacked the airstrips at Lae, Salamaua and Bulolo. Half a dozen mining company aircraft were destroyed on the ground at Lae, several civilian aircraft suffered the same fate at Salamaua along with one RAAF Hudson bomber, and five Japanese Zero fighters followed a Junkers G-31 to Bulolo and strafed the strip. Three G-31s at Bulolo were destroyed, with the crew of the one that had just landed making a lucky escape as Japanese bullets flew all around them. The Morobe aircraft fleet that had been used so effectively to serve the mining airstrips and communities was decimated in the attack. Mining operations ground to a halt, as the threat of a Japanese invasion made evacuating the miners and their families the priority. The gold rush was over, and the Wau-Bulolo Valley would never be the same again. As one commentator put it, with the attack on the goldfields airstrips and aircraft that day in January 1942, a thrilling chapter in world aviation history had ended in flames.[151]

With the strong box secured on board, and the somewhat surly security guards seated in the middle of the Navajo's cabin, I started the engines and prepared the aircraft for departure from Wau's 815-metre-long grass strip. After a quick radio call on VHF to area traffic, and a call on HF to alert Lae ATC of our intentions so they could monitor our flight progress, I taxied up to the top of the strip, had a quick look around for any unannounced circuit traffic and applied full power for take-off.

As we climbed away and I eased back on the throttles to set climb power, Mack pointed out the skeleton of one of the 1930s gold dredges beneath us. I glanced off to the side where he was indicating, catching a faint glimpse of a rusty steel carcass in the Bulolo riverbed's vegetation. Sadly, that oxide-brown skeleton is all that remains of the glory days of the Wau-Bulolo Valley's gold-producing years, an era now largely forgotten.

En route to our next stop, Chimbu in the Simbu Province, Mack motioned for me to turn to the east for some sightseeing. The small detour enabled him to show me the *Grey Ghost*, a WWII Boeing B-17 Flying Fortress wreck. Five miles from Wau, I spotted her, splayed on the side of the mountain in a patch of kunai grass like a giant puffed-up aluminium crucifix.

This B-17E heavy bomber took off with seven others from Port Moresby's 7 Mile aerodrome in January 1943, tasked with attacking a Japanese convoy off the coast of Lae. Japanese fighters pursued the B-17 after her bombing run, inflicting serious damage to her port engines. US Air Force pilots 1st Lt Ray Dau and 2nd Lt. Donald Hoggan nursed the damaged plane back towards Moresby, but with two engines soon completely out of action the four-engine bomber was unable to maintain altitude and the flight crew made the decision to force-land on a mountainside near the head of the Black Cat Pass. 1st Lt Dau put her down in an open grassy patch on steeply sloping terrain. He grasped victory from the jaws of defeat: in the impact the aircraft's back was broken aft of the wing trailing edge and the cockpit section was partially torn away, but the forced landing was a complete success. All nine crewmembers survived and were rescued by Australian troops.[152]

The mountainside has been the B-17's home since that day in 1943. Exposure to the elements has led to a gradual deterioration of the aircraft's US Air Force markings. These faded away to reveal something unexpected: Royal Air Force markings and serial numbers underneath. Conspiracy theorists were quick to jump on this, speculating that the B-17 was a British government aircraft on a clandestine mission. There is a much more pedestrian explanation. Boeing applied the RAF markings in the USA after the aircraft's manufacture, as it was initially assigned to serve with the English Coastal Command as part of the USA/UK lend-lease program. Before the aircraft had left the USA for the UK however it was re-tasked and sent instead to the US 5th Air Force's 43rd Bombardment Group based at Port Moresby. US Air Force markings were simply painted over the RAF ones at this time.

The *Grey Ghost*, as it has come to be known, remains one of the most easily accessible WWII wrecks in Papua New Guinea. North Coast Aviation pilots Colin Hicks, Joe Saba, Herwin Bongers, and Herwin's wife, Gill, made the trip in the mid 1990s. The four drove to the end of the road south of Wau, then hiked about 90 minutes up the ridgeline to get to the B-17. They took a 'shortcut' on the way back, spending three stressful hours in head-high kunai grass trying to find their way back to the road and their vehicle. On their return to Wau they were told by a local helicopter pilot that he would have been happy to fly them there — and it would have taken about two minutes!

After flying a couple of orbits over the Flying Fortress wreck (with the security guards seated in the back probably wondering what the hell we were doing) I departed the area, overflying Bulolo airstrip and township

The 'Grey Ghost' B–17E bomber near Wau.

10 miles NNW of Wau before setting course for Chimbu.

After two more fun sectors — Chimbu to Goroka and Goroka back to Port Moresby — we secured the Piper Navajo on Jacksons Airport bitumen parking apron and I made my way back to the Cathay Club's Chinese Restaurant to meet my colleague Sid Makary for dinner. PNG had one last bit of excitement lined up for us that day. Halfway through our meals, as we sat swapping war stories over a couple of SP Lagers, a very drunk and very angry ex-employee burst in through the front door. He was brandishing a large bush knife, slurring in half English half Pidgin about 'payback' and *'kilim i dai pinis'* ('kill him dead') and ranting about his unfair dismissal. I froze like a cigar store Indian, my chopsticks suspended over a bowl of *chowfan*. The manager, our upstairs neighbour in the Cathay Club's accommodation, appeared and negotiated with the man, skilfully talking him down from his rage. Sid and I nervously continued eating our sweet and sour pork and fried rice, our eyes glued to the intoxicated aggressor and his weapon. It seems inconceivable now, looking back on such events many years later, but we considered this to be a fairly normal occurrence, and after the machete-waving maniac was placated and escorted out of the restaurant we continued as if nothing had happened. We hadn't been mangled in an aircraft crash that day, Sid and I had both put some good flying hours in our logbooks, I'd learned a bit more about PNG's history, and we'd avoided being hacked to death with a machete over dinner. It had been a pretty good day.

●

— Chapter 12 —

Needles and Haystacks

As soon as we left the ground, I knew I myself had to fly.
AMELIA EARHART, AFTER HER FIRST AEROPLANE RIDE[153]

They could hear the drone of the aircraft long before they could see it. Straining to spot it against the backdrop of the Markham Valley's afternoon cumulonimbus clouds, one bystander finally made out the sleek lines of the inbound Lockheed L-10E Electra, shouting to his mates that he had seen her.

The polished aluminium alloy Electra descended gracefully from the sky and landed at Lae's coastal aerodrome. It was 29 June 1937.[154] The two famous and anticipated occupants of the aircraft clambered out, looking fatigued but pleased to have finally made it this far. Amelia Earhart and her navigator Fred Noonan had departed on their 1200-mile flight eight hours earlier from Darwin, Australia, their previous 39 days having been filled with adventure and challenge as they attempted an eastwards around the world flight. Starting in Burbank California on 20 May they had routed via Miami (Earhart had first landed at the wrong airport in Miami then made a very hard landing at the correct field, Miami Municipal)[155] then on to San Juan, Puerto Rico; Caripito, Venezuela; Paramaribo, Guiana; Fortaleza and Natal, Brazil; across the Atlantic to St Louis in French Senegal (Dakar was their planned destination but they couldn't find it), then on to Khartoum in the Sudan; Eritrea;

Karachi; Calcutta; Burma; Rangoon; Singapore; and finally Bandoeng in Java, the Dutch East Indies. They had been delayed for five days in Bandoeng, waiting as their unserviceable exhaust gas analyser (used to set maximum fuel efficiency) was fixed by Royal Netherlands East Indies Airline engineers.

From Bandoeng the Electra had routed via Surabaya to Timor and so on to Darwin.

In Lae, Guinea Airways' general manager Eric Chater had been trying all day to receive transmissions from the inbound Electra on the high frequency (HF) channel Amelia Earhart had informed him she'd be using. She had cabled ahead instructing that she would be sending and receiving on a wavelength of 36 metres, but Chater had heard nothing on this frequency. She had given him incorrect information — her calculations converting HF kilocycles into wavelength in metres (a conversion from the American system to the British system) were inaccurate. The HF channel she was actually transmitting on, 6210 kilocycles, converts to 48.3 metres, not 36 metres. In fact the Electra could only transmit and receive on two HF frequencies: 3105 and 6210. Not only was the Lae station listening out on the wrong frequency, but Lae could only transmit on 6522 kilocycles, meaning Earhart could not receive transmissions from them either. She didn't seem to be particularly proficient in radio navigation or radio procedures in general, and was on record as having said of her long-range direction finding radio equipment — "I don't need that! I've got a navigator to tell me where I am!"[156] The confusion with the Lae HF comms was an ugly omen of what lay ahead on the critical last stage of Earhart's around the world attempt.

Earhart and Noonan spent three days in Lae, with Earhart's husband back in California becoming more and more frustrated that their departure was delayed. He was anticipating her triumphant return to the US, and had arranged a guest spot for Amelia on a popular US radio program, scheduling it just six days after her arrival in Lae.[157] The couple's financial wellbeing depended on a successful and well publicised end to Amelia's epic journey, and this latest delay threatened to derail their plans. The last three legs of her around-the-world journey were the most dangerous of the trip: from Lae to equatorial Howland Island, in

Amelia Earhart and her Lockheed Electra.

the middle of the Pacific Ocean (Howland is north of Samoa and east of Nauru); then a north-easterly leg to Hawaii; and finally the leg to the US mainland. The pressure was on.

In Lae, Earhart was having problems obtaining weather forecasts prior to the challenging 18+-hour over-water leg to Howland Island. When planning her trip she had presumed that there would be a meteorologist at Lae, but she had presumed incorrectly. More ominously, delays were put down to 'radio misunderstanding',[158] as Earhart struggled to ensure that all parties were using the appropriate radio frequencies. The US Coast Guard had stationed the ship *Itasca* at Howland Island to help her home in on the airstrip there, and another ship, the *Ontario*, was stationed halfway along the route to act as an aid to Noonan's navigation. A failure to establish contact with either of these ships would make the Electra's search for the airstrip on remote Howland Island like looking for the proverbial needle in the haystack. Howland was a tiny pinprick of land in the vast expanse of the Pacific Ocean, and even with precise navigating during the long over-water flight, Earhart and Noonan would need to make contact with the *Ontario*, and more importantly the *Itasca*, to have any chance of finding it. Incredibly, these radio 'misunderstandings' were not resolved prior to her departure from

Lae. The *Itasca* at Howland was informed that Earhart would be able to receive and transmit on HF frequencies 500, 3105 and 6210. This information was incorrect. The Electra's HF 500 trailing antenna had been removed in Miami,[159] meaning that HF 500 could be used as a direction finder only, over very short distances. Earhart could therefore only transmit on HF frequencies 3105 and 6210 during her long over-water flight. To make things worse, she was of the opinion that her Electra could home in on signals in the ranges 200–1500 kilocycles and 2400–4800 kilocycles. The aircraft was actually equipped for accurate direction finding in the 200–1500 kilocycle range only. There was much confusion. The bottom line was that she planned to navigate her way to Howland Island by homing in on a signal sent by the *Itasca* for which she had no means of reception. The *Itasca* could not home in on her signal either — *Itasca*'s on-board direction finder had a frequency range of HF 270–550,[160] yet, as we have seen, Earhart had no capacity to transmit on HF 500 due to the Electra's missing antenna. There was an additional HF direction finder on Howland Island that the Electra would have been able to utilise, but Earhart was never informed it was there. She was doomed.

Amelia Earhart and Fred Noonan took off from Lae at 10 am on 2 July 1937. Guinea Airways Engineers described the take-off of the fuel laden Electra:

> ... the Lockheed took off towards the sea, taking the full run of the airstrip. As the wheels left the end of the drome, which would be 12 to 14 feet above sea level, the plane actually dropped a few feet, skimming over the water until it gradually rose, gaining height. Those watching kept the plane in sight until it was a speck in the blue of the morning sky. Lae's residents were the last to wish them 'bon voyage' . . .[161]

Before she left Amelia had sent her last press release to the *Herald Tribune*:

> Not much more than a month ago I was on the other shore of the Pacific, looking westward. This evening, I looked eastward over the Pacific. In those fast-moving days which have intervened, the

Amelia Earhart 's last takeoff. Lae aerodrome, 2 July, 1937.

*whole width of the world has passed behind us — except this broad
ocean. I shall be glad when we have the hazards of its navigation
behind us.*[162]

The ocean was to prove broad indeed. The Electra found plenty of
haystack, but no needle. The radiomen on board the *Itasca* heard
Earhart's transmission 19 hours and 27 minutes into the flight: "We are
circling but cannot see island cannot hear you . . ."

And then, 20 hours and 14 minutes into the flight, in an obviously
strained voice: "We are on the line of position 157 dash 337 will repeat
the message on 6210 kilocycles. We are now running north and south."[163]

And then silence.

By now navigator Noonan must have calculated that they were far
enough east to be close to Howland Island. When they couldn't see it,
and with their fuel running low, in desperation they resorted to flying
north and south on the same line to try and establish their position.
The sun had risen two and a half hours earlier, with the Captain of the
Itasca reporting smooth seas, clear weather and an unlimited ceiling. It
was a beautiful clear day, and yet the crew of the Electra couldn't see the

Itasca's signal smoke, the boat, or Howland Island (if they were flying below 1000 feet, their maximum visual range to the horizon would have been approximately 45 miles).[164] Earhart and Noonan were lost. One hour after Earhart's last transmission all involved knew the incontrovertible truth: the Electra's fuel tanks must by now be dry.

The resulting search-and-rescue operation lasted a week, covering some 250,000 miles of open ocean, at a cost of four million dollars — about $60 million today. But the most extensive sea search in US history (involving nine ships, 66 aircraft and over 3000 sailors and airmen)[165] failed to find any trace of the fliers or their aeroplane.[166] Amelia Earhart and Fred Noonan were never seen again.

Five years after Earhart and Noonan departed from Lae on their fateful flight, WWII arrived on the town's doorstep. Japanese troops invaded Lae unopposed in March 1942, striking from their base at Rabaul to occupy strategic sites along the coast of New Guinea, including ready-made airfields at Lae and Salamaua (airstrips constructed in the 1920s by the mining operator GGNL, described in the previous chapter). A witness described the first air raid on the airstrip at Lae by Japanese Zeros: *Wave after wave they came in with their guns crackling as they blazed away at sitting targets. The thudding of the bullets as they struck could be easily heard. With no opposition they could come as low as they wished. There were no fighter planes to intercept them and no anti-aircraft guns to fire against them. What an easy raid it was for these Japanese pilots.*[167]

The Japanese land grab was the precursor to Japanese Imperial HQ's plans to occupy Port Moresby, New Guinea's capital, as well as Tulagi in the Solomon Islands, giving them control of the shipping routes through the Coral Sea, and denying America the use of Australia as a major base in the Pacific. These outposts would serve as the southern boundary of Japan's planned 'Greater East Asian Co-Prosperity Sphere', a misguided aspiration to rule over much of Asia and use the Pacific Islands as a defensive perimeter. The 'co-prosperity' angle was pure spin. In reality, Japan wanted to rule Asian lands for their own agricultural and manufacturing needs and the islands to the south (the Dutch East Indies, Borneo, and Malaysia) were coveted for their petroleum reserves. The Japanese naively believed that by acquiring territory quickly they could subsequently agree to a negotiated peace with their newly conquered and occupied neighbours. *Asia for the Asiatics* was their battle cry, but the end-game was really *Asia for Japan*.[168]

Although frightfully slow to react, the Allies were eventually cognisant of the serious threat posed by the Japanese advance: forward bases in Port Moresby and in the Solomon Islands would give the Japanese a springboard for strikes against the Australian mainland. Thereafter, in an attempt to halt the Japanese southerly creep, RAAF and USAAF aircraft subjected Lae to almost daily bombing attacks from Allied bases in Port Moresby and northern Australia. Almost as soon as the first Allied ordinance fell on Japanese positions at Lae, exuberant press releases raving about the pinpoint accuracy of the attacks were issued from the General HQ of the Allies' South West Pacific Area (HQSWPA) in distant Melbourne, Australia.[169] The press department here was firmly under the control of Allied Commander General Douglas MacArthur. US history books generally make MacArthur out to be a military genius,[170] a lionised leader oozing with personal charisma and battle-won experience, but the perspective from those who worked with the man is somewhat different. A British liaison officer at HQSWPA said of him: "(MacArthur is) shrewd, selfish, proud, remote, highly strung and vastly vain. He has imagination, self-confidence, physical courage and charm, but no humour about himself, no regard for the truth, and is unaware of these defects." The US Navy called him 'that brass-hatted bastard',[171] and considered him a 'supreme egotist and grandstander.'[172] (MacArthur went on to serve as US Army Chief during the Korean War. He was fired in 1951 by then US President Harry S. Truman, who was less than complimentary of the military icon: *I fired him because he wouldn't respect the authority of the President. I didn't fire him because he was a dumb-son-of-a-bitch, although he was, but that's not against the law for Generals.*)[173]

But back to the bombing of Lae. Despite the propaganda coming from General MacArthur's sycophants at HQSWPA, the truth was many times the Allied bombs dropped on the Japanese at Lae fell into the sea. One Australian soldier spoke of how he had been privy to the real damage statistics: "A native from a coastal village told us with a grin that more often than not the raids made from high altitude were ineffective — except that they saved the Japanese the trouble of fishing, for the explosions stunned or killed thousands of fish, and small boats were always held ready to pick them up when the raid was over."[174] The glaring discrepancy between the press releases coming out of HQ in Melbourne and actual damage reports from spotters on the ground led to the installation of cameras in the Allied bomber fleet — after this only photographic evidence was used to compile reports on enemy targets destroyed.[175]

Despite some wayward ordinance, the unrelenting Allied air raids were ultimately so disruptive that the Japanese had to change the way their Lae garrison was resupplied. Initially this was done by air, then via barges from ships off the coast, and finally via submarine. Eventually, losses from Allied air raids were too much to take, and the Japanese bombers stationed at Lae's airstrip were withdrawn to fortress Rabaul.[176] From here they faced much longer flight times to reach targets in and around Port Moresby.

Two months after the Japanese occupation of Lae, Australian ground forces were brought in to needle the Japanese there and at Salamaua, although in small numbers. Troops were airlifted into Wau, the mining settlement 40 miles SSW of Lae, to form the 450-strong Kanga Force, adding to a skeleton unit of the New Guinea Volunteer Rifles (a territorial force made up of volunteers from Wau's pre-war mining-boom expatriate population) already there. While not large enough to present an offensive threat to the Japanese in Lae and Salamaua, Kanga Force was highly effective as a guerrilla unit: reporting on enemy troop, shipping, and aircraft movements; aiding in Allied target selection; harassing enemy patrols; holding off a Japanese advance on Wau; and most importantly bluffing the enemy into believing that a much larger force opposed them.[177]

Within 18 months of their Lae invasion, the tide had turned against the Japanese in the Pacific war. 1942 saw the height of their triumphs, with victory after victory, but by early 1943 their fortunes had turned — they had by then fought and lost the battle for the Kokoda Trail, had their Moresby invasion fleet turned back in the Battle of the Coral Sea, and lost four aircraft carriers and countless veteran pilots in the Battle of Midway. In September 1943 they lost control of Lae when Australian and US troops executed a bold pincer movement (codename Operation Postern) against the 2500-strong Japanese garrison stationed there. Australian soldiers advanced from the mountains of Wau and Tsile Tsile to the south-west, Australian and US soldiers advanced from beachheads to the east and south, and the first use of paratroopers in the Pacific theatre saw 96 C-47 transport aircraft disgorging 1700 paratroopers over the Markham Valley to the north-west. Large quantities of equipment and stores were captured when the Allies retook Lae, but the majority of the Japanese troops had already withdrawn into the rugged Saruwaged Range to the north, hoping to escape to the coastal towns of Madang and Saidor.[178] It was not to be an easy retreat. Japanese soldier Ogawa Masatsugu revealed the horrors of the withdrawal in his 1983 memoirs:

Soldiers who had struggled along before us littered the sides of the trail. It was a dreadful sight. Some were already skeletons — it was so hot that they soon rotted — or their bodies were swollen and purple . . . The whole mountain range was wreathed in the stench of death. That was what it was like . . . It was a death march for us. It had rained for more than half a year straight. Our guns rusted. Iron just rotted away. Wounds wouldn't heal. Marching in the rain was horrible. Drops fell from my cap into my mouth mixing with my sweat. You slipped and fell, got up, went sprawling, stood up, like an army of marching mud dolls. It went on without end, just trudging through the muddy water, following the legs of somebody in front of you . . . All battlefields are wretched places. New Guinea was ghastly. There was a saying during the War: "Burma is hell; from New Guinea no one returns alive" (Masatsugu sailed for New Guinea in January 1943 with over four thousand men. Three thousand more were later assigned to his unit. Only 67 survived the war).[179]

After its recapture Lae became a vast army camp for Australian and US troops, and engineers began construction of an aerodrome at Nadzab, 20 miles out of town on a track towards Goroka. In his book *Fear Drive my Feet*, soldier Peter Ryan, who was there, relates a funny story about the enterprising Australian troops (and gullible Americans) after the Allied victory:

> *Lae was found nearly empty when our forces stormed the place. Many Japanese had been drawn off to reinforce Salamaua, and the others had made good use of their prepared escape-routes through the mountains . . . The next day I wandered round among our troops . . . Australians were doing a brisk trade in counterfeit Japanese flags, made by painting a bright red disc on a piece of parachute silk. Some copied characters from Chinese Epsom-salt bottles, and we frequently saw an American proudly displaying his 'Japanese' flag, which bore the words, had he known it, 'Two teaspoonfuls in warm water, followed by a cup of warm tea.'*[180]

Post-war Lae flourished as the country's second largest city and largest port. Today the town is the capital of Morobe Province, with a population of some 80,000.[181] Lae's success has been very much linked to the establishment of the Highlands Highway in the 1960s,[182] an 800km potholed artery that links Lae and the coast with the towns of the Highlands provinces in the PNG interior.

My first trip to the Lae province was with Mack Lee in Cessna 402 P2-CBC. The flight was a part of my 402 training, with a light load of freight to be dropped off at Lae's 'new' airport, Nadzab. We departed on 17 October 1992, routing on an instrument flight plan via the waypoint *Starfish* 35 nm to the west of Port Moresby, onwards via the NDB (non-directional beacon) at Kubuna, then a visual segment to the disused airstrip at Maipa and overhead Aseki. Patchy low cloud obscured most of the terrain en route. We then tracked via the NDB at Tsile Tsile and finally flew visually down the Watut Valley, banking over the wide gravelly braids of the Markham River to land at Lae's Nadzab Airport. As we made our final approach to runway 09 I could see ahead to the coast, with the hazy outlines of Lae city nestling on the edge of the Huon Gulf. In 1937 Amelia Earhart had landed at Lae Airport, the airstrip on the coast, but when I was in PNG this airstrip was no longer in use, having been closed to commercial flights in 1987. Lae's replacement aerodrome, Nadzab, was the site of the major offensive support base and airfield used by the American Air Force after the Allies recaptured Lae in 1943. Post-war, it was upgraded (in part with Australian Government aid money) and opened as a commercial airport in 1977. At 2438 metres long it is PNG's second longest runway: rumour has it the post-war improvements were done so Nadzab could be used as a forward staging strip for the RAAF's fighter squadrons, should there ever be a need for Australia to engage in battle with one of her northern neighbours.

After landing, Mack directed me to taxi to the General Aviation apron on the eastern end of the terminal, past two Air Niugini Fokker F-28s, and beyond the hangars, offices and cargo sheds of Lae's dominant third-level charter operator, North Coast Aviation.

We dropped off our cargo, refuelled, and after engine start taxied back across the apron towards the runway for departure. I was still getting used to the 402's tendency to accelerate quickly on the ground at idle power, especially when empty. One of the Air Niugini F-28 jets was just rotating as I looked towards the runway — its stubby white fuselage powering off the deck in a fluid transition from earth to sky, a twin line of black exhaust trails spewing from its raucous Rolls Royce RB183-2 Spey engines. As we taxied to the holding point I noticed faint outlines of WWII-era taxiways snaking off into the disused areas of the extensive airport. These now-vacant grass-choked aprons and dispersal areas are reminders of the role the airfield played in the later stages of WWII, as the Allies harried the Japanese withdrawal from PNG to the Dutch East Indies (Indonesia), onwards to the Philippines, and eventually all the way back to their homeland.

The tower cleared us for take-off, and we departed Nadzab on a direct track for Port Moresby, climbing to 12,000 feet just to avoid all the terrain. I was still getting my head around the extreme nature of the landscape in PNG: everything was on such a grand scale.

The morning cloud cover over the ranges had largely lifted and a blue sky smiled down on the mountains, giving me the opportunity to take in all the landmarks that Mack was pointing out to me.

As we climbed on track to Port Moresby, the flat Markham Valley quickly gave way to the thickly wooded mountains of the Kuper Range, running north-south like a finger protruding from the north-western end of the famed Owen Stanley Range. Our Cessna passed over the Black Cat Gap, giving views to the airstrip at Wau less than 10 miles to our west, and Bulolo airstrip behind us. Soon we were over the heart of the Owen Stanleys, and the topography changed. Termite-trail veins of narrow mountain streams dissected the high country grassland plateau that had risen to meet us. Flanked by 8500 foot-high ridgelines we took a small detour to our left and flew over the azure waters of Lake Trist, with Mack mentioning how the Lake got its name. In 1931 pilot Les Trist gained the dubious honour of becoming the first pilot to be killed in a plane crash in Papua New Guinea. In May of that year, Trist took off in a Junkers W-34, a single-engine transport aircraft owned by Guinea Airways, on a flight from Lae to Bulolo. When he failed to arrive in Lae, search parties were sent out on foot and into the air, but after a two-week search no trace of Trist or his aircraft was found. Two months later, a pilot from the same company was approached at Lae aerodrome by a group of natives. They appeared out of the forest next to the airstrip, animated and gesticulating. One of the natives pointed to a *bilum* (a traditional string bag) he carried, then pointed to his head, and then to the airstrip. He stopped in front of the Guinea Airways pilot and opened the *bilum*, letting its contents fall to the ground at his feet. It was Les Trist's head. These tribesmen later led a ground party to the site of Trist's W-34 — he had crashed straight into the side of a mountain in the Wampit Gap, between Zenag and the Markham Valley; pilot Trist had been decapitated in the violent impact.[183] The lake in the Owen Stanley high country bears his name to this day.

With the turquoise teardrop of Lake Trist at our six o'clock, Mack

Les Trist, the first pilot killed in PNG.

told me to set course for the distinctive flat-topped peak of 10,700ft high
Mt Yule, standing like an obelisk to the NNW of Port Moresby, 40 miles
ahead of us. Having left the high country grasslands behind, I marvelled
at the rugged nature of the terrain now below us — a riot of green, with
jungle clinging impossibly to near vertical dogtooth ridgelines. Sheer
limestone cliffs created a maze of narrow white-water laced gorges,
with angry torrents bulling their way through to the lower ground of
the coastal plains beyond. I wondered how any crashed aircraft could
ever be found once swallowed up by the inhospitable country beneath
us. During WWII hundreds of Japanese and Allied crash sites were never
found. In one case in recent history it took the dense jungle of the area
three years to give up its secret . . .

In early 1979 New Zealand pilot Graham Walker departed Wau on a
freight run to Port Moresby in a Cessna 206 operated by Elomair Ltd.
His route was to have taken him over the same terrain I now looked down
on from the left seat of Mack's Cessna 402. Classic PNG tiger country.
Graham was new to PNG, and although he had a total of 880 hours and

outside of PNG would have been considered a reasonably experienced pilot, he had only arrived in PNG ten weeks earlier and had held a PNG Commercial pilot's licence for just 13 days. He was a PNG newbie. His Cessna 206 was observed departing from a climbing turn overhead the Wau airstrip towards the Kudgeru Gap, which lies 10 nm to the SSE, and is the normal VFR (visual flight rules, i.e. staying clear of cloud and in sight of the ground) route that is followed to cross the Owen Stanleys before descending on the Moresby side of the range. Terrain within ten miles either side of the Kudgeru Gap rises to over 9000 feet. Once through the Kudgeru Gap pilots normally track via the deep gorge of the Korpera River to the flat floodplains of the Gulf Province, a further 25 nm to the south-west. When the weather closes in this is a tricky route to navigate successfully — the valleys are tight, the mountain peaks high and unforgiving and there is little room for error. An RAAF Caribou crew had learned this the hard way in August 1972 (seven years before Walker arrived in PNG) when they crashed into a ridgeline near the Kudgeru Gap in bad weather while attempting a low-level reversal turn, killing the three-man crew, two adult civilians, and 20 of the 24 PNG schoolboy Army Cadets on board.[184]

The weather in Wau was fine on the morning of Walker's departure in 1979, but the pilot of a Fokker F-27 Friendship reported that there was a line of thunderstorms and associated bad weather lying between Wau and the Port Moresby side of the Owen Stanley Range. A Cessna 206 pilot operating south of the Kudgeru Gap reported that the weather in the area made it *too dangerous to attempt VFR*, and that he was faced with *thunderstorms, rain, reduced visibility and generally rat-shit* conditions on his side of the Range.[185]

Graham Walker failed to make contact with Port Moresby air traffic control service after his hand-off by Lae ATC, and 30 minutes later the search-and-rescue phase was activated.

It was presumed that Walker had first tried to get through the Kudgeru Gap and, failing that, tried the secondary VFR route, to the south-east of Wau, crossing ridgelines to get to the Lake Trist plateau and then tracking south via the Biaru Valley (known as the 'false Kudgeru') to the lower country.

Over the next four days an extensive air search was undertaken. Eleven fixed-wing aircraft and five helicopters spent a total of 117 hours in the air looking for Walker's Cessna 206, concentrating on these two routes across the mountains. Initial promising reports of emergency beacon signals could not be confirmed, and despite leads on the third day the nature of the terrain prevented any sighting of a crash site. The aircraft was not found and the search abandoned, Walker presumed dead.

Three years passed.

In late November 1982 villagers on a hunting trip in the Kudgeru Gap came across the wreckage of a light aircraft. It was found impacted into near vertical terrain, 5900 feet above sea level. Fifteen village men were employed to cut a helipad as close to the accident site as possible, and a week later CAD staff inspected the wreckage. The shell of the Cessna was overgrown, deep beneath a tall and dense jungle canopy. The engine and propeller were buried in the ground and the fuselage had been burnt open in a post-accident fire. The tail section was gone, having rolled down a steep cliff face, and the emergency beacon was found in the fuselage — having been rendered inoperative by impact damage. There were remains of a pilot on board and personal effects recovered included a shirt, a pair of socks, a toothbrush and a bank passbook. These items identified the pilot as Graham Walker. It was clear that the Cessna 206 had hit the mountainside with considerable force, and that that Walker had been killed instantly.

I knew nothing of the grim history of this area as I transited overhead in the Cessna 402 on that day in 1992. On a clear day the terrain looked benign and beautiful; it was easy to forget how easily life could be rubbed out down there when the weather was bad and a pilot took chances he shouldn't be taking.

It was a stunning view from the office as Mack and I left the Kudgeru behind us. Forty miles later we hit Air Manubada's familiar hunting ground, the strips of the Goilalas. We over-flew the Tapini Valley and looked down on Fane and across to Ononge as we began our descent into Port Moresby.

●

Chapter 13

Missionaries, Mercenaries and Misfits

When I obtained my private pilot's licence, I briefly considered a career as a commercial pilot as I appeared to have the necessary attributes . . . with a heart like Phar Lap and a brain like a pea, however I would probably have failed the pilot's medical with my blood pressure and IQ too high.

JOHN RALSTON WILD[186]

In 2007 I sat at the bar of the Port Moresby Aero Club, yarning over a few beers with PNG pilot Norm Bramley. At the time he was working for Airlines PNG (formerly known as Milne Bay Airways — MBA), but inevitably talk turned to 'the good old days' and his previous life as a pilot for legendary PNG airline Talair.

The arrival of Johnny Walker, himself a PNG aviation veteran, turned the evening into something of a boozy Talair story fest. A couple of their tales stood out and I remembered them long after our chat, even as other details of the night were blurred by multiple rounds of icy cool SP lager.

The first concerned orchid fanciers and obscene photos. In Talair's heyday, when their aircraft crisscrossed the airways of PNG with a multitude of aircraft, a bunch of adventurous elderly American ladies embarked on a tour of the PNG interior, taking in highlights such as the Goroka Show and Tari's Ambua Lodge, with side trips to focus on their particular fascination — PNG's extensive range of endemic orchid species. A Talair aircraft ferried them between stops, and the pilot would generally remain with the aircraft while they were bussed to a local attraction. At one such stop the pilot, who shall remain nameless, noticed that a few cameras had been left in the aircraft. He decided to leave them some 'special' images of Papua New Guinea, and secretly snapped away, making sure to return the cameras to their original positions so as not to raise any suspicion.

Weeks later the orchid fanciers, now back home in the US, arranged a get-together to compare the photos they'd taken on their epic trip to deepest darkest PNG, excitedly hovering over the freshly developed images (this was back in the dark days of photographic film and processing), going gaga at the wild and wonderful snaps. I wish I could have been a fly on the wall at the meeting:

"*Here's a picture of the rare* Orchidaceae Acianthus vulcanicus."
"*Outstanding!*"
"*Wow, look at the distinctive lateral sepals on this* Calanthe triplicata!"
"*Delightful!*"
"*Now what's this one of, dear?*"
"*That orchid looks just like a man's thingy!*"
"*Oh my Lord, that is a man's thingy!*"

Yeah — *Orchidaceae Phallus maximus.* On several of the rolls of film the pilot's rather large penis made an unexpected but spectacular appearance, lying al fresco on top of an open aircraft logbook. His man-bits may well have been larger than his brain though — the aircraft's registration, the date and his name were clearly visible in the photos! The offended orchid fanciers, with perhaps a curious mixture of outrage and titillation, wrote a stiff letter of complaint to their tour agency; this eventually found its way to the desk of Talair's Chief Pilot back in PNG. Norm told me that Captain Big Dick was summonsed to Talair HQ in Goroka for a bollocking. It was suggested to him that if he wished to keep his job, he should refrain from taking snaps of his wiener with passengers' cameras, and that it would be best if his man-orchid was *not* permitted to experience any al fresco moments in future. The hardest part of the Chief Pilot's job during the disciplinary meeting was keeping a straight face!

With stories flowing as thick and fast as the handles of SP arriving on the bar-top, Johnny Walker shared one about his early days with Talair. Very soon after being hired, and checked out in the BN-2 Islander, he dropped into Wanigela with a near-full load of passengers and freight to pick up one punter. It took the ground staff longer than usual to board the passenger — he was an elderly man, and from his reluctant shuffle out to the aircraft and the look of fear in his eyes, was obviously a nervous flyer. Walker waited as the Talair agents manhandled the passenger onto the plane, reassuring him in Pidgin English that all would be well with the flight. Eventually Johnny departed Wanigela for his destination, Gurney. Soon after he established the Islander in the cruise a passenger leaned forward and tapped him on the shoulder, yelling, "Smoke!"

Johnny shouted back over the din of the Islander's engines: "No mate, you can't smoke!" The passenger tapped him a few minutes later — same thing — "Smoke!"

Bloody hell, these local passengers just don't listen. Johnny ignored him. Then the passenger repeated the process, this time looking alarmed, pulling on Johnny's shirt sleeve and pointing to one of the engines. Johnny tracked the man's gesture with his eyes — shit! There was smoke billowing from the rear of the port engine! At that very instant said engine coughed, spluttered and stopped running. Johnny threw in a bootful of rudder to keep the machine straight while carrying out his engine securing drills, extremely concerned there might be an uncontrollable fire somewhere inside the engine cowl. But the smoke cleared; the dead engine was safely shut down. His thoughts then turned to fuel balancing — they had a 30-minute flight on one engine ahead of them — and he thought it best to feed the running engine from both wing fuel tanks to prevent the build-up of a lateral weight imbalance. Johnny had a very careful think about how to achieve this — the Islander fuel system had three settings per engine: *tank to engine, off,* and *tank to opposite engine.* He mentally rehearsed the required movement of the respective fuel selectors, then did it. In the heat of the moment he buggered it up and accidentally shut off the supply of fuel to the good engine. The starboard engine started coughing and spluttering too, with the aircraft now yawing left and right like a life boat in stormy seas. This was not good for the mental health of his passengers, who must have been convinced the BN–2 was about to become a glider and crash-land in the patchy scrub below. It took Johnny a few moments to sort it all out — he reconfigured the fuel system, this time properly — and the good engine burst back into life. The rest of the flight went OK and he performed an uneventful single-engine landing into Gurney. The passenger disembarkation process was anything but uneventful though — one passenger simply didn't. It was the elderly nervous flyer Johhny had picked up in Wanigela. He was dead. An understandably rattled Johnny, who suspected the *lapun* (old man) died of a heart attack during the acute stress and excitement of the near-double engine failure, called his boss in Lae and passed on the news. With a money-comes-first attitude not atypical of management stiffs, the boss seemed entirely uninterested in the death of Johnny's passenger, and far more concerned with the financial implications of the death of the engine!

There are a million Talair anecdotes, and this is no surprise when you realise the importance of the airline to the development of domestic aviation in Papua New Guinea in the 20th century. In a rugged landscape so utterly dependant on air transport, its ubiquitous aircraft and its symbiotic embrace became irrevocably intertwined with daily life in PNG. There would be no one who lived in PNG between the 1960s and 1990s unfamiliar with the aircraft of Talair: their orange-and-white livery with the company logo on every tail — a stylised Highlands warrior in feathered headdress holding a long barbed spear. This was an image that came to be synonymous with PNG bush flying. No discussion on the nation's flying scene would be complete without at least a brief exposé on the company.

It all began in 1952 when a small aviation company by the name of Territory Airlines (TAL) started operations in the Highlands port of Goroka. In 1958 the struggling airline (consisting of just two aircraft, a clapped-out old de Havilland DH-84 Dragon and a Cessna 170) was purchased by 25-year-old Dennis Buchanan, who had started his PNG aviation career as a cargo manager for Gibbes Sepik Airways. Buchanan may have been young, but he was a born businessman and had already shown his entrepreneurial nous with the sale of his half share of a Bena Valley coffee plantation at a 400% profit. Buchanan was to become the preeminent figure in PNG aviation for the next 35 years, with TAL (renamed Talair in 1974) gobbling up its competitors and going on to become one of the largest third-level airlines in the world. In its prime the airline was flying to 193 PNG airstrips with over 600 scheduled flights per week. Talair aircraft over the years included a plethora of Cessna models — the 170, 180, 185, 205, 206, 207, 336, 402, and Cessna Citation Jet; the Dornier Do27; Beechcraft Barons and Queen Airs; the de Havilland DH-84 Dragon; de Havilland Canada DHC-6 Twin Otters and DHC-8 Dash 8s; the Piper PA-23 Aztec; Pilatus PC-6 Porters; Britten-Norman BN-2 Islanders; Embraer EMB-110 Bandeirantes. More than a thousand staff worked behind the scenes, with pilots at bases including Madang, Kundiawa, Mt Hagen, Mendi, Port Moresby, Lae and at company HQ in Goroka.

Dennis Buchanan's services to tourism and aviation in PNG were rewarded with an MBE in 1975 and a knighthood in 1991, but his personal and financial success, and that of his airline, was never without drama. Throughout his long career he was involved in endless running battles with the PNG Civil Aviation Department, constantly fighting for what he believed to be Talair's rightful share of the domestic air transport market. He was incensed that preferential treatment seemed to be given to the 'big boys' (Trans-Australia Airlines, Ansett-MAL and later Air Niugini) and refused to let his airline be pushed into a subservient position by local politics and bureaucracy. Things came to a head in 1988 when the PNG Government under Prime Minister Paias Wingti announced a move to cancel licences of 'foreign' air operators unless they sold a 75% controlling interest to nationals by the end of the year.

Buchanan, an Australian by nationality but a man heavily invested in the PNG tourism and transport sector, was outraged. Never a man afraid to fight for his patch, he publicly announced that unless the Wingti Government withdrew their nationalisation policy he would ground his airline within 30 days in protest. Wingti held firm; so did Buchanan, and Talair was grounded as promised. Overnight most of the domestic air services in the nation were terminated. The travel plans of thousands of passengers were thrown into disarray, as were the lives of villagers in the many isolated mountain and island communities for whom Talair was the sole lifeline. Within four days the resulting chaos and public uproar led to a vote of no confidence in the Wingti Government. They were ousted, and the new government under Rabbie Namaliu promptly returned the status quo.

Buchanan's hard-nosed gamble had paid off. But Talair's halcyon days were over, and sadly PNG skies were only to be graced with his flying Highlands warrior-tails for another five years. In May 1993, with financial difficulties mounting, Buchanan announced that Talair would cease operations. The aircraft were transferred to one of his subsidiary companies, Flight West Airlines of Australia and, in the blink of an eye, the airline that had contributed so much to PNG's domestic aviation sector simply disappeared.[187] As someone who had always looked up to Talair, its pilots and managers and staff, initially it seemed inconceivable to me that it was all gone. I had watched TAL's Bandeirantes and Twin Otters come and go from the tarmac at Jacksons Airport in Moresby from my first day in-country; starry-eyed in admiration and drooling with envy as the Talair pilots, gods of the bush, launched into battle. For me the morning procession of orange-tailed aircraft trundling out to the holding point in a heavenly cacophony of hissing turbine engines and growling reverse-pitch propellers was a central vignette in the country's rich aviation tapestry. PNG aviation without Talair was like Kermit without Piggy; Starsky without Hutch; macaroni without cheese; Kool *sans* Gang. But one man's loss is another's gain, and Port Moresby-based airline Milne Bay Airways (MBA) moved quickly to fill the void — snapping up Talair's route network, honouring outstanding TAL tickets to curry favour with the Buchanan faithful, and ordering new aircraft quicktime to take up the slack. Until their competitor's downfall, MBA had played second fiddle to Sir Dennis Buchanan and his massive Talair fleet. Not anymore.

Milne Bay Airways (MBA, known tongue-in-cheek by pilots and staff as 'Married But Available') began commercial operations in 1987. The airline was formed when John R. Wild, a Port Moresby-based architect who had always held an interest in aviation, agreed to a 50% partnership with the Milne Bay Provincial Government to establish an air service catering to the needs of the local people. MBA started off with a Grumman Goose seaplane imported from the USA and soon added to their fleet, operating a Piper Aztec and a Beech Excalibur Queen Air between Milne Bay and Port Moresby. The Grumman Goose proved unsuitable for PNG operations and was expensive to maintain, so was swapped for an Aero Grand Commander in a deal with Paradise Air in Palau.[188] (When I first arrived in PNG the Grand Commander sat idle on the tarmac near the MBA hangar. It was known as the *Ground* Commander as it never flew.) From these relatively low-key beginnings MBA expanded quickly, and by 1990 they had become a turbine operator, with their first de Havilland DHC-6 Twin Otter on line, followed by two Dornier 228-212s in 1991 (airframes previously with the failed 'Tranzair' in New Zealand). MBA in the 90s was a Wild family affair, with patriarch John Sr as Managing Director, son Simon as General Manager, son Michael as Engineering Services Manager, daughter Victoria as Special Projects Manager and son John Jr as a senior pilot.

Talair's downfall was a gift of immeasurable value to MBA, and it presented me with an opportunity too. Soon after the orange tails disappeared I heard whispers at the Aero Club bar that Milne Bay Airways needed co-pilots for their expanding fleet of Dornier 228 turboprops. I wanted in on that deal, and approached MBA's chief pilot, Mike 'Jeeves' Butler, with my resume. By this time I had 1509 total flying hours, including 1041 hours of PNG time: 351 hours on Mack Lee's twins (the Cessna 402 and Piper Navajo) and 690 hours in the Cessna 206, most of it in challenging mountain strip ops. Jeeves hired me on the spot. I handed in my notice to Mack Lee, thanking him for giving me my start in PNG aviation. His generosity, sage counsel and excellent route and strip training could not be faulted. Without the latter it is doubtful I would have survived my first 1000 hours of PNG flying. It had been a pleasure to work for Mack and his business partner Godfrey Seeto as a bush pilot for Air Manubada, and I count my days working with them as some of the best of my career.

I joined MBA in October 1993, by which time I had been in-country for 18 months. The co-pilots who joined MBA at around the same time included the lads from Moresby and Kamusi-based Malaysian logging company Rimbunan Hijau Trading (Massimo 'Max' Lombardo, Paul Walsh, Dave 'Sloppy' Alsop), North Coast Aviation's Brian Hoskinson and Sanjay Tikary and Ian Jeremy, Trans Niugini Airways' Cameron Gibbs and Gerry Krynen, Colin Hicks from Island Airways, and newbies Shane Wedding and Kris Randall, who were the only MBA co-pilots with no prior PNG experience. I had to wait a few days for my Dornier ground school, as well as pass the PNGDCA Basic Gas Turbine exam, so in the interim was assigned as a non-rated co-pilot on the Twin Otter. This meant I sat in the right seat of the aircraft on revenue flights and observed the operation, although I was not legally allowed to do any flying. My first flight was with 24-year-old Captain Grant Le Lievre, the golden boy of MBA. Grant had experienced a stellar ride to a quick command with the company, partly because of his good timing (joining MBA just as they began their expansion into turbine ops) and also because he was a switched-on unit: a good operator with an air of Errol Flynn *je ne sais quoi* about him. Grant and I launched on a morning MBA Gulf run, the daily loop of coastal strips between Port Moresby and the central Gulf Province: Kerema, Ihu, Baimuru and Kikori. Strapping into the Twin Otter, I could see John Wild Sr pacing up and down the flight line. This was a sight that was to become very familiar. 'Old Man' Wild began each and every day outside the main maintenance hangar, arms crossed, brow furrowed, scrutinising the aircraft movements on the apron like Caesar inspecting centurions on a battlefield. He was known for his short temper and explosive outbursts, and although I was never on the receiving end I'm told they were hairy and scary indeed. The quickest way to have your MBA career curtailed was to be involved in a heated disagreement with the Old Man.

Within a few days of starting at MBA, I had met most of the captains. They were a motley bunch. In addition to Chief Pilot Mike Butler and Grant Le Lievre, the roster included John Wild Junior, Ivan Popek, Bill Purcell, Stu Hannah, brothers Xavier and Daren McHugh, Tom Karlsborn, John Thomas, Clive Morgan, Johnny Walker, John Bruce, Mike Douglas, Joe Kumasi, John Everett, Andrew Hursthouse, Peter Yasi, Drew Salter, Henry Goines, Ross Fieldus, Rob Rachinger, Jim Millar, Warwick Rankin, Peter Jones, Tony Gridley, Neil Brooker, and father and son duo Gerd and Michael Franck. Included in their ranks were more than a few ex-Talair pilots and between them they shared many decades and thousands upon thousands of hours of PNG flying experience.

When I first arrived in PNG, Br Damian had told me about the three 'M's. Expatriates in New Guinea were half-jokingly pigeonholed into three groups: Missionaries, Mercenaries and Misfits. I'd arrived as a Missionary, but by the time I joined MBA I was firmly in the Mercenary camp — gaining experience I'd be unable to obtain back in my home country of New Zealand, frantically accumulating as many flying hours as I could. The problem with the lifestyle in PNG was that the longer you stayed, the more likely you were to join the ranks of the Misfits, and the harder it would become to reintegrate back into a more normal existence in one's home country. In PNG's wild-west free-for-all tropical paradise the boundaries between what was acceptable behaviour and what was not became blurred, with expats living like kings and, at times, acting without regard for conventional social rules and practices. The white *masta* was top of the tree, and if so inclined could behave very badly indeed, generally free of consequences. This was a very 'un-PC' legacy of the country's colonial past. The hard-core Misfits, especially the pilots, got a glazed look in their eye, an addiction to South Pacific Lager twist-tops (or something stronger), and a pathological aversion to how things were done in their home countries. The moral compass tended to drift too, firmly in the direction of the local *meris* (girls). This affliction was known as going *troppo*. Errol Flynn spoke of the *troppo* effect in his 1960 autobiography: ". . . if you spend more than five years in New Guinea you were done for, you'd never be able to get out, your energy would be gone, and you'd rot there like an aged palm."[189]

MBA had the odd Misfit on the payroll, but in the 1990s the cuckoo's nest's head loony was Captain X (it's best if the reader doesn't know his real name). If you looked up *troppo* in the PNG dictionary, there'd be a picture of X next to the definition, grinning inanely. He was nuts. Captain X was extremely full of himself and his skills as a pilot, and was a total FIGJAM ("Fuck I'm Good! Just Ask Me!"). There was no doubt in his mind he was the ace of the base: the best pilot in the company. The Chinese have a saying for people like this: *Great doubts, deep wisdom. Small doubts, little wisdom.* His body was his temple, and was another outlet for him to express his awesomeness. X was borderline anal about the healthiness of the food and drink he consumed, and spent countless hours in the gym pumping up his pipes and his guns. He was known to strip down to his running gear in between scheduled flights and jog around the airfield perimeter (even in the intense heat of Moresby's dry season) as a further masochistic punishment to himself and no doubt to appear bigger and stronger than anyone else. X didn't stroll into a room; he would glide in like a Spanish galleon — his half-open shirt revealing his man-fur and a cluster of gold chains and trinkets between his man-cleavage. He was one hell of an intense character, and I was never sure if he was going to high five me as a fellow aviator and 'dude,' or punch me in the face just because he could.

My first flight with X was soon after I started as a co-pilot at MBA. He was the chief pilot on the Dornier 228 fleet at the time, and I was paired up with former Rimbunan Hijau pilot Paul Walsh (who had joined MBA the same day as me) so X could give us our initial Dornier endorsements. Paul and I were good boys the night before the flight and turned up at the MBA offices at Moresby's airport at dawn's crack, hangover free, excited and ready to begin our Dornier training. I was in awe of the machine as X talked me through the cockpit prep and the engine start procedure. The 228, a 19-seat high-wing unpressurised turboprop commuter aircraft from the Dornier factory in Oberpfaffenhofen, Germany, was equipped with twin Garrett TPE331-5 engines, with 715 horsepower per side. The nine-seater Piper Navajo and Cessna 402 I'd been flying for Mack Lee each had less than 620 hp with their two engines combined, so I expected the Dornier to be a real beast. It sure was. X gave me control as we climbed away from Moresby's runway 14R. The first thing I noticed was the extreme lightness and sensitivity of the controls, and the crispness of the ailerons. The Dornier 228 had a fantastic wing and remains the only aircraft I've flown that can pick up the dropped wing in a stall with aileron alone (for non-pilot types, this means that it has an aerodynamically advanced wing design). The machine was almost impossible to stall — the wing was so efficient that the nose had to be raised to a ridiculously high attitude and the speed washed back to below 60 knots before the airflow would break away from the top surface and start rumbling across the tailplane. This was incredible handling for a 19-seater turboprop commuter aeroplane. Captain X ran me through all the normal upper air handling exercises — steep turns, climbing and descending, stalls in a clean and approach configuration, stalls with power on and power off, and a dive to the maximum operating speed (V_{NE}) of 200 knots. This was the only odd thing about the Dornier 228 — there was a much smaller band than most aircraft between the cruise speed (170 knots) and the maximum operating speed. I was told this was something to do with the lack of robustness in the design of the aircraft's empennage (stabiliser, elevator, fin and rudder assembly). It was a lovely aircraft to pole around the sky, however, and the Garrett engines with their direct link between the turbine section and the prop driveshaft were responsive and powerful. In approach configuration, with the aircraft dirty (with flap and gear extended), X showed me how the 2.7 metre disc of the Hartzell props acted as a huge speed brake when the power levers were at flight idle (closed). This de facto speed brake was a great recovery tool to be used when a pilot got high on approach (too steep) and needed to correct and get back on an ideal descent path. Another nifty bit of kit was the RSDI (Reference Speed Deviation Indicator), a gauge on the captain's side of the instrument panel. It was a real-time green-arc indicator of the angle of attack, calibrated for landing speeds, labelled SLOW on one end and FAST on the other. On short-field landings one could fly an airspeed that put the pointer on the letter W of 'slow' and be assured of the ideal

The Dornier 228.

minimum approach speed. Later, when I was a captain on the aircraft, I was to use this technique often.

Once my turn in the co-pilots seat was up, I swapped with Paul Walsh and moved to the middle of the empty passenger cabin to enjoy the ride as X began running Paul through the same exercises I'd just experienced. I didn't pay much attention to what they were doing — but Paul told me about the handling exercises years later. He said that they'd finished off the approach configuration stalling exercise (with the aircraft configured for landing, with gear and flap out) and then moved into the V_{NE} demo. Paul pushed the nose forward into a steep descent, but could not accelerate the aircraft into the barber's pole (the beginning of the red section of the airspeed indicator). He pushed and pushed, but the aircraft wouldn't accelerate. "Push more, push more!" yelled X. Paul tried, and with a near kamikaze angle of dive the aircraft finally accelerated close to its top speed. As they recovered from the dive and the aircraft decelerated back to cruise speed, Paul noticed that the flaps had been left in the extended position after their low speed handling exercise. The flaps had been oversped by 70 knots! This was an excursion well outside of the aircraft operating limits and required an entry in the aircraft logbook and a post-flight inspection by ground engineers to confirm the structural integrity of the flaps and the flap extension system, as they were not designed to be operated at these extreme speeds. Captain X didn't put the overspeed in the log book. He brushed it off and pretended it hadn't happened. It's quite possible that for the rest of its life that particular Dornier flew around with the strength of its flaps compromised. X was covering his ass, but the correct thing to do would have been to put safety above the embarrassment of the cock-up and let the MBA engineers know about the overspeed.

My line training began, again with X as my training captain, the following week. My first flight was a Moresby — Gurney — Missima — Gurney — Moresby flight. It was one of MBA's regular scheduled services, with a load of passengers and freight. This is how a new pilot is introduced to the handling of an unfamiliar aircraft — in a normal line-flight situation.

I learned that day that Captain X had no awareness of passenger comfort. In an unpressurised aircraft, like the Dornier, a pilot should take care not to exceed a 1000 feet per minute descent (as indicated by the vertical speed indicator in the cockpit — the VSI), as anything steeper doesn't give the inner ear a chance to equalise and generally leads to pain and discomfort in the ears as you descend into more dense air. The pain is most acute for those on board the aircraft who have a head cold or nasal congestion. If you have ever been in a high-speed elevator, or in a train passing through a tunnel, you will know what I am talking about: discomfort as you attempt to unblock your ears as they are affected by rapid pressure changes. X either had no idea about this, or simply didn't care. The whole of the south-eastern coast of the country was clagged in that day, and as we descended into Gurney through broken cloud layers it was obvious to me that we'd have to fly overhead the airstrip and track outbound on the instrument letdown procedure in order to get below the cloud and become visual with the airstrip. X and I were not on the same wavelength. He was flying the sector to introduce me to normal Dornier ops, giving me a chance to relax on our first flight together and watch and learn from him. He exhibited nothing but bad technique and was clearly rattled by the bad weather. Approaching the descent point for Gurney he was all Neanderthal grunts and mumbles, twitchy and sweaty as he readjusted the position of his hands on the thrust levers over and over again. His nervous tic of repeated shoulder shrugging further displayed his anxiety (X was not the only senior MBA pilot with a nervous tic. I was later to fly with another who, when weather conditions were bad, would nervously pick at his greying chest hair, transferring plucked hairs to his mouth and chewing on them as his uneasiness grew).

As we flew overhead Gurney's VOR navigation aid a hole opened up over the strip. It was clear all the way to the ground and I could see one end of the runway, but the hole was too small for my liking, and certainly too small to be manoeuvring a six-tonne aircraft down through. Or so I believed. Before I could say anything, X cranked the aircraft into a steep turn, closed the power levers and shot down through the hole. Very soon the rate of descent was approaching the 2000 feet per minute mark and as he rolled on more bank angle to stay in the clear air of the narrow gap I felt my body press downwards into the seat as the G-force increased. This guy was a frikken nutter. As I held my nose and blew to equalise my ears I looked back into the cabin to check on our passengers. Their eyes were wide with fear, some were holding their hands to their ears in obvious pain, and most had a "WTF?" expression on their face. X clearly needed reminding that Japanese troops had been turned back from Gurney by the Australian Army and the RAAF in 1942, and that there was really no need for him to dive-bomb the strip.

I chatted with fellow PNG pilot Colin Hicks over a coffee in Sydney's Darling Harbour in August 2012. Colin told me that Captain X had done exactly the same thing to him — a dirty dive into Gurney airstrip — when Colin was a co-pilot with MBA. After landing and pulling up at Gurney's parking bay, Colin expressed to Captain X that he wasn't impressed with the manoeuvre and didn't think it was an appropriate way to manhandle the Dornier, especially with passengers on board. Captain X was not receptive to the criticism — he was clearly very proud of his performance and couldn't see any fault with what he had done. He dismissed Colin with a tsk and a roll of the eyes, muttering, "It's hard to soar like an eagle when you are surrounded by turkeys." What a fruit loop!

While I was researching this book Captain X's name made an unexpected but not surprising entry in PNGDCA's accident files. When he was a younger, fitter and unfeasibly better looking FIGJAM he was working for Douglas Airways, flying the BN-2 Islander. At this time he'd been flying in-country for over seven years, so was considered a very experienced PNG pilot. One day he did a charter from Port Moresby to Bodinumu, a short, steep, clay strip in the Koiaris. The weather was good, with little cloud and no wind. On his return to Port Moresby, a routine post-flight inspection by an engineer revealed extensive and shocking damage to the aircraft. The right undercarriage was displaced rearwards, the same-side engine mounts were distorted and the right wing was a mess. Its leading edge was buckled, its top and bottom surfaces were wrinkled and an internal inspection revealed the rear spar was fractured. Marks on the right door indicated that at some point the propeller had made contact with the fuselage. The aircraft had obviously experienced a VERY hard landing. Captain X was subsequently interviewed by PNGDCA Accident Investigator N W Yonge who sought to establish the reason for the hard landing (which X admitted had taken place in Bodinumu) and the reason that X thought it was acceptable to fly an obviously badly damaged aircraft back to Moresby while carrying two fare-paying passengers. X said that there had been a large rate-of-descent increase on his final approach into Bodinumu, but that he had not applied any power to correct this. He said, "It was the shortest landing I have ever done . . . (I) needed a lot of power to get to the top of the strip."

I can imagine the shock experienced by his passengers during the firm landing in Bodinumu, with one perhaps turning to another and asking: *"Dispela balus i kam daun? Or wanpela man em i sutim?!"*(Did we land? Or were we shot down?!).

Yonge's Q and A session continued:

"Did the aircraft handle OK on the return flight?"

"Yes, but it did pull to starboard slightly."

"So you can offer no reason as to why the aircraft landed heavily?"

"None at all, I can't work out what happened."

Yonge was shocked at X's lack of comment on, or explanation

for, his heavy landing. The final line of his report was blunt: *When a pilot is involved in an accident such as this, and is unable to offer any explanation as to a possible cause, then serious doubt must be placed on his suitability to operate aircraft in a similar role in the future.*[190] When I did my Dornier line training with Captain X, more than ten years had elapsed since his hard landing at Bodinumu. It *was* the future Accident Investigator Yonge had spoken of, and here was X, in charge of pilot training on MBA's Dornier fleet. X's rise to a position of responsibility reminded me of an old adage: The higher a monkey climbs, the more he shows his bottom.

After one more line training flight with Captain X (Moresby — Tabubil — Kiunga — Moresby), I was 'checked to line', meaning I was released to normal line duties as a Dornier 228 co-pilot and OK to operate MBA's flights in that role with any of the captains.

It was an exciting time. I was a part of a real airline — MBA operated their Twin Otter and Dornier fleets throughout PNG from their Moresby base; they had a satellite base at Mendi in the Southern Highlands; they managed a crew-change contract for the gold and silver mine at Misima for Placer Pacific Ltd,[191] using aircraft and crews wet leased[ix] from TransAir Australia. I was soon head down and bum up with a busy roster, crewing scheduled RPT (Regular Public Transport) flights that covered the Highland ports of Goroka, Chimbu, Tari, Mendi and Mount Hagen; Lae's airstrip at Nadzab; as well as Kerema, Daru, Balimo, Kiunga, Tabubil, Gurney, Misima, Losuia in the Trobriand Islands, and Popondetta. Popondetta (also known as Girua) was the only airstrip I had not flown into during my time working for Mack Lee and Air Manubada.

Popondetta town is 70 nautical miles north-east of Port Moresby, on the far side of the Owen Stanley Range. The town is served by Girua airstrip, which on initial inspection appears something of an anomaly — a 1700m-long tar-sealed runway, not something you'd normally see at a small regional town in remote Papua New Guinea, a country lacking

---

[ix] Industry term: a wet lease is when the aircraft comes with crews (pilots and sometimes cabin staff) included. A dry lease or 'normal' lease is when the lessee gets just the aircraft.

in major infrastructure. There is an explanation. Girua was built by US military engineers for use by the US Air Force in late 1942. The site had been selected for its strategic location — bringing an Allied bomber and fighter base within closer proximity to the Japanese-held strips at Lae, Salamaua and Rabaul — as early as July 1942, but the Japanese landings at Buna had forestalled these plans.[192] Girua airfield was built after the Allied victory over the Japanese troops at Gona and Buna later that year, at the conclusion of the Kokoda Track campaign, and had several names including No.7, West 7, Horanda No. 7, and Kenny Strip.[193] It lies on a coastal plain ten miles inland, with the beaches of Buna to the north and the slopes of 5500 foot-high Mt Lamington to the south. It was one of the few strips that were laid with bitumen during the war. I first went there three weeks after joining MBA, with taciturn Captain Stu Hannah. Flying overhead Girua and joining the circuit area, I could clearly see the outline of several wartime airstrip complexes nearby. Dobudura drome was most prominent, made up of three strips north-east of Girua, once used as the advanced base for the US Fifth Air Force. The largest runway here was 2700 metres long. A smaller intersecting strip was covered in Marsden matting and used as a fighter base. Another 1800m-long runway was built parallel to the main strip and surfaced with bitumen. The whole area around Girua and Dobodura was covered with miles of taxiways and aircraft dispersal hard stands during WWII. Flying overhead I could still see horseshoe shaped aircraft revetments clustered near the runways. These were used by the 58th Fighter Group's Republic P-47 Thunderbolt fighter-bombers. Beyond Girua and the deserted Dobodura dromes I could see the outline of yet more aerodromes further to the east, near the shores of the Embi Lakes. The whole complex was truly massive: by the end of 1942 American Army engineers had prepared a total of 15 landing strips in the Popondetta area. According to author Bill James, in the late 1940s there were over 1000 aircraft wrecks here.[194] Parts of aircraft can still be found in nearby fields, especially during the dry season burn-offs, but all the major wrecks are long gone, most of them chopped up by scrap metal dealers soon after the end of the war. It's a real shame that more weren't preserved, as yesterday's junk has become today's priceless WWII relics (as an example, an airworthy P–47 Thunderbolt is now worth over 1.5 million US dollars).

In the 1970s and 80s several wartime aircraft wrecks were set up on display at the side of the terminal at Girua — static gate guardians. By the time I was operating in and out of there, 1993–95, there were only two left: a North American B-25 Mitchell sitting on its undercarriage, and a Republic P-47D Thunderbolt standing on its nose. At the time of writing only the B-25 remains, the rest having been removed over the years by private restorers — some with and some without permission.

As I settled in to the new job I quickly came to appreciate how different MBA's scheduled RPT Dornier operation was from Air Manubada's ragtag GA ops. The Dornier 228 fleet was a very professionally run operation — exactly as it should have been. There were full-time MBA agents at all stations and they took care of all the commercial aspects. What a change for me not to have to collect the tickets and cash fares, load the aeroplane and argue with the locals over the size and weight of their luggage. These duties fell to the ground staff and once the aircraft was loaded and ready to go they passed the pilots the passenger/freight/fuel load weights, and we referred to the plasticised charts in the cockpit and calculated the performance data for our departure (the decision speed, rotate speed and emergency climb-out speed). It was a pleasure to have moved on from my previous life flying overloaded and chronically underpowered aircraft into dangerous airstrips. The take-off and climb performance of the Dornier was impressive, even with full loads out of the Highlands airstrips of Hagen, Goroka, Mendi and Chimbu. Even with an engine failure just after take-off we'd be OK to either continue or return. This was in complete contrast to the twins I flew for Mack — if I'd lost an engine just after take-off in Air Manubada's Cessna 402 or Navajo with a full load of veges on board out of Mendi or Hagen the operating engine would only have been good for escorting me to the scene of the resulting crash.

One aspect of the operation that took a bit of getting used to was the two-crew cockpit environment. Other than the training trips I flew with Mack Lee, all my flying in PNG had been single pilot. I had been in charge of everything, a real *boss man balus*, but I now found myself in a support role as a co-pilot to MBA's captains. Losing my former position as head honcho, and having to run all decisions through the captain, was initially a bit weird. Captain Ernest K. Gann, in his epic aviation tome *Fate is the Hunter*, summed up this quirk of the co-pilot position well: *He is not exactly mortal. Existing in a sort of purgatory, he waits with all the patience he can muster for the day when he will no longer be a co-pilot. Until then he must mind his manners, ever balancing the obedient against the obsequious, salving his pride and temper only in his most hidden thoughts. For a number of reasons, not the least is his eventual promotion to captaincy, he must observe the code of master and apprentice. The rules are fixed and catholic. I am, in all eventualities, supposed to know more than he does, a theory we both secretly recognise as preposterous.*[195] My take on my position in the right-hand seat of the Dornier was this: I was there to make the captain look good, to assist him any way I could, and to be an extra pair of qualified eyes to keep watch over things and make sure we didn't make any silly mistakes and crash the thing. But it was ultimately the captain's aircraft, and I always made a special effort to let them run the operation their way. Most of MBA's captains were great — relaxed confident proficient aviators — and my adaptation to the co-pilot role was an easy one.

Included in the paperwork when I joined MBA was an application to the Department of Civil Aviation for my partial ANO28 exemption. The holder of an ANO28 was exempt from the normal route and airstrip training requirements — you could literally go anywhere, to any airstrip you had never been to before, without the need to be checked out there first by your airline's training pilots. A partial or full ANO28 was a real badge of honour, a tangible validation of a pilot's PNG experience and credentials. I called it the 'licence to thrill'. Talair pilot Charles Perry summed up nicely what it *really* meant: "After about two and a half years I was given an exemption from needing to be route and strip trained . . . it was called an ANO28 exemption. I had probably operated into 50 strips at that point in time and from then on I was completely on my own . . . we called it the licence to be lost and afraid." Mine came through a few weeks after I started on the Dornier — an AN028 covering the Western, Gulf, Central and Oro Provinces.

I wasn't a Dornier co-pilot for long; in the end just shy of six months. One day I walked past the Operations room and saw my name on the wall — I'd been assigned the next Twin Otter command training course. MBA had plans for me, and were to make good use of my AN028 and my background as a bush pilot.

●

Chapter 14

Dodge City and the Cheshire Cat

*You love a lot of things if you live around them, but there isn't
any woman and there isn't any horse, not before nor
any after, that is as lovely as a great aeroplane.*
ERNEST HEMINGWAY[196]

**The de Havilland of Canada DHC-6 Twin Otter is a beast. If you want
to hear a pilot rave about how great his or her machine is, have a
chat with a 'Twotter' pilot.**

The DHC–6 is a 19-seat unpressurised high-wing twin turboprop
STOL (short take-off and landing) utility aircraft. The prototype first
flew in 1965 and was designed as a replacement for the renowned
single Otter, with its twin-engine design allowing improved safety (the
reliability and performance of twin turboprop power plants vs a single
piston engine) and an increase in payload while retaining the type's
impressive STOL qualities. The Twin Otter was a wildly successful utility
aircraft (available from the de Havilland factory equipped with tricycle
landing gears, floats or skis), with over 800 examples in service before
the type ended its production run in 1988. When I joined MBA, they
operated two models: the –200 series (powered by twin Pratt & Whitney
550 shaft horsepower PT6A-20 engines), and the –300 series (powered

by two 620 hp PT6A-27 engines)[197].

I was lucky enough to do my command on the aircraft in 1994. It remains the most amazing, impressive, adrenaline-spiked and testosterone-infused aircraft I have flown (I've since flown the Boeing 747-400, Boeing 777, and the Airbus A330/340 wide-body airliners, and three ex-military jets: the BAC Strikemaster, de Havilland Vampire and Czechoslovakia's L-29 Delphin. The Twotter is top of the list for me). The Twotter was the perfect aircraft for Papua New Guinea's bush airstrips — with its oversize low pressure tyres and low landing speeds permitting operations into short rough landing grounds, its rear cargo door and spacious cabin allowing ease of cargo and passenger loading, and its grunty turbine engines enabling the airframe to carry an impressive payload (1,500–1,800 kg) out of most airstrips. My training was done by MBA Captain Ross 'Shags' Fieldus, a PNG old-timer who had been flying in-country since 1979. We started with three sorties of upper air work and circuits, introducing me to the normal and emergency handling of the aircraft, before the line training began. This also included ground handling — Ross showed me how the aircraft could be taxied backwards using a touch of reverse propeller pitch on the ground. During the following two weeks we flew together on regular MBA passenger flights, involving multiple sectors up and down the Highlands and Gulf runs out of Port Moresby. I acted as aircraft commander while Shags sat in the co-pilot's seat and trained me in the routine operation of the Twin Otter. Within three weeks of starting my Otter endorsement and having accumulated 37.5 hours on type (involving 40 sectors of line flying, a line check, an instrument check and a night circuit check) Ross signed me off as a Twin Otter captain. Becoming a skipper with MBA was an important milestone. (Ross Fieldus retired from PNG flying in July 2011. When he left he was a training captain on Airlines PNG's fleet of Dash 8 turboprops, and had amassed a total of 25,065 hours in a 47-year flying career. Shags flew for Talair for 15 years and MBA/Airlines PNG for 18 years. It is a testament to his professionalism that he survived so long in Papua New Guinea when so many others did not. I have great respect for Ross, and for the other old-timers like him. They are a rare and fine breed indeed).

There was nothing I didn't like about the Twin Otter. She was a big girl, standing 19 feet 6 inches tall, 51 feet 9 inches long, and with a generous 65-foot wingspan. I loved that you had to climb up to get into the aircraft — like a trucker monkeying up into the cab of a big rig. Direct access through the cockpit's left-hand door was achieved using a step bolted to the lower forward fuselage and a hand-hold on the side of the aircraft, allowing the pilot to hoist himself up into the sharp end of the machine. The flight controls were unusual, with a central pedestal coming up from the floor branching into a Y-shape, and a control yoke on each side for the captain and the co-pilot. Most of the time the MBA Twin Otters were flown single pilot, i.e. no co-pilot, just the captain. The other unusual feature of the cockpit was the location of the engine controls — the power levers, propeller pitch levers and fuel control levers were suspended from the roof. This, too, was unorthodox, as most aircraft house the engine controls in a central floor-mounted console (the Otter's high-wing design lent itself to this layout). Having your hand up on the power levers in the roof gave the aircraft a biker-gang vibe — it was like reaching up for the throttle on a custom Harley's ape-hanger handlebars.

Steering on the ground was via a tiller mounted on the back of the captain's control yoke. The tiller controlled the hydraulically actuated nose wheel, with a maximum deflection of 60 degrees left and right of centre giving the aircraft great manoeuvrability on the ground. The interior of the cockpit not crammed with controls, gauges, and circuit breakers was lined with a grey quilted vinyl fabric — a cockpit design feature from the 1960s — showing the aircraft's vintage. Yeah baby! I loved it.

The Twotter was my first command on a turboprop powered aircraft. This was a big step up from the piston engines I had been operating so far — a turboprop is basically a jet engine, but instead of the thrust coming from the hot efflux out the back end of the jet pipe, the exhaust gasses pass through a compressor that powers a thrust-producing propeller. The Twin Otter's Pratt and Whitney PT6 power plants are free turbine engines equipped with a single annular combustion chamber and a four-stage compressor. The same engine, or variants of it, are found in some other great turboprop aircraft: the Beechcraft Super King Air and 1900D, the Embraer Bandeirante, the Pacific Aero Cresco 750XL, and Pilatus' PC-6 Turbo Porter, PC-9 Turbo Trainer, and PC-12.

The de Havilland Canada DHC-6 Twin otter.

Flying the Twin Otter was a physical and auditory workout. The controls could not be considered light, and the beast really had to be manhandled around the sky. In a tight turn you needed two hands on the control wheel to force her where you wanted to go. An engine failure (I never experienced a real one in the Otter, but did practise them) involved an awful lot of rudder and a thigh of steel to hold it in on the 'live' side. She was noisy too, but emitted sounds that reminded the pilot how rough and ready and awesome she was. During engine start, with the axial flow compressor making the same high-pitched winding-up noise as a military jet, and the glow-plug igniters clicking away in the heart of the hot section, you'd hear the guttural roar of the fuel combusting as you opened the cockpit fuel master lever for light-off.[x] The next sound was the whap-whap-whapping of the 8 foot 6 inch diameter feathered props as the P&W power plant spun them up. As you taxied for take-off you'd hear the high-pitched whirring of the hydraulic pumps, like staccato bursts

---

[x]   Industry term for the point of ignition in a jet engine.

from a dentist's drill, as fluid was diverted to the nose wheel steering assembly through the captain's steering tiller. You'd hear the same noise as you selected flaps for take-off. On take-off from rough strips there was a metallic banging and crunching sound from the nose wheel shock strut, and the sprung steel arms of the main undercarriage talked to you as they crackled through the compression urethane shock absorbers bolted to either side of the fuselage. As you landed, if your speed was where it should be on a length-limited bush strip, the stall warning horn would scream at you just as the main wheels touched down (with that big wing and 37.5 degrees of flap out the stall speed was a wonderfully low 56 knots). When you took a hint of reverse thrust on the ground the props reverberated with an angry growl over the underlying hiss of the gas turbine. These were the sounds of short-field ops heaven.

The Otter was, on paper, a much bigger and more complicated machine than my previous ride, the Cessna 206, but an absolute joy to operate. The pairing of the Twin Otter and the PNG bush was Yo-Yo Ma with a cello; Matisse with a paintbrush; Federer with a racquet. The Otter was simple and reliable. It had no vices. It was a great engine–airframe match too: talk to anyone who has operated a PT6 engine and they will say the same. Pratt and Whitney's *Reliable Dependable* slogan is not just a catchy marketing phrase — it's a fact.

My first solo trip as Twin Otter Captain was on 29 April 1994. I was 23 years old. It was a morning gulf run: Moresby — Kerema — Baimuru — Kikori — Baimuru — Kerema — Moresby, with MBA co-pilot Morris Rondeau. It was so nice to have the training behind me, have the check-and-training monkey off my back, and be free to operate the aircraft my way. And it was pure pleasure to be in command of such a magnificent aircraft. *There are some days when I think I am going to die from an overdose of satisfaction.*[198] I think when Salvador Dali penned these words he was referring to an image of me in the captain's seat of the Twin Otter, my grin wide and unflappable.

I thought I'd be given a bit of time to settle into flying the Otter, and settle into the routes out of Moresby (although I'd been to all destinations already during my time with Air Manubada), but this was not the plan that MBA had for me. One week after checking out as captain I was called into Chief Pilot Drew Salter's office. He told me I was to be transferred to MBA's Base in Mendi, the provincial capital of the Southern Highlands Province. The senior MBA pilots at that stage were almost entirely ex-Talair pilots, with a collective experience of many thousands of hours of PNG Twin Otter flying, but none of them were keen on a transfer away from Port Moresby. They had all been asked if they wanted the transfer and all had turned it down. Drew Salter had looked down the seniority list and found the most junior Twin Otter captain with a solid background of flying into one-way mountain strips — a pilot who could easily transition to single-pilot ops flying in the Highlands with minimal training — and most importantly one who was too junior to turn down his request for a Port Moresby to Mendi transfer. That pilot was me, so I packed my bags and prepared for the move.

I had flown in and out of Mendi many times, operating Air Manubada's chicken runs in the Cessna 402 and the Piper Navajo, but had never flown into any of the multitude of other strips in the Province. I knew anecdotally that there were gnarly mountain strips scattered throughout the Southern Highlands, and from my Air Manubada Mendi experience I knew that afternoon bad weather would make flying in the area *challenging* — PNG code for *bloody dangerous.*

The Southern Highlands Province is defined by a roughly triangular boundary: its base is an east-west line between Mt Bosavi in the west and the Purari River delta in the east; its northwest apex is Lake Kopiago; and the triangle's longest side runs from Kopiago, along the mountains north of Tari and Mendi, then across the northernmost edge of 14,527 foot-high Mt. Giluwe, PNG's second highest mountain. With an area of 23,800 square kilometres (roughly the same size as Israel) the Southern Highlands is the most highly populated of PNG's provinces, with the 2000 national census registering over 500,000 inhabitants.[199] It is also the province with some of the lowest literacy rates in PNG, low levels of economic development, and it has serious law and order issues.

Until fairly recently the Southern Highlands Province was, as far as Europeans were concerned, uncharted inhospitable wilderness. Right up until the mid-20th century, the label UNCONTROLLED TERRITORY was stamped across most of the Highlands on Government

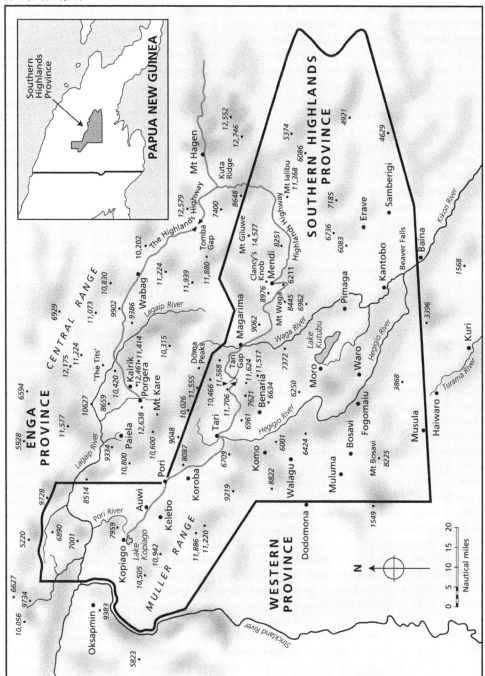

The airstrips and terrain of the Southern Highlands Province.

maps, this being the equivalent of drawings of sea serpents and other mythological creatures on the blank areas of nautical charts, warning sailors: *Here be Dragons.* A government officer explained the meaning of 'uncontrolled territory' to a new recruit in 1948: *That country is not under Government control. They're still fighting in there, and I haven't got the staff to send in patrols to stop them. We made a good start before the War, but it's been years now since anyone went in there, and it's going to take us a long time to get them to stop chopping each other.*[200]

The first European penetration of the Southern Highlands was in 1935, during an overland government patrol led by two officers of the Papuan Magisterial Service, Hides and O'Malley. Government Patrol Officers, or *Kiaps,* were often the first Europeans to go into previously unknown regions. Once an area had been explored, and they had made contact with the local tribesmen, the Kiaps were responsible for repeat trips to make the government's presence felt on a regular basis. The Hides and O'Malley patrol led to the establishment of the first government post in the Southern Highlands, at Lake Kutubu, which was supported logistically by Junkers seaplanes. For four years patrols set out from the Kutubu outstation, exploring the remote wilderness of the province and extending the influence of the government, until the outbreak of WWII led to its abandonment. Kutubu was reopened in August 1949 when civil administration returned to the Territory. Post-war the Australian-run Administration of PNG was keen to explore and survey all remaining uncharted pockets of the country and initiated an ambitious program to bring the whole Territory under control by the end of 1955. The process was sped up through the intelligent use of aircraft. Aerial surveys quickly located areas of dense local population, found sites for new airstrip construction and identified potential overland routes for the Kiap-led patrols that would follow.

To the Australian Administrators the so-called *pacification and development*[201] of the Highlands Provinces was necessary for the country to move forward. Through indigenous eyes, the program might have looked more like *control and subjugation.* The world they inhabited could not be further removed from that of the *mastas* (white men). The Highlanders of PNG, having been completely isolated from the rest of the world, were frozen in the Stone Age. They lived as Europeans had at the beginning of the Mesolithic Age, some six to seven thousand years earlier. It was never going to be an easy transition, being pulled kicking and screaming into the modern age by the Australian Administration of the day.[202] Inevitably, there were problems: the imposition of Western law and forced abandonment of the age-old tribal laws began a breakdown in traditional values. Tribal leaders, once the backbone of the community, lost their authority as it was usurped by Government-appointed village heads and District Officers. European contact also brought with it the triple scourge of introduced diseases, alcohol, and firearms.[203]

Today, for those on the outside, it appears that Papua New Guinea (especially the Highland Provinces) is a backwards nation, slow to adapt to the modern age. I have always felt the opposite, and been impressed how the locals have coped with so much change in such an impossibly compressed time frame. Missionary Aviation Fellowship pilot Tom Teale-Sinclair, who flew extensively in PNG in the 1990s, told me about one of the local pilots he trained, a talented young man who worked his way through the junior pilot ranks to become a Twin Otter captain. He said to Tom: "You guys just don't get it. I grew up in a bush hut. My mother and father are simple villagers who don't speak Pidgin or English. And here I am, a MAF Twin Otter captain!" The people of PNG have gone from grass huts and headhunting to iPhones and the internet in less than 100 years. I think that's something for them to be very proud of.

If you Google PNG's Southern Highlands Province, you will be led to a small number of tourist websites. Mention will be made of the Province being home to the Huli wigmen, warriors with famously elaborate and colourful dress. Beautiful Lake Kutubu will rate a mention, as will highly regarded Ambua Lodge in the Tari Basin, with its luxury rooms fashioned from bush materials, rainforest walks, bird-of-paradise watching, and traditional *singsings* (cultural performances by local tribesfolk). The town of Mendi, the Provincial capital, is conspicuous in its absence from these websites: if it is mentioned at all, the headlines are more likely to be about crime and civil unrest and roaming gangs of *raskols* than of any tourist must-dos. "Must avoid" might be the best advice. Mendi has an edgy frontier-town feel, a sort of Dodge City-meets-Mogadishu vibe.

There's not much to the place: a scruffy central main street with a bank and tradestores and fast food shops; an open-air produce market on the banks of the river; *buai*-stained government buildings; a public hospital. It's worth a trip to the hospital just to read the pricelist for various medical procedures on a prominent signboard near the entrance. Included on the list is *Childbirth K55; Broken limb K30; Gunshot wound K20;* and my favourites (in a tacit admission that tribal fighting is rife) *Spear/Arrow removal K15* and *Knife/Axe wound K20.* Good grief.

The site of Mendi's airstrip was chosen in September 1950, when Government Officers Smith and Clancy, who were on patrol between Lake Kutubu and Mt Hagen, located a flat area beside the Mendi River. Local labourers were enlisted to flatten and prepare the site, and pilot Bobby Gibbes made the first landing there in an Auster in October 1950. Author and ex-Kiap James Sinclair first visited Mendi in 1954, and commented on his first impressions of the town: *There was an indefinable aura of the primitive about Mendi, a rawness, a crudeness even, that stimulated and excited. There were no frills here.*[204] I felt the same way, arriving in Mendi in the 1990s — evidently not much had changed!

In 1994 the MBA Base in Mendi was run by Captain Jim Millar. Ruddy-faced, hard-working and affable, Jim had been flying in PNG forever, and at the time had over 20,000 hours of flying experience. You knew you were working with a true old PNG hand if the pilot was mentioned in James Sinclair's *Balus* series of books chronicling the history of PNG's aviation industry, published in the 1980s. Jim was one such pilot, featuring in Volume II: . . . *Jim Millar (was) a real character. Good stick-and-rudder man, a bush flier . . . used to have an alarm clock under his seat, and to do a position report, he'd reach under the seat and grab this great alarm clock. Carried his lunch in a flour bag — a tin of baked beans. Some passengers thought him a bit of a hick, but he was a good pilot.*[205]

Millar was a superstar in Mendi, as one night years earlier he had flown a desperately sick European child on a night emergency Medivac flight from Mendi's airstrip direct to a town in Northern Australia. There are no runway lights at Mendi's airport, so under normal circumstances this night flight would have been both impossible and illegal. Jim put the wellbeing of the child ahead of the legality of the flight, and improvised. He got all the Mendi-based expats to line their cars up along the edge of the airstrip at 100-metre intervals, with headlights on to illuminate the runway, and took off into the blackness of the Southern Highlands night. After that he could do no wrong in the eyes of Mendi's expatriate population.

Jim, as a senior MBA pilot, was on 'tours of duty,' meaning that he worked one month in PNG then had one month off — in his case a month spent at home with his wife in Melbourne, Australia. This was, and still is, common practice for multinational companies in PNG, especially those involved in the mining, oil and gas industries. The daily international flights in and out of PNG have passenger manifests full of foreign skilled workers either on their way home to begin their tour break, or inbound to begin their work duty. It's a subculture that most people are not aware of: I've sat on flights out of Port Moresby and chatted with chopper pilots from the US, fitters and turners from rural Queensland, chefs from New Zealand, and mechanics from the UK — all on their way home on a tour break after spending a few weeks at some remote location in the PNG wilderness. Tours of duty for expatriate employees can be month-on-month-off, or six-weeks-on-four-weeks-off, or even two-on-two-off. Later, as I became more senior in the Milne Bay Air pilot ranks, I was to be offered the same month-on-month-off deal as Jim Millar.

I arrived in Mendi in May 1994 in MBA Twin Otter P2-MBS to be checked into the Southern Highlands strips by check Captain John 'JB' Bruce. JB, another long-time PNG resident, was also ex-Talair, and was a very experienced Twin Otter and bush-flying pilot. I liked him, but he was a bit of an oddball. Tall, in his mid-thirties, with a thick, close-cropped beard, a brush with hepatitis and other tropical diseases had left him looking like a bag of bones. He was so thin he was almost invisible viewed side-on. JB's passion, outside of flying, was recreational diving. There were whispers that he had done one too many deep dives and was suffering from permanent nitrogen narcosis (this occurs when divers go below depths of 100 feet, when an increase in the pressure of nitrogen in the compressed air produces an altered mental state similar to alcohol intoxication. Nitrogen narcosis is also known as the *martini effect*). No doubt the rumourmongers were in search of an explanation for the Cheshire Cat grin he wore 24/7 and his intense, almost maniacal, stare. He also had the slightly disturbing habit of pulling a pistol from a concealed holster and fondling it like it was his baby, often in inappropriate settings like barbeques, or at remote airstrips, or even sometimes in the aircraft cockpit. En route to Mendi he sat silently in the co-pilots seat of the Twin Otter, watching my every move with his dark shark-like eyes while he stroked his beard and fiddled with this and that in the cockpit. He couldn't sit still — he was a bit of a MacGyver — and would pull out his pocketknife and disassemble parts of the aircraft instrumentation as he flew along, inspecting them and cleaning them before reassembling them and screwing them back in their housing.

There were two famous stories about JB. In the first he was at a remote outstation, waiting with his aeroplane for a load of passengers to arrive at the airstrip. Not able to stop himself from tinkering, he passed the time with his MacGyver tool kit, removing the igniters from the Pratt & Whitney PT-6 turboprop's hot section: *just to have a look.* The passengers turned up earlier than expected, and JB scrambled to put the engine back together. But he had misplaced part of the igniter assembly on one engine, and his unauthorised tinkering rendered the aircraft unserviceable. Oops. JB and his passengers had to wait until another Twin Otter was dispatched from base with an engineer and replacement parts to fix the problem. It was apparently a long wait.

In the second story, he was flying with a friend of mine, who was acting as JB's co-pilot on a Highlands run out of Moresby in one of MBA's Dornier 228 turboprops. As he was known to do, with the aircraft established in the cruise at 9000 feet, JB pulled out his pistol in the cockpit and began fiddling with it. He was doing his best Dirty Harry impersonation ("... *You've got to ask yourself one question: Do I feel lucky? Well, do ya, PUNK?*"), pointing the gun at the cockpit windscreen and mimicking firing it, when BANG! the gun discharged. This left a bullet hole in the plexiglass in front of him, and the co-pilot in need of a change of trousers. As they made their way back to Port Moresby airport, with airflow whistling in through the hole, JB came up with a plan to avoid blame for the destruction of the windshield. A plan so cunning you could put a tail on it and call it a weasel. He called up the

A 2007 photo of the damage caused by the Rabaul eruption of September 1994. The cone at the centre is Mt. Tavurvur.

Steve Saunders

Rabaul's ash and lava-covered runway is visible at centre left.

MBA Captains John Wild Jnr. and Clive Morgan were the first to fly into Rabaul after the '94 eruption.

Steve Saunders

Rocky Roe

The 'Grey Ghost' USAAF B-17 Flying Fortress wreck near Wau. Note the RAF markings on the wing and fuselage.

Colin Hicks

Rusting hulks of the Wau and Bulolo gold dredges from the 1930s gold rush.

Rocky Roe

Rocky Roe

Miners in the mud. The Mt. Kare goldrush of the late 1980s.

Richard Leahy

Dean Boatman

Kairik airstrip, servicing the gold mine at Porgera. Elevation 7450ft, slope 7%, length 1200m.

Mike O'Byrne

The author's favourite PNG airstrip, Paiela.
Elevation 6200ft, slope 0%, length 487m.

MAF archives

Typical Southern
Highlands passengers.

MAF archives

The aftermath of the machine gun attack on Gerry Krynen's Twin Otter. Blood on the aircraft floor, and the bottom section of the rudder shot away.

Troop and ammunition charter flights to Buka in Bougainville Province for the PNG Defense Force.

Jim Millar lands a Milne Bay Airways Twin Otter in Mendi.

Erin Leslie

Clancy's Knob, the only major obstacle in Mendi's circuit area. Jim Millar's crashed Twin Otter is visible at the centre of the picture.

Mack Lee's final ride: his Cessna 402, registration P2–SAV.

September 1983: Betsy, Cathay Pacific's original DC3, at Sydney airport with a company 747.

Martin Willing

Right: Betsy undergoing maintenance, date unknown.

Above: Today Betsy hangs from the ceiling of the Hong Kong Science Museum.

Post Courier archives

"Pure pilot nirvana". Cathay Pacific 747 Jumbo Jets on approach to Hong Kong's famous runway 13.

Above: The 'Kai Tak heart attack', aka the 'checkerboard turn'.

Below: A 747-300 on final approach viewed from the streets of Kowloon.

company operations room on the HF radio and told them he'd just had a bird strike, that the windshield had a hole in it, and that he was bringing the crippled Dornier back to base. He then made sure the co-pilot's lips would be sealed, swearing him to secrecy, and convincing him to go along with the bird strike cover story. "But John," said the co-pilot, "that little hole doesn't look anything like a bird strike."

"Don't worry," replied JB, his cat-got-the-canary grin spreading from ear to ear, "it will."

He then whipped out his MacGyver pocketknife and set about picking away at the edges of the bullet hole, slowly making it bigger by removing small sections of the cracked plexiglass windscreen. By the time he was done the hole was bigger all right, but all this did was make the co-pilot even more nervous. As the air whistled even more noisily through the enlarged hole the co-pilot had visions of the whole weakened windscreen caving in on them, exposing them to the full force of the 300 km/hr airflow as they descended into Port Moresby. But they made it and after landing taxied up to the MBA hangar, where quite a crowd had formed, all wanting to take a look at the damage caused by the 'bird strike' JB had reported. A burly Australian aircraft engineer approached the two of them as they stepped out of the Dornier. He looked at the hole in the windscreen, looked at JB, and then looked at the windscreen again. "Shit, John," he exclaimed. "It doesn't look like you hit a bird mate — it looks like you've been fuckin' shot!"

With JB guiding me, I was introduced to Southern Highlands flying over four hectic days in May 1994. I had never seen anything like it, and in all my years of flying since nothing has matched the Mendi base flying in terms of the volume of sectors, the variation in the types of airstrips and the challenges each one posed: the terrain, the weather, the inherent danger of such operations, and the hassles along the way dealing with the passengers and the airline agents at each strip. The Mendi flying was some of the most challenging flying that PNG could offer; perhaps some of the best and most demanding flying in the world. In just four days we operated 52 flights, visiting 21 different airstrips in the province. We were in the air for a total of 18 hours during the four days and had to fly from sunrise to sunset every day to fit in all that work. When I say 'we' did all that flying, I mean me. JB hardly touched the controls. He sat in the co-pilot's seat, observing my operation, saying little, stroking his beard, and smiling a lot. At least he didn't get his gun out.

No airstrips in the Southern Highlands were equipped with lighting, so flights could only legally be done during daylight hours. On day two there was so much work that we literally flew until we ran out of daylight — we were en route to Mendi as the sun set and had to make an unscheduled stop at Chevron's base camp airstrip at Moro (on the shores of Lake Kutubu) and ask them if we could stay the night. Staying at one of the oil and gas camps was always a treat. While the accommodation was basic — shipping containers kitted out as living quarters — the food was first rate. We made pigs of ourselves at the mess-hall buffet that night, and reappeared the next morning for round two. After breakfast we fuelled up the Twin Otter and took off for Mendi and continued with the rostered flying.

One of the flights that day was a Mendi–Waro (to drop off 12 passengers and their freight, mostly tradestore goods) followed by a dead leg (no passengers or freight) from Waro to Tari. As we flew between Waro and Tari we came to the Agogo gas field north-west of Chevron's base camp — a crazy compressed jumble of karst pinnacles, jostling for space like Austin Powers' dental work. The flames of the gas field's flare stacks dotted the chaotic limestone landscape, their incongruous fiery torches a symbol of man's intrusion into this remote and hitherto pristine wilderness.

JB turned to me and said, "I have control."

"You have control," I replied, as his spidery hands crept out and wrapped themselves around the Otter's control yoke.

"Ever seen a Twin Otter upside down Matt?" he asked, looking across at me as smug and self-assured as a tiger scrutinising a tethered goat.

"Uh, no," I replied, not sure I was happy with the direction this conversation was headed. "Then you'll like this," he said. With an imperceptible nudge forward on the control column JB eased the Otter into a shallow dive. When we had lost about 300 feet and gained 20 knots of speed, he pulled the nose through the horizon to about 20 degrees nose-up, then rolled the aircraft through the inverted position and back to wings level! He finished his barrel roll at 1500 feet above the terrain, the altitude where we had been cruising. He had held 1G throughout, and the aircraft had remained perfectly in balance. Before I could say anything he did two more barrel rolls as we sailed along over the Agogo gas field, the earth and the sky a blue-green tumble dryer as he performed his aerobatics. The Twin Otter was in no way designed for such manoeuvring, but he had done a real nice job of it. He was loving the aerial ballet, and beamed at me:

"You won't try that on your own now will you?"

I didn't know what to say.

"And of course" he added, "if you tell anyone about this I'll personally see to it that your career is destroyed."

Pregnant pause.

"You have control," he said.

I took over the flying and we cruised along in an uncomfortable silence for the rest of the sector. After I landed in Tari, and taxied over to the parking bay, I shut down the port engine and went to climb down from the cockpit to meet with the MBA agent and get the next load of passengers and cargo on board. Before I left, JB yelled to me over the turbine hiss of the still-running starboard engine:

"Matt, I was kidding about wrecking your career!" He gave me a Chinese politician's smile — his mouth had curled into something resembling a grin, but his eyes remained cold. I knew he had not been kidding at all.

JB had one more surprise in store for me before my highlands training was complete. Our last assignment that day was a flight from Lake Kopiago to Paiela.

Paiela remains my favourite PNG bush strip. It's a cracker. Asking a gaggle of PNG bush pilots to come up with their favourite mountain strip is a bit like asking a bunch of alcoholics to name their favourite liquor — there will be lots of hot air, a beating of chests and gnashing of teeth, and no consensus. At the end of the process each pilot will still believe that his choice is best, and that the airstrips nominated by his mates are poor cousins to his chosen favourite. I will argue with any of them that Paiela is a classic.

The strip at Paiela is 85 nm west-north-west of Mt. Hagen, on a tabletop mountain that stands solitary in a narrow basin (think Richard Dreyfuss' pile of potatoes in *Close Encounters*). The wee tabletop, 6200 feet above sea level, is completely hemmed in by a circular range of mountains soaring from 7000 to 9000 feet — giving the impression that the mesa on which Paiela airstrip sits is surrounded by a jungle-choked moat. The brown gravel airstrip is plonked on top of the miniature mesa, taking up all of the available real estate: it's 487m long, dead flat, with a 1000 foot drop to the basin floor at each end. There are no landmarks or visual references with which to judge or calculate a normal approach path. In the afternoons the strip is mauled by swirling winds that create crosswinds, tailwinds, updrafts and downdrafts. Is there a go-around option? Yes. But if you land long and fail to pull up by the end of the strip you and your aircraft and your passengers will be on a quick trip to death as you slide off the sheer end and plummet 1000 feet to the jungle floor below. Even getting into the basin can be a challenge. In the wet season, and in the early morning all year round, cap cloud sits on the peaks that encircle Paiela, preventing all but the most determined/crazy pilots from entering the tight basin and making an approach to land.

I later became experienced at finding a way into the basin: my preference was to attack Paiela from the Porgera/Kairik side. I'd follow the Lagaip River on the north-eastern outer side of the Paiela basin until I saw a particular gap in a ridgeline, a small 'v' just before the river turned to meander along a more westerly course. My gap was identifiable by a series of unique bare rock patches on the vertical face of the ridgeline — if I could see this landmark I knew I had the correct 'v'. I'd stooge through there in shocking weather, at ridiculously low level, and transit the gap blind into the Paiela basin beyond. This was only dangerous if I somehow misidentified the ridge line and flew at low level through the wrong gap. This I never did, but two other chaps had.

In September 1976 a MAF Turbo Cessna 206, P2-MFR, flown by the Chief Pilot David Grace (49 years old, with over 14,000 hours of flying experience) and a new pilot, Warwick Walesey, was on its way from Porgera to Paiela with a load of cargo and two passengers. Walesey was undergoing route familiarisation training. They didn't make it.[206] An account of the flight appears in Sinclair's Balus Vol. III:

> *David wanted to show Warwick the direct route, and as there was considerable cloud on the ridge, looked for a gap underneath the clouds. Thinking he had found one, he steered in that direction, only to find that the gap was in reality a patch of light cloud. He threw MFR into an extremely tight turn, but to no avail. It entered the cloud and almost immediately struck a tree which tore off the starboard wing. Another tree struck the engine, and that too was separated from the fuselage. The port wing then hit another tree, and was torn off, and this caused the aircraft to change direction and move backwards. A tree was driven through the floor just behind the rear seat and further movement lifted MFR off the tree which was then driven through the seat between the two passengers, a seat which was to have been occupied by a third person, who, at the last minute, decided he would walk! The crash beacon had been activated by the impact, and the aircraft came to rest almost dead level on the side of a steep mountain. There was no fire, as the fuel tanks and engine had all gone . . .That there were any survivors of such a fearful crash was little short of a miracle. All survived. Walesey later told the accident investigators that after MFR hit the first tree, he heard David Grace exclaim, "Here we come, Lord". Both men were certain they were about to be killed.*[207]

The CAA Investigation into the crash was less than complimentary about Captain Grace's piloting that day. The report pointed out that an alternative route to Paiela, clear of the high ground and clear of cloud, was available. It went on to state that the cause of the accident was the pilot (a) continuing VFR flight into adverse weather conditions; and (b) making an improper in-flight decision.[208]

The day I was checked into Paiela by JB the weather was fine and I had no dramas finding the airstrip. I did find the approach to land quite challenging though, with the strip looming up at me like a 1000-foot tall aircraft carrier in a sea of green vegetation. I fell back on my many hours of experience flying Mack Lee's Cessna 206 into mountain strips, and managed to get away with a respectable short-field landing, hitting full reverse as the main wheels touched down, and pulling off to the eastern side of the strip into the parking bay. JB didn't say a thing, which I took to mean he felt I knew what I was doing.

We dropped off some tradestore goods and punters, and picked up more of the same for the next leg, from Paiela to Tari. On take-off, just as the Twin Otter gained flying speed, JB reached up and pulled back one of the power levers. He was giving me an engine failure drill with a load of passengers on board! This was not something that was supposed to be done. But there was little time for me to think — I booted in a massive wad of rudder to keep the aircraft straight as the live engine tried to yaw us off our course, and struggled to hold the engine-out climb speed.[xi] If the speed is allowed to decay in this situation the rudder loses its aerodynamic ability to counter the asymmetrical yaw from the engine failure and the aircraft rolls onto its back and falls out of the sky. It's not something you want to stuff up. I managed to keep it all under control as the Twin Otter sank off the end of the strip into the basin below. After we had lost a couple of hundred feet, JB powered up the other engine again, and I restored the aircraft's trim and climbed away to set course for Tari. I should have been upset with him, but wasn't. He sat there, grinning like a madman, and said, "Yeah, that's how you handle an engine failure on take-off Matt. Pretty good mate." JB was just being JB.

At the end of the four days of flying, he signed me off as competent to operate into any of the Southern Highlands strips, adding, "You're not a bad pilot, Matt. You'll probably get into the airlines one day." Coming from him, these understated words were a huge compliment. His training mission complete, John Bruce returned to Port Moresby, Jim Millar disappeared on his tour break (one month off) and I was left to run the Mendi base solo.

●

[xi]   The engine out climb speed is manufacturer mandated, and keeps the aircraft above V_{MCA} — the minimum control speed.

— Chapter 15 —

"The bus drivers want to cut his head off"

Come to Papua New Guinea — The Land of the Unexpected!
PAPUA NEW GUINEA DEPARTMENT OF TOURISM SLOGAN

The Mendi-based flying was spectacular. Most of the sectors involved combined freight and passenger runs into the satellite airstrips around Lake Kutubu.

Village income in these places was supported and sustained by royalties from the Chevron oil and gas work in the area. A lot of the Mendi flying involved *ad hoc* charters, flying fuel drums and construction materials: corrugated iron sheets, timber, nails, rolls of fencing wire, plus tradestore goods. In many ways it was just like the Cessna 206 flying I had done into the Goilalas and Koiaris, but it was less hands on, as Wafi, the MBA office manager, and the cargo boys would do all the loading, the fuel truck in Mendi would refuel the aircraft for me in between flights, and generally the accounts were taken care of by Wafi too.

Wafi also always knew where the passengers were and on which day I was supposed to pick them up — he was very professional and efficient, and never sent me off to the wrong airstrip. The schedule and confirmation of passenger numbers and freight weights was coordinated via HF radio broadcasts between Wafi and the MBA agents at each strip. Each morning he'd lay out my trips for the day, and off I'd launch. When I got back to Mendi the next load was always on the tarmac ready to go, and the passengers were ready too. After telling the refueller how much Jet A1 fuel I needed for the next sector, and instructing him on the fuel split between the forward and aft fuel tanks, all I had to do was unload the thick wad of cash from my shirt pockets from the cash fares I had picked up on the previous sector, pass it on to Wafi, then clamber back up to the cockpit and launch again. It was a very smooth operation.

Just as I had during my training with JB, most days I flew from sunrise to sunset. In the first five days of my solo flying in the Southern Highlands I flew 47 sectors. Later, an average day in Mendi came to mean operating 14 or 15 flights. Airstrips serviced from the Mendi Base included Erave, Waro, Fogomaiu, Kaipu, Moro, Benaria, Tari, Auwi, Lake Kopiago, Oksapmin, Walagu, Dodomona, Muluma, Bosavi, Mt. Hagen, Paiela, Kairik, Pimaga, Kantobo, Baina, Samberigi, Haiwaro, Kuri, Musula and Kikori. I'd fly Monday to Saturday, then fly the aircraft to Port Moresby on Saturday afternoon (this leg took 2 hrs 30 mins). Sunday was a rest day in Moresby, then on Monday I'd fly back to Mendi via Kikori and Moro and then get straight back into the weekly Mendi charter schedule. The greatest number of sectors I ever flew in a single day was 19, all single pilot in the 200 series Twin Otter. I achieved this number more than once, but 2 August 1994 was typical of the crazy–busy days of MBA's Mendi Base.

As usual, I started work early. I was out at Mendi's airport not long after daybreak, preparing the aircraft for departure. The more flying I could fit in before lunchtime the better — as it was in the afternoons that the cloud would roll in, closing some of the valleys, bringing reduced visibility in isolated rain pockets, and creating unpredictable wind shifts. All these things made my job much harder and a lot more dangerous. The conditions that morning were near perfect, with light winds from the east, a temperature of about 20 degrees in Mendi, and wide open blue skies. My first sector, from Mendi to Tari, was a pleasure. I decided to route at low level, following the Waga River between Mendi and Lake Kutubu, tracking north-west at 500 feet AGL and picking up the Margarima–Tari road when the river fishhooked at the base of the Engensh Range. Visibility was almost unlimited, with the ridgelines to port and starboard etched against the big blue in Peter Jackson

48-frames-per-second HD; the line between earth and sky sharp like a cardboard cut-out. In stable conditions like this, Highlands flying was a piece of cake, a complete contrast with the stressball it would become later in the day as the weather turned nasty. Fifteen miles out from my destination I scooted through the Tari Gap at lose-your-licence low altitude, buzzing the grass-hut villages clustered in the lee of the multi-peaked massif that looms over the Tari basin's eastern flank.

I keyed the mike when five minutes out from landing at Tari, informing any circuit traffic that I'd be joining downwind for runway 14. There was little chatter on the radio that morning; the only traffic I heard was on area HF frequency, a MAF Twin Otter cancelling SARWATCH at Komo, a village airstrip some 15 miles to the south-west. There were almost always other pilots on the radio, but it was possible to fly from sunrise to sunset in the Southern Highlands and not actually *see* any other aircraft. On days like this I felt like Will Smith in *I Am Legend* — flying New Guinea's skies solitary in a post-apocalyptic world; my Twin Otter the only piece of machinery to have survived the post-nuclear electromagnetic pulse.

Rolling downwind at 1000 feet AGL I was surprised to see what looked like at least 200 people on the runway beneath me, a swarm of ant-like dots on the airstrip. I remembered something Wafi had mentioned the day before — there had been a period of civil unrest at Tari, and there was a NOTAM to that effect warning pilots about a possible blockade of the runway. I'd seen this at mountain airstrips before. It was tribal fighting referred to colloquially as 'Highlands Football', and today the two tribes or clans had decided to use Tari airstrip as their arena. In these tribal battles the opposing sides, armed with traditional axes, bush knives, spears, shields, and occasionally shotguns and crude homemade firearms, came together in ritualistic warfare — with more of a threat of battle than actual man vs man close-combat fighting. It was like an armed dance-off, with the sides alternately advancing on their opponents, doing their best to intimidate each other. These performances, while largely theatrical, were always based however on some real or fancied wrong — a conflict sparked by homicide or political disagreements, or by disputes over land, possessions (often pigs), or women. These conflicts were driven by PNG's ubiquitous undercurrent of payback, the belief in revenge. One villager spoke of this in a 1998 study on tribal fighting:

Now I will talk about warfare. This is what our forefathers said: When a man was killed, the clan of the killers sang a song of bravery and victory. They would shout "Auu" (hurrah or well done) to announce the death of an enemy. Then their land would be like a high mountain, and that is how it was done down through the generations. The members of the deceased's clan would become small. They would be nothing. But when they had avenged the death of their clansman, then they would be alright.[209]

MAF archives

Highlands football attire.

While Highlands Football seemed like a harmless show of strength, and while casualties and fatalities were usually limited, the peripheral violence and mayhem associated with tribal warfare came with consequences that were real and of lasting impact — the indiscriminate burning of village buildings, the destruction of subsistence gardens, and the killing of livestock.[210]

There was another convenient, and almost amusing, side to Highlands Football — the warring sides would usually ignore outsiders. So it was on this particular morning. As I turned onto a final approach for the runway I saw the two sides withdraw from their 'game' of armed bull-rush, moving to separate sides of the gravel strip and allowing me to land, taxi past them, and turn into Tari's parking apron. As I pulled off the runway a euphoric Highlander warrior ran towards my aircraft, waving his spear at me like I was a long lost friend. He wore nothing but a skirt of dried grass, his chest was smeared with mud, and a plume of bird-of-paradise feathers danced atop his headdress. A seven-inch-long horizontal piece of reed protruded from a hole in his nose, and a broad smile burst through his vivid yellow face paint as I taxied past. I gave him a nervous wave out the port-side cockpit window and continued to the apron. This really was the land of the unexpected.

At the parking bay, some 100 metres from the airstrip and well clear of the battle zone, I was totally ignored by warriors on both sides as I met with the MBA agent, picked up the tickets and money from the morning's cash fares, and supervised the unloading and re-loading of the Twin Otter during the turnaround. The whole process took less than 15 minutes. As they had when I arrived, the tribes put down weapons and withdrew from their skirmish long enough for me to taxi back out to the runway, back-track, and depart. There was no sign of my yellow-faced spear-wielding mate from earlier.

My next scheduled stop was the airstrip at Auwi. The nav from Tari to Auwi was hardly in the difficult basket — I climbed to about 1000 feet AGL and tracked to the north-west, following the dirt road that connects Tari and the airstrips at Koroba, Pori, Kelebo, Auwi and Lake Kopiago. Within 10 minutes I could see Auwi, a cluster of buildings in a distinctive red clay clearing. I manoeuvred the Twin Otter to fly overhead the village airstrip to clear the runway of livestock and people, check the windsock, and set myself up for an approach and landing towards the south. Jim Millar had warned me to be careful here — Auwi's 540m-long grassed loamy strip was in fair condition, but the ground bordering the airstrip could become extremely waterlogged and boggy after any rain. He'd told me to keep my wheels well and truly confined to the airstrip, and not cut any corners. Years earlier, a RAAF DHC-4 Caribou crew had been unaware of this, and as they made a 180 degree turn at the end of the strip to line up for take-off they had allowed one of the main bogies to track off the airstrip into the grass and mud beyond. The Caribou had sunk to the axle immediately, becoming firmly bogged in the soft and sticky clay at the side the strip. Trying to use the aircraft's engine power to free the bird just made the situation worse. The engines were shut down and the crew exited to survey the situation, deciding that manpower was to be the solution. A long length of rope was produced and attached to the undercarriage. The Caribou crew and 70 or 80 bystanders, mostly young village men, formed a line on the rope. Included in the tug-team was a European nun from a missionary group stationed at Auwi at the time. She had decided to do her bit to help try and free the RAAF aircraft. On the captain's command the masses heaved and pulled and tugged. The Caribou was slowly extricated from the bog, but just as it became completely clear of the mud — *ping!* — the rope snapped. The entire tug-team was unceremoniously launched backwards, ending up as a pile of bodies in the grass behind the aircraft. Somewhere amid the heap of sweaty brown bodies lay the nun. She was eventually pulled from the pile of men — the story goes that, while it took several days to tend to her bumps and bruises, it took two weeks to get the smile off her face!

I did a quick turnaround at Auwi — dropping off people and supplies and picking up a handful of punters who wanted to be shuttled to my next port. From Auwi I climbed towards the north-west and set course for Lake Kopiago, where my manifest indicated I was due to pick up a party of eight and fly them to Paiela. The strip at Kopiago is 12 miles from Auwi, in the lee of the western end of the Muller Range. The gravel runway sits at 4300 ft AMSL in a cultivated green valley, and at 820 metres long and with a modest 2.5% slope is one of the easiest Southern Highland airstrips. I called area VHF traffic and advised I'd be making a straight-in approach for runway 32. I often flew to Kopiago on the Medi Base, and there was always a lot of work there — passengers with cargo keen to be transported to the other ports. Pulling up at the parking bay, I looked at the crowd standing outside the MBA office — a faded grey weatherboard shack — and saw our agent fighting his way through the throng to get to the aircraft. I shut down the left engine, pulled the propeller control on the still-running starboard engine to feather, and climbed down to meet him.

"Morning, Boss!" He smiled at me through a rotten mouth full of crimson *buai*-stained teeth.

"Gidday, mate, what have you got for me today?" I replied.

Sure enough, there were eight pax waiting, but the agent explained there was a problem with their cargo. "Boss, they have a pig to take to a wedding at Paiela, but I think it is *bikpela tumas*!" (too big).

I couldn't see the pig anywhere, so walked over to the passengers and asked them about it. "Morning *tru wantok. Dispela pik belong yu, em i lik lik o bikpela o wanem*?" (Is this pig of yours small or big or what?).

"*Em lik lik tasol*" (It's a small pig, that's all), said a pygmy of a man in a blue hat and red striped shirt. Clearly it was his pig.

"OK," I said to the agent. "Let's load her up and go."

The agent gave me a funny look, as if to say *you don't know what you are getting yourself into.* Suddenly there was some cheering and hollering tribal-style from the mob at the side of the strip and the crowd parted like Moses and the Red Sea to reveal a team of men carrying a pig trussed to a pole. A *very* big pig, over 300lbs of live wriggling pork, on a *very* big pole — four inches in diameter and at least 10 feet long. Oh shit. Before I had time to comment, they hoisted the screaming hog up to a 45 degree angle and tried to fit it and its pole into the Twin Otter's cargo compartment. This was like trying to stuff an elephant into a phone booth. I politely suggested they might have more success if they cut the ends off the pole.

"Hey, *wantoks. Sapos yu kissim wanpela akis na cuttim dispela diwai na mekim lik lik, olrite?*

After much jabbering and yelling and commotion a bush knife and an axe were produced by the crowd, and a couple of young chaps began hacking into each end of the pole with demented enthusiasm. I almost couldn't watch as the blows rained down mere millimetres from the now extremely nervous and agitated pig. Once the job was done, to the great amusement of the watching masses, the men tried again to get the pig and the pole into the cargo compartment. It was still a no-go. I wasn't about to stuff up their wedding celebrations at Paiela by leaving their *lik lik* pig behind, so without any other option, I asked the passengers if they would mind if the pig was carried inside the aircraft cabin. No one objected, so that's what we did. The pig was strapped to the floor in between the seats in the aisle in the middle of the cabin, and the passengers entered via the back door and climbed over the pig to get to their seats. The pig wasn't a great passenger — the old boar clearly wasn't used to flying coach, and wriggled and screeched and made a good effort to break free. I decided to charge the pig's owner the full price of a passenger ticket to carry the pig. Sorry, no frequent flyer miles. He was happy enough with the deal, and forked out the cash fare.

The crowd that had spilled onto the strip and around the aircraft while we sorted out the trussed-pig situation were now herded back behind the fence by the MBA agent, and he gave me a thumbs-up to start the port engine. I looked across to the mob of bystanders, smiling and waving at me as the PT6 power plant spun up the stationary left propeller. They pushed up against the airstrip's wire fence, and crowded around the large aircraft engine and propeller that was mounted like a monument strip-side. This gate guardian is clearly visible in the pictures I took that day. I only discovered the radial engine's origins while researching this book in the 2000s.

In June 1957 Gibbes Sepik Airways pilot Helly Tschuchnigg force landed a Noorduyn Norseman (a Canadian single-engine, high wing, fabric-skinned utility aircraft) in a swamp near Lake Kopiago after his engine failed. Tschuchnigg and his three European passengers were stranded in the middle of what was then classified by the Australian Administration as 'Restricted Territory', surrounded by armed and possibly hostile tribes, and spent a nervous night in the cabin of the downed aircraft. The next day they were led by Kopiago tribesmen to a Government camp at the Lake, and were eventually rescued by a Qantas Beaver floatplane.

Bobby Gibbes, the owner of the Norseman, was eager to return it to flying condition rather than write it off (it wasn't insured), and boldly decided to salvage it. He brought together a massive party at Tari airstrip: 120 tribesmen, an engineer, a carpenter, a Government Patrol Officer and 12 members of the Royal Papua and New Guinea Constabulary. They trekked to the crash site near Lake Kopiago and dismantled the aircraft (the heavy engine, a Pratt and Whitney Wasp SIHI-G,[211] was left in the swamp). Over the next 18 days the carriers manhandled the components of the disassembled Norseman over 35 miles (65 km) of rugged country between Lake Kopiago and Tari — moving in relays and cutting a 15-foot-wide track as they went (there were no roads in the Southern Highlands in the 1950s). It was an incredible effort, hailed at the time by the Director of the Department of Civil Aviation as an "amazing feat, unique in the history of Commonwealth aviation."[212] The engine and propeller were later recovered from the swamp and erected at Kopiago strip as a monument to those involved in the 1957 salvage effort.

I departed from Lake Kopiago, the shrill squeal of the still-wriggling pig audible over the drone of the Otter's engines, and climbed to the east,

The Lake Kopiago 'lik lik pik'. Behind the pig is the monument to the 1957 salvage of a Sepik Airways Norseman.

following the Pori River to its confluence with the Lagaip. The next stop was my favourite PNG strip, Paiela, and the Lagaip River valley would take me there.

The Pori meandered east, cutting through the chiselled cliffs of the Central Range, before swinging north to meet the Lagaip. The sun, now mid-arc in the still-clear sky, was hot and hard like a fist, beating down at me through the Perspex of the Otter's cockpit. The wind had picked up as the morning katabatic air currents swung anabatic (from down-slope to up-slope), and we were buffeted by light chop as I steered the Twin Otter to the Pori-Lagaip river junction.

The Lagaip River was impossible to misidentify due to its odd appearance (bright rust-red waters) and its dramatic topography, running deep within a steep-walled canyon, turning and twisting about a predominantly east–west course. Having a distinctive weird-coloured river in this neck of the woods was a great aid to pilot navigation, but the source of its colour was a topic of heated debate. The Lagaip was downstream of Placer Dome's gold mine at Porgera, 25 nm NNE of Tari. The mine was a massive project, one of the world's largest gold producers, beginning production in 1990; by 1991 Porgera mine revenue made up nearly one third of PNG's total export earnings.[213] The Porgera gold mine discharged mining waste directly into the river, a process known as riverine tailings disposal. Placer Dome, the Canadian company running the mine, had chosen this method of tailings disposal over a more conventional tailings storage facility because of the site of the mine — in steep mountainous terrain in a high earthquake, high rainfall, high landslide environment. They argued that these factors made safe construction and operation of a conventional facility unviable.[214] While the mine was, and still is, operated in line with guidelines laid down by the PNG Government, environmental watchdog groups have always argued that this method of tailings disposal has an immense negative impact on the local ecology. In 2006 ownership of the gold mine at Porgera passed from Placer Dome to Barrick Gold Corporation, the world's largest gold mining company. The new owners continue to dump tailings into the river, and the mine continues to be controversial. A 2012 report by Earthworks and Mining Watch Canada warned that the Porgera mine introduced *6 million tonnes of tailings and more than 12 million tonnes of sediment eroded from the waste rock dumps into the river in 2008. The tailings contain high concentrations of toxins including cyanide . . . dumping has contributed to increased sedimentation, changes in flow and depth in the rivers, and contaminated them with large quantities of arsenic, lead, mercury, and other toxic chemicals . . . fish populations are less plentiful than before and people in the area fear the mine is causing contamination of fish and livestock. The tailings appear to be responsible for inputs of mercury into southern Lake Murray . . . even after mining stops, impacts on the rivers are expected to continue for several hundred years.*[215]

I continued on to the Paiela basin, turning south away from the terracotta-red waters of the Lagaip and setting up for a straight-in approach and landing on the one-way strip perched on the Paiela tabletop. There was a huge crowd waiting abeam the parking bay. The women obviously did all the work here, as a throng of *meris* sat beside the strip, surrounded by large bags of produce and cargo that they had lugged up from the village. The place was a sea of brightly coloured *meri*-dresses and multi-hued *bilums*. One preschooler munchkin, holding the hand of his mum, stood out in the crowd — he was dressed in full military-style khakis complete with a chest full of sewn-on medals, shoulder rank slides, and a matching peaked hat with gold braid. He looked like a dwarf African dictator! As soon as I had shut down the left engine the crowd surged forward, and there was a melee as Paiela's MBA agent did his best to keep it all under control. As the Kopiago passengers emerged out of the Otter's rear stairs, manhandling their *lik lik* pig, the Paiela passengers began stuffing their luggage into the cargo hold and cabin. The agent told me there were passengers and freight for three runs to Kairik (the airstrip that serviced the Porgera gold mine — a 1991 landslide destroyed the original Porgera airstrip), and that the same number of people were waiting at Kairik to come back to Paiela. It was lucky that the weather was holding — three Paiela–Kairik shuttles on a shitty day would be very stressful indeed, as both of these strips were notoriously difficult to get into in foul weather. I departed Paiela with the first load and set course for Kairik, which is only 14 nm to the east-south-east, climbing to 8000 feet to scrape across a ridgeline abeam Mt Pangalin, ducking over to the next valley and following the Porgera River to my destination. Kairik airstrip lies on the eastern side of the dead-end Porgera valley, wedged at 7450 ft AMSL onto the shoulder of a 12,500 foot-high wall of mountains. It was constructed by PJV (Porgera Joint Venture, a partnership between the owner of the mine, the PNG Government and local landowners), so is a well-maintained, wide and relatively long bitumen airstrip, a rarity in PNG. But the location the engineers were forced to place it was hardly ideal — the airstrip and environs were carved out of the side of the mountain, with towering peaks overshadowing the runway to the immediate east, steep downslopes to the west, and a sheer drop off the end of the runway to the valley floor below. There was no chance the site could be levelled, so the runway was simply laid on the land as it stood — level for the first 20% of its 1200 metres,[216] then sloping up the hillside at a crazy 7%, like a concrete ski jump. The top of the runway was nearly 70 feet higher than the threshold. This sort of slope was common at the short one-way dirt runways of the PNG mountain villages, but operating into a first-world-quality bitumen runway built like this, at such an extreme elevation and amidst such rugged topography, was a real eye-opener. It was routine to see not only bush aircraft (Twin Otters, BN-2 Islanders, Cessna 185s and 206s) operating in and out of Kairik, but aircraft not normally seen at these extremes of elevation and slope — Beechcraft King Airs and Dornier 228s. These aircraft either operated into Kairik on a special dispensation from PNGDCA, or DCA had turned a blind eye and put the necessity of servicing the port above the legal considerations. Take-off and landing performance calculations (precise calculations of the safety margins for specific aircraft types at airstrips of different altitudes and slopes, at varying weights, and at varying ambient temperatures and winds — normally calculated using the manufacturer-supplied performance charts from the respective aircraft flight manuals) were simply not available — the Kairik data was literally 'off the charts'. Kairik was just too high, too hot, and too steep.

I joined for a right base for the one-way runway 23, aligning my base leg with a local landmark — the twin peaked summit on the Porgera–

Wabag road, known affectionately by local bush pilots as 'the tits'. Landing at Kairik reminded me of landing at Sopu, the steepest village strip in the Goilalas behind Port Moresby — I ignored the flat bit and set my aim point at the beginning of the slope. After touchdown, and a hint of reverse to slow to taxi speed, I had to add power to maintain the momentum and make it all the way up to the parking bay and the PJV-built terminal building. I didn't have to wait long for the first load of passengers, and watched as the MBA agent shepherded them from the terminal to the stairs at the back of the Twin Otter. They had just undergone what was at the time PNG's most extensive airport security screening. The whole Porgera valley was dry — no alcohol allowed in or out — so they had been screened for illicit booze. They'd also undergone another security check — a search to make sure that they were not carrying any gold surreptitiously 'liberated' from the mine.

The weather held for my return to Paiela and a further two Paiela–Kairik shuttles, although cloud had started to build on the mountains to the east of the airstrip, and the gold mine was now completely obscured by low stratus and drizzle to the west. Most of the passengers I flew between these strips that day were mine workers, PNG nationals known as FIFOs (fly-in fly-out). The punters headed to Paiela were going home for some time off after completing a tour of duty in the mine; those headed to Kairik had finished their break and were returning to begin a new tour.

By about 2pm I had finished the last of the shuttles, and departed Paiela for the fourth time that day, this time headed for Tari, 30nm SSW. My route to Tari would take me across some of the highest terrain in the Southern Highlands, a cluster of six peaks with an elevation of over 11,000 feet, a 10 mile by 10 mile chunk of terrain looming over the southern approaches to the Porgera Valley. My precise route choice that day had been made for me by the weather — the only clear path to the south was via the head of the valley, climbing up and over a gnarly ridgeline between two massive peaks. After take-off from Kairik I rolled the Otter into a lazy orbit over the strip, climbing through 9000 feet before pointing the ship towards the ridgeline. Again, the navigation wasn't difficult — the plan was to climb up and over the ridgeline to

10,500 feet, follow the Porgera–Tari power lines, and transit the high country at low level for 20 miles before descending into the Tari basin and the circuit height at 6500 feet. As I continued the climb towards the ridge, something made me feel uneasy.

I peered out the front of the Twin Otter's windshield, not entirely happy with the climb rate. The picture out the front of the aircraft during a comfortable (safe) ridge crossing was like looking at a floor disappear below you as you go up in a shopping mall elevator — the ground would drop away beneath you at a steady rate as you progressed towards the ridge, the ridgeline would become lower in the windshield, and there would be more and more air between you and the terrain. On this day the vertical component seemed a tad insufficient — as the aircraft came closer and closer to the lip of the ridge I could just see over it, but I was uncomfortable with the vertical component of the climb. I'd crossed plenty of ridgelines with this sort of minimal clearance before, but this day, at the very last second, my gut told me something wasn't right. I rolled in an armful of aileron and turned the Twin Otter away, lowering the nose to hold my present altitude while carrying out a reversal turn. The new plan was to orbit at the head of the valley and gain some more height before trying again. My gut instinct saved me and the punters that day. No more than two or three seconds after I made the decision to turn away I was hit by a significant downdraft. The aircraft fell out of the sky as if held in the fist of a giant and hurled towards the mountainside. In the blink of an eye I'd gone from fine 'n' dandy to impending disaster. Without thinking I pushed the prop levers and power levers to full power, struggling to suppress a sudden flash of fear. The airspeed dropped from my 90 knot climb speed to 70 knots as the Otter sank towards the trees, and I focused on holding the speed and continuing the turn as we came within 30 feet of the treetops, barely clearing the steep slope of the mountainside and tracking back towards Kairik. If I hadn't made the decision to turn back we would have bought the farm. Shit that was close.

Ridge crossing was a PNG bush pilot's bread and butter — a standard technique used on almost every flight — but it came with risk and had to be managed and flown with care. I later had a chat with PNGDCA Director of Air Safety Mike Feeney about this incident. In his role as an accident investigator he'd done the maths on the expected downwards component of the airflow (the downdraft) in strong wind conditions in the lee of a significant ridgeline. A 20 knot wind crossing a ridgeline and deflected downwards by 20 to 30 degrees will produce a downdraft of between 600 and 1000 feet per minute. My Twin Otter that day had been climbing at about 800 feet per minute — not enough to outclimb the sort of severe downdraft I encountered. What had saved me? Did I get away with it through experience, or luck? Probably a dash of both. Others had not been so lucky. PNG's aviation accident files were full of reports of pilots crashing perfectly good aeroplanes into ridgelines while attempting low-level transits, often losing control in a last minute split-arse turn away from the terrain (see the death of Richard Rowe in Chapter 8).

I crossed the ridgeline comfortably on my second attempt, and held 11,000 feet on the altimeter, which put me about 1000 feet above the terrain en route to Tari. A few minutes later, as the jungle-clad peaks surrendered to open high country tussocky swamplands, I passed abeam Mt Kare, the site of a modern-day Klondike gold rush. Gold was discovered here in 1988. Lots of gold. Three geologists from Australian mining company Conzinc Riotinto set up camp in the Pinuni Valley, in the shadow of the mountain, and began a preliminary survey of the area. Gold was found before they'd even had a chance to undertake any solid scientific investigation. When they began digging the camp toilet hole, gold fell from the soil on their shovels; not flakes of gold like the ones they'd panned from the nearby streams, but actual nuggets. News of the discovery travelled fast, and within months there were up to 10,000 miners crammed into this one isolated muddy valley, panning the creeks and churning up the sticky black soil. The scene was complete chaos, with local men back-to-back and shoulder-to-shoulder, a mass of picks, shovels, sluices and buckets. Tradestores soon set up shop in the valley too, selling everyday commodities (all flown in via helicopter) at criminally inflated prices. There was no infrastructure to support the huge numbers of miners and entrepreneurs in the valley; no fresh water; no sanitation. In the bitter alpine cold and rain people became sick.[217] But gold fever pushed them on. Geologist Stephen Promnitz was there, and witnessed what has been called one of the great alluvial gold rushes of the modern era: *It was the most astounding thing I have ever seen. There was more gold than you could poke a stick at . . . the locals were shaking gold nuggets from the roots of the grass. Some of the nuggets were the size of goose eggs. It was on for young and old.*[218]

Helicopter pilots I spoke to in the 1990s had been there too, and told tales of charter flights to pick up villagers and their gold at Mt Kare and fly them back to Porgera or Tari. The miners often paid the pilots in nuggets; one Pacific Helicopters company pilot told me he'd later had the gold melted down and cast into innocuous shapes (engine parts) and smuggled it into his home country on his subsequent tour break. The gold rush brought wealth — US$100 million or more — to the surrounding communities[219] but material benefits were overshadowed by tribal clashes, murder, rape, theft, extortion, and an almost total lack of government control. The Mt Kare gold rush was largely over by 1990, after the removal of most of the easily retrievable gold made the cost of remaining in the helicopter-supplied goldfield unsustainable. The day of my overflight, in 1994, a brave and stubborn few still worked Mt Kare — I could see them beneath me as I transited the Pinuni Valley — the green and yellow tarpaulin squares of makeshift tents; a handful of prospectors knee-deep in mud, still searching for their PNG Highlands El Dorado.

The rest of the day became a bit of a blur. On arrival at Tari there was no sign of the Highlands football match combatants — they must have had an extended break for lunch, or perhaps they'd had enough fighting for one day. From Tari I flew onwards to the Chevron-run base camp for oil and gas exploration at Moro on the shores of Lake Kutubu, then a short flight back to Mendi, with a lazy climb over the craggy ridges of Mt Pulim. Wafi had lined up another mission for me — a six-sector run to Erave — Kikori — Waro — Moro — Pimaga and finally home to Mendi again. By late afternoon, worried that I might run out of daylight before completing all the days flying, I started cutting corners. The most significant timesaving technique was to not shut down any engines on arrival at the airstrips, and to just leave them idling and the propellers feathered (at a zero-thrust setting). I just had to be careful not to walk into the spinning left prop as I climbed down out of the cockpit, and make sure that no passengers or villagers walked anywhere near the whirring propellers as they approached the rear passenger stairs and cargo door. The health and safety boffins would have blown a gasket had they been a fly on the wall at any of these stops, seeing an unattended aircraft strip-side with both engines running, but it was a vital timesaver on the hectic days in the Southern Highlands. This dodgy technique also made for highly expeditious departures once the aircraft was loaded and the doors were closed. I'd just unfeather the props, make an all stations call on area VHF and a taxi call to the area HF controller, and power out to the runway for take-off.

There was one area where there were no shortcuts — the pre-take-off standard aircraft checklists and performance calculations. For each of the 19 take-offs that day I had to do a quick calculation of the torque limit for the engines. The power plants on the -200 series Twin Otter were flat rated, meaning that within a defined range of altitude, temperature, and aircraft weight full power could be used for every take-off. If the aircraft operated outside this range, like in the hot and high conditions of the mountain airstrips of PNG's Southern Highlands, then using max power for take-off would overstress the engine — leading to hot section component distress that would reduce the life of the engine and affect its reliability. I carried a Pratt and Whitney torque calculator in the cockpit — a circular plastic slide-rule — and worked out the max torque that I could set on the primary engine gauges for each take-off.

At the end of the 11-hour day at the office (19 sectors; 6 hours and 40 minutes of turbine time for my logbook), as I clambered down from the Otter's cockpit, I ran into Tom Peninsa and Mark Smith, pilots with Southwest Airlines, also based in Mendi, who flew their company BN-2 Islander and DHC-6 Twin Otter into many of the same strips as me. Mark asked me where I'd been. "I can't remember!" I said. "It's been a long day — let me check the flight log!" It was head-spinningly busy work.

At the close of the day's flying I'd secure the aircraft for the night then jump into the MBA ute with Wafi and the cargo boys. It fell to me to drop them off at their homes in the village on the far side of the airstrip before driving myself home, as MBA only had the one vehicle in Mendi. Their village was nestled at the base of the range that overshadows the town to the west. A steep dirt road led into a rabbit warren of corrugated iron shacks, tradestores, and bush-material huts. Blue-black smoke from cooking fires curled up from the thatched grass rooftops. Seemingly idle villagers milled about in the age-old PNG way, most of them stopping to watch me pass, and I got wide-eyed stares from naked toddlers leaning in shack doorways, with their distended tummies and muddy legs and snot-encrusted faces. Every now and again I'd get a *tap tap tap* from one of the boys in the back on the rear windshield, and I'd come to a halt by the side of the road. It was someone's stop — one of the cargo boys would jump out the back of the ute and disappear into the village. From the looks I got it was clear that not too many white folks came this way. There was an Australian Army presence in Mendi at that time (the Engineering Corps of the Australian Army were involved in much of the Province's civil infrastructure development from 1971 until their withdrawal in 1996, and on their watch it was said that Mendi had the best Public Works Department in the whole country) but other than Australian Army personnel and the odd pilot and missionary, I saw few Europeans in Mendi. Although I was a bit of a novelty to the kids in Mendi's satellite villages, my presence didn't elicit the same response as the first white men in this area. The first European penetration of the New Guinea interior came in the late 1920s when miners came in search of new goldfields, and Lutherans came to establish missions. One woman recalled her first contact (in 1928) with Europeans: *When they came, people ran into the forest in fear — they thought the missionaries were ghosts. They also smeared pig blood and grease over their hands, face, hair, etc. to protect themselves. They feared they would die because they were seeing the dead.*[220]

The Europeans in the great exploratory patrols of Leahy, Dwyer and Taylor in the 1930s had similar experiences with first contact. The villagers saw these white men as spirit-beings, and believed that they and their possessions were endowed with magic properties. After witnessing their first aircraft landing and watching the European occupants clamber out, locals were heard to mutter that they would like to eat the human waste and the genitals of the visitors from the heavens. The Leahys and the other Europeans in their party had to post guards when they relieved themselves in the bushes, as locals were known to pick up their excrement and roll it into leafy packets that would become conversation pieces in the village.[221]

Having dropped off Wafi and the boys, I had other things to worry about as I stopped outside the MBA pilot's house in the Mendi suburbs. By now the sun had set. I was acutely aware of the high crime rate in Mendi and the fact that if anyone wanted to rob me and steal the car now would be a perfect time. I was always on edge as I got out of the car to unlock and open the gate: senses alert, just waiting for a *raskol* attack. This was easily the most dangerous part of my day. Luckily for me I was never held up, but I admit now that I nervously anticipated an attack every time I drove home. My stomach is in knots just writing about it.

My initial basing in Mendi lasted three months. At one point Jim Millar had a marketing brain wave and decided to squeeze a new service into our already tight flying schedule. He thought it would be a good idea to offer a once-daily late-afternoon flight from Mendi to Tari and back, and he set local tongues wagging by setting the airfare the same as the cost of a one-way bus trip to Tari. Which would you rather do as a passenger: Pay K40 (at the time, about US$40) for a 6-hour torture-fest in a clapped-out old bus with hard bench seats and dodgy suspension, or pay the same for a 30-minute flight in a Twin Otter flown by an experienced PNG hand (Millar) or a keen young Kiwi (me)? Market forces spoke loud and clear, and the afternoon Tari flights were a huge commercial success. Jim Millar's marketing genius came at a cost to his personal safety though. One day, soon after we had started offering the Tari flights, I was accosted at the airport gate by an angry mob of local bus drivers. They were not impressed that we were eating into their revenue stream, and demanded to speak with Jim Millar. *"Em I no stap,"* I told them (He's not here), *"You laik lukim em long wanem?"* (What do you want to see him about?). As the mob yelled and cursed and tried to push their way past airport security staff a bystander explained the tense situation to me: *"Boss, it is about Jim Millar's new flight to Tari. The bus drivers want to cut his head off!"* He was not kidding.

The new service to Tari was bad for Jim's standing among the local bus drivers, and bad for my nerves. The Tari Gap, like the Kokoda Gap, is an aircraft graveyard. The thought of doing late-afternoon flights from Mendi to Tari and back would send shivers down the spine of any PNG aviator.

Mendi and Tari are at the same approximate elevation (5250 feet for Mendi, 5500 feet for Tari) and are 45 nautical miles apart. The terrain that must be negotiated to get from one airstrip to the other is formidable, even on a blue-sky day. Climbing out from Mendi's runway 17 (which was my preference, as it was a shorter taxi from the apron and the strip sloped 0.65% downhill in that direction), my route to Tari took me south for a few miles before a 180-degree turn to head north-west, passing overhead the old airstrip at Nipa. The climb continued, paralleling a concertina of narrow valleys towards the small village and disused airstrip at Magarima. Here the terrain levelled off, and I turned to the west over a broad highlands plateau and followed the Magarima–Tari road, a few miles later passing through the Tari Gap. Tari lies 14 miles beyond the gap, in a wide and open basin.

To a layman, calling it the Tari 'gap' perhaps invokes images of a wide and deep valley that facilitates easy and safe passage in between two mountains. It is far from this. The gap itself is a mere one-mile wide by one-mile long corridor that squeezes through the extensive wall of mountains forming the Tari basin's eastern flank: the Doma Peaks (11,700 feet AMSL), Mt Kerewa (11,624 ft), and Mt Ne (10,900 ft). You need to be cruising at a minimum of 8500 feet to edge between these mountains and descend into the Tari basin beyond — at this altitude you will be at low level through the gap, due to the expansive 8000-foot-high plateau on its eastern approach. Terrain is not the only concern. The Tari Gap is notorious for its skittish and unpredictable weather. The narrow gap can appear to be clear, only to close seconds later in dark low-level cloud and scud and heavy rain. There are no navigation aids to help pilots determine their position in or near the gap — this must be done visually, and there are limited landmarks. Apart from the road from Magarima to the gap, the only useful landmark is Ambua Lodge, a distinctive circular cluster of bush-material hotel rooms and outbuildings nestled on the western flank of Mt Kerewa, but this is below the level of the gap and is only useful as an aid to navigation when the weather is clear.

The Tari Gap is littered with the mangled and burnt-out shells of many aircraft, and the list of accidents in the area over the years makes for depressing reading:

January 1976: a Talair Cessna, piloted by John Absolon, approached the gap beneath a dark rain-shot cloud base. What had been a clear lane through the gap closed in on him, and he crashed while attempting a low-level reversal turn. The aircraft was destroyed and Absolon was seriously injured. He spent two days and nights without food or water before the emergency locator transmitter (ELT) fitted to his Cessna guided searchers to the wreck.[222]

May 1980: pilot Mark Garlick, flying a Provincial Air Services Beechcraft Baron from Mendi to Tari, disappeared en route. The resulting search failed to locate any sign of the missing aircraft. Two years and four months later villagers found the wreckage of an aircraft in the Tari gap. It was Garlick's Baron. The aircraft had hit the ground at full speed and Garlick and his passenger, local man Kipa Yagugu, had been killed instantly.[223]

July 1980: Pilot Raymond Hoffman, captain of a Talair Baron, disappeared on a flight from Tari to Mendi. On departure from Tari he was heard on the radio saying he was . . . *climbing up towards the gap*. Another pilot asked him about his planned cruising altitude and Hoffman replied, *Stand by, I'm having weather problems*. It was the last call he ever made. The next day the wreckage of the Baron was found on a ridge in the Tari Gap, close to the road. A ground party reached the accident site to find Hoffman and all his passengers dead. One was Mr Andrew Andaija, the recently elected Premier of the Provincial Government.[224] It was Talair's first fatal crash in 22 years of operations into the Southern Highlands and caused them considerable strife. It was feared that the clan of the dead Premier would seek revenge (payback) with an attack on the Talair Mendi-based staff. Talair's General Manager was dispatched from HQ and offered the family compensation, which they accepted, defusing the tense situation.[225]

September 1982: Cessna 206 P2-SEG crashed north of the Doma Peaks during a flight from Lake Kopiago to Mendi via the Tari gap. Three people died in the post-impact fire, including the Southern Highlands

Education Minister and his wife. The survivors spent the night on the frigid slopes of the Peaks before being rescued the following morning.

November 1990: Greg Cox, flying a Missionary Aviation Fellowship Cessna 206, crashed near the Tari Gap. Cox and his three passengers were killed.

Of all the Tari gap accidents, that of Greg Cox in 1990[226] was the most disturbing. I am glad that I knew nothing of this crash when I began the afternoon Mendi — Tari — Mendi runs in the MBA Twin Otter during my basing in the Southern Highlands. It is such a sad story.

Australian Greg Cox, 32, began his aviation career as a gas turbine engineer with Qantas. He had been a Missionary Aviation Fellowship (MAF) pilot in Papua New Guinea for the past five years, in his most recent role as the pilot/manager of MAF's Twin Otter operations out of Tari. He was an experienced PNG aviator, with extensive experience in the Tari and Southern Highlands area. His total flying experience was 4715 hours, the vast majority of it earned in PNG.

In November 1990, Greg Cox and his family were on vacation in Australia. While there, Cox and his wife, Sue, met with the General Manager for MAF Papua New Guinea to discuss with him reports that Cox had been flying in weather that was considered less than appropriate for MAF operations. Cox admitted that he had been feeling the pressure of the responsibility for the economic viability of the Twin Otter operations out of Tari, and that this pressure had led him into flying in poor weather as reported. It was clear that Cox had been under some mental strain. As a result of these discussions, Greg Cox agreed to step down from his flying position and accept a posting back to the hangar as an engineer at Mt Hagen for the next 12 months. Cox and his wife were reportedly happy with this decision. They returned to Papua New Guinea on 22 November 1990. MAF PNG's Engineering manager, Grant Dixon, met the couple on their arrival in Port Moresby, stating later that he *had never seen Greg and Sue looking so well. They seemed so enthusiastic about this new term of service at Mt. Hagen.*[227] It seemed that Cox's transfer from dangerous and stressful Tari-based flying operations back to the Engineering Department was like a weight lifted from his shoulders — a burden he was glad to get rid of.

Cox and his family spent the night in Port Moresby, staying with some MAF friends, and travelled to Mt Hagen (MAF's main base in PNG) the next day.

On arrival at the MAF hangar in Mt Hagen, Cox was told to fly himself and his family to Tari in a Cessna 206, so they could pack up their things and return to Mt Hagen to begin the posting to the Engineering Department the following Monday (this was a Friday). This would also give the Cox family a chance to say their farewells to the staff in Tari. Greg Cox had not flown a Cessna 206 for quite some time, but due to his extensive prior experience on the type (3000 hours, which is a great deal, especially in PNG flying), he was not subjected to a check flight prior to his departure for Tari.

The weather forecast for Tari, obtained in Mt Hagen prior to his departure, was for 8/8th cloud (meaning a solid overcast), visibility OK in the Tari area and to the south, and smoke haze to the north and on the ranges. Prior to Cox's departure from Mt Hagen, the Meteorology Officer at Tari airport was contacted and reported back that Tari weather was indeed fine. Mt Hagen weather that day was also fine. Post-accident pilot reports stated that there was an inversion layer at 9000 feet over Tari, with cumulus cloud building up and protruding through. Visibility was poor under the inversion layer due to smoke beneath the cloud. There were build-ups to the north and east, but the approach into the Tari basin from the east was clear.

Not long after lunchtime Cox departed Mt Hagen with his wife and two children on board the six-seater single-engine Cessna 206: wife Sue (34), daughter Stacie (6) and son Cameron (4). The aircraft was 312kg (20%) below its maximum certified take-off weight (MTOW).

The flight seemed normal enough until Greg Cox approached the Tari Gap and began looking for a way through to the Tari basin. Another MAF aircraft, P2-MFS was in the Lake Kutubu area that day. Cox made contact with the pilot of MFS at 1258, saying that he was in the Tari gap, . . . *having a bit of fun trying to get down.*

He then made a radio call to another aircraft in the area, P2–FHR, a Talair Islander. FHR was descending into Tari, and Cox inquired about the Tari weather. The Talair pilot, Tony 'Bigfoot' Thirnbeck, said,

Standby, as he was unable to talk at that time. He couldn't get in touch with Cox after that to pass on the Tari weather. If he had, he would have told him that south of Tari there was a big break in the build-ups and blue sky.

For the next three minutes Cox made radio calls to the pilot of the other MAF aircraft (MFS). It was clear that Cox's predicament was deteriorating fast. He told MFS's pilot that the situation was *not good*, and that he was in trouble and did *not think they were going to make it*. In another transmission Cox raised his voice and said, *It's not good at all*, followed by . . . *have descended in the wrong place*. Another pilot in the area, who was flying the Tari–Porgera track, was monitoring the conversation between Greg Cox and the pilot of MFS. He too heard the . . . *have descended in the wrong place* call, as well as another desperate call from Cox: . . . . *unable to climb over trees*. Finally, at 1301, he heard the most chilling radio call of all from Cox: *We're going to crash*. Talair pilot Tony Thirnbeck also heard this call and was struck by the way Greg Cox said these words — without emotion and with such a matter-of-fact tone, like he was leaning over the garden fence shooting the breeze with a neighbour. The three pilots in the area listening to Greg Cox's transmissions were hearing the last words of a man about to kill himself and his whole family.

Cox's Cessna never arrived in Tari. A search-and-rescue (SAR) helicopter was sent up to the Tari Gap area immediately, and found burning wreckage two miles south-west of the Doma Peaks. A ground party abseiled in from the chopper and confirmed there were no survivors. Accident investigators later established that the Cessna was on a westerly heading at extremely low level when the left wing struck a tree with great violence. The crash site was in a narrow, steep, heavily wooded gully at 8400 feet AMSL. Trees in the gully were 50–60 feet high. At impact the Cessna's flaps were up — the aircraft was not in a low-level bad weather configuration.

How had this tragic accident happened?

Cox had most recently been flying MAF's DHC-6 Twin Otters, aircraft with excess power and an impressive climb rate. In all but the most dire of circumstances, the Twin Otter's performance surplus can be used to get a pilot out of trouble if they get stuck in an awkward and potentially dangerous situation, such as being forced into a dead-end valley by deteriorating weather conditions. The Cessna 206, although it is well suited to PNG bush flying ops, has limited excess performance and in certain situations (like the one Greg Cox got himself into that November afternoon) has absolutely no capability to outclimb terrain. All PNG bush pilots have to be extremely cautious when entering an area of bad weather at low level amongst high terrain, and must always keep an escape route open. Most especially those flying underpowered single-piston-engine aircraft like the Cessna 206. Greg Cox, with 3000 hours of Cessna 206 experience in PNG, should have known this. Not having flown the Cessna 206 for quite some time, had he forgotten about this performance differential? Did he remember after it was too late, after he had already backed himself into a corner?

Cox had been suspended from his pilot role for flying in weather conditions deemed unsuitable by MAF management. Yet here he was, in an underpowered aircraft, pushing his luck in bad weather again. And his luck ran out.

Post-accident, commentators wondered why he hadn't made a 180-degree turn and returned to Mt Hagen when he experienced bad weather in the Tari Gap. Why hadn't he slowed the aircraft, extended some flap, and set the machine up for low-level slow speed manoeuvring, in case he needed to do a reversal turn in a narrow valley? Why had he gone past the point where he still had an escape route open, and committed himself to a one-way low-level flight (surrounded by gnarly unseen terrain) up a narrow gully in deteriorating weather?

Given the stress he had been under, it is highly likely that he became cognitively overloaded. He abandoned his decision-making process. He stopped flying the aircraft and let the aircraft fly him. Stress can have play havoc with normal thought processes, and in this case the pilot became a passenger by relinquishing his role as commander and letting external factors (the aircraft's lack of performance, the nature of the terrain, the deteriorating weather) decide his destiny. In doing this, his fate was sealed. As the old line goes: *You took a risk and the risk took you.*

The accident investigation looked to answer one key question. Why had a pilot who had so recently been removed from flying duties been tasked with an afternoon flight in a Cessna 206 through the Tari Gap with his whole family on board? Crazy! This flight held challenges for any PNG pilot, but a mountain of them for a pilot who had just been relieved of his flying duties due to stress and mental strain. It was like sending a jumpy retired gladiator back into the arena to fight one last time –*Oh shit! Not again!* Greg Cox had been sent out to face the demons once more; just days after he had appeared so happy and relieved when informed he was to be taken off flying duties.

The final words in this tragic and wasteful accident come from PNG's Department of Civil Aviation. The DCA report into the accident was blunt when it came to the glaring oversight by MAF management — that of asking Greg Cox to fly himself and his family to Tari that November afternoon in 1990: *If the more drastic action had been taken, that of grounding the pilot, this accident would have been prevented.*[228]

As nerve-racking as the afternoon Tari flights were, I flew them when they fell to me, as did Jim Millar. Flying in PNG, especially on a run like this, involved balancing the risk, accepting the challenge, and just getting on with it. For me, balancing the risk meant always making sure I had an escape option, or a plan B. If I couldn't make it through the Tari Gap I'd turn back and stooge around off the southern flank of 11,624-foot-high Mt Kerewa and see if there was a break in the cloud over an airstrip called Benaria. If there was I'd transit overhead the poky Benaria Valley and set course for Tari via the wide basin to Tari's south-east. If the weather was really bad, and cloud tops extended well above the point where I could stay visual and outclimb them, I'd climb to 14,000 feet and transit the range in cloud (blind) and hope to find a gap into the Tari Valley on the other side. This was my least preferred option: firstly, because oxygen levels decreased significantly above 10,000 feet and I had to keep an eye on any elderly passengers for signs of hypoxia (oxygen deprivation — the Twin Otter has an unpressurised cabin); secondly, because I didn't want to get into a situation where I was flying in cloud while unsure of my exact position. There were simply not enough navigation aids in the area for me to confirm my position while flying blind, and I was reluctant to rely too much on the Garmin GPS unit in the cockpit (the Global Positioning

System — GPS — is a space-based satellite navigation system developed by the US Military. In the early 1990s the signal made available for civilian use was of downgraded accuracy and had reliability issues). If you were unsure of your exact position when over the mountains in cloud then you couldn't descend again until you were 100% sure you were clear of terrain. This was a problem in the Papua New Guinea Highlands — there were mountains everywhere! The nightmare scenario here was being stuck in or on top of cloud, unable to descend, chewing through your fuel reserves and having nowhere to let down. Thankfully, due to equal measures of good luck and good management, I always managed to get in and out of Tari without scaring myself too much.

●

Chapter 16

Cowboys and Dickheads

Alas! The dung beetle eats shit and rejoices.
A fish swimming in a kettle forgets the water is boiling.
CHINESE JOURNALIST WRITING IN 1908[229]

**After three months of exclusive Mendi Base rotations I returned
to Port Moresby for a short period of training. Drew Salter wanted
me checked into the Goilalas and the Koiaris in the Twin Otter, as
bush pilots were a bit thin on the ground in the Moresby-based MBA
ranks (the ex-Talair bush pilots ahead of me on the seniority list were
almost exclusively flying the Dornier 228, doing the gentlemen's
runs to the major ports, and most had no desire to climb back into
the Twotter and service the short rough mountain strips).**

I was checked into the Goilalas in August '94 by Twin Otter training
captain Bill Purcell, and the strips of the Koiaris (the Jungles) the
following month by Warwick Rankin. I only needed to fly two trips —
one with Bill into the Goilalas and one with Warwick into the Jungles —
and they signed me off as competent to operate into any of the airstrips
solo. What a pleasure it was to operate this wonderful aircraft into my
old Air Manubada hunting grounds — strips that I had such extensive
Cessna 206 experience on. The Twin Otter really was in her element in
these kinds of operations and was the perfect aircraft for once-daily milk
runs out of Moresby, carrying punters, tradestore goods, construction

materials and livestock to the isolated mountain communities. Soon I was flying daily Moresby — Ononge — Woitape — Fane — Tapini — Moresby missions, just like in the good old days of Air Manubada. And in the Jungles — flights to Naoro, Manari, Kagi, Efogi, Myola, and over the Owen Stanleys to Kokoda. Some of the villagers remembered me from *taim bipo* (the past — literally 'time before'), and I received a warm reception everywhere I went: *Wantok! Ass-day yupela boss-man lik lik balus bilong Air Manubada . . . nau yu save dispela bikpela balus! Em nau!* (Brother! Before you were the captain of Air Manubada's small planes . . . now you fly the big planes! Cool!).

These villagers, despite their primitive appearance, were canny, and would generally avoid flying with new, unfamiliar pilots, especially when the weather was bad. I was a known quantity, and they seemed happy to be on board my aircraft again. I even caught up with double agent Alex Gusi at Fane, who still strutted around the top of the strip, clutching his dog-eared clipboard to his chest, directing the minions like he owned the place. Srs Martha and Gerard were still there too: their coffee and scones remained fresh and flavourful. They were happy to see me and catch up with happenings in the real world while they killed me with kindness in their humble tin-roofed abode.

Flying in PNG had undergone a transformation of sorts as I had moved up the ranks. The introduction of two-crew ops by some of the country's airlines, most notably MBA, had led to vast improvements in safety, as had the installation of GPS-based navigation units in PNG's cockpits. The GPS units, while still hamstrung by the occasional loss of signal from the US-owned satellite network, were an invaluable navigation aid when utilised in turboprop commuter aircraft like the Twin Otter and Dornier 228, especially in ops involving flying from coastal destinations up into the mountains. The power and excess performance of the turboprops gave pilots the capability to climb over the terrain and some of the inclement weather, and the GPS gave track guidance on the exact location of the destination. You could get on top of the lower and middle cloud layers, use the GPS to position yourself over or near the destination, then look for a break in the weather and descend to the destination airport. This was very different from the boys in the Cessna singles and BN-2 Islanders, who still had to stooge out to the mountains at low level and fight their way through the scary weather and terrain to get to the destination.

Another change in PNG aviation was the move away from the exclusive hiring of pilots with PNG experience. This was a paradigm shift — in the Talair days there was just no way a pilot would get a turbine job without first cutting his teeth in the PNG bush for at least 1000 hours. In the mid 90s it was possible to join MBA as a turbine co-pilot with zero PNG experience. I was not convinced that this was a great idea, but the co-pilots rostered to fly with me were generally very good operators, and their co-pilot position could be viewed as an apprenticeship of sorts — an exposure to PNG turbine ops under the tutelage of experienced New Guinea aviators. MBA's new batch of co-pilots in these days included expatriates Jay Noori, Simon Rollston, Marty Lobert, Richard Vincent, Chris Hammond, Sven Steube, Phil Marshall, S. MacLeod, J. Davis, Sid Makary (my old workmate from Air Manubada, with plenty of bush pilot time), Anthony Rich, Tim Parer, Mick Wilson, Travis Gibson, Terry McMahon (Travis and Terry had prior PNG experience with RH Trading), Paul Paschke, Karen Butcher, Mike Salam, Ed Terry and PNG locals Morris Rondeau, Johannes Pilamp, James Yanda, T. Orok, Ed Niggea, Peter Christenson, P. Kalo, Russel Yapa, Felix Opa, Sylvester Namalok, and Nancy Wii. I got to fly with all of these new pilots when I had the good fortune to be a captain on both the Twin Otter and the Dornier 228 fleets: just after my one-year anniversary with MBA I was promoted to Dornier captain after completing the conversion course and operating 25 sectors with Training Captain Henry Goines.

While it is true that the two-pilot standard crew complement now adopted by MBA was statistically safer than single-pilot ops (this is discussed in more detail in Chapter 19), the cowboy spirit of my bush flying past was an impossible light to extinguish. Doing battle with the weather and the terrain had become the norm during my first 18 months in-country with Air Manubada, and I'd continued with that combative risk-taking mindset on MBA's single-pilot Twin Otter Base in Mendi. I therefore thought it entirely reasonable for me to continue to push it in order to get the job done when operating MBA's Goilala and Jungle runs out of Port Moresby. One day I got to see myself through another pilot's eyes. It was a regular early morning run out to the Goilala ports in the Twin Otter, and in the co-pilot's seat was PNG newbie Simon Rollston. He was due to begin his MBA Dornier co-pilot training that week, but as he was a total virgin to PNG ops he was flying with me to gain some exposure and get an idea of what being a *boss-man balus* was all about. I think it was a flight he will always remember.

First stop was Fane. The sector from Jacksons Aerodrome to the Fane area was routine, with the mountains of the Goilalas etched clearly against New Guinea's morning sky, the Mt Yule obelisk at my 10 o'clock, and the southern approaches to the Owen Stanley Range all clear, but descending to the destination I could see that the narrow Fane valley was still in shadows and swirling ramparts of mist and cloud clogged the bottom half of the ridges. Excellent. I relished the challenge presented by shitty weather in and around the mountain airstrips, and descended into the Fane Valley buzzing with anticipation and excitement. I had come to share the attitude of Formula One legend Ayrton Senna, who had once said, "Fear is exciting for me."[230] Flying into the mountains, especially if I had to do an early morning wet-season flight or any afternoon mission into the Goilalas or the Koiaris, I felt like John Wayne on the white horse — arriving out of the mist and the cloud and the shit when others were turning back or not even departing Moresby. It was empowering. I strapped on the Twin Otter and wielded it like a weapon, to do battle with the weather and the terrain. I was Dr Strangelove's gung-ho B-52 commander Major T J Kong, except instead of a nuclear warhead I was delivering a rather more pedestrian payload: boxes of tinned fish, soap powder, salt, razor blades, Ramu sugar, Twisties, kerosene, Trukai rice, Nambawan crackers and frozen New Zealand lamb flaps.

I dropped into the cloud-choked Fane Valley and set myself up on final approach, with the bare earth of the Fane's small open-cast gold mine on the ridge out my port window and the Kailope River in the bowels of the valley beneath me out the starboard side. I knew Fane's runway threshold was dead ahead at 4400 feet on the altimeter, but the mist rolling down-slope in the morning katabatic airflow blocked any clear view of the airstrip; ahead there was nothing but a patchy wall of white. No problem

— let's have another go and see if the cloud clears up on our next pass.
The valley was just wide enough to allow an orbit staying level with the
end of the strip, so I selected half flap, full forward on the prop levers,
and simply did a 360 degree steepish turn at 4400 feet, maintaining a
safe speed of 90 knots. We were in clear air for the turn, hemmed in on
all sides by the 6000-foot-high ridges of the surrounding range, and
the aircraft passed close to the edges of the scuddy mountainside cloud,
but in my estimation the manoeuvre was safe. At the completion of the
360 I rolled out again on final approach — but still there was no clear
view of the strip. I pushed it a bit more than the first attempt, pointing
the Otter towards where I though the strip should be and entering the
first wisps of the cloud, but again I couldn't make out the strip environs
so pulled hard into the same right-hand orbit. On the third pass I could
see the bottom two cone markers, with the airstrip threshold peeking
at me through the patchy low stratus that hung as raggedy fingers from
the mountainside; the fleeting view of my destination now teasing and
tempting me like the thigh-high split in a Chinese girl's cheongsam.
I slowed the Otter to the approach speed of 65 knots and was about to
commit myself to land when in a flash the view was gone, the airstrip
again masked by rolling mist, and I was forced to make an orbit in the
valley once more. As I went around I applied power to hold my selected
safe holding speed, with the twin Pratt & Whitneys growling through
the airframe, their drone building up like the nascent wail of an air raid
siren; the controls mushy as we accelerated back towards 90 knots. This
time I elected to descend 100 feet beneath the level of the strip and make
my attack from slightly below. The plan was to get under some of the
patchy cloud and mist and hopefully see a bit more of the threshold and
get away with an unorthodox *climbing* approach. I rolled the aircraft out
for the fourth time on the final approach track, again slowed up to 65
knots, took full flap, and stooged once more into the mist. It worked.
This time I could just make out the bottom of the strip 100 feet above
me, with a cone marker on each side. I climbed up to meet the end of
the grass runway and threw the machine on the ground, selecting full
reverse a heartbeat before we made contact with the damp earth. The
whole airstrip was still in cloud, so we careened up Fane's 12% slope in

near whiteout conditions; the barely visible line of cone markers in my left and right periphery guiding the way. I manhandled her up to the top of the strip and slid the aircraft through a 180 degree turn on the tiller to park adjacent to the priest's house, the nose pointed back down the strip. Awesome. Job done. Simon Rollston, sitting ashen-faced in the co-pilot's seat, turned to me. I had scared him, and he was most unimpressed: "You're a bloody cowboy!" he snapped.

He was right. I *was* a cowboy, and my years flying in PNG had conditioned me to wholeheartedly believe that my approach into Fane was perfectly acceptable. So I took his words as a compliment!

I like to pretend that I don't have much of an ego, but of course we all do. I was always chuffed when praised by locals for my ability to get into the mountain airstrips in inclement weather when other pilots had turned back. I still remember the reaction of the MBA agent that morning in Fane. After securing the port engine and filling out the aircraft logbook I'd clambered down from the cockpit to supervise the loading. Mist still swirled over the aircraft, and anything outside of a 50-foot radius was blurred and indistinct, people and their freight floating into view like ghosts from an ethereal fog. The agent came up to me and shook my hand with great vigour, his face lit up with a wide smile: "Captain! We knew it was you! We hear the *balus* in the valley; we see your lights come up the mountain. Only you can find Fane in this bad cloud!" This sort of ego-fodder did nothing but encourage cowboy antics. The extreme flying that resulted was like running an egg and spoon race with a nitro-glycerine egg: if you got away with it, flying at the absolute edge of the aircraft performance and the outer limits of your own skill, you felt great, elated, bursting with adrenaline and professional satisfaction. If you mishandled it, it would blow up in your face. There was a fine line between pushing it and getting the mission accomplished, and pushing it and backing yourself into a corner and crashing. Pulling off approaches and landings in these extreme conditions was the sort of cowboy stuff that would get you killed one day. Lose an engine while carrying out an in-cloud low speed go-around, orbiting in a tight valley with no escape option? You are dead.

I knew that there was no shame in diverting a flight due to bad weather — continuing on to another port or simply returning to Port Moresby — but I always did my damnedest to get in. Mack Lee had never questioned my decisions in the mountains, nor had MBA Chief Pilots Mike Butler and Drew Salter. These guys expected me to fly a successful mission, but trusted I wouldn't push it too much and crash. As the MBA Operations Manual clearly stated: "An aborted flight is a sign of prudence, not of cowardice."[231] Fellow PNG bush pilot Giles Rooney had this concept explained to him well by one of the senior pilots when he joined North Coast Aviation in Lae in the 1990s. It was a sage bit of advice, and stuck in my head when he relayed it to me during research for this book: *If you're the only pilot in the company who can't make it to your destination, and you return to Nadzab, you're a dickhead for a day. If you crash and write off the aeroplane and kill yourself and your passengers while trying to get in, you'll be a dickhead forever.* I was in no hurry to be a dickhead forever, but in a total of 881 flights between the mountain airstrips of the Goilalas and the Jungles during my PNG years I was only ever unsuccessful (unable to land at my destination due to bad weather) six times. Was this the record of a bold cowboy with a well-honed skillset, or that of a reckless dickhead with unnaturally good luck? While my Fane co-pilot Simon Rollston would suggest it was the latter, I would say the jury remains out on this one.

One pilot for whom the jury came to a clear decision was PNG pilot S. Kale, who in mid 1993 crashed a BN-2 Islander (registration P2-ISC) at Kiriwina airstrip. This strip services the Trobriand Island group, a cluster of small islands off PNG's eastern coast. The Trobriand Islands have been known since the early 1900s as the 'Islands of Love', based on exaggerated tales of the annual yam festival, a sexually charged celebration of harvest season. PNG folklore has it that during the festival roaming gangs of horny women run amok on the islands, dragging unsuspecting men into the bushes and having their wicked way with them. Unfortunately for captain S. Kale, yam festival-endorsed copulation was not the reason for his infamy.

The day he crashed it was a fine and beautiful day on Kiriwina Island, with a blustery 25 knot wind running straight down the 1630-metre-long gravel strip. Kale went to start his engines for departure to find that only one would start — the other engine had a buggered starter motor — so it looked like he and his lone passenger were stuck there until his company could fly in replacement parts and an engineer. The strong headwind blowing down the barrel of runway 14, and the fact that it was a very long strip (it was built by US Army Engineers and used by Royal Australian Air Force Kittyhawks and Spitfires in the 1940s) inspired Kale to try something a little bit wacky. He decided to do a high-speed taxi run down the strip and use the acceleration from the good engine and the stiff on-the-nose breeze to try to reach a safe engine-out speed and attempt a single-engine take-off. This 'safe speed' is known as V_{MCA}, the speed below which the airflow over the flight control surfaces is insufficient to keep an aircraft controllable with one engine failed. The BN-2 Islander's V_{MCA} is 65 knots. Kale's plan was pure madness! On his first attempt, hooning down the airstrip, holding in a bootful of rudder to keep the aircraft straight, he failed — the airspeed was just too low. On the second attempt, near the end of the runway, a lucky gust of extra headwind pushed the indicated airspeed over 65 knots, and Kale thought: *I may as well just keep going!* He pulled the aircraft off the deck with an incorrect assumption the Islander would keep flying. Just as he got airborne the aircraft lost a few knots (perhaps due to being out of ground effect, or because of the adverse drag from all the rudder he had in to keep the aircraft tracking straight on one engine, or because the headwind reduced), thus decelerated below V_{MCA}, and became completely uncontrollable. The good engine yawed the aircraft towards the dead engine and Kale had no more rudder left to prevent it. The BN-2 Islander fell from the sky and crashed into the bush off the end of runway 14, with the right wing clipping a tree and bending backwards, the same-side undercarriage leg twisting towards the fuselage, and the nose wheel and the nose cone deformed rearwards in the impact. Thankfully there were no injuries to either occupant. The best bit of this crash came after it was investigated by the PNGDCA. Safety Investigator Mike Feeney, on learning that Kale had crashed while attempting a single-engine take-off, wrote on the accident report: "I recommend urgent suspension of his Pilot's licence".[232] Attempting a single-engine take-off in a twin-engine aircraft? There was no doubt here — this guy was a 100% guaranteed-or-your-money back dickhead.

Once a year the heavy hitters of Papua New Guinea's powerful oil and gas industry would get together for a night of cocktails and fine dining at the black-tie Petroleum Ball at Port Moresby's Travelodge Hotel. MBA operated a crew-change contract for Chevron, who ran the gas fields at Lake Kutubu, and were generally invited to attend. In 1994 Simon Wild, MBA's GM, kindly arranged for tuxedo rentals for a few of the lads, myself included, and we had the pleasure of dressing up and pissing with the big boys the night of the Petroleum Ball. The star of the night turned out to be Dornier captain Grant Le Lievre. He was a baby-faced killer any day of the week, but on this occasion he got some of Port Moresby's expat ladies fizzing at the bung even more than usual. Before he left for the ball he strapped a faux penis to his lower inside leg (it was a gift from his father, a joke-shop lifelike dick attached to a calf-muscle strap). At the ball, with the oil and gas industry husbands off at the bar smoking cigars and hobnobbing with their associates, he flitted amongst their seated wives, casually lifting one leg up onto a vacant chair while he chatted them up. As he did so he purposefully let his trousers ride up his calf and expose the business end of the skin-toned monster penis. I sat at the MBA table with Simon Wild, Paul Walsh, Shane Wedding and Dave Alsop, watching the magic unfold. We were on the edge of our seats, waiting to see if the ladies noticed the heavily veined schlong peeking out from Grant's trouser leg. Most of them did, and their wide-eyed reaction was clear, with the befuddled wives struggling to remain composed as Grant nonchalantly continued his chitchat. It was comedic gold! Le Lievre was a joker of epic proportions, and during my all-too-brief former life in the RNZAF would have been a good man to have in the Officer's Mess (provided he promised not to burn any pianos!).

After a short stint in Port Moresby I returned to the Southern Highlands Base at Mendi to fill in once more for Jim Millar, who was due to depart for his one month off in Australia. The cowboy stuff continued, albeit backed up by a currency-based skill picked up in the course of hundreds and hundreds of sectors in the Twin Otter. During the first few days back I decided to try a Twotter challenge that I'd heard about from John 'Disco' Everett. Apparently it originated from his Talair days — the challenge was to set the power leavers in one spot when downwind, then not touch them again until after landing (guessing the exact amount of power required to get you all the way to touchdown). This required great familiarity with the aircraft, which most of us possessed in spades. I was successful on my first attempt, selecting about half power when downwind into Pimaga, an 885m-long clay strip at 2568 ft AMSL at the southern extremity of Lake Kutubu. With the power now set, and unable to be changed (that would be admitting defeat!) I used the aircraft's pitch to control the speed, and the aircraft's drag (flaps and a bit of sideslip as necessary) to control the glide angle. No problem. I touched down neatly on Pimaga's strip, reached up to the power levers for the first time since being downwind (closing them), selected prop levers full forward, and twisted the throttle grips to the forward detent[xii] to allow me to take a hint of reverse thrust.

The next challenge was something I'd seen on TV. I'd recently watched a video of the Australian Bicentennial Airshow and been impressed by the RAAF DHC-4 Caribou display. On one of its low passes the aircraft came in nose-down, fully configured for landing, and did a touch-and-go on the nose wheel only. Caribou pilots called this stunt 'the wheelbarrow'. I figured the Twin Otter should be able to do that too, so one day on approach into the Chevron camp at Moro airstrip I gave it a go. It turned out to be a messy bit of flying. I came in on a normal approach at 70 knots, but instead of raising the nose in the flare for landing and reducing the power, I gingerly pushed the nose forward and increased the power. The nose wheel alone made contact with the white gravel of Moro's airstrip, and I successfully wheelbarrowed the aircraft down the first third of the runway, holding it there with a touch of forward elevator control, modulating the power to hold my landing speed. But

---

[xii] The detent is a lock that prevents inadvertent selection of reverse thrust.

now the tricky bit. Unlike the Caribou display pilot, I wasn't planning on applying go-around power and launching into the air again — I had to make a full stop landing and unload my cargo. What followed was a very awkward transition from 'the wheelbarrow' to a normal landing. I pulled the nose off the deck, reduced the power, and fought the controls as the Otter bounced roughly onto first the left main wheel, then the right, then settled on all three. It was not pretty. Moro airstrip was always busy — with the comings and goings of lumbering Southern Air Transport C-130 Hercules aircraft, Columbia Helicopters' Boeing 234 Chinooks, and Pacific Helicopters' Aerospatiale Lamas and Bell 206 Longrangers; the choppers buzzing about the strip like bees around a hive. A Chinook crew had observed my ugly post-wheelbarrow touchdown, and without knowing that I'd done the whole thing on purpose as an experiment, couldn't keep from commenting. The radio came alive with a Texan drawl as I taxied past the hovering twin-rotor: "Son, that was the worst landing I have **ever** seen!"

A few days later I arrived overhead Pimaga to find that wet-season rains had led to a nearby tributary of the Kikori River bursting its banks, and the threshold of Pimaga airstrip was now fully submerged, although still clearly visible through the floodwaters. I'd read of daring topdressing pilots doing touch-and-go landings on rivers, so decided to give this a shot too. I selected my aim point just before the demarcation line between the water and the dry section of the airstrip, and landed on the main wheels in the shallow water with about 30 feet between me and dry land, careful to keep the nose wheel from making contact. The landing was exceptional — the Twin Otter aquaplaned across the smooth surface like she was sliding on a flawless icesheet, or an oiled pane of glass — there was almost no perception that the aircraft was no longer flying. It was eerily quiet and smooth as silk. As the Otter's main wheels made contact with the grassed clay of the strip the normal aural and tactile sensations of landing returned, somewhat surprising and exaggerated, like the sensory shock when a car leaves a smooth tar-sealed road and hits an unexpected section of gravel.

A final bit of cowboy flying took place one afternoon on a dead-leg sector back from far away Timbunke, where I had dropped a group of tourists who were joining a Trans Niugini Tours multi-day cruise on the Sepik River. It was rare to fly a sector completely empty — no passengers and no cargo — and I was inspired to emulate the Twin Otter aerobatics of my Highlands check captain John 'JB' Bruce, Mr Cheshire Cat himself. How hard could it be to barrel roll the Otter? JB had made it look so easy.

The track from Timbunke back to base at Mendi saw me heading SSE, climbing to 12,000 feet to get over the Central Range, and overflying Lake Surunki in Enga Province, the highest freshwater lake in PNG. Thirty miles from home the land dropped beneath me to 8000 feet, and ahead I could already make out the Mendi Valley, nestled on the flanks of monolithic Mt Giluwe, whose 14,527 foot peak hid in a patch of puffy fair weather cumulus. I decided to try a barrel roll over the Kandep Valley, and eased forward on the control column to put the Otter into a gentle dive. Once she picked up a bit of speed I pulled up through the horizon and rolled her around the longitudinal axis. Fully inverted it went pear shaped. I had subconsciously let the roll rate drop, failing to keep enough aileron in to sustain the manoeuvre, and the Otter simply stopped. Upside down over the Southern Highlands. The aircraft froze in a zero-G state, with me hanging in my seat harness, the shoulder straps cutting into my shoulders, and everything that was not bolted down now floating around the aircraft like a NASA astronaut training session. I forced myself to put in a big handful of aileron to finish off the manoeuvre, and as the aircraft came right way up the nose scooped out the bottom of the roll and the airspeed rapidly increased to a marginally scary figure. As 1G (normal gravity) conditions returned everything that had been floating around the cabin came crashing down, flotsam littering the interior of the aircraft like a bomb had gone off. I sheepishly flew on to Mendi, noticing that my flying briefcase was missing from its normal spot on the floor between the cockpit seats and was now at the back of the cabin, having left a messy trail of maps, pens, stationary, my logbook, an old RNZAF issue navigation ruler and my circular E6-B flight computer. All of the floor panels (light three-ply wood sheets placed between the seats to protect the metal floor of the aircraft) had popped up and floated around the cabin along with everything else during my failed roll; they now sat propped at crazy angles throughout the cabin like a jumbled pile of firewood. I landed at Mendi and shut down the machine on the apron. Before I could stop them, the cargo boys opened the rear airstair. Wooden panels and pens and bits of paper and assorted shit fell down the stairs on top of them, and they looked at me with a curious mixture of surprise and suspicion. I climbed down from the cockpit and offered the best explanation I could come up with: "Sorry about the mess boys, there was some really bad turbulence between here and the Sepik." They didn't look convinced.

Despite the now-widespread use of GPS units in the cockpits of PNG's aircraft, and the supposed safety of turbine ops over piston-engine ops, aeroplanes continued to crash, and pilots and passengers kept on dying. At the end of 1994, just as I became qualified as a captain on MBA's Dornier 228 fleet, two more PNG pilots fell off the knife edge.

In late November Andrew McDonald, a South West Airlines pilot with over 1500 hours of PNG time, was on a routine flight from Selbang to drop off six passengers at Bolobip, a gnarly airstrip nestled in the lee of the Hindenburg Range. This mountainous wall blocks the northern approaches to the OK Tedi copper and gold mine at Tabubil, on PNG's western border with Papua (Indonesia), and is a treacherous region of limestone pinnacles, sink holes and harsh vertical cliff faces; the spine of the range averaging 11,000 feet AMSL. McDonald's as-the-crow-flies track from Selbang (5054 ft elev.) to Bolobip (5000 ft elev.) was a mere 5 nm (less than 10km), but involved crossing a significant spur off the eastern side of 9100-foot-high Mt Sari. The weather on the day in question had been reported as "marginal" for visual flight, with forecast scattered showers of rain and thunderstorm activity and reduced visibility in heavy rainfall, haze and fog. The forecast and actual reports from other aircraft in the area at the time confirmed that visual navigation in this heavily mountainous area would have been problematic.[233] McDonald, in BN-2 Islander P2-SWC, never arrived at his destination, and deteriorating weather conditions in the area prevented any search until the following day. After some initial confusion, with numerous false emergency beacon signals due to the precipitous terrain and the altitude of the crash site, the aircraft was located at 6900 ft AMSL on the eastern face of Mt Sari in an area of vertical limestone cliffs. Rescue personnel rappelled down the mountainside — it was impossible to cut a helicopter pad anywhere near the crash site — and found no survivors. It was an especially grisly scene. The aircraft had impacted in a wings level climbing attitude, and suffered catastrophic compressive disintegration. The abseiling party informed the rescue coordination centre (RCC) that the wreckage was in a very precarious position, with a whole section of the cliff in danger of slipping to the valley below due to the unstable nature of the limestone topography. Two days later a heavy-lifting Kamov KA-32 helicopter arrived on-site and attempted to retrieve the accident aircraft using a specially designed and constructed grapnel device, but during the lift the Islander's compressed fuselage broke into pieces. Horrifically, this allowed all the bodies in the main part of the wreckage to fall out onto the mountainside. The only body to remain was that of the pilot, trapped in the front section of the aircraft. The instability of the crash site led to an RCC decision not to attempt the retrieval of the fallen bodies and the rescue team were forced to leave them where they lay.

Investigators had no problems coming up with an opinion as to cause. They determined that McDonald had lost situational awareness and flown in poor visibility straight into the cliff face. It was a black-and-white example of what aviation accident investigators term CFIT — controlled flight into terrain.

Does lightning strike in the same spot twice? In PNG bush flying it does. Three and a half weeks later, 28 people died in a crash in this same area, less than 10nm from McDonald's accident site.

In mid December '94 veteran PNG pilot Roy Hoey was en route in a Missionary Aviation Fellowship DHC-6 Twin Otter, ferrying a load of 26 passengers from Tabubil to Selbang, the very airstrip McDonald had departed from prior to his fatal flight the previous month. Weather conditions were again marginal for visual flight, with visibility decreasing to less than 3 km in heavy showers and thunderstorms. Somewhere south of the direct Tabubil–Selbang track Hoey found himself trapped in an extensive area of broken cloud, and manoeuvred to find a clear patch through which he could descend. He found what he thought was a suitable hole and, for reasons unknown, continued a reduced-power tight descending turn all the way to treetop level. His aircraft impacted a mountainside at 6400 ft AMSL in a steeply banked nose-down attitude. Hoey, his cabin attendant and 26 passengers all perished. This was the worst crash during my time in PNG and brought the number of people killed in aircraft accidents in the mountains around Tabubil to 63. Hoey's accident was yet another case of CFIT — investigators surmised that while in the descending spiral the experienced MAF pilot misjudged either the height of the cloud base or his proximity to the ground, or attempted to avoid a ridgeline at low level and struck trees in a panicked steep turn. In their words, "the pilot failed to maintain adequate clearance from the terrain."[234]

As was always the case in the wake of an aircraft accident, especially one involving such large loss of life, the newspapers and TV screens across the country were plastered with coverage of Hoey's crash for days. Whenever someone 'went in' there was an uproar in the press and a conspicuous public unease, despite the fact that per kilometre travelled flying was still the safest way of travelling around the country (and often the *only* way to travel, given the paucity of national roads). Sadly, it remained the case that most accidents were due to pilot error, often involving CFIT — controlled flight in perfectly serviceable aeroplanes into clouds containing vertical real estate. There was nothing new here. As one senior PNG pilot had pointed out way back in the 1970s, most accidents occurred through the toxic combination of pilot inexperience and/or risk taking and bad weather. If every pilot in the country flew according to regulations, he pointed out, there would be no crashes. This was true, but as another senior PNG aviator had rebutted, "then there would be no flying."[235]

The cowboy antics of PNG flying weren't just restricted to shenanigans in aircraft. One morning, when I was once again based in Port Moresby, I awoke to find I'd missed my four am alarm and was now 30 minutes late for a scheduled pre-dawn departure operating MBA's daily *Post Courier* newspaper charter to Nadzab. I threw on my uniform and barrelled out the door in a blur, leaping into my trusty Suzuki SJ410 jeep. There were a few traffic lights to negotiate at the intersections between my MBA accommodation and the airport, and on this particular morning the green-light gods were against me — it seemed at every set the lights were red, despite the total lack of traffic at this hour of the morning. I did what had become standard operating procedure in Moresby when one was in a hurry at night — I turned off my headlights just before arriving at the intersections and simply drove straight through the red lights. I did this at the 3 Mile traffic lights, slowing up as I approached the intersection with Wards Road to check for traffic, the floodlit buildings of PNG Motors to my right and the dark void of the Taurama Barracks' parade ground off to my left. Once safely through I turned my lights back on, only to sense a vehicle accelerating behind me, swerving into the lane to my right, and aggressively pulling level with my jeep. My sixth sense told me that something was wrong. I looked across in the darkness to the vehicle — it was a beaten up Toyota LandCruiser ute — and leaning out the passenger door window was a man with a shotgun to his shoulder. A shotgun that was pointed squarely at my face. He waved the barrel at me, motioning for me to pull over. It's amazing how quickly the human CPU can process information when under stress. The Sherlock Holmes part of my brain had two immediate explanations for this gun-to-the-face predicament, and instantly mapped out the consequences for each. The first was that these guys were *raskols* out for a score and that I was about to be robbed/raped/killed. The second was that they were plain-clothes cops and I was to be scolded for running a red light in the pre-dawn darkness. Whatever the truth, one certainty was the fact that my diminutive Suzuki could never outrun their LandCruiser. So I calmly decided to pull over and see which fate was to befall me. There's not much else to be done when you have a shotgun six feet from your face. I eased the jeep to a halt in the dusty verge at the side of the Hubert Murray Highway and watched as the tatty Toyota did the same, crunching to a stop in the gravel just ahead of me. Three guys jumped out, and Mr Shotgun ambled over, pausing at my open window. He wore jeans, a pair of scuffed combat boots, and I noticed with no small amount of relief that he had somehow squeezed his stocky frame into a too-tight PNG Police shirt. It was explanation two — these guys were cops. Mr Shotgun no longer pointed his weapon at me, but waved it about with one hand as he spoke, like an angry tribal chief might wag a spear at a recalcitrant warrior. "Why you no use lights? *Yu mas yusim* lights!" He spat a mishmash of English and Pidgin at me

COWBOYS AND DICKHEADS

—————————◦—————————

321

through heavily stained teeth, his mouth full of blood-red *buai* juice. "*Sapos yu no stopim, mi sutim kar bilong yu!*" (If you hadn't stopped, I was going to shoot at your car).

"I'm very sorry," I apologised as meekly as I could muster. "I'm really late for an important flight". He looked me up and down, no doubt taking in my white shirt, the MBA wings pinned to my chest, and the gold stripes on my shoulders. A light came on in my head: "I have to fly a charter for the Prime Minister in 30 minutes, and I'm running late," I offered. *Genius.* His demeanour completely changed. The angry tribal chief now had an important mission as one of Port Moresby's finest, tasked with a vital mission helping out the nation's Prime Minister, *boss-man namba wan.* "OK Captain. *Em i no problem. Nau mipela givim yu Police escort long* 7 Mile!"

And they did. One of his *wantoks* produced a red/blue emergency strobe light, which was placed with urgency on the dashboard of the LandCruiser. The trio of cops piled back into their vehicle and I was escorted to the airport in fine style, still ignoring the red traffic lights, but this time leaving my lights on, 1000 cc of petite Suzuki power plant struggling to keep up with the speeding LandCruiser. Our convoy of two raced through the dark city, past Boroko, up and over 5 Mile hill and down to the Airport entrance on Morea Tobo Road. As I broke left to go past the Air Niugini Offices and onwards to the MBA buildings the Police LandCruiser stopped under the airport gate guardian, the three cops smiling and waving as I accelerated out of sight. What a great service they had done for their country that morning! And how fortunate for me that they didn't decide to hang around and escort the non-existent Prime Minister out to my aircraft . . .

Although it was kind of self-inflicted, this shotgun-in-your-face experience reminded me that sometimes it was safer to go flying in the nation's unforgiving mountains than it was to spend time on R & R in PNG's main centres. The towns, Port Moresby in particular, remained dangerous and chaotic, with major law and order problems. If you were in the wrong place at the wrong time terrible things could happen to you. One week later the chaos became incarnate. A bunch of us had decided to kill a few South Pacific lagers down at the Port Moresby Yacht Club — the original Yacht Club, on the western side of Touaguba Hill, on Champion Parade across the road from the shipping container terminal. The 'Yachtie' was one of Moresby's top watering holes, and its Saturday night disco was always standing room only. That night the place was heaving, with the entranced masses gyrating to the latest hits by M People, Real McCoy and Ace of Base. I stood near the club's open windows, chatting away with the MBA boys. The crowd behind us danced in a perfumery: the ocean breeze carried the scent of frangipani blooms from the garden outside, and this mixed with the smell of the coconut oil on the hair of the local girls, permeating the place with a potpourri of sweetness. The disco finished late, and my girlfriend and I made our way back to my MBA shared accommodation at 2 Mile. It was well after midnight, and the drive through Port Moresby was eerie. By day the city hummed with activity — a vibrant harbour front, busy roads, PMVs crammed with *bilum*-totting *meris* on their way to market, and lethargic *buai*-chewing men on their way to nowhere in particular. By night the city was different. Cool. Quiet. It was like Port Moresby had peeled off its grubby coat of humanity and lay naked under the tropical night sky, supine and relaxed. It was a beautiful city by night. They all are. Come nightfall, the flaws and untidiness and uncomfortable truths of a metropolis's daylight hours morph into an unsullied nocturnal blanket of twinkling lights, like a treasure chest spilled across the landscape. Viewed from above, a two dollar light bulb in the porch of a tin shack shimmers and shines just as well as the lanterns of the Champs-Elysees, or the apartment lights of the Manhattan skyline. That night the city slept fitfully. Moresby stirred, rolled over to scratch itself, and exposed its dark underbelly. I arrived back at the house about 30 minutes after a fellow MBA pilot, who had also been at the Yacht Club disco with his girlfriend. The four of us were part of a group that'd been drinking together, taking in the sounds of the disco, and enjoying each other's company. I pulled into the drive and was surprised by the flashing lights of two police cars. This was a bad sign. I soon found out why the cops were there: half an hour earlier, as my colleague opened the gate to enter the MBA compound, he had been held up by a gang of *raskols* armed with knives and firearms. The pilot was robbed and held at gun point, then physically restrained and forced to look on while his girlfriend was gang raped in front of him. Gang raped. Here again was the hand of fate — if I had arrived home any earlier that might have been me and my girlfriend. To a Western brain this attack seemed barbaric, but it had strong cultural underpinnings and was far from an isolated incident in a city like Port Moresby. It may have been a *payback* rape — retribution for some real or imagined wrong that had been committed either by my friend, his girlfriend, or even by a completely different MBA pilot. Alternatively, it could have been completely random, and the attack and rape was considered a fun way to kill some time by a roaming gang of *raskols*.

The following Monday I was due to fly back to Mendi for another stint in the Southern Highlands. This rape had left me feeling sick to my stomach. Not for the first time I wondered why I was exposing myself to the dangers of PNG life. But my march up the career ladder again took precedence, so there was nothing to do but push the horror of the attack to the deepest darkest recesses of my mind (filing it next to the memories of the bloody aero club attack of '92), and just get on with it.

I didn't know it yet, but my time in PNG would soon be coming to an end. My next Mendi rotation presented me with the opportunity to prove that, while I had pulled off plenty of stunts and lucky escapes as a bush-flying cowboy, I was still more than capable of making a dickhead of myself. A few days after settling into the Southern Highlands flying, Wafi, the MBA office manager, sent me off on a standard punters-and-freight charter to the satellite strips of Lake Kutubu: a nine sector Mendi — Moro — Kantobo — Baina — Haiwaro — Musula — Fogomaiu — Waro — Moro — Mendi mission. The weather was stable but shitty that day, with low cloud and patchy pockets of drizzle falling in dark curtains from beneath a low cloud base, and I had to work hard to get into all of these airstrips. The most challenging sector of the day was the one from Baina, a short boggy grass strip downstream of Beaver Falls, to Haiwaro. Haiwaro lies 40 nm to the west of Baina, on the southern perimeter of Mt Bosavi, the Southern Highlands' last topographical hurrah, where the mountains finally surrender to the wide soggy expanse of the Western Province's flat wetlands. The weather was really clagged in on the south-eastern flanks of Mt Bosavi that day and departing Baina I could see a dark wall of rain and scud between me and Haiwaro. Flying the direct track between airstrips wasn't going to be possible due to the inclement weather and the terrain — a spur of 4000-foot-high limestone pinnacles straddling my route. The Garmin GPS unit in the -200 series Otter I was flying had been removed prior to my departure from Port Moresby days earlier, so I flew without any navigation aids, old-school, using the eyeball and distance/time calculations scribbled on my flight log to estimate when I should descend to the destination. I dodged patchy stratus for the whole 20 minute flight, careful to stay clear of solid cloud, and tried to keep track of just where I was on the map using the limited peeks I got at the landscape below. I found myself pushed further and further left of track due to the heavy showers and limited visibility over the limestone spur I was attempting to traverse. Visual navigation in this area was hard — unlike Southern Highlands mountain flying, there were limited landmarks here, and all the rivers and rolling hills looked the same, most especially at low level. For this reason navigating the featureless wetlands could be quite intimidating. The landscape was intimidating too — stretching out from the base of Mt Bosavi, the Western Province took in 97,000 square kilometres of heavily timbered plains, steamy jungle, twisting mazes of crocodile-infested rivers and waterlogged marshlands. Ecologically the area was something of a "lost world". In 2009 a BBC Natural History Unit film crew working in the dormant crater of Mt Bosavi discovered several new species, including fanged frogs, grunting fish and the Bosavi woolly rat — a large silvery-grey rodent almost one metre long, weighing 1.5kg.[236] Happily, right on the expected elapsed time, I found a break in the cloud near where I thought Haiwaro airstrip should be, in the shadow of Mt Bosavi's lost world, and kept sight of the ground as I spiralled down through the gap. I popped out beneath the cloud base about 500 feet above the deck, close to a river. My map indicated this twisting sinew of water must be the Turama River, the only landmark in the area, on whose banks I'd find the village and airstrip of Haiwaro. Sure enough, there it was, a couple of miles downstream, a clear patch of clay and grass on the river's edge. Smoke curled up from the roofs of the nearby village houses, drifting south, indicating I should land in the north-easterly direction. I manoeuvred for a straight-in approach while cancelling SARWATCH on HF radio and calling circuit traffic on VHF. So far so good. On short finals, with the aircraft moments from touchdown, something just didn't feel right. I had to make an especially steep approach to avoid some rather tall palm trees between the river and the airfield perimeter — I didn't recall these trees being a feature of landing at Haiwaro — and the airstrip seemed a lot greener and grassier than I remembered. Wasn't it supposed to be a sparsely grassed brown clay strip? As I touched down, expecting to see the parking bay flash by me on the right side of the strip, it went by out the left side window. What the hell? This was *really* confusing. My brain did a 180 degree turn inside my skull at this major *glitch in the matrix*, and I struggled to make sense of this perplexing picture. Finally the penny dropped. I looked down at the map on my lap and realised that I'd just landed at the wrong airstrip! This wasn't Haiwaro at all — it was Kuri, a similar airstrip with a similar altitude, length and runway orientation, also in the lee of Mt Bosavi and on the banks of the Turama River. The claggy weather over the limestone spur had pushed me further left of track than I'd realised, and instead of landing on runway 06 at Haiwaro I'd landed on runway 09 at Kuri, 14 nm downstream. Dickhead.

A major secret of doing well in aviation is looking at all times, no matter what, like you know what you are doing. The way you are perceived by others is paramount. I'd always been pretty good at this. I nonchalantly pulled the Twin Otter into Kuri's parking bay, idled both engines, put the park brake on, feathered the port propeller, and leaned back into the passenger cabin, cool as a bloody cucumber. I yelled out to the cabin load of Haiwaro-bound passengers: "I'm supposed to pick up two passengers here." I feigned looking out the window for my fictional Kuri punters. "I'm going to wait for five minutes, and if they don't show up we'll continue on to Haiwaro — OK?" I got a couple of understanding nods from the cabin then put on a great show of checking my watch every minute or so, continuing to scan the airstrip for the imaginary passengers. Soon enough the charade was complete: "*Olrite, twopela man em i no stap. Nau dispela balus em bai kirap na go long ples belong yu.*" (OK, the two passengers didn't show, now this aeroplane is departing for your village). I'd got away without letting the punters know my mistake — now I had to maintain the deception with air traffic control too. So I made no radio calls other than a quick one on the area VHF frequency (to warn any inbound traffic that I was about to take off from runway 09 at Kuri) and departed on the five minute flight to my *real* destination. ATC were none the wiser. The only catch was that if we crashed en route, somewhere between Kuri and Haiwaro, there would be no search-and-rescue follow-up — as far as ATC were concerned I was already safely on the ground in Haiwaro. That was a risk I was willing to take — anything to prevent the lads from finding out that I'd cocked up and landed at the wrong airstrip!

This may be an amusing stuff-up in hindsight, but on one occasion a landing at the wrong PNG airstrip proved fatal. In 1977 iconic 61-year-old PNG and WWII aviator Bobby Gibbes (owner of the aircraft that crashed at Lake Kopiago described in Chapter 15) returned to PNG to fly for Talair after a spell in semi-retirement in Australia. The man was a living legend, not only for his pioneering work as owner of Gibbes Sepik Airways in the 1950s, but for his earlier adventures as a dashing P40 Kittyhawk/ Tomahawk pilot with the RAAF in North Africa during WWII, where he took part in countless battles against the Luftwaffe and the ground forces of Rommel the Desert Fox. Gibbes was the Commanding Officer of 3 Squadron in this theatre and his impressive service record saw him credited with 10.25 aircraft destroyed, five probables, 16 damaged, and two destroyed on the ground,[237] making him one of the RAAF's leading fighter aces. In December 1942 he famously went 'above and beyond' to rescue one of his pilots. Gibbes watched as a colleague was hit by flak as they strafed an enemy airfield, crashing his Kittyhawk a mile off the end of the runway. With the other Squadron pilots flying cover, Gibbes landed his P40 in a rough clearing close to the enemy base. The downed pilot ran to Gibbes's machine, and Gibbes (a short nuggetty man), got the downed pilot to sit in his P40, with Gibbes climbing into the cockpit and sitting on his lap. They took off successfully, with one man operating the rudder pedals, the other the stick and throttle. They made it back to base, although only just. Gibbes later said of his rescue: *I landed about three miles away and picked him up after he had a long run. Burst tyre and broke left leg of kite getting off. Were damned lucky to make it.*[238] This episode of 'double dinking', with two pilots crammed into the cockpit of the single-seat fighter, made Gibbes a hero.[239] Post-war, Bobby Gibbes moved to PNG and worked for Mandated Airlines and by 1948 had started his own aviation company, Gibbes Sepik Airways (GSA). GSA quickly became a vital lifeline for the Government Patrol Officers (Kiaps), with their aerial supply drops into remote corners of the Highlands enabling the long exploratory foot patrols of the Colonial Government. He sold his airline a decade later, moving into the business of coffee growing and running hotels. By the 1970s he was based in Australia, but did make the occasional trip up to PNG to do a spot of flying for MAF, Macair and Talair.[240] And so it was 61-year-old Gibbes found himself in PNG in 1977 on a one month Talair contract. After a week flying out of Madang he was transferred to Wewak for three weeks of flying a Cessna 402 into the airstrips of the Sepik. This region was his old hunting ground — few pilots knew these airstrips better than Bobby Gibbes. What happened next was almost beyond belief. One day Gibbes, who by this time had amassed 8000 hours of PNG flying, mistook the short strip at Brugam for the longer strip at Nuku (these airstrips are, respectively, 50 and 70 miles west of Wewak, in the lee of the Torricelli Mountains). Brugam was nowhere near long enough to allow a safe landing in a Cessna 402 (with this aircraft's high landing speeds) — at 486 metres long it was suitable for Cessna singles and BN-2 Islanders only. Gibbes landed normally but soon put the aircraft into an uncontrollable skid, no doubt realising he wasn't going to pull up in the runway remaining. He attempted a ground loop but overran the strip and crashed into a village house, the starboard wing bursting into flames. All occupants of the burning Cessna 402 escaped with minor injuries, but the fire quickly spread through the house, killing five villagers trapped within. The veteran pilot's mistake had come with terrible consequences. Talair were censured for failing to ensure that the 61-year-old pilot was properly route-endorsed and checked, and had to pay compensation to the relatives of those killed at Brugam. Author James Sinclair, a friend of Gibbes, spoke of this accident in the third volume of his *Balus* books: "That a pilot of Bobby Gibbes' experience and reputation could suffer such an accident was further proof — if any was needed — of the traps that await the unwary aviator in PNG".[241] Gibbes never again flew in New Guinea skies, his error at Brugam sadly punctuating his otherwise exemplary career.

Those of us who lived and breathed PNG bush flying flew with a mix of skilled cowboy and lucky dickhead to the end — you really needed a bit of both in your genetic make-up to not only get the job done, but to survive. Thorough training, hands-on experience and good joss were the only things keeping us from becoming a part of the accident statistics. One stark display of these statistics hangs from the wall of the Port Moresby Aero Club.

In the mid 90s the aero club moved from its old position (the site of the vicious aero club attack of 1992) to a new site, a soulless building attached to a large aircraft hangar on the south-western end of Jacksons Airport. The new venue held little of the charm of the old location, but by the time the framed aviation pictures, the glass boxes containing aircraft models, and stale SP Lager-scented beer mats were transplanted to their new home, it was still a pleasant enough spot to enjoy a cold one after a day's flying. The wreckage of a WWII American Bell P-39 Airacobra fighter in the garden, relocated from the grounds of the original aero club, lent the venue a further slice of authenticity. Hanging from the wall in the corner of the bar closest to the aerodrome apron was a cold reminder of those damn statistics — the Roll of Honour. It's still there today. It's a simple framed list of all the civilian pilots killed in Papua New Guinea since the first, Les Trist, in 1931; it lists the pilot's name, the date of their crash, the aircraft type, and the location of their fatal accident. The first time I took a close look at the Roll of Honour was when I stopped by in November 2007 on a research trip for this book, by then separated by more than ten years from my own PNG experiences. I never read it during all my visits to the old and new aero club bar when I was in PNG between 1992 and 1995. You would expect a PNG bush pilot to be curious about the Roll of Honour, but my conscious decision to stay detached from the list once again showed my attitude towards those who crashed and died in PNG. It was a way of keeping distance from the harsh reality of what could happen if I made a mistake in the mountains — consequences that were just too chilling to contemplate.

●

Chapter 17

Bagpipes, Blood, and Farewell

*". . . it appears that (Papua New Guinea) will survive as a functioning
independent democratic state with strong
prospects of economic and social progress. However,
something unexpected could happen tomorrow."*

ANN TURNER[242]

**When I was a new co-pilot on MBA's Dornier fleet one of my first trips
was an early morning PNG Defence Force (PNGDF) coffin charter
from Port Moresby to Balimo, an airstrip and major village on the
northern banks of the mighty Fly River in the Western Province.**

Captain Tom Karlsborn and I prepared the aircraft for departure;
Karlsborn setting up the cockpit and monitoring the refuelling while
I did the walk-around safety inspection, watching as a solemn group
of uniformed PNG Defence Force troops loaded a flag-draped coffin
through the rear doors and quietly took their seats inside the cabin. The
flight time to Balimo was about 1 hr 25 mins, the direct track from Port
Moresby taking us across the Gulf of Papua. Tom was flying the sector
and levelled the Dornier off at 8500 feet, trimming the machine out
nicely so he could fly hands free. Tom was another of MBA's characters
— a short stocky Scandinavian rogue who wouldn't have looked out
of place dressed in animal pelts, sporting a horned helmet and a long-
handled axe. The man smoked like a Copenhagen chimney, and was

known to get a bit fidgety on longer flights, busting for his next nicotine fix. When we first met I thought him a gruff and grumpy chap, but he was just economical with his words, and when he thought it an appropriate time to string a few together he displayed a dry wit, accessorising it with a gravelly chuckle. Still, it wasn't difficult to imagine the man leaping off the front of a longboat, wading ashore to get into a bit of slashing and pillaging and general Viking mischief. After an uneventful climb and cruise we descended in clear crisp morning skies to the verdant Fly River floodplains. Beneath us ground-hugging cloud and patches of fog masked random chunks of the countryside, dotting the landscape like tufts of cotton candy. Luckily Balimo airstrip was still visible, and Tom set up an approach and landing on the grass and clay runway 10. As we pulled into the parking bay and shut down both engines, low cloud moved in from the east, sitting snug over our half of the airstrip like a cap, shrouding us in misty light drizzle. I moved from the cockpit back through the cabin, past the soldiers and the coffin and opened up the rear doors. I'd flown plenty of coffin charters during my time with Air Manubada into the airstrips of the Goilalas and Koiaris, and thought I knew what to expect. The arrival of a coffin charter was a noisy affair, with loud and public displays of grief. I expected a chaotic scene to unfold as soon as the doors dropped open, with howling villagers throwing themselves about the airstrip, a theatrical display of chest-beating and hair-pulling, muddied faces and bodies, and general bedlam. Our reception at Balimo was entirely different. The Balimo villagers moved soundlessly out to the aircraft, standing silent and with great reverence as the PNGDF troops unloaded the coffin and hoisted their fallen brother onto the shoulders of an eight-man honour guard. The only sound was the drip drip dripping of the drizzle running off the Dornier wings onto the sodden earth of the airstrip, the skies seemingly joining in and lamenting the soldier's loss. Suddenly the hush was broken by the reedy drone of a lone military bagpiper, and the haunting notes of an ancient Scottish tune washed over us, eerie and beautiful. He stood beneath the tail of the aircraft, sheltering from the light rain, his cheeks full, his elbow gently pumping the bag in the crook of his arm, dew dripping from the beret atop his head and the red tassels of his pipes. I hadn't noticed this soldier or his instrument during the aircraft loading in Moresby, so this was a completely unexpected and surreal soundtrack. The crowd engulfed the PNGDF coffin bearers, carrying them away from the airstrip as silent and stealthy as a storm tide, trickling through a narrow gate at the exit from the parking bay like sands through an hourglass. Down a muddy track towards the village they moved, the camouflage patterned uniforms of the honour guard visible in snatched glimpses through the crowd, the still-playing piper bringing up the rear. The mournful bagpipe melody faded away to nothing as the throng disappeared from view behind a row of waterlogged nipa palms. It was an incredibly moving scene, and I felt great empathy for the dead soldier's silently suffering *wantoks*. To be completely honest I found the whole thing quite emotional, and I blinked back tears as I turned back towards the aircraft. "Are you OK?" croaked the Viking, sucking hard on a cigarette. "Yeah," I said, "I'm fine. There's just something stuck in my eye. Let's fire this thing up and get back to Moresby." I didn't know how the soldier died, but I knew where. This young man, a son of Balimo, had fallen in the civil war on the island of Bougainville.

The Conzinc Riotinto Australia (CRA) copper mine at Panguna on the island of Bougainville was the most important economic development in the lead-up to Papua New Guinea's self-rule in 1973, when the newly independent nation finally broke free of its colonial shackles. Huge copper deposits had been discovered on Bougainville back in 1964, and drilling began within the year. Receipts from the project, which exported its first batch of copper in 1972, were expected to be a significant contributor to the new nation's coffers, but possible *complications* had been anticipated. One observer wrote in 1972: 'It can be expected that (CRA) will completely overcome the physical problems of mining copper on Bougainville. Its major test is in the realm of human relationships — political, economic, social, cultural and environmental.'[243] How prophetic these words would prove to be. No sooner had the copper started coming out of the ground than angry landowners confronted CRA, with rioting at the mine site. Some were totally opposed to any mineral extraction; some would only allow it if environmental concerns associated with the open-cut extraction methods were addressed, and if they and the provincial government received a more significant share of the profits. In 1974 the agreement between parties was renegotiated on terms that were considered, by world standards, very generous[244] but many Bougainvilleans still felt they were being cheated. Their disillusionment ultimately led to the formation of the Bougainville Revolutionary Army (BRA), a group who, by 1988, were demanding 10 billion kina compensation (at the time, roughly US$10 billion) — an unrealistic figure many times the mine's gross earnings since its first copper export in '72.[245] When CRA and its subsidiary Bougainville Copper Limited failed to meet their demands, the BRA resorted to sabotage and terrorism, linking their attacks to earlier demands for an independent Republic of Bougainville. Their guerrilla tactics led to the closure of the mine in 1989, at which time the government declared a state of emergency, sending Defence Force troops and armed riot police to crush the rebellion. They failed and the conflict escalated. Bougainville was gripped by a secessionist civil war for the next nine years, with control of the island see-sawing between government forces and the armed BRA rebels. The social cost was huge — some 30,000 refugees moved from areas controlled by the BRA into government care centres during the conflict, and on top of those killed in armed skirmishes, thousands were thought to have died as a result of the strategic denial of medical supplies to treat malaria, pneumonia, tuberculosis and other preventable diseases. The Bougainville civil war was dirty on both sides, with allegations that 'neutral' villagers were subjected to mortaring, aerial bombardments, assassinations, rape, extra-judicial killings, and torture.[246] Between 1989 and a final ceasefire agreement brokered by New Zealand in 1998 it is estimated that 10,000 to 20,000 people lost their lives on Bougainville.[247] The economic cost to the nation was significant too — the year prior to its closure the mine had provided 30% of PNG's export earnings, 11% of GDP, and 15% of national government revenue.[248]

The Bougainville conflict also gave rise to what was perhaps the biggest political scandal in PNG history, 'the Sandline Affair'. In 1997 the Prime Minister of PNG, Julius Chan, entered into a secret contract with British-based mercenary group Sandline International. They were promised US$36 million in return for sending foreign mercenary troops and equipment to Bougainville to help government forces defeat the BRA. Soon after the mercenaries arrived (44 of them, guns-for-hire from the UK, South Africa and Australia) Brigadier General Jerry Singirok, the head of the PNG Defence Force, withdrew his support for this cloak-and-dagger arrangement, announcing publicly that the armed forces refused to work with Sandline. The Brigadier General clearly 'did not want a private army on the loose in his patch'.[249] He also accused the Chan government of corruption and called on the PM to resign. Chan's reaction was to sack Singirok, which caused widespread violent anti-government protests. The nation teetered on the edge of a constitutional crisis. When the dust settled the Sandline mercenaries had been arrested by Singirok's men and ejected from the country; Julius Chan was forced to resign and lost his seat in parliament in subsequent elections.[250] The most outrageous chapter of this political scandal was yet to come — the following year Sandline sued for breach of contract, and an international tribunal ruled in their favour. It was reported the British mercenary group was expected to ultimately receive more than US$40 million of PNG public funds for a US$36 million contract that was never fulfilled.[251]

My years in PNG were smack bang in the middle of the Bougainville rebellion. The war was not something that had ever affected me — it was a topic in the local newspapers and was constantly smouldering away in the background, but it had no tangible impact on my life or on flying ops out of Port Moresby. The only physical sign of it was the movements of PNGDF aircraft on the military apron on eastern side of Jacksons Airport, a steady flow of troops and ammunition and supplies to the affected area. It wasn't until I operated as crew on the PNGDF coffin charter to Balimo and saw for myself the collective anguish of the village, that I appreciated the civil war had a far greater impact than I'd realised.

One of the lads had a *very* up close and personal experience of the Bougainville conflict. In February 1995 New Britain-based Airlink pilot Gerry Krynen (an old mate from my Air Manubada days and a previous employee of MBA) launched on a routine Twin Otter Bougainville Island milk run — Hoskins to Buka; down the east coast of Bougainville to Wakunai; Wakunai south to Arawa (a coastal airstrip adjacent to the closed copper mine at Panguna); Arawa back to Buka; Buka home to Hoskins. Although the Bougainville civil war was still in full swing, Airlink bravely continued their scheduled passenger services on the Island. They were the only company still doing so, basing their decision to keep flying in the war-torn Province on assurances from the BRA that Airlink's civilian humanitarian operations would be exempt from any acts of violence. That day Gerry got as far as Arawa before the plan changed. Here he was asked if he could shuttle some military personnel and Government officials to Oria, a strip on the southern end of Bougainville. Apparently there was a peace ceremony taking place in Oria later that day. There was nothing unusual about a schedule change like this, and Gerry did as requested. It was a stunning day aloft and he flew the sector from Arawa to Oria without incident. On the ground in Oria the Airlink cabin attendant supervised the passenger disembarkation while Gerry filled out the paperwork and enjoyed the views from the airstrip across to the Shortland Island chain to the south. Soon enough the aircraft was ready for departure, with a load of nine passengers for the next destination, Buin, just 10nm to the SSE. In a 2013 email Gerry described what happened next:

I powered up, ensuring we had take-off power, and released the brakes. The Otter lurched forward eagerly, gaining speed quickly, and in no time I eased the control column back, and we were airborne. Within seconds, as if in slow motion, I was transfixed by the vision of a piece of white fibreglass about the size of a fist fly over the top of the windscreen. To my great surprise I heard what sounded like three savage hammer blows on the fuselage. We were only about 50 or 60 feet high, and for some strange reason I realised we were receiving ground fire. Instinctively, without thinking, I violently banked the aircraft right, pushing the nose forward, and descended into a ravine that ran roughly north– south immediately ahead of me. I still had my right hand on the power levers, which I retarded. From the ground, it probably looked like I had lost control of the aircraft, because the shooting suddenly stopped. All I could hear now, above the engine noise, was screaming and yelling from behind me. I quickly checked the engine instruments, but I already knew both engines were okay. We popped out of the ravine, and flew low and fast over a ridgeline ahead, heading straight for Buin. The aircraft felt good, there was a very slight vibration through the rudder pedals — that was a concern — but otherwise everything seemed fairly normal. I called down the back for the flight attendant to come up and let me know what the situation was in the cabin. He was clearly shaken, and informed me that one of the passengers had been hit in the chest, and appeared dead, and a female passenger had received a wound to her arm. I remember looking down the aisle, and seeing a lot of blood on the floor. I asked the flight attendant to move the body to the rear of the cabin. This was really to help calm the passengers down, and he quickly came back to let me know it had been done. I also asked him to have a look at the aircraft through the windows to see if there was any obvious damage. He returned and said there was no damage that he could see.

Gerry now had a decision to make — to continue on to Buin or divert to another airstrip. He decided that the BRA rebels could be in the Buin area too, so elected to fly all the way back to Buka. As he climbed away to the north-west on track to Buka he had a chance to look back towards Oria. Far below he saw a group of grass huts in flames, with a thick pall of smoke drifting inland. That peace ceremony was turning out to be anything but peaceful. He heard a helicopter call on VHF inbound for Oria and warned them he'd just taken ground fire on departure. He also called Moresby on HF and amended his destination to Buka, giving an estimated sector time of 45 minutes, advising them that he'd been hit, and requesting urgent medical attention upon arrival.

On descent into Buka the vibration from the rudder pedals increased, so Gerry reduced his airspeed. The Twin Otter handled OK and the approach was normal, but on landing the right main tyre deflated. He carefully taxied the aircraft off the runway and parked close to the terminal building. With great relief he shut the machine down, watching as medical and military and police personnel swarmed around the

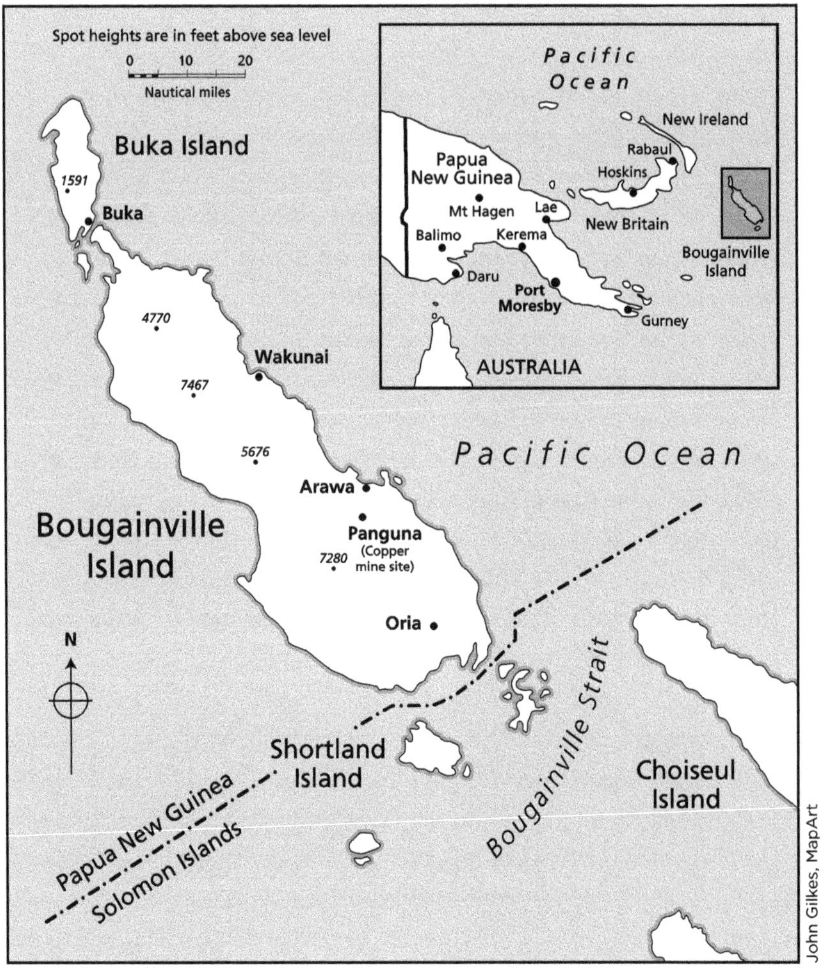
Spot heights are in feet above sea level
0 10 20
Nautical miles
Buka Island
1591
Buka
4770
Wakunai
7467
5676
Arawa
Bougainville Island
Panguna
(Copper mine site)
7280
Oria
N
Shortland Island
Papua New Guinea
Solomon Islands
Bougainville Strait
Choiseul Island
Pacific Ocean
Pacific Ocean
New Ireland
Rabaul
Papua New Guinea
Hoskins
Mt Hagen
Lae
New Britain
Balimo
Kerema
Bougainville Island
Daru
Port Moresby
Gurney
AUSTRALIA
John Gilkes, MapArt

Bougainville Province.

aircraft. It was time to take stock.

The right main wheel had been holed by a bullet. One passenger, Joachim Kaima, was indeed dead, shot right in the chest when the rebel gunfire raked through the cabin. One other passenger, teacher Joyce Ika, seated next to Mr Kaima, had been hit in the arm by the same volley. Bullet holes peppered the top of the fuselage forward of the right wing and the tail cone, rear navigation light and the bottom of the rudder had been shot away (this was the source of the vibration). The aft floor of the cabin was awash with blood. Most gruesome of all, significant amounts of blood had seeped through the floor panels and been sucked out the rear door by the en-route pressure differential, leaving a wide bloody smear on the aircraft's aft port-side exterior. It was only once he was on the ground that the enormity of the morning's events hit Gerry: *I disconnected my headset, grabbed my flight bag and walked to an area away from the crowd. It started to dawn on me how lucky we had all been to escape with our lives, and how tragic the incident had been for at least one of my passengers and the rest of his family.*

That night Gerry was back in Kimbe town, Airlink's base in Hoskins, knocking back a few rum and cokes at the San Remo Club "becoming comfortably numb as the shock wore off." The very next day he was back in the saddle, in command of an Airlink Cessna 402 picking up punters and baggage from the southern airstrips of New Britain, as if nothing had happened. There was no such thing as stress leave or touchy-feely trauma counselling in PNG. Today Gerry Krynen still flies New Guinea skies — as a captain with Air Niugini. As far as I'm concerned, his calm actions under fire that day on Bougainville in '95 make him a PNG aviation hero.

Two months after the attack on Gerry's Airlink Twin Otter I was scheduled to operate as part of a four-ship Dornier 228 charter for the PNG military to Buka, the northernmost island of Bougainville Province (Buka and Bougainville Islands are separated by the Buka Passage, a 200m-wide tidal channel). Northern Bougainville was supposedly under government control (Gerry Krynen had taken hits while flying in southern Bougainville), but it was common knowledge the whole area was still *hot*. I'd had this confirmed personally during a recent chat with a PNGDF helicopter pilot who'd just finished a tour of duty out there. I met him late one afternoon in the grass verge between the MBA apron and the airport taxiway, a chunky highlander in a green zoom-bag struggling to secure the weighty main rotor of his Bell UH-1 Iroquois to the tail boom with a canvas strop. I gave him a hand, and asked him how things were going on Bougainville. He described in detail his daily missions — flying at low level over the jungle watching tracers from rebel gunfire drifting up towards his ship; his door gunner returning fire with the staccato tat-tat-

tat of the chopper's heavy machine gun. I knew this helicopter was one of several supplied by the Australian Government on the strict condition they were to be used on humanitarian missions only.[252] He knew this too. "Should you be telling me this?" I asked. He just grinned, shrugged his shoulders, and finished telling his war stories about gunship missions over Bougainville.

The day of the Buka charter arrived. I left my co-pilot Tim Parer with the other crew members preparing the four aircraft on the MBA apron and drove to the flight briefing office at Jacksons control tower to file our flight plans and check the weather and NOTAMs. The forecast en route and destination weather reports were fine, but one NOTAM for Buka caught my eye:

> *Caution due civil unrest. Small arms fire reported in area. Do not overfly Bougainville Island. Minimise time in Buka circuit area.*

Small arms fire reported in area? Wasn't northern Bougainville safe? Was there a chance we'd be shot at too? This was a worry, but hardly reason enough to put four gung-ho MBA Dornier crews off carrying out the mission. I'd never heard of anyone getting gunned down anywhere near Buka and besides, the risk of getting strafed seemed no more dangerous than the bush flying I'd been doing for the past few years. Truthfully, the prospect of flying troops and guns into a war-torn province was terribly exciting, another thrilling adventure in this *land of the unexpected*. I left the flight briefing office and got back to the MBA hangars just as Unimog truckloads of uniformed PNGDF soldiers arrived. They were marshalled out to the waiting line-up of Dorniers — 60 of them in full combat fatigues, boots and backpacks, camo caps and helmets; M16 assault rifles slung over their shoulders. These guys were loose and chatty and seemed far too relaxed for a bunch of lads about to see some real action. They were as blasé about heading off to war as we were about flying them into a hot airstrip. The troops were split into four groups of 15, each group was assigned to one of our four ships, and we saddled up and headed off on a direct GPS track to Buka. Before we'd left I'd asked the senior soldier on my Dornier to make sure that magazines were removed from all weapons and chambers cleared. I could only presume the PNGDF grunts did as they were asked.

As the four captains had pre-briefed, we descended early for Bougainville, some 430 miles along the 500 nautical mile/two-and-a-half-hour leg, and arrived at 500 feet over the water in loose line astern formation into the uncontrolled Buka circuit area. The lads kept it tight, arcing around with a neat base turn to the north-east and soon enough all four aircraft were on the ground clear of the runway, the crews waiting for the flight manual mandated three minute cool-down period before hitting the stop button and shutting down the Dornier's Garrett TPE331-5 power plants. It took some time to unload the troops and all their gear, and this delay, on top of our slightly late departure from Port Moresby, meant we were now pushing ECT. ECT (Evening Civil Twilight) is an officially published time band, specifically calculated for any global location on any given day of the year, for the transition from day to night. It begins when the sun is on the horizon at sunset and ends when the centre of the sun is six degrees below the horizon. In aviation the beginning of ECT is the time after which the sun's illumination is no longer considered sufficient for daytime flying: it's the legal demarcation between day ops and night ops. Published ECT for Buka that day was 1754. There was no problem with us arriving in Port Moresby after dark — Jacksons Aerodrome was fully equipped with the necessary lighting and navigation aids for night flying — but we had to be airborne from Buka *before* 1754, as the airstrip had no lighting and was approved for daytime ops only. If we weren't wheels-up by 1754 we would be stuck here overnight — any take-off even one second past the start of ECT would be unlawful. By 1715 all four aircraft were unloaded but we had a problem — there was no sign of the refuelling agent. Sod's law — the rule whereby if something can go wrong, it will — was against us this day on Buka. One of the co-pilots was dispatched to comb the airstrip looking for said tardy agent. By the time he sputtered into view, his clunky old tractor towing the Jet A1 fuel tank, it was almost 1730. There was no way four Dorniers could be refuelled and fired up and launched off the end of Buka strip in the next 24 minutes. The four captains got together for a powwow while the FOs hurried along the refuelling process. We quickly decided on the lesser of two evils — rather than leave four aircraft and eight crewmembers at Buka overnight, exposing our machinery and personnel to possible ground attack from the BRA rebels, we'd lie about our departure time to Air Traffic Control. We'd just have to massage our reporting times en route, and make sure that by the time we got within range of Moresby radar our position reports matched our actual position. It was a canny plan, and it beat the pants off staying in Buka overnight. By 1754, the start of ECT, the refuelling of the last Dornier (mine) was almost complete, and the other three were just closing doors and would soon be ready to roll. We needed to get out of here ASAP — the airport apron was bathed in the golden light of the dying fireball on the far horizon, shadows lengthening as the curtain of night crept in from the east.

I called Port Moresby ATC on HF radio: "Moresby, Moresby, this is Mike Bravo Papa on 8861."

The controller came back almost immediately over the hiss and crackle of the high frequency radio channel: "MBP Moresby, go ahead".

Time for the deception to begin: "Moresby four Dorniers, MBW, MBQ, MBR, MBP, POB (persons on board) eight, departed Buka time five three, tracking direct Port Moresby, climbing 10,500 feet, will call you time two three, and at position AKYA."

"Roger MBP call time two three".

Now on paper at least our flight was legal. Within 10 minutes our Dornier too was refuelled, and all four aircraft *really* departed Buka, rotating off the end of the runway in near darkness and turning south-west for home into the fading light over the Solomon Sea.

We got away with the ruse — calling 30 minutes after our fake take-off time and at AKYA and VEVEK (two compulsory en route reporting points from the instrument navigation charts) a few minutes before we actually got to them; only giving real times when we arrived over the PNG mainland two hours later, flying overhead Girua and obtaining permission to climb to 12,500 feet to transit the Kokoda Gap in the dark. The only stuff-up was when one of the captains (who shall remain nameless) got his maths wrong and transmitted an en-route position report based on his actual location and actual (illegal) departure time from Buka. Within seconds of his slip-up he received some fairly curt radio calls from the rest of the formation on our company air-to-air frequency (including more than a few 4-letter words!) and he quickly corrected his call to Port Moresby ATC based on our fabricated departure time. The four Dorniers were safely on the ground at MBA HQ in Moresby by 2040. We were relieved to have gotten away with an incident-free Bougainville mission. In the end our biggest concern had not been tracers fired from rebel guns floating up towards us from the Bougainville jungle, Gerry Krynen-style, but the ill-considered radio call fired off by captain doofus.

I left PNG for good in July 1995 when I got a job as a pilot with an international airline based in Hong Kong. As my remaining time in-country ticked down (June '95 was my last full roster month at MBA) I was overcome with an irrational fear of an impending calamity, like Fate or the Grim Reaper knew that their opportunities to have me hurt or maimed in an aeroplane crash were becoming more and more limited and they were contemplating doing something about it: *If we are going to get this guy we'd better do it soon!* I'd experienced this paranoia before when working for Mack Lee at Air Manubada, an uneasy niggle in the back of my mind when I flew into the mountains in the days preceding my few-and-far-between vacation breaks. I wasn't the first to have these premonitions of looming doom closely tied to the end of a period of stressful and dangerous flying — there are accounts of this same fear being experienced by combat pilots as they approach the end of a tour of duty in a war zone. US Army helicopter pilot Chuck Carlock described his feelings as he neared the end of his service in Vietnam in his book *Firebirds*: "I never had much hope of getting out of Vietnam alive. I just took it for granted that I wouldn't make it. With about 30 days left, I began to think seriously about going home and started to worry about getting killed . . . I thought I was destined for an untidy demise."[253]

I *was* to receive one more scare in PNG before I left, but it was to be Port Moresby's law and order problems that delivered it, not aviation.

The last place I lived in before I departed was a shared house at the

MBA compound on Port Moresby's Korobosea Drive, a short way down the hill from 2 Mile. The compound was as well protected as it could be — an eight-foot high steel mesh fence topped with razor wire encircled the group of five houses, and we had *Kukukuku* (pronounced 'cookah-cookah') security guards living on-site. These were lads from the famed Kukukuku clan from the back country of the Papuan Gulf, the most feared tribe in all of PNG. Their ancestors had practised headhunting and cannibalism as recently as the early 1900s, and these wiry wee men were still considered the most bloodthirsty and vicious tribal group in the nation.[254] To PNG eyes, a Kukukuku tribesman with a bush knife and a bow and arrow was more intimidating than a Highlander with a shotgun, or an armed member of any other ethnic group. These 'hard men' of PNG were given a wide berth by all other tribes so were a natural choice to be employed as security guards. But high fences and Kukukukus couldn't protect against everything.

I was woken one morning by bloodcurdling screams from the top of the compound. In an instant I was fully awake, flesh crawling, heart racing, adrenaline surging, 100% certain we were being attacked by *raskols*. *Here it comes*, I thought. My premonitions had been right after all. I grabbed the baseball bat I kept under my bed and inched towards my front door, peering through the security grill to see what was going on. The screams were coming from the stilt house at the top of the compound — Ross 'Shags' Fieldus's place. I knew Shags was in there with his wife, Lagri, and I shuddered to think what calamity had befallen them. The screams were Ross's: *"Get out! Ahh, ahh, get out!"* I thought his house had been overrun by weapon-wielding *raskols*, and I was sure there would be blood. Fortunately my instincts were wrong. There were intruders alright, but luckily for Ross and his wife it was a pair of petty crime *raskols*, not slit-your-throat-for-two-dollars *raskols*. He told us the story later. He'd come out of his bedroom to make a pot of tea and disturbed two intruders. They'd used a car jack to prise open the security bars on his living room windows and as he walked in one was squeezing his way out through the gap with Ross's stereo in his arms while his accomplice helped pull him and his booty onto the balcony. Ross's screams had sped up their exit and the *raskols* disappeared through a hole in the security fence behind his house, along the rear fence line where our compound backed onto a squatter settlement. No one was hurt in the robbery.

Two years after I left PNG this same house was again targeted by the *raskols* from the squatter settlement. MBA pilots Mike Wilson and Dean Boatman were woken in the dead of night by the agitated barking of their Rottweiler. Mike went to the door to investigate and opened the front door only to come face to face with a *raskol* pointing a pistol at him. Without thinking he pushed the would-be assailant away and slammed the door shut. Mike and Dean barricaded themselves in the house, listening in horror as a group of *raskols* carried out a frenzied attack. Several began hacking away at the rear windows of the house with axes and machetes, trying to rip off the security bars, while another got under the house and swung a bush knife through a section of thin particle board between exposed wall studs. Inside the house the *raskol's* knife blade slashed into view through the back of the pantry, the hole in the particle board becoming bigger and bigger with every stroke. The besieged pilots were paralysed by fear — if the attackers got in, how would they defend themselves? They grabbed a pot and a pan as makeshift weapons, and set about boiling a jug of water on the stovetop, planning to pour it over any *raskols* who appeared in the jagged hole in the back of the pantry. They were that desperate. Help arrived when a pilot in another house was awoken by the commotion and activated his personal panic button. The *raskols* fled over the back fence when a rapid response security vehicle arrived noisily in the compound minutes later, its floodlights bathing Mike and Dean's house in blinding light. Neither pilot had been hurt, but their nerves were never the same again.

One of my last flights in PNG was a Jungle run in the Twin Otter with MBA First Officer Jay Noori. I'm not normally one to throw stones, well aware that I live in a glass house myself (none of us are immune to the screw-ups, omissions, miscalculations and lapses of concentration that in the aviation game can lead to an incident or an accident), but I will make an exception for Jay and lob a few pebbles of criticism his way. He was a bouncy little fellow, small and hairy, with plump fingers and a balding pate — a bit like a Middle Eastern version of Radar from the 1980s TV's show

MASH. Jay looked like he was straight out of flying school — he'd turn up at MBA's flight dispatch in a crisp starched pilot's shirt, a pair of too-large-for-his-wee-face Ray Ban aviator sunglasses, lugging a spanking new black pilot's briefcase almost bigger than him. He was probably the guy least suited to being a pilot I ever met, but his heart was in the right place and he was *uber* excited about all things aviation. Young Jay was a permanent co-pilot on the Twin Otter. He had failed his first-officer upgrade to the Dornier 228 after a dodgy instrument check with Captain Henry Goines, who had replaced madman Captain X as the chief pilot of the Dornier fleet. Henry told me that Jay had become confused while trying to intercept a radial during an instrument approach procedure and turned the wrong way, descending in the completely opposite direction to the published track (this could have fatal consequences, as the aircraft could be descending into terrain). After this he was relegated back to Twin Otter co-pilot and picked up the unfortunate nickname "Wrong-way Jay." MBA's Twin Otter Captains avoided flying with Wrong-way. He had the annoying habit of masturbating his headset boom microphone with his mouth. The intercom (the only way pilots could communicate with each other over the engine noise) was noise activated, and as you flew along with Jay there'd be endless staccato bursts of amplified sucking and scraping noises in your ears as his wet lips probed and teased his microphone like a pair of copulating worms. It was not pleasant. On top of this, he was a wildly verbose chappie, and there was a near-endless stream of jabbering from him as he fidgeted in the co-pilot's seat. This guy had more rabbit than Sainsbury's!

The morning of my flight with Wrong-way Jay we departed Moresby under blazing blue skies and set course with a full load of punters and freight for Manumu in the Jungles, the site of the three unfortunate crashes covered in Chapter 7. After that we were due to make stops in Kagi and Efogi, with the typical payload of people and Triffids expected for the trip back to base — the normal Jungles milk run. Jay was still very new to PNG, so I decided to let him do most of the day's flying. As we levelled off in the cruise at 5500 feet, there was a sudden burst of air noise and commotion in the cockpit, on Jay's side. Instantly I knew what had happened — I'd flown this particular Twin Otter (P2-MBS) many times before and knew if the co-pilot's door wasn't locked shut just so, it would work its way loose and open in flight. Jay had been more shocked than me by this unexpected event, and was all arms and legs as he struggled to fly the aeroplane, gather up the charts and paperwork that had become dislodged in his panic, close the door, and regain his composure. I found his overblown reaction highly amusing. Once things had settled down, Jay realised that he was missing one chart — his personal Port Moresby visual terminal chart (VTC). This map displayed all the airspace boundaries in the area, the significant terrain, the visual routes, and limited details of the airstrips out to a 60 nm radius from Jacksons Airport. Jay was most upset. "Oh shit!" he said, "I think my Moresby VTC's gone out the bloody door".

I bit my lip.

"Shit!" he moaned, "I just had it laminated. That thing cost me ten kina".

This was priceless.

"Oh well, it does have my name and address on it so maybe someone will find it and post it back to me".

Really? I don't think so, mate. We were flying over solid jungle, halfway to the base of the Owen Stanley Range, effectively in the middle of nowhere. Had he just seen *The Gods Must Be Crazy*? Did he think a villager hit on the noggin by a falling aviation chart would set off from his grass hut on a quest to return the thing to its owner? Perhaps the chart is still where it fell — as the centrepiece of a shrine to the airspace gods of Papua New Guinea in some remote jungle village! I dined out on this story for years — it was a classic.

I lost track of Jay after I left PNG in 1995 and found out in 2010 that he persevered with his career and is now an Airbus A330 captain with a Middle East-based airline. Good for him. For the sake of the travelling public, I hope his nickname is now *Right*-way Jay. *Insha'Allah.*

The last thing to arrange before I left PNG was a going away party. In PNG, these are called *go pinis* parties (*go* = leave, *pinis* = finish, final). Fellow MBA Dornier captain Colin Hicks had also snagged an airline job, so we teamed up and had a combined farewell piss-up. It was held in the TV room of MBA's tour-pilot compound on 2 Mile Hill and we ordered a couple of kegs of SP lager and put on a BBQ dinner. The party provided a last opportunity to catch up with fellow flyers as well as my non-aviation Port Moresby friends like Br Damian and some of the boys from the PNG Surfing Association. It was a great send-off, and on 6 July 1995 I departed PNG shores for good. Career-wise I was moving onwards and upwards to greener pastures, unaware at the time that I'd never experience such challenging and exciting flying ever again. I'd been a PNG bush pilot for almost three and a half years. In that time I had flown 3,392 revenue flights into 98 of the nation's airstrips for a grand total of 2,484 hours on the New Guinea knife edge.

Sadly the high spirits of the *go pinis* party and my excitement for the future, the Holy Grail of an airline job finally in my hot little hands, was tarnished by yet another tragedy. Just six days later MBA pilot Ed Terry was killed when his Twin Otter P2-MBI crashed and burned on the Gurney foreshore. This was a horrible accident. Ed took off from Gurney on an early morning flight to Wedau with a load of 13 passengers and one MBA cabin attendant. It was a crappy day, with a low 200 to 500 foot cloud base and visibility less than three kilometres in rain mist. Soon after take-off, as Ed's Twin Otter crossed the coast, witnesses heard an explosion and saw smoke coming from the tail section. Moments later the aircraft was observed in a steep turn, onlookers aghast as it descended almost vertically and smashed into the shallow water of the rocky foreshore. The Otter hit with such force it left an impact crater several metres across and nearly one metre deep. All 15 souls on board were lost, including 34-year-old Ed Terry. His loss was hard to bear. He was a popular member of the MBA staff; just two weeks earlier he'd been partying hard at my farewell, and I still remember standing by the barbeque with a group of the lads, spellbound as Ed spun yarns and rattled off jokes like a pro.

I read the details of the crash from my new home in Hong Kong. Ed Terry's Twin Otter was so severely damaged that what remained of the aircraft was of little use to the investigation in determining whether or not the engines or flight controls had been contributing factors in this accident. The tail section was still intact enough however to provide evidence of an in-flight fire, which, when coupled with the eyewitness accounts of the crash, led investigators to the most probable cause. Ed had been terribly unlucky. A fuel source, either from a faulty aircraft fuel tank or a passenger's leaking flammable liquid container (the origin could not be determined) had ignited when it had leaked from the cargo bay into the tail section and come into contact with an electrical terminal board between the inverters and the inverter control relay. An explosion and fire in this area would have saddled Ed with two immediate problems. Firstly, it's likely that the explosion caused panic among a number of school children who were on board and it's quite possible that some may have attempted to run forward to the front of the passenger compartment. He may have been struggling to keep passengers out of the cockpit while also trying to keep the aircraft under control. Secondly, with both inverters on fire he would have lost all AC power, which would have resulted in the total loss of his directional and attitude gyro information. Ed's primary instrument, his artificial horizon indicator, would have been useless; he would have been left with what is known as a limited panel (the turn and slip indicator, wet compass, vertical speed indicator and the airspeed indicator). This was a horrific combination of events — a rush of passengers forward into the cockpit, a loss of critical instruments when outside visibility was very limited, and a fire raging in the tail.[255] This combination led to the death of Ed and all those on board.

Another crash. Another colleague dead. Another traumatic event in a chapter of my life that had been defined by fear and trauma and loss. I was very sorry that we had lost Ed, and I felt, as always, sympathy for the families of those killed, but I can't say I was surprised.

It was, after all, still Papua New Guinea.

●

Chapter 18

Fate is the Hunter

My candle burns at both ends;
It will not last the night;
But ah, my foes, and oh my friends –
It gives a lovely light
EDNA ST VINCENT MILLAY[256]

**Consider this: *A New Delhi labourer survived getting hit by one bus,
only to be struck and killed by a second bus 20 minutes later. Raj
Kumar, 38, was on his way to work when a bus hit him from behind.
Locals put Kumar in a three-wheeled taxi to take him to a hospital,
but before they got there they said he felt fine and jumped out. Then
when he was crossing the road another bus hit him and he died on
the spot.* (Associated Press, January 2009).**

Having seen what I saw in New Guinea I firmly believe that when
your number's up, your number's up. The unfortunate Mr Kumar would
probably agree with me, if he could. Death reaches up from the bowels
of the earth, or materialises out of the ether, or comes from wherever
it is Death dwells, and takes you. You cannot turn away from your date
with Death; you cannot run nor hide; your end is upon you. This was very
much the case with two of my PNG friends and colleagues: the avuncular
veteran and Mendi superstar Jim Millar, with whom I had shared MBA's
Southern Highlands-based flying, and Mack Lee, Chief Pilot and co-

owner of Air Manubada, the gregarious Chinese–Australian pilot who gave me my first real break in aviation.

One year after I left PNG I heard through the grapevine that Jim Millar had become the latest PNG pilot to have his name added to the Port Moresby aero club's Roll of Honour.

On the afternoon of 9 July 1996 Jim was returning to Mendi in MBA Twin Otter P2-MBB from the last of his 12 charter flights for the day, a run to Bosavi and back. On board — a full load of 19 passengers. Both Jim and his aircraft were well travelled: Jim with over 22,000 hours of flying experience; the aircraft with just shy of 30,000 hours in service. Another pilot in the area reported typical late-afternoon Mendi weather — large blue-sky patches to the north and the west, but deteriorating weather in the Mendi circuit area with a low cloud base and dark and stormy conditions to the east and the south, the direction from which Jim approached Mendi. A prominent feature of Mendi's circuit area is the steeply rising terrain on either side of the airstrip. To the west, Mt Pulim and a razorback ridgeline looming over the town make circling on that side of the airfield impossible. To the east there is just enough room to manoeuvre for an approach and land, although one mile from the airfield terrain slopes up towards the flanks of nearby Mt Giluwe, rising from 5300 feet at the airstrip to over 10,000 feet within eight miles. A potential danger in the Mendi circuit area is Clancy's Knob, an isolated pimple of rock rising 500 feet above the sloping floor of the Mendi Valley, situated three miles from the threshold of runway 17. On this day Clancy's Knob was enveloped in cloud.

At 4.17pm a village pastor who lived at the base of Clancy's Knob heard an aircraft fly overhead. The noise stopped suddenly, punctuated by a loud explosion, and he realised the aircraft had crashed. Jim Millar, descending in cloud, had flown directly into the only significant obstacle in Medi's circuit area — the vertical face of Clancy's Knob, 100 feet from the top. The aircraft disintegrated in the violent impact and there were no survivors.

Jim had been Mendi-based with MBA for the past three and a half years, since just before I joined him on the Mendi basing in 1994. Post-accident, there were rumours that Jim, who was well into his 50s, may have had a heart attack, or been in some way incapacitated prior to the fatal crash. The rumours were understandable — fellow pilots, aware of Jim's wealth of PNG flying experience (he was one of MBA's most seasoned PNG veterans), were struggling to find reasons for the terrible accident. What else could possibly explain Jim flying a perfectly good aeroplane straight into Clancy's Knob, a well-known danger in Mendi's circuit area? An autopsy discounted the rumours — Jim was medically fit at the time of his death. The CAD accident investigation revealed the true reason: for years Jim had been pushing his luck, and his luck ran out.

It was common knowledge that Jim used a self-made GPS cloud break procedure to get into Mendi in shonky weather conditions. He had inserted waypoints off the end of each runway into his on-board GPS unit and used a timed leg from overhead the airstrip to position himself downwind and turn towards one of these points, thus aligning himself with the runway centreline in poor weather/limited visibility conditions (I had flown with him once into Mendi and had seen him use this technique). The problem on the day of the accident was that he was flying a 300 series Twin Otter, rather than the 200 series Otter he normally flew out of Mendi. He had last flown a 300 series Otter four years prior, and had never flown a 300 series Otter while based in Mendi with MBA. The 300's cruise speed is 30 knots (55 km/hr) faster than the 200. So when Jim descended into cloud over the airstrip that day and timed his turn onto a downwind point in Mendi's circuit, he failed to take into account the extra groundspeed of the more powerful 300 series aircraft. His extra speed meant he flew approximately one mile further from the airfield than he thought he had. Unfortunately for him, this put the aircraft on a collision course with the top of Clancy's Knob, lying unseen in the cloud directly ahead of him.

A common contributor to fatal aircraft accidents in PNG is when the poor performance of an underpowered aircraft means a pilot is unable to get himself out of a sticky situation, e.g. flying up a blind valley in poor weather and attempting a reversal turn only to stall and crash during the manoeuvre. For Jim, the *opposite* was the case — too much performance killed him. If he had been flying a 200 series Twin Otter, flying 30 knots slower, he probably would not have crashed that day. After the accident it was revealed that he'd handed in his notice to MBA and intended to quit PNG flying just three weeks later. But for flying a 300 series Twin Otter that day, he'd now be living in the Victorian countryside in Australia, enjoying a well-deserved retirement. Instead, I'm writing about his death in these pages.

As the years passed after my departure from PNG, I heard less and less about accidents in my old hunting grounds. This was good — no longer was I hearing about friends and acquaintances dying in aircraft crashes. This was partly because I no longer had any close contacts in the industry there, and partly because the nature of the operations had changed. As the 21st century dawned there were fewer and fewer small operators in PNG skies, with the largest of the third-level airlines (Airlines PNG, Airlink, Nationair and others) having taken over most of the flying, squeezing out the small piston-engine charter operators in the process. In many cases the larger airlines began servicing the remote airstrips with Twin Otters, which allowed less frequent services for the same weekly payloads than in the hectic days of multiple flights in BN-2 Islanders and Cessna singles. The epic Goilala and Koiari *bomb bursts* of the 1990s were no more. Safety levels had increased too, partly because there were fewer sectors per year (so less exposure to the dangers of PNG flying); because the turbine-powered aircraft had better performance therefore better safety margins; because many of the twin turboprops now utilised were no longer operated single pilot but with two crew. Two-crew ops (more akin to the way jet airliners are operated, with a captain and first officer) are statistically safer. This is tied to issues of monitoring (with the non-flying pilot crosschecking the actions of the flying pilot) and to a reduction in instances of pilot risk-taking and unsafe behaviour when an aircraft is manned by two crew.

By the year 2000, a full five years since my departure from New Guinea skies, I lived in hope that never again would I receive a phone call or email informing me that one of my former colleagues had bought it. I was almost convinced that Jim Millar's crash would be the last I'd hear of. Events were soon to shatter my premature optimism.

In June 2000 Mack Lee took off from Port Moresby in his Cessna 402 *Koiari Kekeni* (P2-SAV) on the first leg of a charter for the Papua New

Guinea Banking Corporation (PNGBC). Mack, 38 years old, had a total of 8713 hours in his logbook, the vast majority of which was PNG time, and had approximately 3000 hours on Cessna 402s. He was scheduled to fly Port Moresby — Bulolo — Kerema — Daru — Port Moresby, picking up cash from the regional bank staff at each airstrip. Mack had been doing these PNGBC Bank runs once a month for the past four years, so it was a routine flight for him. As large amounts of cash were involved, PNGBC provided two armed security guards to accompany Mack on the flight, and there was a third passenger also. Young Australian pilot David Tunney was tagging along for the ride. Tunney was in PNG on a job search — he had no experience flying in-country — and Mack had offered him a free ride to experience some PNG flying first hand. This was typical Mack — always happy to help out a rookie pilot, especially those looking for work in PNG.

The first sector Moresby–Bulolo was flown without incident. In Bulolo Mack changed his flight plan, deciding to proceeded first to Nadzab rather than flying direct to Kerema. This was because he had learned there was no fuel available in Kerema or Daru that day (stops two and three of his planned flight), so had sensibly decided to re-route via Nadzab to pick up a full fuel load before continuing with the charter. As Mack had taught me, there was no such thing as having too much fuel when flying in PNG.

He took off from Nadzab at 1439 and set course for Kerema via the Tsile Tsile non-directional-beacon (NDB), climbing to 12,000 feet. Mack knew the track between Tsile Tsile and Kerema well — it crossed PNG's central divide, with peaks within 20 miles left and right rising to 11,000 feet. Once past the airstrips at Menyamya and Aseki mid-route, his track crossed multiple river gorges and ranges, with terrain varying between 3000 and 6000 feet. Only within 10 miles of Kerema did the landscape become less threatening, with a coastal lowland band of swampy scrubland stretching from Kerema's seaside township into the foothills.

His estimated time of arrival (ETA) for Kerema, passed to Air Traffic Control as he departed Nadzab, was 1517. The area forecast read as follows: Isolated cumulonimbus clouds 1800 to 40,000 feet; Scattered cumulus clouds 1800–15,000 feet with isolated clouds up to 20,000 feet; Scattered stratocumulus cloud 3000 to 8000 feet forming an overcast layer with rain; scattered altocumulus 12,000–18,000 feet. This indicated typical scuddy conditions for the Gulf at this time of the year. The kind of conditions where you would have two options to successfully sight Kerema's airfield and land: 1) carry out an IFR descent and instrument approach to break visual beneath the cloud base, or 2) do a cloud break through a hole in the cloud off the coast and then scud run back to the airfield, keeping the coast in sight and staying visual beneath the cloud base. Mack of all people knew this — he trained me, and I had seen him put both options into practice in the past in the very aircraft he was flying that day, in similarly scuddy weather.

The last call from Mack was at 1508, when he reported leaving 12,000 feet on descent for Kerema. He was expected to arrive in Kerema nine minutes later.

There were two instrument aids in Kerema, a non-directional beacon (NDB, an aid like a homing needle that enables a pilot to track towards the station) and distance-measuring equipment (DME, an aid that provides suitably equipped aircraft with a digital readout of real-time distance from the aircraft to the station). The Kerema NDB was unserviceable that day, and had been so since the beginning of the month. A NOTAM that it was out of action had been released so Mack knew it would not be available. The Kerema DME had in recent weeks been unreliable, but was not NOTAM'd as being unserviceable. On the day of the accident however it was determined that it was not working. With both of Kerema's ground-based navigation aids unserviceable Mack found himself on top of a solid cloud layer, attempting to find an airfield on the coast, effectively flying blind. Although not an ideal situation, this would hardly have been a first for Mack, as flying in PNG involves just this kind of challenge on a regular if not daily basis, and he would have flown such a sector literally hundreds of times in the past. In this situation you simply had to fall back on the basics — using the mark-one eyeball where possible to determine your position, coupled with an awareness of where you 'should' be based on dead reckoning (time-groundspeed-heading calculations) since your last known fix. If there was ever any doubt about your position, you had to observe three simple rules in PNG in order to stay alive:

Rule 1: Do **NOT** fly in cloud in PNG, as cloud has a nasty habit of containing mountainsides.

Rule 2: If you have to fly in cloud — make sure you know **EXACTLY** where you are.

Rule 3: When you feel tempted to fly in cloud in order to complete a mission: see Rule 1.

Another pilot, in BN-2 Islander P2-ALM, passed south of and abeam Kerema one hour earlier than Mack's planned arrival time and reported that Kerema had a cloud base of 2500 feet, with continuous heavy drizzle inland of the coast. The hills north of Kerema were covered with build-ups but the pilot of the Islander couldn't estimate the height of the tops because of a low layer of stratocumulus and cumulonimbus clouds. It was a shitty day in the foothills and mountains, but below the 2500-foot cloud base Kerema was clear. This pilot reported the Kerema DME was not working at the time of his transit, confirming the fact that Mack had no ground-based navigation aids to help him find Kerema that day.

Some time after Mack commenced descent into Kerema, several people in the village of Ivandu, 22 miles north of Kerema, heard the Cessna 402 pass overhead. A villager tending his garden at an elevation of 5100 feet stated that Mack arrived from the NNE. Witnesses heard the aircraft, but most never saw it due to the extensive cloud cover in the area. The direction they heard Mack arrive from was consistent with his arrival track from Tsile Tsile. They heard the aircraft pass overhead, then heard it again over Kamina, a village and airstrip two miles north of Ivandu. The aircraft was in the area for approximately five minutes. The gardener heard the 402 again, coming from the same direction as the first time, but lower. The 402's flight path was consistent with Mack flying a direct entry into the published DME holding pattern overhead what he thought was Kerema. As he had no ground-based navigation aids to confirm the position of Kerema, it's not known if he was using a back-up hand-held GPS unit (the Garmin 100 GPS unit normally fitted in Mack's C402 became faulty some time prior to this flight and had been sent to Australia for repair) to establish his position or whether he relied on a raw heading-time-speed calculation to reassure himself that he must be over Kerema and clear of the terrain.

He was not overhead Kerema. He was not clear of the terrain. Mack's Cessna 402, the *Koiari Kekeni*, my old steed, was descending in cloud into the mountains well behind Kerema. The aircraft impacted the side of a 60 degree slope at 5300 feet in close proximity to Ivandu village. A witness caught a glimpse of the aircraft on descent just before it hit. Wreckage was strewn over a 50 square metre patch of the mountainside; the majority thrown up-slope in the direction of travel and slightly to the left of the initial impact point. It was not survivable. Photos from the scene show little that resembles an aircraft — a wheel here; a section of the fuselage there; broken branches and tree trunks in the impact zone. The ground is littered with what looks like confetti. It is not — it is small pieces of shredded Cessna 402 fuselage. The accident investigator, Sid O'Toole, stated that the wreckage pattern suggested that Mack may have attempted to avoid the terrain at the last second when he realised an impact was imminent. I pray that this wasn't the case. I can only hope that Mack Lee, the legend, the man who gave me my start in PNG aviation, did not see his windscreen fill up with a view of that mountainside and did not know that his end was upon him. I would like to think that the four occupants of the Cessna 402 knew nothing of their fate until impact, whereupon they were killed instantly by the severe deceleration force.[257]

Like the death of Jim Millar four years before, Mack's accident was different from a lot of the crashes I researched in that it really was a classic manifestation of what is known by safety researchers as a 'Swiss cheese model' of accident causation. In this model, complicated safety-critical human systems (like aviation, engineering, nuclear power generation, and healthcare organisations) are likened to multiple slices of Swiss cheese, stacked together. Each slice of cheese represents an organisation or system's defences against failure, with the holes in the cheese representing individual weaknesses in the lines of defence. The organisation or system presents the possibility of an accident when all the holes align, giving 'a trajectory of accident opportunity.'[258] So it was with Mack's crash, with a series of external and internal factors aligning to almost guarantee an accident. One could argue that Mack, like Jim Millar before him, was destined to die that day. To die in that place, at that time, and under those circumstances. Fate, cruel fate some would call it. Mack's Chinese ancestors would have called it bad joss. I called it a complete absence of luck.

The series of events and conditions conspiring to end Mack's life (and the lives of the two security guards and the young pilot who was tagging along to take in the scenery) were linked to Mack's personal life in the days and hours before the crash.

The engineer who worked for Mack saw him on the morning of the accident. He knew Mack extremely well and reported that Mack looked gloomy, and that it seemed something was troubling him. He was not his normal self. His financial state may have been the reason. Although Air Manubada was a successful air charter company, just as it had been when I was flying Mack's fleet of *Kekenis*, Mack had other business interests, one in particular that had not gone well. He had opened a Jollibee fast food restaurant in Port Moresby (Jollibee is the Philippines' version of McDonald's), and although it had started off well, the business had been performing poorly in recent months. A rival fast food chain had spread malicious rumours that Mack's Jollibee was sourcing its meat supply from Port Moresby's stray dog population, doing his sales figures no favours. Additionally, four weeks before the accident, Mack had started legal proceedings against a local company who had agreed to purchase the business but had reneged on the deal. Mack was under a lot of financial pressure. On the Air Manubada front, he was due to fly his Cessna 402 to Cairns the next day for some overdue maintenance: this would have added to his financial woes when added to the debts from the under-performing restaurant. Mack was also in hot water with the PNG Civil Aviation Department — he was under scrutiny as it had been brought to CAD's attention that Mack had arranged in-house maintenance on the Air Manubada fleet without holding appropriate facilities or CAD approvals. On top of this, his Cessna 206 was 30 hours over the engine overhaul period without any dispensation. Stress plus stress plus stress: something had to give and unfortunately, and with fatal consequences, on this day it was his attention to just where his aircraft was in relation to the terrain when he commenced descent into Kerema. The Accident Investigator stated: *It is probable that these pressures and his financial*

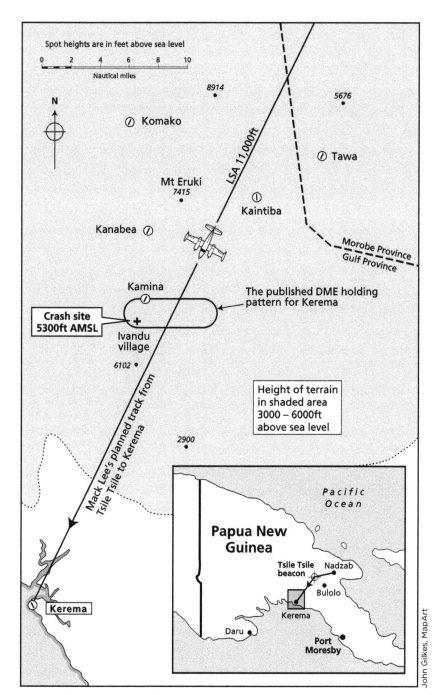

Spot heights are in feet above sea level

0 2 4 6 8 10
Nautical miles

N

8914

⑦ Komako

5676

⑦ Tawa

LSA 11,000ft

Mt Eruki
7415

① Kaintiba

Kanabea ⑦

Morobe Province
Gulf Province

Kamina
①

The published DME holding
pattern for Kerema

**Crash site
5300ft AMSL**

+

Ivandu
village

6102

Height of terrain
in shaded area
3000 – 6000ft
above sea level

Mack Lee's planned track from
Tsile Tsile to Kerema

2900

*Pacific
Ocean*

**Papua New
Guinea**

Tsile Tsile
beacon

Nadzab

Bulolo

Kerema

① **Kerema**

Daru

**Port
Moresby**

John Gilkes, MapArt

A map of Mack Lee's last flight.

difficulties combined to affect the pilot's decision-making capability causing him to make fundamental errors. It didn't help that he was robbed of both of Kerema's navigation aids that, on any other day, would have been available to help him confirm his position.

The unexpected unserviceability of the Kerema DME was a significant contributor to Mack's death, and the reason behind it received major attention in the accident report. The DME set-up in Kerema, like all others in PNG, ran continuously on battery power, kept fully charged by a regulator/charger in series with the mains power supply. The batteries lasted only five hours if not recharged. The investigation found fault with the power supply — the Kerema power station had been experiencing fuel supply problems during the month of the accident. This led to rolling blackouts and power surges, which meant the DME batteries were progressively discharged. Post-accident it was recommended that PNG's navigation aids be connected to town emergency power supply lines to ensure a constant supply of power. This was a good idea, and a sensible recommendation, but it came too late to save Mack Lee.

We can only speculate about the final link in the accident chain of events, the final hole in the final slice of the Swiss cheese. Whatever it was, it led to Mack believing he was overhead Kerema and commencing a descent into cloud clear of terrain, when in fact he was still over the mountainous country of Ivandu and Kamina villages.

It's possible that Mack used an incorrect groundspeed figure to calculate the expected elapsed time to fly from Nadzab to Kerema. At the flight planning stage, Mack had indicated that his groundspeed for the Moresby — Bulolo leg would be 162 knots, and the Bulolo — Kerema leg would be 140 knots. This made sense, as the forecast winds at his level were indicating a tailwind when heading north, and a headwind when heading south. After his change of route and departure from Nadzab he based his arrival time in Kerema (the estimate he passed to air traffic control) on the higher groundspeed (162 knots), rather than the 140 knots he had originally calculated. Had he forgotten about the headwind that would have been affecting him between Tsile Tsile and Kerema? Overestimating his groundspeed by 20 knots over this distance would have seen an error in his calculations of approximately six minutes, which at the Cessna's descent speed equates to 17 miles. Mack crashed 20.5 miles inland from Kerema. Is this the reason he descended into cloud while still over the mountains — because he wasn't as close to the Kerema coast as his calculations suggested he was? Did he initiate his descent for Kerema six minutes too early?

Another possibility is that Mack was navigating exclusively with his hand-held GPS unit. If so, there was the possibility of a fatal error here too. There was dangerous ambiguity in the three letter codes used as airstrip designators by the PNGDCA, IATA (the International Air Transport Association), and Jeppesen (a global navigation database supplier). The IATA code for Kerema was KMA. Confusingly, the Jeppesen code for Kerema was different (KRM), while in the Jeppesen GPS database and PNGDCA publications KMA represented another airstrip entirely — Komako, a mountain airstrip some 14 miles from Mack's crash site. Had Mack accidentally entered KMA as his 'go-to' point in the GPS and wrongly believed he was descending into Kerema? Or had he somehow entered the code for Kamina (Jeppesen code KMN, the airstrip closest to the crash site) instead? Either of these two GPS data entry errors could help explain why he descended into the tiger country behind Kerema — he may have been convinced he was safely over the coastal lowlands of the Gulf Province and clear of the high ground. No GPS unit was recovered from the accident site, so this theory could neither be proved nor discounted.

Like the accident of Peter Gill in Chapter 6, we will never know exactly what happened, and how such an experienced PNG pilot came to fly a perfectly good aeroplane into the side of a mountain.

On the day of Mack's death I was at my home in Hong Kong. Mark Hampton, an Australia-based pilot who had done some work for Mack in the past, phoned me with the sad news. It was a shock. Within the week I flew to Brisbane, Australia, to pay my respects at Mack's funeral. I tried to find kind words to say to Joanne, Mack's wife, who had their two-year-old daughter, Jolene, at her side and was pregnant with their second child. I saw the pain in the eyes of Mack's parents, and the look of shock and disbelief on the face of Godfrey Seeto, Mack's business partner and best friend. I helped carry Mack's coffin from the chapel to the hearse, then joined the funeral convoy to the cemetery, dropping a handful of earth onto his coffin as he was lowered into the ground under clear Queensland skies. I said goodbye and Godspeed to my old friend and mentor.

It was awful.

●

Chapter 19

Rubber Dog Shit

"I gotta do something here, I still can't believe it. I gotta give you your dream shot. I'm gonna send you up against the best. You two characters are going to Top Gun. For five weeks you're gonna fly against the best fighter pilots in the world. You were number two, Cougar was number one. Cougar lost it, turned in his wings. You guys are number one. But you remember one thing: You screw up just this much — you'll be flying a cargo plane full of rubber dog shit out of Hong Kong!"

LT. DAVIS TO MAVERICK AND GOOSE, TONY SCOTT'S FILM *TOP GUN*[259]

During my time in the RNZAF (it's cringe worthy admitting it) I'm sure I watched Top Gun at least 20 or 30 times. The movie, starring a cocky Tom Cruise as a cocky US Navy F-14 Tomcat pilot (back in the day, when Cruise was cool, before Scientology made him weird), was played in the 2 Mess TV room every Sunday night.

It was cheesy, but was an enshrined 2 Mess ritual, and served as cheap and accessible motivational material for us budding military aviators. We weren't the only ones on whom it made an impression — after the release of the film it was reported the numbers of young men enlisting with the US Navy hoping to become pilots surged by 500%.[260] When fictional naval officer Lt Davis uttered the above words 15 minutes into the film, a collective shudder passed through the pilot trainees in the 2 Mess TV room. How dreadful, we thought, to be relegated to the lowly ranks of cargo pilots — trash haulers with zero adrenaline in their lives. Transport guys were BLUNT (Bloody Useless, Non Tactical). We were destined to become fighter pilots, to be SHARP (Shit Hot And Real Potent), to fly low and fast with our hair on fire!

It's funny how perceptions change over time.

Fast forward a few years to when I was a turboprop captain in PNG, always looking ahead to the day when I could snag an interview with a major airline. The reaction to the same lines was markedly different: "Hmmm, a slot as a cargo pilot in Hong Kong. That would mean flying Boeing 747s for Cathay Pacific Airways' freight division. How much are they paying? Sounds great! How do I apply?"

Cathay Pacific Airways was founded in 1946 by two WWII-era C-47 pilots, American Roy Farrell and Australian Syd de Kantzow. The two met while flying cargo missions for the China National Aviation Company (CNAC) over the treacherous mountains of the eastern Himalayas (known as 'the Hump') between Calcutta and Kunming, in the last four years of the War. CNAC was a Sino–American airline, owned by Pan American Airways and the Chinese Government. When Japanese troops closed the Burma Road (the primary Allied supply route into China) in 1942, the pilots and planes of CNAC were tasked with the airborne resupply of China's Generalissimo Chiang Kai-shek, whose Nationalist Army shared the same goal as the Allies — the defeat of Japan in South East Asia.

After the War, Farrell, sensing a business opportunity, purchased a C-47 (the military version of the venerable Douglas DC-3) in Augusta, Georgia, and ferried it to Shanghai. His inaugural commercial flight was a freight run from Sydney to Shanghai, the war-surplus aircraft bursting at the bulkheads with three and a half tonnes of woollen clothing for the Chinese market. On arrival in Shanghai the entire cargo load was sold within six hours, with one author likening the sales frenzy to "throwing fish to hungry seals."[261] The profit from the flight, US$70,000,[262] was more than twice as much as he had paid for his aircraft! Clearly Farrell was on to a good thing. He was soon joined by his old flying colleague de Kantzow, and the airline (which had been trading as the Roy Farrell Export-Import Co.) was renamed Cathay Pacific Airways. In an interview published in 1988 Roy Farrell told the story behind the name: "The name was to have 'Cathay' in it . . . Cathay has a kind of magic, doesn't it?. . . Pacific is another kind of romantic name, and anyway we thought we might be flying the ocean one day."[263]

The embryonic airline soon moved its HQ to Hong Kong, with a ticketing office in the lobby of the Peninsular Hotel in Tsim Sha Tsui. By the end of their second year of operations Cathay Pacific Airways was on its way to success, operating a fleet of seven DC-3s and two Catalina flying boats between Hong Kong and Shanghai, Manila, Sydney, Bangkok, Macau, Rangoon (Burma), and Singapore.[264] But there was turbulence ahead. That same year, in a direct attack on co-owner Roy Farrell's American citizenship, the Hong Kong Government stipulated that the airline must reduce their 'foreign' element to just 10% or lose their landing rights in the then staunchly British colony. Farrell and de Kantzow were forced to look for a local investor, a Hong Kong-British company, whose inclusion as a part owner would dilute Farrell's ownership to the 10% requirement. At this point an old New Guinea connection surfaced, a link between Syd de Kantzow and the explosion of air freight in PNG's goldfields in the 1930s (described in Chapter 11). This link facilitated a new partnership that would eventually see Cathay Pacific Airways become one of the world's most successful and admired airlines.

Before he became a pilot, Syd de Kantzow dabbled as a gold prospector in Papua New Guinea's Morobe Province goldfields at Roaring Creek, between Wau and Bulolo.[265] The remote airstrip near his claim was serviced by Guinea Airways, and one of their pilots was a fellow Australian by the name of Ian Grabowsky. Grabowsky and de Kantzow came to know each other in the course of Grabowsky's regular flights to the mining settlement airstrips in the 1930s (Grabowsky was the Guinea Airways pilot who had been presented with the decapitated head of Les Trist by the side of Lae airstrip in 1931). Fast forward to December 1947, when Butterfield & Swire (B&S), one of Hong Kong's principal colonial trading houses, was lining up as a potential investor in Cathay Pacific Airways. Ian Grabowsky, by now based in Australia with Australia National Airways (ANA), was called in as an advisor on a proposed partnership between B&S, Farrell and de Kantzow of Cathay Pacific Airways Ltd, and Grabowsky's employer ANA. He reported back to his bosses at ANA, and to the Hong Kong *taipan* of B&S, Jock Swire, that he personally knew de Kantzow from their PNG days and strongly recommended the deal go ahead. It did, and de Kantzow and Grabowsky continued their friendship as two of the Directors of the re-jigged company.

For B&S, who later became John Swire & Sons (HK) Ltd, and today trade as Swire Pacific, the decision to become financially involved in Cathay Pacific Airways has proved prudent. The airline has consistently been one of the most profitable in the world, and today covers an extensive global network serving 188 destinations in 46 countries and territories. Cathay Pacific's milestones over the years have included its first turboprop, the Lockheed L188 Electra, in 1959, its entrance to the jet age with the arrival of the Convair 880 in 1962, its first Boeing 707 in 1971, and its first Boeing 747 'Jumbo Jet' (a –200 model) in 1979. In

Ian Grabowsky (right) in a Guinea Airways Junkers G-31.

the early years of the new millennium the airline cemented its place as one of the preeminent airlines in the Asia–Pacific region with the delivery of its 100th wide-body jet (an Airbus A330-300, in 2006).[266] In 2011 the airline was ranked first in the world for the volume of scheduled freight carried, and sixth in the world for the volume of passengers flown.[267] At the time of writing (2014) the airline boasts 142 wide-body jets,[268] including Boeing 747-400s and 747-8Fs, Airbus A330s and A340s, and Boeing 777s. Future orders include another 89 jets, including 48 Airbus A350s, with deliveries of this brand-new type expected in 2016, and the airline's most recent order for 21 Boeing 777-9X airframes, to be delivered from 2021 onwards. The airline employs more than 2900 pilots and 9700 cabin crew, and has a global staff numbering over 22,000. Today the airline is owned by Swire Pacific Ltd (45%), Air China (30%), and a public shareholding through the Hong Kong stock exchange (25%). Management services are provided by Cathay Pacific and Swire Hong Kong.

Another connection between Cathay Pacific Airways (CX) and Papua New Guinea has to do with aeroplanes. CX had humble beginnings in Shanghai, operating cargo flights in a sole WWII vintage C-47, nicknamed *Betsy*. This war-surplus airframe was soon joined by another C-47/DC-3, *Nikki*. By the 1950s the airline had expanded, operating a fleet of DC-4s, pressurised DC-6s and two turboprop powered Lockheed L188 Electras. The faithful old DC-3s were surplus to requirements and in August 1955 *Betsy* was sold to Mandated Airlines (MAL) in Lae, PNG. For the next 18 years she flew as a workhorse on PNG strip ops, flying passengers and freight into some of the same airfields I would operate into in the 1990s. MAL was taken over by Australia's Ansett Transport Industries in 1961, and by the late 1960s *Betsy* found herself in the livery of Ansett Airlines of Papua New Guinea.[269] In 1973[270] her PNG sojourn ended when she was purchased by Bush Pilot Airways in Queensland, Australia. Eight years later she was put up for sale again, at which point nostalgic and prescient Cathay Pacific staff realised not only was she Cathay's first aircraft, but she was the only one of the airline's old DC-3s still in flying condition. Recognising her provenance, CX bought her, changed her exterior to Cathay's 1940s livery, and had her ferried from Cairns to Sydney. She was destined to begin her Australia–Hong Kong homecoming flight in ultimate style. On 18 September 1983 *Betsy* sat on the runway at Sydney's Kingsford-Smith airport next to a Cathay Pacific 747 — the airline's *today* and *yesterday* together in a piquant moment of juxtaposition. *Betsy* took off first, her graceful lines wobbling into azure NSW skies; the roaring and bulky mass of her Boeing 747 stable-mate powered into the heavens just moments after her. The 747 touched down at Hong Kong's Kai Tak airport eight hours later, but the journey home was to take *Betsy* a full five days, with stops en route at Coolangatta, Cairns, Port Moresby, Wewak, Biak, Davao, and Manila. The graceful old bird then sat in a HAECO hangar at Kai Tak airport for three years, almost invisible under dustsheets, until she was fully refurbished and gifted to the Hong Kong Science Museum[271] in 1989. She remains there to this day, suspended from the ceiling, a monument to Hong Kong's airline pioneers and a silent nod to the little-known links between Cathay Pacific Airways and the aviation scene in Papua New Guinea.

The final link between CX and PNG, tenuous and cheesy as it is, is me. I first applied to join the airline when I saw an advertisement in global aviation periodical *Flight International* when I was a part-time flying instructor and charter pilot at Air Gisborne in 1990. Cathay Pacific's recruitment process was a real test of my determination and patience — I updated my CV with them every six months or so between 1990 and early 1995, when I was finally invited to attend the first stage of the recruitment process. My initial interview was in Auckland, New Zealand, where I was alternately grilled by Cathay Pacific Captain Colin Pierce (tricky technical questions about swept-wing jets, GPS, and high-speed aerodynamics), then made to feel at ease by chatty recruitment manager Stephanie Heron-Weeber. The pair played a mean game of good cop/bad cop. After success at this first round I was flown to Hong Kong three months later for four days of interviews, tests, psychological profiling, a comprehensive medical, and a simulator check. As I had after my initial Auckland interview, I returned to PNG and to the flying roster at MBA, the second time on a two-week posting to MBA's Mendi Base. I really wasn't sure how well my interview had gone, and the days seemed to grow longer as the wait to hear back from Cathay Pacific stretched ever on. One day I returned from an afternoon Tari trip to be told there was a phone call for me in the MBA office at the edge of Mendi's airstrip. It was Cathay Pacific's recruiting department, and down a crackling line I heard the news that I got the job. I was the first Papua New Guinea bush pilot to be hired by Cathay Pacific as a Second Officer. Happy days.

I departed Papua New Guinea with my eyes fixed ahead, on a new beginning with an international airline, but I was aware even then that my three and a half years as a *boss-man balus* in PNG were special — incredible adventurous times that I would never see again. PNG gave me a lot. I was an ordinary young man experiencing truly extraordinary things. Ever-humble champion of Mount Everest, iconic New Zealander Sir Edmund Hillary, evidently felt the same way about his formative experiences as I did about mine: *I discovered that even the mediocre can have adventures and even the fearful can achieve.*[272] I was fortunate to have the opportunity to live and work in Papua New Guinea, fortunate to meet so many warm and wonderful people, fortunate to only ever be peripherally affected by the nation's ubiquitous law and order problem, and fortunate to be put in a position where I could test my mettle; really learn that my professional flying skills were up to scratch. Not many pilots get tested like that. More than anything else, I was fortunate to survive.

I moved to Hong Kong in September 1995. Hong Kong was a culture shock, but a welcome one. The imposing mountain ranges, rifts and ravines of PNG's rugged topography had been replaced by the steel and glass monoliths of Hong Kong's *Blade Runner* skyline. The city was like an Asian New York, a crossroads between East and West, a British-run *laissez faire* colonial thorn in the underbelly of China, the (then) sleeping communist giant a mere stone's throw from Hong Kong's New Territory borders. The city teemed with life, a hustle and bustle of humanity, with 6.4 million people crammed into an area less than 3% of the size of Papua New Guinea. Modest *dai pai dongs* (open-air food stalls) wedged between glitzy boutiques for designer fashion labels, 24-hour convenience stores, mum-and-pop hardware stores and velvet-curtained stripper bars. Hong Kong was high tea at the Peninsular Hotel, Nathan Road neon signs brighter than the sun, swanky mega-clubs, a bustling harbour where rickety sampans elbowed with the sleek mega-yachts of the rich and the richer; Hong Kong was Friday nights in Lan Kwai Fong, with a crowd of bankers, models, *Tai tais* and tycoons spilling into the street outside Oscars and California Bar and Midnight Express; Hong Kong was alcohol-fuelled naughtiness at any one of many dark and dodgy bars in Wanchai on the main island, including prime den of debauchery for the budding Lotharios of the expatriate community — Joe Bananas bar on Luard Road. Hong Kong was brash and ostentatious — JJ's nightclub at the Grand Hyatt, with a queue of Porsches and Ferraris and Lamborghinis at the entrance; a city awash with bling, with the world's highest per-capita ownership of Rolls-Royce automobiles.[273] If you wanted it to be, Hong Kong was a town of excess, of extravagance, of self-indulgence. If the expression to sum up life as a bush pilot in Papua New Guinea had been, "It couldn't happen to me," the one for my first couple of years in Asia would have been, "Forgive me Father, for I have *Hong Konged*."

I joined Cathay Pacific as a Second Officer (S/O) on their Boeing 747-400 fleet, meaning I would receive the same training as the airline's captains and co-pilots, but I would only be qualified to operate the mighty Jumbo Jet in the cruise portion of the flight (i.e. no take-offs and landings). This is a common entry position in many international airlines (in North America the role is termed 'cruise pilot', or 'cruiser'), and serves two purposes. Firstly, it can be seen as an apprenticeship in a wide-body airliner — a chance to observe the operation for a while, gaining experience on the aircraft via osmosis, watching the captains and co-pilots managing and manipulating the big jet on international flights. Secondly, it offers the airline a financial advantage — hiring a cheaper category of crew, thereby saving on crew wages at the bottom end of the seniority list.

My initial training took three and a half months, comprised of seventeen four-hour simulator sessions (including three check rides), five training flights (to Vancouver, London Heathrow, Paris Charles de Gaulle x 2, and Amsterdam), and one check flight to London and back. At the completion of the training I was released to operate as a Second Officer on Cathay Pacific's fleet of 19 Boeing 747-400 aircraft. Even though I was just a cruiser, I couldn't believe that my new workplace was the cockpit of the mighty -400. My roster had suddenly become a lot more glamorous than it had been in PNG too. Destinations I was to become familiar with included those I'd seen in my initial training, as well as Johannesburg, Sydney, Adelaide, Melbourne, Auckland and Los Angeles. My first line flight was a five-day trip from Hong Kong to Frankfurt with Captain Neil Hassel, two Cathay Pacific first officers, and 19 Asian air hostesses. Huzzah! In those days we always had 48 hours off at the long-haul outports, so there was plenty of time to socialise with the crew. On the second day of the trip the pilots and half the cabin crew met in the lobby of our hotel, the Hilton in the town of Mainz, and departed on a half-day cruise up the Rhine River to the picturesque German winemaking town of Rudesheim, part of the Rhine Gorge UNESCO World Heritage Site. We spent the afternoon sipping local Rieslings and Pinot Noir under a sun-dappled awning, feasting on Schweinshaxe (pork knuckle) and sauerkraut, taking in the views of Rudesheim's 15th-century cobblestone Drosselgasse Lane.

Pinch yourself. Dreams do come true.

Cathay Pacific Airways also had a fleet of dedicated 747–400F freighter aircraft (all cargo; no passenger seats fitted), and I soon had the opportunity to fly them too. A year after I was checked to line I was rostered for a mid-December freighter trip to Anchorage, Alaska. The aircraft was packed full to the gunnels with Chinese-made goods being re-exported out of Hong Kong for US retailers. On board, a large last-minute shipment from Chinese toy manufacturers for the North American Christmas market: a huge consignment of plastic knick-knacks and stocking fillers. One could argue I really was flying a cargo plane full of rubber dog shit out of Hong Kong!

Within two years I was promoted to co-pilot/first officer (FO) on the 747-400. This upgrade involved another full conversion course — 12 simulator sessions, three check rides, 28 training sectors flying the -400 around Cathay Pacific's short and long-haul ports (including my first look at Taipei, Tokyo, Singapore, Bangkok and Fukuoka), and a three-sector check flight.

In any flying career there are a few exceptional moments that stand out. My FO conversion course gave me perhaps the best day of my flying career — Base Training. This was sandwiched between the simulator sessions and the line-flying training sectors. Base Training is when a trainee flies circuits in the actual machine, rather than just in the simulator. Circuits in a 747-400! I turned up with fellow trainee FO Rod Provan at the airline's flight planning and briefing rooms at Hong Kong's Kai Tak airport and met with Base Training Captain Brian King, who was to run the sortie. He discussed with us what the session would involve and we took a crew bus out to a remote parking bay on the airport's south apron and climbed the stairs up to our waiting aircraft, tail registration B-HOW. The last time I had flown a training mission like this, with an empty aeroplane, was during my Dornier command training with Henry Goines in Port Moresby. Now here I was about to launch in an empty 387-seat 270 tonne Boeing 747-400, the queen of the skies, an aircraft I'd always dreamed of flying. It was almost inconceivable — the training department of one of the world's most admired airlines was saying to us, "Here's a 200 million US dollar jet — take it out for a few laps and get comfortable with it." Incredible! We flipped a coin and Rod won the toss and elected to fly first. He and Brian took the aircraft from Hong Kong to Shenzhen (an international airport on the shores of the Pearl River delta, a short 27 nautical mile hop from Hong Kong), and Rod flew 12 circuits while I sat in one of the cockpit jump seats. Once Rod's training was done it was my turn. I had experienced an identical flight profile in the flight simulator a few days earlier, so I was well prepared and rearing to go. I strapped into the right-hand seat and listened to Brian's instructions as we configured the aircraft for my first take-off. Checklists complete and clearance from the tower received, Brian stood the thrust levers up to 60% thrust, allowed the engines to stabilise, then hit the TO/GA button to engage the auto throttle. The immediate acceleration rate as the throttles moved through to max thrust was incredible, like a kick in the pants, with the massive aircraft launching down the runway like a wild beast and the engines spooling up in a roaring crescendo like the Starship *Enterprise* punching through to warp speed. Each of the four mighty Rolls Royce RB211-524G engines were producing 58,000 pounds of thrust. To put this into perspective, the queen of the skies was putting out roughly the same amount of thrust as two hundred and fifty Cessna 206 Stationairs, the 6-seater from my PNG bush pilot days. Manhandling an empty 747-400, with all that thrust and inertia, around a 1500 foot AGL circuit pattern was like riding a wild rodeo bull, and my first circuit was a bit messy. I settled in pretty quickly though, and soon found that the aircraft was easier to fly than the simulator, probably because there was so much more immediate sensory feedback and a much wider field of view out the cockpit windows than the 180 degree screens in the Boeing sim.

The aircraft reminded me of the Twin Otter — it was heavy on the ailerons and needed firm and positive control. The trickiest thing to master was the landing technique. This was hardly surprising, as the perspective from the flight deck was totally different to anything I'd experienced before. The 747 cockpit, perched on the top deck of the huge aircraft, placed the pilot a whopping 8.7 metres (28.5 feet) above the runway. After a few circuits I got the hang of it — holding the approach descent rate until the audible "60" foot call from the radio altimeter system, starting to ease back on the stick and commence a flare just before the "30" foot call, and bringing the thrust levers to idle at the "10" foot call. If you got all that right she'd gently rumble onto the runway no trouble at all. Brian was happy with my progress, but also wanted to make sure I could consistently land the jet on the same spot on the runway — the *aim point*. The standard landing zone, or aim point, is a pair of white painted rectangles 1300 feet in from the runway threshold. All ICAO and FAA certified runways have these markings. Just past them there is normally a large irregular black triangular patch on the tarmac, formed by rubber deposits from the multitude of aircraft wheels that have landed 'in the zone.' Brian called the dark patch the *beaver*, and told me to make this my aim point. On my first attempt I missed the beaver, flaring late and floating 2000 feet down the runway before the 16 main wheels rumbled onto the deck. On my next attempt I was looking good, descending through the last couple of hundred feet before touchdown, making subtle adjustments to the pitch attitude to hold the approach angle and small corrections on the throttles to hold the correct approach speed. Brian's voice came across loud and clear in my headset: "That's it,

Matt, aim for the beaver." After landing in the right spot, and having him take control, stand the power levers to take-off thrust, and set the flaps and elevator trim wheel for a touch-and-go, it was impossible to stifle a smile as the headset crackled with a complimentary purr: "Nice beaver!" I took over and eased back on the control column, launching the Boeing into the air again, and off we went for another lap.

I spent an hour flying circuits onto Shenzhen's runway 15 — some at low level, some with flight directors on, some in raw data, even some with one engine inoperative (Brian simulated an engine failure by pulling an inboard engine back to idle downwind, only reinstating it after landing and before the next take-off). Just when I thought it couldn't get any better he told me I could fly the jet back to Hong Kong and shoot the IGS approach for runway 13 to conclude the Base Training session. This was like telling a rookie pro surfer they had been selected to compete at the Banzai Pipeline, or an amateur golfer they'd been chosen to tee off at St Andrews. The IGS approach at Hong Kong's old airport was the ultimate test for any airline aviator. It was pure pilot nirvana.

At the time, Hong Kong's IGS (Instrument Guidance System) approach for runway 13 was probably the world's most famous international airport arrival procedure. The approach began with an intercept of the localiser and glideslope beam at 4500 feet over the northern tip of Lantau Island, near Discovery Bay. This gave precision guidance to aircraft all the way down to the minimum altitude of 675 feet over the crowded suburb of Kowloon City, at which point the tricky bit began. From here pilots had to make a tight visual right turn through 47 degrees (to avoid a collision with Lion Rock and the hills of the Ma On Shan Country Park), while continuing the descent, and line up on extremely short final (at about 150 feet above the deck) for a landing onto Hong Kong's relatively short runway 13, an 8000 foot-long sliver of tarmac jutting out into the harbour. This quirky low-level dogleg was known as the 'checkerboard turn', as there was a large red-and-white checked signboard plastered onto the side of a hill near the Lok Fu cemetery acting as a visual aid to identify the correct turning-in point. Passengers called the hair-raising last-minute manoeuvre the 'Kai Tak heart attack,' a turn so low that laundry on the washing lines of the cheek-by-jowl Kowloon tenement buildings was clearly visible from the starboard cabin windows as the aircraft swooped in over the packed cityscape; some passengers swore they could see the flickering TV screens inside individual apartments as their aircraft barrelled past in frightening proximity. Aviation enthusiasts drooled over this approach, with its thrilling spectacle of large aircraft in steep banked turns at low altitude over the city, and it was like crack cocaine to the camera-wielding addicts of the global plane-spotting fraternity.

IFALPA, the international association representing airline pilots, saw the airport in a different light. Kai Tak had been placed on its 'Black Star' list of dangerous airports, due to its tricky topography and challenging low-level turn, and for most airlines it was a captain-only approach. Not for Cathay Pacific. It was our home port and there were no restrictions on co-pilots operating the aircraft. I was fortunate to manhandle the 747 around the IGS approach many times before Kai Tak closed and we moved to Hong Kong's new Chek Lap Kok airport on Lantau Island in 1998. If the 747 reminded me of my favourite aeroplane, the Twin Otter, then the IGS reminded me of PNG bush flying: it was a white-knuckle adrenaline-fest every time, especially so in typhoon season and in strong crosswinds, when it became extremely challenging.

If the reader ever had the pleasure to arrive in Hong Kong during the Kai Tak era, they will be very familiar with the other memorable feature of the airport. In the 1988 TV series *Noble House*, based on the James Clavell book of the same name, a character arrives at Kai Tak. "What's that smell?" he asks. His host replies with an all-knowing smile, "Oh, that's Hong Kong's very own . . . that's the smell of money." It's a canny bit of screenwriting, summing up Hong Kong's colonial-era status as a living breathing wheeling dealing embodiment of Deng Xiaoping's famous catchphrase, "To get rich is glorious." Kai Tak Airport did have a signature scent, but its pungent reality was somewhat different to Clavell's fiction. Immediately after landing passengers were overwhelmed with the odour from the oily waters of the Kwun Tong typhoon shelter and nullah, a sewage-choked waterway on the north-eastern side of the runway. It was not pleasant. There's a famous anecdote about this Hong Kong-style assault on the senses, involving legendary Hollywood actor and comedian Bob Hope. The story goes that Hope, on his first visit to Hong Kong, was exiting the aircraft down the stairs at a remote bay when he noticed the smell. He turned to his travelling companion, his nose wrinkled up in disgust, and asked the inevitable question: "What is that smell?"

Hope's associate replied: "That's *shit* Bob, that's *shit*."

"I know," replied the celebrity, still recoiling from the stench. "But what have they done to it!?"

I spent nine years as a first officer on the 747–400 with Cathay Pacific Airways, then made captain on the Airbus A330 fleet in 2006. By then I had been a professional pilot for nearly 18 years. That may sound like a long stretch, but unlike other occupations, it really does take an awfully long time to get towards the top of the tree in aviation.

I was 36 years old when I got my wide-body command. That's not a bad run. I sent an "I made it" email to my RNZAF/PTS nemesis, the prickly Squadron Leader McWilliam, with a subtle jab that I was the first of the 189/589 officer cadets to qualify as a captain with an international airline. He was by then like the rest of us, a mere civilian, employed as a manager with Pacific Aerospace in Hamilton, New Zealand, no longer looming large over the fate of junior pilot trainees. I received a warm and pleasant reply, something along the lines of, "I am pleased to hear that you have been so successful in your career." Yeah right. As John F. Kennedy said, *"Forgive your enemies, but never forget their names."*[274]

My first flight as an airline captain was an overnight sector from Hong Kong to Dubai in the Middle East. On board my 230,000 kg Airbus A330: 29 tonnes of freight and luggage, 55 tonnes of fuel, a full load of 264 passengers, 13 crew members and my most precious cargo — my wife, Anna. She joined me on the trip, sitting in the cockpit jump seat en route to Dubai, and we spent two wonderful days together before I operated the flight home to Hong Kong.

So I had made it. The dream I'd had for my future when I was 13 years old had become reality. This was to be the chapter filled with stories of international airline travel stories: of landing an Airbus in a sandstorm at

Jeddah's King Abdulaziz Airport on the shores of the Red Sea; of sliding around in a 394-tonne Boeing 747-400 on ice and snow covered taxiways in Anchorage, Alaska; of fighting with Bombay air traffic control to obtain permission to make an approach to land in an Airbus A330 in near zero visibility conditions in a torrential Indian monsoon-season downpour; of landing a Cathay A340-300 in Hong Kong in the middle of a super typhoon, with a 65-knot headwind on base turn and a 40-knot blustery crosswind on short final approach. But writing this book has reinforced for me that most of this is routine, procedural and predictable. Modern airline ops can't hold a candle to the excitement and inherent danger of the PNG bush flying of my past. And rightly so!

This of course is the essence of modern jet airliner ops. Airlines are not attempting to mislead you when they say that air travel is very, very safe. Their claims are more than borne out by the statistics. Industry watchdog website AirlineRatings.com determined that 2013 was the safest year for flying since 1945, with only 269 deaths from 29 accidents.[275] Contrast this with the number of deaths per annum attributable to automobile accidents in the USA: over 30,000 fatalities per year.[276] This means at the current accident fatality rates for airline travel vs car travel it would take over 100 years of *global* airline fatalities to equal just one year's worth of US auto-related fatalities. Tragically these feel-good numbers were shat on from a great height in 2014, when the aviation industry crash and fatality stats were blighted by the twin calamities of Malaysia Airlines. A total of 537 souls were lost in the perplexing disappearance of MH370 in the remote expanse of the southern Indian Ocean and the explosive decompression of MH17 in the skies over the Russian–Ukraine border. While the cause of the former remains a mystery, the latter appears to have been caused by the twitchy finger of a rebel fighter less sophisticated than his lethal surface-to-air weapon.

While the job of an airline pilot remains fundamentally safe (the terrible anomaly of Malaysia Airlines' losses aside, along with that of Air Asia, whose Airbus A320 was lost in the Java Sea on December 28 2014 just as this book went to press), it still holds certain challenges. As the skipper of a big jet, my enemy is no longer the terrain, short one-way airstrips, the weather, or marginally performing aircraft, as it was when I was flying in PNG. Now, enemy number one is fatigue. Unfortunately the wide-bodied long-haul passenger jets in use today are not solar powered. If they were I wouldn't have to go to work at night! A characteristic of the airline pilot lifestyle is irregular shift work and disturbed sleep cycles, resulting in what the lab-coated ones term circadian dysrhythmia, or desynchronosis. The man in the street knows this unpleasant affliction as jet-lag. Many flights depart at or near midnight, and there is not always an opportunity to get rest beforehand. Airline crews operating intercontinental trans-time-zone flights must be one of the few professional groups worldwide engaged in a safety-critical role scheduled on wildly irregular day/night work schedules. While it is to be expected that human rest requirements must be balanced against the commercial demands of running an airline, some argue that the pendulum has at times swung too far in favour of the airline bean counters and away from the crews' physiological needs. It is not uncommon for an airline crew to land not having had what most of us would consider 'normal rest' in 20+ hours. In body-clock terms, their work schedule may have placed them in a state where it was impossible to achieve a normal sleep cycle in between duties. The effects of this cumulative fatigue shouldn't be underestimated (we all know the effects of extreme tiredness — drowsiness, irritability, a lack of focus, a degradation in mental acuity), but are often ignored, with the status quo simply accepted as 'the way it has to be'. Russell Foster, professor of circadian neuroscience at Oxford University, is one of many experts concerned by this: "Sleep is a fundamental part of our biology . . . yet we've pushed sleep back into a box, like it's an inconvenience."[277]

So how is enemy number one to be tackled? It is a commercial reality that airlines are required to operate 24 hours a day, to global destinations across a broad swathe of time zones. Crews are required to operate these flights, so clearly the problem is not going to go away. The only panacea available to the aviation industry is what one researcher has called 'enlightened crew scheduling,'[278] finding the delicate balance of work and rest cycles that minimises crew fatigue without inflicting too severe a financial penalty on airlines' bottom lines, and most importantly has no negative impact on safety. This continues to be a challenge for pilots, airlines and regulators worldwide.

The other major challenge faced by airline industry pilots is paradoxically one that was created when technological advances removed another threat. In the first 50 years of aviation, when men were men and airline flying was unregulated and the chaps got by on sheer guts and adrenaline, most flying was done manually. Basic autopilot installations were used in the cruise only, and even then were not always reliable. Many pilots hand-flew their steeds from take-off to landing (I was without the luxury of an autopilot for all my years of flying in New Zealand and PNG). This is OK for small unsophisticated aircraft — for short flight times and for those conducted at lower altitudes — but as newer aircraft were developed that flew much higher and had a much increased range, the concentration required to physically fly the machine while simultaneously controlling a lot of the aircraft's systems (such as fuel, hydraulic, electrical and pressurisation) just became too much. The fix has been the design and introduction of sophisticated automatic systems that now control almost everything on board today's long-haul wide-body jets. For large portions of the flights the human crew has been relegated to being systems managers and monitors. This comprehensive use of automation was supposed to free the pilots from manual tasks and allow a wider view of the operation, freeing up cognitive capacity and enabling crews to focus on the macro, the 'big picture', rather than doing everything themselves and becoming bogged down in the micro. But automation has proven to be a double-edged sword, and while enhancing safety in many phases of flight it has spawned a new elephant in the room, a clear and present threat to flight safety known as *automation complacency*. This occurs when a pilot 'over-relies on and excessively trusts the automation, and subsequently fails to exercise his or her vigilance and/or supervisory duties.'[279] This insidious abdication of responsibility can lead to unsafe conditions and, in the worst-case scenario, to tragic accidents.

Tied in with automation complacency is the issue of boredom. The business of getting 300 passengers from A to B along the world's multiple airways has become so routine, so regulated and controlled, and the operation of the aircraft so strictly governed by rules and procedures and 'mouth-music' (a company-prescribed standardised script of verbal challenges and responses used by flight crews during all manipulations of the aircraft controls and systems) that there is little room for variation. Very little happens that departs from the tight framework of rules and regs and company standard operating procedures. There is good reason behind this (enabling crews who have never before flown together to quickly mesh as a team; to keep things predictable and familiar), and I'm not suggesting it should be done differently, but this does make the cruise portion of most flights generally quite bland. Our primary role remains as system managers and monitors, manipulating the aircraft through the autopilot's controls in order to follow a line in space predetermined by air traffic control and our flight plan. The biggest decisions I am likely to make while in the cruise on a routine flight is whether to turn left or right to safely deviate around a large weather build-up on track, followed closely by whether I will have the beef steak or the grilled salmon for dinner (I thought that a BCF was a type of fire extinguisher until I joined an international airline to discover it stands for the crew menu on almost every flight: Beef, Chicken or Fish).

But before I talk down our role any further: we are there for one very important reason. Someone once said that airline flying involves hours of boredom punctuated by moments of sheer terror. On that one day in a million when one of the engines disintegrates in a fireball, throwing hot shards of metal into the lower wing surface and shearing fuel and hydraulic lines; on that one day in a million when we take off and fly through a flock of birds and they are ingested into the engines and our 250+ tonne aircraft turns into a glider; on these thankfully rare days when the accident gremlins strike and our modern airliner falls from the ever-present knife edge that routine and complacency had led us to foolishly believe we no longer negotiated, we are called on to follow a strict set of well-practised emergency procedures, to fall back on our years of experience, to improvise when we wind up in critical situations not covered by the manuals, and, come what may, to nurse the stricken aircraft and her precious human cargo back to terra firma in one piece. This is our *raison d'être*, and is why we have not yet been replaced in the cockpit by a computer. It's been suggested, rather tongue-in-cheek, that the advanced largely automated aircraft of today no longer need two pilots. The replacement (and airline accountants would love this one, as it would save money on crew wages) would be a single pilot and a dog. The pilot is there to watch the autopilot, and the dog is there to watch the pilot, and to bite him (or her) if he touches anything!

Even with the challenges posed by fatigue, and the issues of automation complacency and boredom, the positive still outweighs the negative. Working for an international airline makes the world a very small place indeed. In one month I might be in Amsterdam, Tokyo, Sydney or Saudi Arabia. Curry laksa in Singapore; *nama-biiru* and sushi in Osaka; *borscht* on the banks of the Moscow River, a stone's throw from the Kremlin. The job also affords me opportunities to catch up with the old PNG flyers. On Rome trips I catch up with Massimo Lombardo, now with Alitalia. On Australian overnights I see Colin Hicks and Giles Rooney; in Dubai I catch up with Sid Makary, Xavier McHugh, and MBA's golden boy Grant LeLievre. Work trips also enable family catch-ups in New Zealand, the US and the United Kingdom. And the view out of the office window isn't bad either: the Orion Nebula rising in a clear night sky over the Tien Shan mountains on the China–Kyrgyzstan border; crystal clear views of the magnificent Adriatic coastline on southern European flights, limestone buttresses rising like nature's skyscrapers from shimmering emerald waters; sunset over Mount Fuji, the day extinguishing in a final pinpoint of light on the horizon like the *hara-kiri* of a cathode ray tube; the Great Wall of China snaking into the dusty mountains on northerly departures out of Beijing, a craggy barrier between the ancient capital and the intimidating expanse of the Gobi Desert; dawn over the dead heart of central Australia, with golden rays creeping tentatively over the barren blue-brown landscape, unfamiliar and alien like it's the first sunrise ever. Of course, the chance to experience this lifestyle and its perks is what attracted me to the job in the first place, but just because my profession generally delivers what it says on the tin, I shouldn't appreciate these moments any less. Standard airline pilot whining aside (airline pilots can be a cantankerous bunch!), it's still very much an industry worth being a part of, and most days I really enjoy my work.

I once read an article by Englishman Brian Lecomber — professional aviator, aerobatic champion and author — where he described what it means to be a pilot. One passage resonated with me: *A very wise pelican once said to me: "If you don't have to think about the airplane, if you go where you wanna go and do what you wanna do, and the airplane just comes with you — why then, and only then, are you truly are a pilot."* This is how I feel, whether I'm sitting up the front of a wide-body jet, upside down in a Yak-52 during an aerobatics routine, or flying a four-seat Cessna 172 for fun with friends and family. What makes me a pilot is not my role as a commander of a passenger jet on international operations. Having struggled to obtain my flying qualifications after the shock of an early exit from the RNZAF, and having persevered in the face of what some would call the 'shit' conditions in Papua New Guinea, when I became an airline captain I realised that what made me as a pilot was not the destination — the shiny four gold bars on my shoulders, the captain's salary, the respect I garner from my crew, the responsibility for the safety of the souls on board my jet — but the journey. Perhaps less than 10% of my total flying knowledge has come from my airline flying. Sure, I've learned how to better lead and manage my crew. Flying the big jets, I've learned effective energy management; the effect of inertia on speed and configuration changes of large aircraft. But that's about it. Let's say another 20% of my total flying knowledge came from my time in the New Zealand military. All the rest, all the important stuff — my decision-making process, my hands-on skill as a pilot, my gut instinct on whether something is safe or not — these vital components of my flying DNA were forged in the fire of my PNG flying experience. Having this experience to fall back on is the difference between being a cadet pilot (an airline-sponsored trainee who goes from a basic commercial licence straight into the cockpit of a passenger jet with no hands-on commercial flying experience whatsoever, a common practice in the industry these days) and being a Sully Sullenberger, the Captain of the US Airways Airbus A320 who successfully executed a dead-stick landing into the Hudson River off Manhattan in 2009. This experience is what a pilot falls back on when the excrement makes physical contact with the electric powered air distribution device and there's nothing on the dials but the maker's name. Papua New Guinea gave me that; the flying there made me as a pilot. The 'shit' was the best part of my career.

As I hope I have illustrated, PNG flying is extraordinarily dangerous, especially operations in single-engine piston aircraft. I spent just under three and a half years there, flying over 3300 take-offs and landings in close to 2500 hours of flying, and I survived while others perished. How? Not because I was better, but because I was trained well, because I had an OK pair of hands, and most importantly because I was really, *really* bloody lucky.

Luck is a small word. A wee four letter word. But luck, or fate, or providence, or the guiding hand of some greater entity or being — call it what you will — was the difference between life and death for the pilots of PNG. More experienced and skilled pilots than me died there. The twisted remains of their aircraft, beginning with the 1931 crash of Les Trist's Guinea Airways Junkers W-34, lie there still, scattered throughout the country. Their stories involve broken bodies and tragic tales and often a seemingly pre-ordained chain of events led to their demise. Chains of events that simply could not be turned away from; chains of events with a fatal conclusion. Luck may be a small word, but it's the most important word in PNG flying, a word you need on your side if you want to survive as a *boss-man balus*, a PNG bush pilot.

So is life like that? Is it a combination of luck and fate that determines whether we make it or not? Do we forge our own path through life, or are we merely passengers, led to believe that we are following our own road, oblivious to the fact that its twists and turns are in fact pre-ordained? Were Jim Millar and Mack Lee and Ed Terry and Dean Hannah and all the others destined to die in a plane wreck in Papua New Guinea from the day they took their very first flying lesson? Why them and not those of us who survived — those of us who took bigger risks and pushed our luck more than they did, yet all we got was an ulcer-spawning fright and a bad case of the shakes after landing?

I never appreciated the PNG flying until it was many years behind me. Writing this book has brought my PNG experiences to life for me again, a conflicting kaleidoscope of memories and emotions: vivid and simultaneously frightening and tragic, thrilling and wonderful. I didn't realise at the time how incredibly fortunate I was to be experiencing life on the knife edge as a bush pilot in one of the world's most dangerous flying environments. My gaze had always been firmly fixed on the prize ahead, a job with an international airline, and I'd never stopped to appreciate the present. I was like an Everest climber making his way along Himalayan mountain paths to get to base camp: forever looking ahead at the distant glimpses of the southern face of Sagarmatha, oblivious of the beauty of the rhododendron forests along the way.

Viewed with the benefit of hindsight, is the journey always better than the destination? I guess everyone is different. In my case, it was the journey that made me.

Enjoy yours.

●

For the PNG bush pilots who didn't make it:

Remember me when I am gone away,
Gone far away into the silent land;
When you can no more hold me by the hand,
Nor I half turn to go yet turning to stay.
Remember me when no more day by day
You tell me of our future that you planned:
Only remember me; you understand
It will be late to counsel then or pray.
Yet, if you should forget me for a while
And afterwards remember, do not grieve:
For if the darkness and corruption leave
A vestige of the thoughts that once I had,
Better by far you should forget and smile
Than that you should remember and be sad.

CHRISTINA ROSSETTI[280]

Endnotes and References

1   © The Estate of Christopher Logue. Used with permission from Rosemary Hill via email 6/8/2014.

2   Quoted in Hanson N. The Unknown Soldier. Doubleday UK, 2005; 238.

3   'Blackadder' created by Richard Curtis, Rowan Atkinson, John Lloyd and Ben Elton, script written by Richard Curtis and Ben Elton. Used with permission.

4   Lewis C. Sagittarius Rising. Yorkshire: Pen & Sword Books, 2009; 31

5   In 189's Wise Owl booklet.

6   Niven D. The Moon's a Balloon. London: Book Club Associates, by arrangement with Hamish Hamilton, 1971; 67

7   www.spykercars.com/heritage

8   http://www.brainyquote.com/quotes/quotes/r/ralphwaldo101322.html

9   Whiting N. Wrecks and Reefs. PNG: Robert Brown and Associates,1994; 109.

10   James B. Field Guide to the Kokoda Track. Sydney: Kokoda Press, 2008; 85.

11   McKinnon, Carillet & Starnes. Papua New Guinea and Solomon Islands. Lonely Planet, 2008; 79.

12   The Economy of Papua New Guinea. Macroeconomic Policies: Implications for Growth and Development in the Informal Sector. 1999 Report (2000). AusAID, Canberra.

13   Turner A. Historical Dictionary of Papua New Guinea. 2nd edn. Maryland: The Scarecrow Press, 2001.

14   Sinclair J. Kiap: Australia's Patrol Officers in Papua New Guinea. Bathurst: Robert Brown and Associates, 1978; 280.

15   Honor Egger, Mack Lee's Eulogy

16   Sinclair J. Kiap: Australia's Patrol Officers in Papua New Guinea, op.cit., p. 35

17   ibid., p.153.

18   http://www.cfr.org/democratization/promoting-democracy-whys-hows-united-states-international-community/p24090; may have been "Yes, but he's our bastard" — http://en.wikiquote.org/wiki/Talk:Franklin_D._Roosevelt

19   PNGDCA File AS-95-1004

20   Sinclair J. Balus: The aeroplane in Papua New Guinea. Vol I: The early years. Robert Brown and Associates Pty Ltd. 1986; 116.

21   www.pngaa.net/bb/viewtopic.php?t=170, and article by Geoffrey Luck in quadrant.org.au/magazine/2011/01-02/how-qantas-became-the-safest-airline

22   DFS-ADF Flying Safety Special: Operations in Tropical Mountainous Areas. Fourth Edition, 2000 p.66

23   PNGDCA File AS-91-1007

24 Pidgin. Lonely Planet phrasebook. 2nd Ed.(1999). Lonely Planet Australia.

25 Nietzsche F. The Gay Science (Die fröhliche Wissenschaft), 1882; Sec. 283.

26 The Unique Catholic Church at Fane. Bikmaus. A Journal of PNG Affairs, Ideas, and Arts. Sep 1987. Vol VII no.3.

27 Perrin A. The Private War of the Spotters: A history of the New Guinea Air Warning Wireless Company Feb 1942–April 1945. Perrin, Cosstick and Lindsay, 1990; 11.

28 ibid.

29 ibid., p.55

30 ibid., p.92

31 ibid., p.93

32 Rothgeb W P. New Guinea Skies. Iowa State University Press, 1992; 205.

33 Levantis T. Papua New Guinea: Employment, wages and economic development. Canberra: Asia Pacific Press; 1.

34 Making Their Own Rules: Police beatings, rape and torture of children in PNG. Human Rights Watch, September 2005, Vol. 17 No. 8 (C).

35 The Economy of Papua New Guinea. Macroeconomic Policies: Implications for growth and development in the informal sector. 1999 Report (2000). AusAID, Canberra.

36 Sinclair J. Balus: The aeroplane in Papua New Guinea. Vol I. op. cit., p.50.

37 Foreword: Directorate of Flying Safety — Air Force, Flying Safety Special Operations in Tropical Mountainous Areas. Third Edition. Feb 1997

38 Statistics from Mike Feeney, email 21/1/14.

39 PNGDCA File AS-92-1008; p. 172.

40 PNGDCA File AS-92-1016; p. 173.

41 PNGDCA File AS-92-1022; pp. 174-6.

42 Brand M. Fighter Squadron at Guadalcanal. New York: Simon & Schuster,1996; 51.

43 The Economy of Papua New Guinea. Macroeconomic Policies: Implications for growth and development in the informal sector. op.cit., p.12.

44 PNGDCA File AS-93-1017; pp. 185-6.

45 PNGDCA File AS 92-1026; pp. 189-93.

46 thinkexist.com

47 Hawthorne S. The Kokoda Trail: A history. Central Queensland University Press, 2003.

48 Fitzsimons P, Kokoda. Sydney: Hodder Australia 2005.

49 Australians at War: War against Japan 1941–1942. Ferguson J, ed. Time Life Books Australia, 1989; James B. Field Guide to the Kokoda Track, Kokoda Press; p.48.

50 Australians at War, op. cit.

51 Willmott H P. The Second World War in the East. London: Cassell, 1999.

52 Hawthorne S. The Kokoda Trail: A history. op. cit., p 196.

53 Fitzsimons P, Kokoda. op. cit., p.100.

54 Hawthorne S. The Kokoda Trail: A history. op. cit.

55 Fitzsimons P, Kokoda. op. cit., p.150.

56 McAuley L. Blood and Iron: The battle for Kokoda. Hutchison Australia, 1991: p.20.

57 James B. Field Guide to the Kokoda Track. op. cit., p. 283.

58 ibid., p.31

59 McAuley L. Blood and Iron: The battle for Kokoda. op. cit., p. 1.

60 Brune P. A Bastard of a Place: The Australians in Papua. Sydney: Allen & Unwin, 2004; p.429.

61 ibid., p. 88.

62 ibid., p. 241.

63 James B. Field Guide to the

64 Kokoda Track. op. cit., p. 49.

64 Hawthorne S. The Kokoda Trail: A history. op. cit., p. 213.

65 James B. Field Guide to the Kokoda Track. op. cit., p. 49.

66 ibid., p. 171.

67 ibid., p. 53.

68 Milner S. United States Army in World War II: The War in the Pacific: Victory in Papua. Dept. of the Army. Washington, D.C. 1957; Papuan Campaign: The Buna-Sanananda Operation, 16 Nov 1942–23 Jan 1943, Centre of Military History (1990), United States Army, Washington DC.

69 James B. Field Guide to the Kokoda Track. op. cit., p. 53.

70 www.anzacday.org.au/anzacservices/poetry/fuzzywuzzy.htm

71 ww2australia.gov.au/asfaras/angels.html; James B. Field Guide to the Kokoda Track. op. cit., p. 505; South Pacific Magazine.

72 www.pngaa.net/Library/Phillips.htm; James B. Field Guide to the Kokoda Track. op. cit., p. 505.

73 Rory Callinan. 'Hopes fade for the lessons of Kokoda crash', The Australian, 31 July 2010.

74 PNGDCA Report AS-09-1005, 31 March 2011, Accident Investigation Commission of Papua New Guinea.

75 ibid., p. 39.

76 Hawthorne S. The Kokoda Trail: A history. op. cit., p. 93 .

77 PNGDCA File AS-84-1014.

78 Hawthorne S. The Kokoda Trail: A history. op. cit., p. 189.

79 James B. Field Guide to the Kokoda Track. op. cit., p. 27.

80 Brune P. A Bastard of a Place: The Australians in Papua. op. cit., p. 113.

81 James B. Field Guide to the Kokoda Track. op. cit., p. 275.

82 www.pacificwrecks.com; James B. Field Guide to the Kokoda Track. op. cit., p. 278.

83 www.pacificwrecks.com; Flightpath Magazine Vol 24, No.1, 2012; 22.

84 Soc Kienzle, email, 19 June 2013.

85 James B. Field Guide to the Kokoda Track. op. cit., p. 277.

86 Used with permission, Fiona Kimbell, email 20 May 2014.

87 PNGDCA File SI-768-1014.

88 ibid

89 PNGDCA File AS-83-1007.

90 ibid.

91 ibid.

92 PNGDCA File AS-91-1002.

93 PNGDCA File AS-93-1003.

94 ibid.

95 www.goodreads.com/quotes/2583-you-only-live-twice-once-when-you-re-born-and-once

96 Gillison D. Royal Australian Air Force, 1939–1942. Adelaide: The Griffin Press; p. 355.

97 ibid., p.354.

98 Australians at War: War against Japan 1941–1942. Ferguson J, ed. op. cit., p. 130.

99 Tanaka K. Operations of the Imperial Japanese Armed Forces in the PNG Theatre during WWII. Tokyo: Japan Papua New Guinea Goodwill Society,1980; 105.

100 ibid., p. 833; Tanaka p.110

101 Moremon J. New Britain 1941–1945: Australians in the Pacific War, Canberra: Dept. of Veteran Affairs; p. 7.

102 Palmer M. Dark Side of the Sun. Ottawa: Borealis Press, 2009.

103 McAuley L. Blood and Iron: The battle for Kokoda. op.cit., p. 19.

104 Boyington G. Baa Baa Black Sheep. New York: Wilson Press; 218.

105 Cook H. T., Cook T. F. Japan at War. New York; The New Press; 419.

106 Holmes T. Aircraft of the Aces: Legends of WWII. Oxford: Osprey Publishing Ltd. 2003; Ch. 11.

107 Bowman M. W. Vought F4U Corsair. Wiltshire: The Crowood Press, 2002; 76.

108 Cox B. Cats Have Only Nine Lives. Tauranga NZ, 2004; 33.

109 Bowman M. W. Vought F4U Corsair. op. cit., p. 43.

110 Wright M. Kiwi Air Power. Auckland: Reed Publishing, 1998; 104.

111 Cox B. Too Young to Die. London: Century Hutchinson Ltd. 1987.

112 ibid., p. 124.

113 Hewson B. Black Monday, History Now, Te Pae Tawhito O Te Wa. Vol. 3 No.2 October 1997. History Department, University of Canterbury. New Zealand; 10.

114 Cox B. Too Young to Die. op. cit., p. 55.

115 Walthers D. 3 January 1988. RNZAF Museum Archives.

116 Cox B. Too Young to Die. op. cit., p. 64.

117 letter supplied by Bryan Cox.

118 Hewson B. Black Monday, History Now. op.cit., p. 12.

119 Archway. archives.govt.nz.

120 Hewson B. Black Monday, History Now. op.cit., p. 12.

121 Rueters.

122 David Morgan. email 8 October 2013.

123 Reuters.

124 Young G. Beyond Lion Rock. London: Century Hutchinson, 1988; ix.

125 Mangold T, Penycate J. The Tunnels of Cu Chi. New York: Berkley Books, 1985; 209.

126 PNGDCA File AS-93-1014

127 Wilde O. Lady Windermere's Fan, A Play About a Good Woman, 1892.

128 Palmer S. A Who's Who of Australian and New Zealand Film Actors: The Sound Era. New Jersey & London: The Scarecrow Press Inc, 1988.

129 Niven D. The Moon's a Balloon. op. cit. p. 174.

130 Flynn E. My Wicked, Wicked Ways. London: Aurum Press, 1960; 6.

131 ibid., p. 66

132 Meyers J. Inherited Risk: Errol and Sean Flynn in Hollywood and Vietnam. Simon and Schuster, 2002; 80.

133 Flynn E. My Wicked, Wicked Ways. London: Aurum Press, 2005; op. cit., p. 84.

134 Meyers J. Inherited Risk: Errol and Sean Flynn in Hollywood and Vietnam. Simon and Schuster, 2002; 80.

135 Flynn E. My Wicked, Wicked Ways. op. cit., p. 55.

136 Godfrey L. The Life and Crimes of Errol Flynn. London; Robert Hale Ltd. 1977; 31.

137 Flynn E. My Wicked, Wicked Ways. op. cit., p. 103.

138 Nalu M. Paradise Magazine, Air Niugini.

139 Flynn E. My Wicked, Wicked Ways. op. cit., p 7.

140 Meyers J. Inherited Risk: Errol and Sean Flynn in Hollywood and Vietnam.

141 Boyington G. Baa Baa Black Sheep. op. cit., p. 132.

142 Sinclair J. Kiap: Australia's Patrol Officers in Papua New Guinea. op. cit., p. 179.

143 Sinclair J. Balus: The aeroplane in Papua New Guinea. Vol I: The early years. op. cit., p. 265.

144 Flynn E. My Wicked, Wicked Ways. op. cit., p. 82

145 ibid.

146 Sinclair J. Wings of Gold. Bathurst: Robert Brown and Associates, 1978; 36.

147 Cooke J. Working in Papua New Guinea 1931–1946. Lara Publications, 1983; 212.

148 ibid., p. 62.

149 Sinclair J. Wings of Gold. op. cit., p. 169.

150 ibid., p. 93.

151 ibid., p. 294.

152 Phil Bradley, pacificwrecks.com

153 Earhart A. The Fun of It. Chicago: Academy Press Ltd. 1978.

154 Cooke J. Working in Papua New Guinea 1931–1946. op. cit., p. 257.

155 Gillespie R. Finding Amelia. Annapolis: Naval Institute Press, 2006; 35.

156 Rafford P Jr. Amelia Earhart's Radio. The Paragon Agency Publishers, 2006; 41.

157 Gillespie R. Finding Amelia. op. cit., p. 71.

158 ibid. p. 69; Butler S. East to Dawn: The life of Amelia Earhart. Da Capo Press, 1997; 403.

159 Douglas Westfall, The Paragon Agency. email 25 January 2014.

160 Goldstein D M, Dillon K. V. Amelia: The centennial biography of an aviation pioneer. Washington D.C: Brassey's, 1997; Ch. 24.

161 Cooke J. Working in Papua New Guinea 1931–1946. op. cit., p. 255.

162 Gillespie R. Finding Amelia. op. cit., p. 79; Butler S. East to Dawn: The life of Amelia Earhart. op. cit., p. 407.

163 Butler S. East to Dawn: The life of Amelia Earhart. op. cit., p. 410.

164 Douglas Westfall, The Paragon Agency. email 25 January 2014.

165 ibid

166 Ware S. Still Missing: Amelia Earhart and the search for modern feminism. W. W. Norton, 1993.

167 Cooke J. Working in Papua New Guinea 1931–1946. op. cit., p. 278.

168 Hinz E. Pacific Islands Battlegrounds of World War II: Then and now. Honolulu: The Bess Press Inc. 1995; 83.

169 McAuley L. Blood and Iron: The battle for Kokoda 1942. op. cit.

170 Hinz E. Pacific Islands Battlegrounds of World War II: Then and now. op. cit., p. 46.

171 Australians at War: War against Japan 1941–1942. Ferguson J, ed. op. cit., p. 120.

172 Rice E. Strategic Battles in the Pacific: World War II. Lucent Books, 2000; 36.

173 James B. Field Guide to the Kokoda Track. op. cit., p. 59.

174 Ryan P. Fear Drive My Feet. Sydney: Angus & Robertson, 1959; 115.

175 Perrin A. The Private War of the Spotters: A history of the New Guinea Air Warning Wireless Company Feb 1942–April 1945. op. cit., p. 58.

176 Ewer P. Storm over Kokoda. Australia: Pier 9. 2011.

177 Perrin A. The Private War of the Spotters: op. cit., p. 50.

178 Bruce Hoy. The recapture of Lae; Paradise Magazine No. 114 March–April 1996.

179 Cook H. T., Cook T. F. Japan at War. op. cit., p. 268; p. 276.

180 Ryan P. Fear Drive My Feet. op. cit., pp. 296–7.

181 National Census 2000, www.morobepng.com.

182 Oseah Philemon; regional editor The National.

183 Sinclair J. Wings of Gold. op. cit., p. 93; p. 169.

184 DFS-ADF Flying Safety Special: Operations in Tropical Mountainous Areas, 4th Edition, 2000. p.76

185 PNGDCA File SI–798–1002.

186 Wild J. The John Ralston Wild Story. PNG Printing, 2004; 31.

187 Howard P. 'Dragon to Dash 8', pngbd.com/forum/archive/index.php/t-658.html; Sinclair J. Balus: The aeroplane in Papua New Guinea. Vol II: The rise of Talair.

188 Sinclair J. Balus: The aeroplane in Papua New Guinea. Vol II: The rise of Talair. op. cit.,

189 Flynn E. My Wicked, Wicked Ways. op. cit., p. 134.

190   PNGDCA File AS-81-1004.

191 Turner A. Historical Dictionary of PNG. Scarecrow Press; 1994; 166.

192 Australians at War: War against Japan 1941-1942. op. cit., p. 147.

193 James B. Field Guide to the Kokoda Track. op. cit., p. 452.

194 ibid., p. 454.

195 Gann K. Fate Is the Hunter. New York: Simon and Schuster, 1961; 4.

196 Hemingway E. 'London Fights the Robots', Collier's Magazine, August 1944.

197 www.pwc.ca

198 brainyquote.com/quotes/authors/s/salvador_dali.html

199 2000 Census, National Statistical Office of Papua New Guinea

200 Sinclair J. Kiap: Australia's Patrol Officers in Papua New Guinea. op. cit., p. 24.

201 Sinclair J. Sepik Pilot. Port Moresby: Robert Brown and Associates, 1971; 134.

202 Maiden P. Missionaries, Headhunters and Colonial Officers. Central Queensland University Press, 2003.

203 ibid.

204 p Sinclair J. Kiap: Australia's Patrol Officers in Papua New Guinea. op. cit., p.112.

205 Sinclair J. Kiap: Australia's Patrol Officers in Papua New Guinea. op. cit., p. 157.

206 PNGDCA File SI-768-1015.

207 Sinclair J. Balus: The aeroplane in Papua New Guinea. Vol. III: Wings of a Nation; 10.

208 PNGDCA File SI-768-1015.

209 Wiessner P, Tumu A. Historical Vines: Enga networks of exchange, ritual and warfare in Papua New Guinea. Washington & London: Smithsonian Institution Press, 1998; 146.

210 Sinclair J. Papua New Guinea: The first 100 Years. Port Moresby: Robert Brown and Associates, 1985.

211 Sinclair J. Sepik Pilot. op. cit., p. 176.

212 Sinclair J. Balus: The aeroplane in Papua New Guinea. Vol I. op. cit., p. 212.

213 Turner A. Historical Dictionary of PNG. op. cit.

214 www.barrick.com/files/porgera/Tailings-Management.pdf

215 'Troubled Waters' How mine waste dumping is poisoning our oceans, rivers, and lakes; Earthworks and Mining Watch Canada, February 2012, p.17

216 www.pprune.org/ (Professional Pilots' Rumour Network)

217 Henton D, Flower A. Mount Kare Gold Rush 1998-1994. Mt Kare Gold Rush Publishers: 2007; Papuan Borderlands: Huli, Duna and Ipili Perspectives on the Papua New Guinea Highlands. Aletta Biersack ed. University of Michigan Press, 1995.

218 www.businessday.com.au/business/back-to-that-gold-in-the-png-hills-20110306-1bjfk.html

219 Papuan Borderlands: Huli, Duna and Ipili Perspectives on the Papua New Guinea Highlands op. cit., p. 343.

220 Brown P. Beyond a Mountain Valley: The Simbu of Papua New Guinea. Honolulu: University of Hawaii Press, 1995; 38.

221 Leahy M J. Explorations into Highland New Guinea, 1930-1935. Bathurst: Crawford House Press, 1994.

222 Sinclair J. Balus: The aeroplane in Papua New Guinea. Vol. III: Wings of a Nation. op. cit., p. 11.

223 ibid., p. 174.

224 ibid., p. 157.

225 Dave Black email 30 September

2013.

226 PNGDCA File AS-90-1024

227 ibid.

228 ibid.

229 As quoted in: Judge J. 'Print and Politics: 'Shibao' and the culture of reform in late Qing China' Stanford University Press, 1996.

230 www.brainyquote.com/quotes/quotes/a/ayrtonsenn201063.html

231 APNG Flight Operations Exposition 119/Vol. 1 Ver. 3.0 Ch. 5.2 May 2009

232 PNGDCA File AS-93-1011

233 PNGDCA File AS-94-1014

234 PNGDCA File AS-94-1015

235 Sinclair J. Balus: The aeroplane in Papua New Guinea. Vol II. op. cit., p. 145.

236 NZ Herald 8 September 2009.

237 Paradise Magazine Vol. 4, 2007

238 Sinclair J. Sepik Pilot. op. cit., p.42.

239 Wilson S. Spitfire, Mustang and Kittyhawk in Australian Service. Aerospace Publications, 1988; Firkins R. Heroes Have Wings. Hesperian Press, 1993; Sinclair J. Balus: The aeroplane in Papua New Guinea. Vol. III: op. cit., 48.

240 Sinclair J. Balus: The aeroplane in Papua New Guinea. Vol. III: op. cit. p.54.

241 ibid., p. 55.

242 Turner A. Historical Dictionary of PNG. op. cit., p. xxxiii.

243 Ryan P. Encyclopaedia of Papua and New Guinea. MUP, 1971; 102.

244 Turner A. Historical Dictionary of PNG. op. cit.

245 ibid.

246 Bougainville Copper Ltd

247 Turner A. Historical Dictionary of PNG. op. cit.; Stone A. 'Little people at the heart of nuclear-free story', New Zealand Herald 25 January 2014.

248 Turner A. Historical Dictionary of PNG. op. cit

249 Barry D. The Sandline Crisis — 10 years on. Woolly Days, 2007; Turner A. Historical Dictionary of PNG. op. cit

250 Turner A. Historical Dictionary of PNG. op. cit. p. 230.

251 Turner A. Historical Dictionary of PNG. op. cit; Peter Byrne, 'Mercenary scandal continues to plague PNG government' 1998 www.wsws.org/en/articles/1998/11/png-n05.html

252 The Sandline Crisis — 10 Years on; Derek Barry, Feb 11, 2007, Woolly Days

253 Carlock C. Firebirds, Chuck. Bantam Books, 1995; 265.

254 Maiden P. Missionaries Headhunters and Colonial Officers. Central Queensland University Press, 2003.

255 PNGDCA File AS-95-1009 plus Addendum.

256 www.poemhunter.com/edna-st-vincent-millay/quotations/page-2

257 PNGDCA File AS-00-1002.

258 Stranks, J. Human Factors and Behavioural Safety. Butterworth-Heinemann. 2007; 130.

259 Used with permission; email from Aaron Sobel, Paramount Pictures, 11 September 2014.

260 http://en.wikipedia.org/wiki/Top_Gun#Effect_on_military_recruiting

261 Young G. Beyond Lion Rock. London: Century Hutchinson Ltd., 1988; 38.

262 ibid.

263 ibid., pp. 55–56

264 ibid., p. 234.

265 Sinclair J. Wings of Gold. op. cit., p. 134.

266 www.swire.com

267 World Air Transport Statistics 56th edition, IATA

268 intracx June 2014

269 Sinclair J. Balus: The aeroplane in Papua New Guinea. Vol II. op. cit., p. 121.

270 Young G. Beyond Lion Rock. op. cit., p. 221.

271 Eather C. The Amazing Adventures of Betsy and Niki. Pacific Century Publishers, 2008; 109.

272 Hillary E. Nothing Venture, Nothing Win. Hodder & Stoughton, 1975. Used with permission from the Hillary Estate. www.edhillary.com

273 Rolls-Royce Owners' Club Fun Facts: www.rroc.org/content.asp?contentid=535.

274 brainyquote.com/quotes/authors/j/john_f_kennedy.html

275 New Zealand Herald, 8 January 2014.

276 Wikipedia; Levitt S, Dubner S. SuperFreakonomics. Penguin, 2009; 149.

277 Collingridge V. 'Rude Awakenings'. South China Morning Post Sunday Post Magazine, 24 June 2012.

278 Hawkins H. Human Factors in Flight. Avebury Technical, 1993; 79.

279 Parasuraman, R, Riley,V. Humans and Automation: Use, misuse, disuse, abuse. Human Factors 39, 230–253. 1997.

280 'Remember' from Goblin Market and Other Poems (1862), www.poetryfoundation.org/poem.174266